BARRON'S

CAHSEE-
ENGLISH-LANGUAGE ARTS

CALIFORNIA HIGH SCHOOL EXIT EXAM

2ND EDITION

D0913799

BARRON'S

CAHSEE-
ENGLISH-LANGUAGE ARTS

CALIFORNIA HIGH SCHOOL
EXIT EXAM

2ND EDITION

Christina Lacie, M.A.

BARRON'S

All inquiries should be addressed to:
Barron's Educational Series, Inc.
250 Wireless Boulevard
Hauppauge, New York 11788
www.barronseduc.com

ISBN-13: 978-0-7641-3995-6
ISBN-10: 0-7641-3995-9

Library of Congress Control Number: 2008013439

Library of Congress Cataloging-in-Publication Data
Lacie, Christina.
    Cahsee English language arts / Christina Lacie.—2nd ed.
        p. cm.
    Includes bibliographical references and index.
    Rev. ed. of: How to prepare for the CAHSEE-English language arts. ©2003.
    ISBN-13: 978-0-7641-3995-6
    ISBN-10: 0-7641-3995-9
  1. Language arts (Secondary)—California—Examinations, questions,
etc.—Study guides. 2. High schools—California—Graduation
requirements—Study guides. 3. Educational tests and measurements—
California—Study guides.   I. Lacie, Christina. How to prepare for the
CAHSEE-English language arts.   II. Title.

    LB1631.5.L33 2008
    371.260973—dc22   2008013439

PRINTED IN THE UNITED STATES OF AMERICA

9 8 7 6 5 4 3 2 1

Contents

Preface

INTRODUCTION TO THE CAHSEE

The California High School Exit Exam is a test that needs to be taken seriously. The purpose of the exam, adopted by the California Department of Education, is to make certain that students graduating from California high schools are competent in reading, writing, and mathematics. It's all about accountability. Teachers need to teach and students need to learn. The exam concept originated with a state law (Senate Bill 2) that was passed in 1999 and authorized the development of the exam (ETS or Educational Testing Service is the company that designed the exam). This basically means that all students in California public schools have to pass the exam to receive a high school diploma.

The exam has two sections; one section is language arts and the other is mathematics. The language arts section (the focus of this study guide) contains two "sessions." Both language-arts sessions consist of multiple-choice questions. There is one writing task included in the exam as well. Over the course of three years, you will take the exam until you pass all portions of it; however, if you pass one section and not the other, you will retake only the portion(s) that you did not pass.

The scoring of the exams is scaled. This means that statistical measures or concepts—using statistical jargon: Standard Error of Measurement, Conditional Standard Error of Measurement, Raw Score to Scale Score Conversion, Weighting of Examination Portions—are used to ensure that a more precise measurement of your achievement is actually achieved. This also ensures that tests given at different times of the year are comparable. What all that boils down to is how it is all made fair in the end. The scoring range of the exam is 250–450. To pass the exam, you must score a minimum of 350 in both sections (language arts *and* mathematics). To pass the writing task, you must score a 3 or 4. The writing task accounts for 20% of your English-Language arts scaled score. The multiple-choice scores are totaled and then weighted to account for the remaining 80% of the scaled score. By the way, each essay or writing task is read by two different readers who are specially trained to do so. To make certain that the readers are consistent, the papers are "back-read" by yet another person who then formally records the scores.

Those are the basics—the ins and outs of the exam. If you have any more questions, please check the California Department of Education's web site devoted to the exam at: *http://cahsee.cde.ca.gov*. You can also look into the ETS (the makers of the exam) web site as well. It is linked from the state's exit exam site listed above.

CONTENT STANDARDS—DEFINED AND ALIGNED TO THE EXAM

The California High School Exit Exam is aligned to the English-Language Arts Content Standards for California Public Schools. The content standards are a list of skills that need to be taught in each grade level and in each subject. Teachers are required to teach the standards and students are required to master them and that's what this test is all about—making sure that everyone is doing their job. These standards were adopted in 1997 by the State of California.

The exit exam covers the content standards for English and language arts for the ninth and tenth grades and very few from the eighth-grade standards. These standards are listed below. They cover very specific things such as: Reading—Word Analysis, Fluency, and Systematic Vocabulary Development; Reading Comprehension; Literary Response, and Analysis; Writing Strategies; Writing Applications (Genres and Their Characteristics); Written and Oral English Language Conventions—Grammar and Mechanics, Listening and Speaking Skills, and Speaking Applications (Genres and Their Characteristics). If you look carefully at the list of standards, you will see how specific and thorough they are in identifying the skills you need to learn at each level. This list, remember, is only for English-Language Arts and only for the ninth and tenth grades. There is a list like this for each subject at every grade level.

English-Language Arts Content Standards for California Public Schools Grades Nine and Ten

READING

1.0 Word Analysis, Fluency, and Systematic Vocabulary Development

Students apply their knowledge of word origins to determine the meaning of new words encountered in reading materials and use those words accurately.

Vocabulary and Concept Development

1.1 Identify and use the literal and figurative meanings of words and understand word derivations.

1.2 Distinguish between the denotative and connotative meanings of words and interpret the connotative power of words.

1.3 Identify Greek, Roman, and Norse mythology and use the knowledge to understand the origin and meaning of new words (e.g., the word *narcissistic* drawn from the myth of Narcissus and Echo).

2.0 Reading Comprehension (Focus on Informational Materials)

Students read and understand grade-level-appropriate material. They analyze the organizational patterns, arguments, and positions advanced. The selections in *Recommended Literature, Grades Nine Through Twelve* (1990) illustrate the quality and complexity of the materials to be read by students. In addition, by grade twelve, students read two million words annually on their own, including a wide variety of classic and contemporary literature, magazines, newspapers, and on-line information. In grades nine and ten, students make substantial progress toward this goal.

Structural Features of Informational Materials

2.1 Analyze the structure and format of functional workplace documents, including the graphics and headers, and explain how authors use the features to achieve their purposes.

2.2 Prepare a bibliography of reference materials for a report using a variety of consumer, workplace, and public documents.

Comprehension and Analysis of Grade-Level-Appropriate Text

2.3 Generate relevant questions about readings on issues that can be researched.

2.4 Synthesize the content from several sources or works by a single author dealing with a single issue; paraphrase the ideas and connect them to other sources and related topics to demonstrate comprehension.

2.5 Extend ideas presented in primary or secondary sources through original analysis, evaluation, and elaboration.

2.6 Demonstrate use of sophisticated learning tools by following technical directions (e.g., those found with graphic calculators and specialized software programs and in access guides to World Wide Web sites on the Internet).

Expository Critique

2.7 Critique the logic of functional documents by examining the sequence of information and procedures in anticipation of possible reader misunderstandings.

2.8 Evaluate the credibility of an author's argument or defense of a claim by critiquing the relationship between generalizations and evidence, the comprehensiveness of evidence, and the way in which the author's intent affects the structure and tone of the text (e.g., in professional journals, editorials, political speeches, primary source material).

3.0 Literary Response and Analysis

Students read and respond to historically or culturally significant works of literature that reflect and enhance their studies of history and social science. They conduct in-depth analyses of recurrent patterns and themes. The selections in *Recommended Literature, Grades Nine Through Twelve* illustrate the quality and complexity of the materials to be read by students.

Structural Features of Literature

3.1 Articulate the relationship between the expressed purposes and the characteristics of different forms of dramatic literature (e.g., comedy, tragedy, drama, dramatic monologue).

3.2 Compare and contrast the presentation of a similar theme or topic across genres to explain how the selection of genre shapes the theme or topic.

Narrative Analysis of Grade-Level-Appropriate Text

3.3 Analyze interactions between main and subordinate characters in a literary text (e.g., internal and external conflicts, motivations, relationships, influences) and explain the way those interactions affect the plot.

3.4 Determine characters' traits by what the characters say about themselves in narration, dialogue, dramatic monologue, and soliloquy.

3.5 Compare works that express a universal theme and provide evidence to support the ideas expressed in each work.

3.6 Analyze and trace an author's development of time and sequence, including the use of complex literary devices (e.g., foreshadowing, flashbacks).

3.7 Recognize and understand the significance of various literary devices, including figurative language, imagery, allegory, and symbolism, and explain their appeal.

3.8 Interpret and evaluate the impact of ambiguities, subtleties, contradictions, ironies, and incongruities in a text.

3.9 Explain how voice, persona, and the choice of a narrator affect characterization and the tone, plot, and credibility of a text.

3.10 Identify and describe the function of dialogue, scene designs, soliloquies, asides, and character foils in dramatic literature.

Literary Criticism

3.11 Evaluate the aesthetic qualities of style, including the impact of diction and figurative language on tone, mood, and theme, using the terminology of literary criticism. (Aesthetic approach)

3.12 Analyze the way in which a work of literature is related to the themes and issues of its historical period. (Historical approach)

WRITING

1.0 Writing Strategies

Students write coherent and focused essays that convey a well-defined perspective and tightly reasoned argument. The writing demonstrates students' awareness of the audience and purpose. Students progress through the stages of the writing process as needed.

Organization and Focus

1.1 Establish a controlling impression or coherent thesis that conveys a clear and distinctive perspective on the subject and maintain a consistent tone and focus throughout the piece of writing.

1.2 Use precise language, action verbs, sensory details, appropriate modifiers, and the active rather than the passive voice.

Research and Technology

1.3 Use clear research questions and suitable research methods (e.g., library, electronic media, personal interview) to elicit and present evidence from primary and secondary sources.

1.4 Develop the main ideas within the body of the composition through supporting evidence (e.g., scenarios, commonly held beliefs, hypotheses, and definitions).

1.5 Synthesize information from multiple sources and identify complexities and discrepancies in the information and the different perspectives found in each medium (e.g., almanacs, microfiche, news sources, in-depth field studies, speeches, journals, technical documents).

1.6 Integrate quotations and citations into a written text while maintaining the flow of ideas.

1.7 Use appropriate conventions for documentation in the text, notes, and bibliographies by adhering to those in style manuals (e.g., *Modern Language Association Handbook, The Chicago Manual of Style*).

1.8 Design and publish documents by using advanced publishing software and graphic programs.

Evaluation and Revision

1.9 Revise writing to improve the logic and coherence of the organization and controlling perspective, the precision of word choice, and the tone by taking into consideration the audience, purpose, and formality of the context.

2.0 Writing Applications (Genres and Their Characteristics)

Students combine the rhetorical strategies of narration, exposition, persuasion, and description to produce texts of at least 1,500 words each. Student writing demonstrates a command of standard American English and the research, organizational, and drafting strategies outlined in Writing Standard 1.0.

Using the writing strategies of grades nine and ten outlined in Writing Standard 1.0, students:

2.1 Write biographical or autobiographical narratives or short stories:
   a. Relate a sequence of events and communicate the significance of the events to the audience.
   b. Locate scenes and incidents in specific places.
   c. Describe with concrete sensory details the sights, sounds, and smells of a scene and the specific actions, movements, gestures, and feelings of the characters; use interior monologue to depict the characters' feelings.
   d. Pace the presentation of actions to accommodate changes in time and mood.
   e. Make effective use of descriptions of appearance, images, shifting perspectives, and sensory details.

2.2 Write responses to literature:
   a. Demonstrate a comprehensive grasp of the significant ideas of literary works.
   b. Support important ideas and viewpoints through accurate and detailed references to the text or to other works.
   c. Demonstrate awareness of the author's use of stylistic devices and an appreciation of the effects created.
   d. Identify and assess the impact of perceived ambiguities, nuances, and complexities within the text.

2.3 Write expository compositions, including analytical essays and research reports:
   a. Marshal evidence in support of a thesis and related claims, including information on all relevant perspectives.
   b. Convey information and ideas from primary and secondary sources accurately and coherently.
   c. Make distinctions between the relative value and significance of specific data, facts, and ideas.
   d. Include visual aids by employing appropriate technology to organize and record information on charts, maps, and graphs.

    e. Anticipate and address readers' potential misunderstandings, biases, and expectations.

    f. Use technical terms and notations accurately.

2.4 Write persuasive compositions:

    a. Structure ideas and arguments in a sustained and logical fashion.

    b. Use specific rhetorical devices to support assertions (e.g., appeal to logic through reasoning; appeal to emotion or ethical belief; relate a personal anecdote, case study, or analogy).

    c. Clarify and defend positions with precise and relevant evidence, including facts, expert opinions, quotations, and expressions of commonly accepted beliefs and logical reasoning.

    d. Address readers' concerns, counterclaims, biases, and expectations.

2.5 Write business letters:

    a. Provide clear and purposeful information and address the intended audience appropriately.

    b. Use appropriate vocabulary, tone, and style to take into account the nature of the relationship with, and the knowledge and interests of, the recipients.

    c. Highlight central ideas or images.

    d. Follow a conventional style with page formats, fonts, and spacing that contribute to the documents' readability and impact.

2.6 Write technical documents (e.g., a manual on rules of behavior for conflict resolution, procedures for conducting a meeting, minutes of a meeting):

    a. Report information and convey ideas logically and correctly.

    b. Offer detailed and accurate specifications.

    c. Include scenarios, definitions, and examples to aid comprehension (e.g., troubleshooting guide).

    d. Anticipate readers' problems, mistakes, and misunderstandings.

WRITTEN AND ORAL ENGLISH LANGUAGE CONVENTIONS

The standards for written and oral English language conventions have been placed between those for writing and for listening and speaking because these conventions are essential to both sets of skills.

1.0 Written and Oral English Language Conventions

Students write and speak with a command of standard English conventions.

Grammar and Mechanics of Writing

1.1 Identify and correctly use clauses (e.g., main and subordinate), phrases (e.g., gerund, infinitive, and participial), and mechanics of punctuation (e.g., semicolons, colons, ellipses, hyphens).

1.2 Understand sentence construction (e.g., parallel structure, subordination, proper placement of modifiers) and proper English usage (e.g., consistency of verb tenses).

1.3 Demonstrate an understanding of proper English usage and control of grammar, paragraph and sentence structure, diction, and syntax.

Manuscript Form

1.4 Produce legible work that shows accurate spelling and correct use of the conventions of punctuation and capitalization.

1.5 Reflect appropriate manuscript requirements, including title page presentation, pagination, spacing and margins, and integration of source and support material (e.g., in-text citation, use of direct quotations, paraphrasing) with appropriate citations.

LISTENING AND SPEAKING

1.0 Listening and Speaking Strategies

Students formulate adroit judgments about oral communication. They deliver focused and coherent presentations of their own that convey clear and distinct perspectives and solid reasoning. They use gestures, tone, and vocabulary tailored to the audience and purpose.

Comprehension

1.1 Formulate judgments about the ideas under discussion and support those judgments with convincing evidence.

1.2 Compare and contrast the ways in which media genres (e.g., televised news, news magazines, documentaries, on-line information) cover the same event.

Organization and Delivery of Oral Communication

1.3 Choose logical patterns of organization (e.g., chronological, topical, cause and effect) to inform and to persuade, by soliciting agreement or action, or to unite audiences behind a common belief or cause.

1.4 Choose appropriate techniques for developing the introduction and conclusion (e.g., by using literary quotations, anecdotes, references to authoritative sources).

1.5 Recognize and use elements of classical speech forms (e.g., introduction, first and second transitions, body, conclusion) in formulating rational arguments and applying the art of persuasion and debate.

1.6 Present and advance a clear thesis statement and choose appropriate types of proof (e.g., statistics, testimony, specific instances) that meet standard tests for evidence, including credibility, validity, and relevance.

1.7 Use props, visual aids, graphs, and electronic media to enhance the appeal and accuracy of presentations.

1.8 Produce concise notes for extemporaneous delivery.

1.9 Analyze the occasion and the interests of the audience and choose effective verbal and nonverbal techniques (e.g., voice, gestures, eye contact) for presentations.

Analysis and Evaluation of Oral and Media Communications

1.10 Analyze historically significant speeches (e.g., Abraham Lincoln's "Gettysburg Address," Martin Luther King, Jr.'s "I Have a Dream") to find the rhetorical devices and features that make them memorable.

1.11 Assess how language and delivery affect the mood and tone of the oral communication and make an impact on the audience.

1.12 Evaluate the clarity, quality, effectiveness, and general coherence of a speaker's important points, arguments, evidence, organization of ideas, delivery, diction, and syntax.

1.13 Analyze the types of arguments used by the speaker, including argument by causation, analogy, authority, emotion, and logic.

1.14 Identify the aesthetic effects of a media presentation and evaluate the techniques used to create them (e.g., compare Shakespeare's *Henry V* with Kenneth Branagh's 1990 film version).

2.0 Speaking Applications (Genres and Their Characteristics)

Students deliver polished formal and extemporaneous presentations that combine the traditional rhetorical strategies of narration, exposition, persuasion, and description. Student speaking demonstrates a command of standard American English and the organizational and delivery strategies outlined in Listening and Speaking Standard 1.0. Using the speaking strategies of grades nine and ten outlined in Listening and Speaking Standard 1.0, students:

2.1 Deliver narrative presentations:

a. Narrate a sequence of events and communicate their significance to the audience.

b. Locate scenes and incidents in specific places.

c. Describe with concrete sensory details the sights, sounds, and smells of a scene and the specific actions, movements, gestures, and feelings of characters.

d. Pace the presentation of actions to accommodate time or mood changes.

2.2 Deliver expository presentations:

a. Marshal evidence in support of a thesis and related claims, including information on all relevant perspectives.

b. Convey information and ideas from primary and secondary sources accurately and coherently.

c. Make distinctions between the relative value and significance of specific data, facts, and ideas.

d. Include visual aids by employing appropriate technology to organize and display information on charts, maps, and graphs.

e. Anticipate and address the listener's potential misunderstandings, biases, and expectations.

f. Use technical terms and notations accurately.

2.3 Apply appropriate interviewing techniques:

a. Prepare and ask relevant questions.

b. Make notes of responses.

c. Use language that conveys maturity, sensitivity, and respect.

d. Respond correctly and effectively to questions.

e. Demonstrate knowledge of the subject or organization.

f. Compile and report responses.

g. Evaluate the effectiveness of the interview.

2.4 Deliver oral responses to literature:

a. Advance a judgment demonstrating a comprehensive grasp of the significant ideas of works or passages (i.e., make and support warranted assertions about the text).

b. Support important ideas and viewpoints through accurate and detailed references to the text or to other works.

c. Demonstrate awareness of the author's use of stylistic devices and an appreciation of the effects created.

d. Identify and assess the impact of perceived ambiguities, nuances, and complexities within the text.

2.5 Deliver persuasive arguments (including evaluation and analysis of problems and solutions and causes and effects):

a. Structure ideas and arguments in a coherent, logical fashion.

b. Use rhetorical devices to support assertions (e.g., by appeal to logic through reasoning; by appeal to emotion or ethical belief; by use of personal anecdote, case study, or analogy).

c. Clarify and defend positions with precise and relevant evidence, including facts, expert opinions, quotations, expressions of commonly accepted beliefs, and logical reasoning.

d. Anticipate and address the listener's concerns and counterarguments.

2.6 Deliver descriptive presentations:

a. Establish clearly the speaker's point of view on the subject of the presentation.

b. Establish clearly the speaker's relationship with that subject (e.g., dispassionate observation, personal involvement).

c. Use effective, factual descriptions of appearance, concrete images, shifting perspectives and vantage points, and sensory details.

How to Use This Book

TIP

Take this exam and all your preparations for it *seriously*—you have to pass this exam to graduate from high school.

The most important thing to remember in using this book is that it is for review purposes. It is a guide and aligned to the California English-Language Arts Content Standards, but it is not a substitute for what you are learning for nine months of the year in your English classroom—that can be done only in an English classroom. The more you read, study vocabulary, write and work on grammar and mechanics during the course of the school year, the better prepared you will be. But this guide should help remind you of what you have learned throughout the course of the year in English, especially ninth and tenth grades.

Begin by taking the diagnostic exam in Chapter 1. The results of this will direct you to the areas that you need to review. Take an honest look at your weaknesses and strengths. For instance, if you read and comprehend well, but struggle with writing, focus more on the writing chapters. Whatever it is that you feel you need to review, spend more time, *quality time*, reviewing those areas.

Good luck in taking the test—be calm, think positively and, most importantly, take it seriously. Always do your BEST.

SECTION I

READING

Answer Sheet

DIAGNOSTIC EXAM SECTION 1

1 Ⓐ Ⓑ Ⓒ Ⓓ
2 Ⓐ Ⓑ Ⓒ Ⓓ
3 Ⓐ Ⓑ Ⓒ Ⓓ
4 Ⓐ Ⓑ Ⓒ Ⓓ
5 Ⓐ Ⓑ Ⓒ Ⓓ
6 Ⓐ Ⓑ Ⓒ Ⓓ
7 Ⓐ Ⓑ Ⓒ Ⓓ
8 Ⓐ Ⓑ Ⓒ Ⓓ
9 Ⓐ Ⓑ Ⓒ Ⓓ
10 Ⓐ Ⓑ Ⓒ Ⓓ
11 Ⓐ Ⓑ Ⓒ Ⓓ
12 Ⓐ Ⓑ Ⓒ Ⓓ
13 Ⓐ Ⓑ Ⓒ Ⓓ
14 Ⓐ Ⓑ Ⓒ Ⓓ
15 Ⓐ Ⓑ Ⓒ Ⓓ
16 Ⓐ Ⓑ Ⓒ Ⓓ
17 Ⓐ Ⓑ Ⓒ Ⓓ
18 Ⓐ Ⓑ Ⓒ Ⓓ
19 Ⓐ Ⓑ Ⓒ Ⓓ
20 Ⓐ Ⓑ Ⓒ Ⓓ
21 Ⓐ Ⓑ Ⓒ Ⓓ
22 Ⓐ Ⓑ Ⓒ Ⓓ
23 Ⓐ Ⓑ Ⓒ Ⓓ
24 Ⓐ Ⓑ Ⓒ Ⓓ

25 Ⓐ Ⓑ Ⓒ Ⓓ
26 Ⓐ Ⓑ Ⓒ Ⓓ
27 Ⓐ Ⓑ Ⓒ Ⓓ
28 Ⓐ Ⓑ Ⓒ Ⓓ
29 Ⓐ Ⓑ Ⓒ Ⓓ
30 Ⓐ Ⓑ Ⓒ Ⓓ
31 Ⓐ Ⓑ Ⓒ Ⓓ
32 Ⓐ Ⓑ Ⓒ Ⓓ
33 Ⓐ Ⓑ Ⓒ Ⓓ
34 Ⓐ Ⓑ Ⓒ Ⓓ
35 Ⓐ Ⓑ Ⓒ Ⓓ
36 Ⓐ Ⓑ Ⓒ Ⓓ
37 Ⓐ Ⓑ Ⓒ Ⓓ
38 Ⓐ Ⓑ Ⓒ Ⓓ
39 Ⓐ Ⓑ Ⓒ Ⓓ
40 Ⓐ Ⓑ Ⓒ Ⓓ
41 Ⓐ Ⓑ Ⓒ Ⓓ
42 Ⓐ Ⓑ Ⓒ Ⓓ
43 Ⓐ Ⓑ Ⓒ Ⓓ
44 Ⓐ Ⓑ Ⓒ Ⓓ
45 Ⓐ Ⓑ Ⓒ Ⓓ
46 Ⓐ Ⓑ Ⓒ Ⓓ
47 Ⓐ Ⓑ Ⓒ Ⓓ
48 Ⓐ Ⓑ Ⓒ Ⓓ

49 Ⓐ Ⓑ Ⓒ Ⓓ
50 Ⓐ Ⓑ Ⓒ Ⓓ
51 Ⓐ Ⓑ Ⓒ Ⓓ
52 Ⓐ Ⓑ Ⓒ Ⓓ
53 Ⓐ Ⓑ Ⓒ Ⓓ
54 Ⓐ Ⓑ Ⓒ Ⓓ
55 Ⓐ Ⓑ Ⓒ Ⓓ
56 Ⓐ Ⓑ Ⓒ Ⓓ
57 Ⓐ Ⓑ Ⓒ Ⓓ
58 Ⓐ Ⓑ Ⓒ Ⓓ
59 Ⓐ Ⓑ Ⓒ Ⓓ
60 Ⓐ Ⓑ Ⓒ Ⓓ
61 Ⓐ Ⓑ Ⓒ Ⓓ
62 Ⓐ Ⓑ Ⓒ Ⓓ
63 Ⓐ Ⓑ Ⓒ Ⓓ
64 Ⓐ Ⓑ Ⓒ Ⓓ
65 Ⓐ Ⓑ Ⓒ Ⓓ
66 Ⓐ Ⓑ Ⓒ Ⓓ
67 Ⓐ Ⓑ Ⓒ Ⓓ
68 Ⓐ Ⓑ Ⓒ Ⓓ
69 Ⓐ Ⓑ Ⓒ Ⓓ
70 Ⓐ Ⓑ Ⓒ Ⓓ
71 Ⓐ Ⓑ Ⓒ Ⓓ
72 Ⓐ Ⓑ Ⓒ Ⓓ

Answer Sheet

DIAGNOSTIC EXAM WRITING TASK

Write your response here:

_____

_____

_____

_____

_____

_____

_____

_____

_____

_____

_____

_____

_____

_____

_____

_____

_____

_____

_____

_____

_____

_____

_____

_____

Diagnostic Exam Writing Task Continued:

California High School Exit Exam

Diagnostic Exam Section 1

READING

Read the following passage and answer questions 1 through 8.

The Dream

"I had this dream, a weird dream," Brett said. "I'll tell you about it. I'm standing at the coffee shop before school. It's really crowded and everyone is talking and animated—everyone's having a good time because it's the last week of school and we can all just taste FREEDOM!"

He rolls down the window in the car, takes a deep breath, then continues. "I'm just standing there like everyone else—feeling good—and suddenly this great-looking, actually, drop-dead gorgeous girl brushes up against me accidentally. She excuses herself, but our eyes connect and then lock. We don't lose the gaze for what seems like hours and I'm thinking to myself, 'You know Brett, this might not be a bad start of the summer.' Part of me knows that this is a dream—you know how it is with dreams—sometimes you are all the way into a dream, and sometimes you are half in and half out, so you don't know if it is real or fake."

With deep concentration and a kind of squint in his eyes that tells me he is reliving this dream as he tells it, Brett continues. "So everything is cool and I've just met the most gorgeous girl on the planet, when in walks this skinny kid. He's kind of wired up. He looks mad as a hornet and he's carrying this bucket of water, at least

Diagnostic Exam

I assumed it was water. He's sloshing it as he walks and he's pushing his way through the crowd and coming right toward me. Suddenly I glance around to see the girl and she is gone. She's nowhere to be seen, and I am thinking, 'How could she disappear so fast?' I look back around and this guy is standing right in front of me. At that moment he throws the bucket of water at me. Everyone in the crowd backs away except for this kid who is grinning this devilish little grin. Meanwhile, I am soaked and my eyes are stinging."

Brett looked at me and smiled a wry smile and again continued to explain his dream. "There I am, standing alone in a puddle of water and I think to myself, 'Why me? What have I done to deserve this?' I know that this just isn't a part of my plans—to be humiliated by a perfect stranger in a coffee shop before school just before summer—this wasn't suppose to happen to me. I figure there has to be some mistake. Then the kid reaches into his pocket. Meanwhile, the crowd is wondering what is going on and you could hear them gasp audibly when he reached into his pocket. You know that they were thinking what I was thinking. But the kid pulls out a handful of change and proceeds to throw it at me while he screams, 'Go buy yourself a toy at the dime store and leave my girlfriend alone.'"

At this point, Brett is stalling and I am wondering where he is going with this dream story when he begins to speak again. "Okay—that's not the end. And you know something else—I've had this dream before, three, four, five times before at least. Each time I have the dream, a new event is added to the scenario. I used to wake up before the bucket of water, and then after the water but before the pocket change being thrown, but this last time . . ."

"Where did the girl go? What happens next?" I prod Brett to continue with the story.

"Well that's the weird thing," he replies. "I'm halfway in and halfway out of this dream, you know that feeling, and I am at the point where I can just wake up and be done with it, or hold on to it and see what happens next. I am curious because this thing is random; I don't really want to let go, but at the same time do I want to witness the ending of something innocent that turned sour really quickly and unexpectedly? Okay, so I stay with it—'Let's finish this thing off once and for all' I am thinking to myself, or my subconscious is thinking it. And the dream continues. Okay, so after the bucket of water and a handful of change are thrown at me, I can't imagine where this is going to go from here. 'Is it going to get any worse?' I think to myself. You won't believe what happens next," he reports as his grin returns to his face.

"Well the next thing I know, the shop manager is trying to grab the skinny kid, because I'm just standing there all bewildered and confused and the crowd is in awe of what has just happened. Within minutes, the skinny kid is down and the manager is calling the cops when in walks . . . oh, you are not going to believe this . . . in walks three cameramen and the host of "You've Been Punk'd" followed by the gorgeous girl. Next thing I know, the manager and the skinny kid are laughing—I'm standing there drenched and shivering—and all I could think to do is . . ."

"What?" I demanded of Brett. "What happens next?"

"Uhhhh," he stammers, "that's what's crazy, I woke up—so I don't know how I responded or what happens next. It kind of makes me crazy!"

I didn't know what to say to him, and shaking my head in wonderment, I said, "Hey, nice dream. Roll the window up—we've got to get to school."

TIP

Take the diagnostic exam in this guide and use them to find your strengths and weaknesses.

1. The words *wired up* and *mad as a hornet* suggest a feeling of—

    (A) disappointment and frustration.
    (B) poor and weakened.
    (C) grand and stately.
    (D) agitation and anger.

2. Read this sentence from the story.

    "It's really crowded and everyone is talking and animated—everyone's having a good time because it's the last week of school and we can all just taste FREEDOM!"

    What does the word *animated* mean as it is used in this sentence?

    (A) lively
    (B) depressed
    (C) disheartened
    (D) disheveled

3. How does the nearing climax to Brett's dream cause a reaction in the narrator's tone toward the end of the play?

    (A) He is anxious to hear the ending and raises his voice to ask what happens.
    (B) He is sympathetic and feels sorry for Brett.
    (C) He thinks Brett is fooling him and doesn't want to hear the ending at all.
    (D) He turns around and walks away without hearing the ending.

4. In what way does Brett's repeated dream foreshadow the ending of the story?

    (A) He changes the ending just for fun.
    (B) Each time he has the dream, a new part is added, which means he will have it again and more will be added next time.
    (C) There is no foreshadowing at this point in the dream.
    (D) He is anxious to see how it ends himself.

5. Which word BEST describes the tone throughout the story?

    (A) ironic
    (B) sarcastic and demeaning
    (C) curious and comical
    (D) frustrated

6. Which of the following BEST represents the intent of the author in writing "The Dream?"

    (A) to explain the dream process
    (B) as entertainment
    (C) to explain friendship
    (D) to express devotion

7. Which of the following BEST represents the time period in which the story is set?

   (A) early 1900s
   (B) early 1970s
   (C) late 1960s
   (D) the present

8. Which of the following BEST describes the diction in the passage?

   (A) informal
   (B) formal
   (C) didactic
   (D) irrational

Read the following passage and answer questions 9 through 15.

Afraid to Let Go

Robert Farley arrives at the Mount Pleasant Hospital to visit his wife. It is his usual routine. "How are you feeling?" he asks as he gently walks in and sits at the bedside close to Sarah. She is smiling up at him, her dark hair a sharp contrast against the white pillows.

"I'm fine," Sarah says quietly. She looks tired and ghostly pale to Robert and he notices the dark circles under her eyes. When she slips her fingers into Robert's hand, he notices brown spots and bruises from various medical procedures.

"You look tired," Robert says. "Are you sleeping well?"

"I had a restless night last night," she responds, but doesn't mention the excruciating pain because she doesn't want to upset her husband. "Have you heard anything from Mary?" she asks.

"She called again last night and I told her that you were just fine and not to worry about anything." Mary, their eldest daughter, is a teacher. Their son David works out of state and hasn't been told that his mother is ill. He is a worrier and they don't want to upset him.

Robert stares across the sunlit hospital ward. Visitors are chatting with their loved ones and offering words of comfort and hope. They bring various flowers and baskets of fruit. "Have you seen the doctor yet today?" he asks his wife.

"Tomorrow maybe, I think," she responds.

"How long are they going to keep you here, do you know?" Robert asks.

Sarah turns away and begins to cough into a tissue, and then settles back into the pillows and takes Robert's hand again. "They'll let me know on Monday, I think. They have to do more tests and gather the results. They won't let me go home until they know. I'm sorry to be such a bother," she says weakly.

Sarah's chest heaves under her nightdress and she reminds Robert of a frightened bird. 'Sweet Sarah,' he used to call her long ago when they were first dating. He would lightheartedly mock her sorrowful eyes and the way that she would take everything to heart and worry. He wonders if she made herself sick with worry all those years. "Sweet Sarah, don't let them move you until you are feeling one hundred percent better," he says holding her hand.

"Are you managing at home all right, dear?"

"Things are just great," Robert responds, but neglects to tell her that he eats all of his meals out and stays away from home as much as possible because he misses her so much. Yes, he's managing all right.

The clock sitting on the table next to Sarah's bed makes him think. He remembers how its irritating ring startled him from his sleep every morning. He remembers how Sarah's clattering of pans and making breakfast noise kept him awake, which served to remind him that there was a full day's work ahead and children to feed and get off to school.

Tic-tic-tic-tic-tic—the clock chatters in the background. The kids are grown up now and their second grandchild will be arriving soon enough. Robert feels that time is running out and thinks to himself, "Why can't clocks just take their time? What's the hurry?"

Sarah's eyelids droop and her mouth opens a little. She appears lifeless. The moments pass slowly. "This must be boring for you, dear," she says to Robert without opening her eyes. "It's not pleasant to have to visit anyone in the hospital, it has to be depressing for you."

"Nonsense" was his only reply.

Sarah settles her dark head back into the pillows and grimaces for an instant, but then valiantly forces a weak smile. "Robert, you should leave now. I think I might sleep for a while."

"Are you sure you want me to go?" he responds hesitantly.

"Positive, I'm positive," she replies.

Robert slowly gets to his feet and kisses his wife's forehead. "I'll come later," he says in a whispered tone.

"Oh, it will be so crowded with it being Saturday, why don't you come tomorrow morning after mass?" Sarah opens her eyes and smiles like a child. It's been so long since she was a child.

"Is that what you want Sweet Sarah?"

"Yes, that's what I want, darling. I'll see you tomorrow." Sarah looks at her husband and notices that he looks tired. "You look tired, Robert, have you been sleeping well?"

"I guess I had a restless night last night," he responds, but he neglects to tell her that he can't sleep at all. The empty house, the quiet, the vacancy that Sarah has left in his heart by being away from home is more than he can take. But he doesn't want to worry her. "I'll go home and rest, and I will see you tomorrow." His heart is breaking as he releases her hand. He is afraid to let go. He is afraid that he won't see her again. Robert tucks Sarah in as though she was a child and kisses her again on the forehead. As he crosses the sunlit ward, he turns back to see Sarah one last time. "I'm afraid to let go," he whispers to himself, and he continues on his way.

9. What does the word *excruciating* mean as it is used in the following sentence?

"I had a restless night last night," she responds, but doesn't mention the excruciating pain because she doesn't want to upset her husband.

    (A) depleting
    (B) antagonistic
    (C) aggressive
    (D) unbearable

10. How does Robert react when his wife asks him to come tomorrow instead of that afternoon?

    (A) He is excited that he won't have to make a trip to the hospital.
    (B) He is crushed and heartbroken.
    (C) He is ambivalent and doesn't seem to care at all.
    (D) He is angry and frustrated.

11. Why does hearing the clock ticking bring back memories for Robert?

    (A) Because he hated getting up to go to work in the morning.
    (B) Because he would rather forget about time.
    (C) He misses his wife and the everyday things that he took for granted.
    (D) He wants to pick it up and throw it across the ward.

12. Which statement BEST describes Sarah's feelings about her husband?

    (A) She worries about him and doesn't want to upset him.
    (B) She is tired of him sitting around all the time.
    (C) She feels that he is pathetic.
    (D) She wants him to be happy.

13. What does the use of a flashback accomplish in the story?

    (A) It raises questions about the couples' past.
    (B) It reminds Robert about how fast time goes by, and how much he misses his wife at home.
    (C) It reminds Sarah of raising children and getting them off to school.
    (D) It raises an issue of resentment that Robert holds for the clock.

14. The ending of the story is—

    (A) ironic.
    (B) comical.
    (C) satirical.
    (D) poignant.

15. How is internal dialogue used effectively in the story?

    (A) It allows the reader to hear the true feelings of both characters.
    (B) It allows the reader to escape from normal dialogue.
    (C) It confuses the reader into believing that the characters are speaking aloud.
    (D) It is frustrating and confusing.

Read the following poem and answer questions 16 through 20.

Sunlight on the Sea

Walking along the shore that evening
While the damp sand embraces my feet
Off and on the waves play "catch me if you can"
As I meander the comforting expanse of shoreline.
Without hope or agenda
My thoughts ramble in countless directions.
The long and exhausting days have taken their toll
And I have reached a crossroads in my life
When a decision needs to be made, a decision needs to be justified
But I don't want to think about that right now.
The sunlight on the sea sparkles and flashes with the waves.
Mesmerizing, it transports me somewhere else for a time.

Minutes pass, and then hours.
My thoughts return to decisions,
Unavoidable and horrifying life choices
That send a once viable life, now vacant,
Into the next, into that mysterious and impenetrable void.
Although the light of day lingers gently in the sky
And the sunlight glimmers on the sea,
Those lights are growing dim.
Presently I saunter between the day and night,
Knowing some must swim when others sink,
And some must sink when others swim.
I miss the voice of one I've heard,
And the sunlight sinks into the sea.

16. How does the imagery of the two stanzas contrast?

    (A) The imagery in the first stanza is dark and mysterious, while the imagery in the second stanza is lighthearted and informal.
    (B) The imagery in the first stanza is comical, while the imagery in the second stanza is serious.
    (C) The imagery in the first stanza is filled with light, while the imagery in the second stanza is much darker.
    (D) The imagery in the first stanza is resentful and angry, while the second stanza imagery is straightforward and aggressive.

17. Read the following two lines from the poem.

    Knowing some must swim when others sink,
    And some must sink when others swim.

    How do these two lines bond with the sunlight and dimming light imagery in the poem?

    (A) The "sunlight" and "swim" equate to life, while the "sinking" and "dimming light" represent death or dying.
    (B) They have no connection at all.
    (C) The two images represent life and vitality.
    (D) The two images contradict the narrator of the poem and his situation.

18. The overall imagery of the poem is—

    (A) friendly and optimistic.
    (B) colorful and animated.
    (C) stressful and tortured.
    (D) intimidating and optimistic.

19. The gradual setting of the sun in the poem is—

    (A) an expression of resentment.
    (B) a metaphor for dying and death.
    (C) a celebration of life.
    (D) a personification of death.

20. Which of the following BEST describes the effect of the tone on the poem?

    (A) It colors the poem with images of joy and celebration.
    (B) It allows the narrative of the poem to move smoothly from stanza to stanza.
    (C) It allows the reader to understand the torment that the narrator experiences as he/she has to make a life-ending decision for someone he/she cares about.
    (D) It takes the reader's hopes and dreams to another dimension.

Read the following passage and answer questions 21 through 26.

Submarines

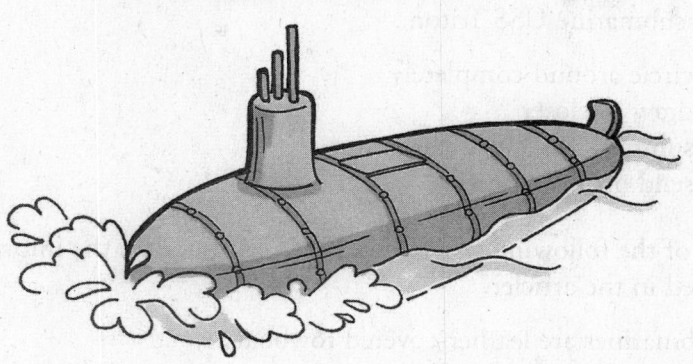

The submarine-like sketches of Leonardo da Vinci, who lived from 1452–1519, are the first known of such a vehicle. A British mathematician actually drew plans for a submarine in 1578. However, the first man who actually built a submarine was Cornelius van Drebbel. In 1620, Drebbel, the Dutch inventor, wrapped a wooden rowboat tightly in waterproofed leather. For air, he used tubes that were attached to floats that hovered on the surface. Because there were no engines at the time, oars were attached through the hull of the boat with leather gaskets. Drebbel's first trip lasted three hours. He took twelve oarsmen into the Thames River in London, where the boat was submerged.

The United States built the first submarine for military purposes. It was built in 1776 by David Bushnell. Bushnell's submarine was called the "Turtle," and it held only one person. It was powered by hand-turned propellers. During the American Revolution, the Turtle would approach British warships, and while it was partially submerged, it attached explosives to the ship's hull. Although the Turtle functioned well, the explosives were less successful.

In the 1890s, two rival inventors, again from the United States, developed the first true submarines. The submarines, built by John P. Holland, were purchased by the United States Navy. Russia and Japan bought the submarines which were designed by Simon Lake. These submarines used gas or steam engines for surface cruising, and electric motors for underwater travel. Torpedoes that were propelled by small electric motors were included with these designs and with these inclusions; the most dangerous weapons of the world at that time were introduced. In Germany, submarines are called U-boats. It is short for "Unterseeboot," which is the German word for undersea boat.

As the submarine evolved over the years, the first nuclear-powered submarine was built in the United States. The USS Nautilus was launched in 1955. In 1958 the Nautilus made the first voyage under the polar ice pack. This monumental voyage was completed in six days and covered about 1,830 miles (2,945 kilometers). The first submerged circumnavigation of earth was made in 1960 by the nuclear submarine USS Triton.

There has been much advancement in technology for submarines over the years, from the leather-covered row boat to the nuclear submarine the USS Triton. The life of the crews of these vehicles certainly has evolved as well. The submarine is an amazing and almost surreal, sci-fi-like creation.

21. What is the synonym for the word *circumnavigation* as it is used in the following sentence?

    The first submerged circumnavigation of earth was made in 1960 by the nuclear submarine USS Triton.

    (A) to circle around completely
    (B) to draw in closer
    (C) to submerge in a circular pattern
    (D) to send off into the air

22. Which of the following statements BEST summarizes the information presented in the article?

    (A) Submarines are leather-covered rowboats.
    (B) Submarines use engines to propel torpedoes.
    (C) Submarines have evolved dramatically since the early sketches of da Vinci to the nuclear submarines of today.
    (D) Submarines have twelve oarsmen on board at all times.

23. Based on the information in the article, which statement about submarines is accurate?

    (A) Submarines are capable of flying, as well as being submerged.
    (B) The first submarine to circumnavigate the earth was the Turtle.
    (C) The first submarine to explore the polar icecap was the USS Nautilus.
    (D) The submarine only uses tubes that float to the surface for air.

24. This article contains the MOST information on—

    (A) the USS Nautilus.
    (B) David Bushnell.
    (C) Leonardo da Vinci.
    (D) the submarines developed in the 1890s.

25. What information supports the idea that the submarine is primarily used for military uses?

    (A) Submarines are used in Germany.
    (B) Since the American Revolution, submarines have been developed and used by the U.S. Navy.
    (C) Submarines can be used for entertainment purposes.
    (D) Submarines can dive for only three hours.

26. What fact supports the idea that the first submarines had no engines?

    (A) Leonardo da Vinci sketched a model of a submarine.
    (B) Germany calls their submarines U-boats.
    (C) Tubes were floated to the surface for air.
    (D) Oars or hand-turned propellers were used to propel the early submarines.

Read the following passage and answer questions 27 through 31.

Languages of the World

Except for references in the Bible, the invention of language is unknown. The language that Adam and Eve spoke is unknown, and the first mention of many different languages is referenced in the Bible and the story of the Tower of Babel. The evolution of language is an extensive and extraordinary phenomenon.

At present, there are more than 2,700 different languages spoken throughout the world and more than 7,000 dialects. There are more than 1,000 different languages spoken in Africa. Throughout the small, but multi-island nation of Indonesia, there are 365 different languages spoken. A singularly isolated language that is considered one of the most difficult to learn is the Basque language, which is spoken in northwestern Spain and southwestern France. Its beginnings are unknown for the most part, and because it is not related to any other language in the world, Basque is unique. The language that is spoken by most people in the world is Mandarin. English is second to Mandarin. However, as a home language, Spanish is the second most spoken language in the world. The only nation in the world whose official language is Latin is the Vatican. It is also the smallest country in the world. Somalia is the only nation in the world whose citizens speak only one language, Somali. The North African Berbers have no written form of their language.

The youngest or newest language is Afrikaans, which is spoken by South Africans. The language developed from the Dutch and German Protestants who fled persecution from the Roman Catholic Church in the 17th and 18th centuries. These groups settled in the Dutch colony of Cape of Good Hope on the southern tip of Africa. The Afrikaans language was developed by the early 20th century primarily from Dutch and German influence. It is now a full-fledged language, complete with its own dictionaries. Within 100 years, it became the second most spoken language in South Africa. The Zulu people are the largest ethnic group, and Zulu is the most spoken language in the region.

When different cultures meet and mix, new languages develop. In London there are about 700 languages spoken. English has become a second language in some suburbs of London. Similar developments are occurring in many large cities throughout the world: New York, Los Angeles, Miami, and Singapore, for instance. Additional cultural influences are the Internet and cell phone texting. As people begin to communicate more easily and more freely, they are influencing the development of languages or the evolution of languages quite rapidly. These technologically inspired developments reach across cultural and regional borders. At present, the fastest growing language in the world is called "Nerdic." It is the language of technology and gadgets.

The world of language is fascinating and extensive. From its beginnings, which are unknown until the present, and the changes and evolutions that occur culturally, along with technological growth, the study of languages is far from short lived.

27. What is the definition of the word *phenomenon* as it is used in the following sentence?

    The evolution of language is an extensive and extraordinary phenomenon.

    (A) occurrence or event
    (B) patterned
    (C) advancement
    (D) mass confusion

28. Which of the following statements BEST summarizes the information presented in the article?

    (A) Languages are spoken all over the world.
    (B) The history and development of language is unknown.
    (C) The number of languages spoken, the history, and the evolution and development of languages is far reaching.
    (D) Spanish and French are the two most popular languages spoken around the world today.

29. Based on the information in the article, which of the following statements is INACCURATE?

    (A) Basque is a difficult language to learn.
    (B) The nation of Somalia has only one language.
    (C) There are more than 1,000 languages spoken in Africa.
    (D) The only language spoken in California is English.

30. This document provides the reader with the LEAST information on—

    (A) the history of writing.
    (B) the development of the Afrikaans language.
    (C) various language facts and information.
    (D) the cultural influences of languages.

31. What information supports the notion that early acknowledgment of languages is referenced in the Bible?

    (A) The first reference to languages is through Egyptian hieroglyphics.
    (B) The first reference to languages is found in the Biblical story of the Tower of Babel.
    (C) The first reference to languages is found in the Dead Sea Scrolls.
    (D) The first reference to languages is found in London in the 20th century.

Read the following passage and answer questions 32 through 36.

How to Write a Movie Review

Some of you may be interested in writing a movie review for fun, for profit, for your blog, or for your school newspaper. Regardless of your reason for wanting to write a movie review, it is not difficult, and making your thoughts known about the latest films will be entertaining in the very least. The following steps will help guide you in writing your first review.

STEP ONE

Select the movie that you want to review, and become familiar with its background and its context. Before you even get to the theater or the DVD player, research the film in advance. Look at the director, producers, and actors first. What have these people previously directed or produced or acted in? Have they won any important awards such as the Oscar or the SAG or the Golden Globe? Are their styles well known? What is the movie based on—was it written for the screen or adapted from a play or a historical event? Has the film been made before—is this a remake? Or, is it a sequel in a series of films? There are many things to learn before you begin watching and then reviewing. All of this information will help you understand the film better. Knowing this information will allow you to have more insight, and you'll pick up on important story elements, details, allusions, and trademarks of the actors or director. Knowing this information will also allow you to tell readers how it has or has not lived up to the original (such as a book). These are the things that readers want to know from critics.

STEP TWO

Watch the film. Once you have seen the film, formulate an opinion in one sentence—kind of like a strong thesis sentence in an essay. This is your job—to give an opinion of the movie. You have no doubt seen the "thumbs up" or "three stars out of five" ratings, but you want to have a specific thesis around which you will formulate your critique. For example, "I hated this comedy" becomes "The plot had its funny ups, but the downside was its length." Or, "This horror film is successful because it builds suspense all the way through to the end." In other words, this sentence is a very specific opinion that will form the foundation of your review.

STEP THREE

Create a good lead. The lead is the first sentence of the review. It is the first thing that your reader sees, and you want to attract attention and get him/her interested right away. There are many ways to grab the reader's attention: begin with a great quote from the movie and explain how it reflects something vital or interesting in the film; refer to the reputation of the actor or director and compare it to the performance that he/she had in this movie; compare this movie to another well-known film in one or two sentences; explain what your expectation was and whether or not it was fulfilled. End that first paragraph with your opinion statement.

STEP FOUR

Write a recap or brief synopsis of the film, but don't give away anything that would ruin the story for your readers—they may want to see it on their own. Professional reviews always include a brief summary. Because some readers like to know what they're getting into before they pay the price of a ticket, these brief summaries will either pique their interest or drive them away. Tell your reader the basic premise of the movie and how the story or plot builds but, again, don't give away the ending or key moments that would ruin the story for them. Most importantly, keep it brief.

STEP FIVE

Be able to back up your opinion with specifics from the film. The reader already knows how you feel about the film from your thesis-like statement early in the critique. But now is the time to support it with more specific details, such as: the film was too long, the actors had good timing, the writers did a fantastic job with the parody, there were too many scenes in the family room, etc., etc., etc. Use specific details to prove to the reader that what you said back in the beginning was accurate.

STEP SIX

Make it interesting. Not all reviews are made alike, and being boring is not going to get you many readers. From the beginning lead sentence to the ending paragraph, make the review engaging—use metaphors, analogies, specific adjectives, and adverbs that liven up the writing and create the image that you are hoping to portray. At the same time, however, be succinct and concise—a film review is not the place to write a dissertation on the meaning of life.

STEP SEVEN

No two opinions are alike, so you need to be honest with your appraisal. Some of your readers will disagree with your review, and everyone has a right to their opinion. However, being honest is going to get your readers to return to your HONEST critiques. You may dislike an actor in the film, but if he did a great job, be honest about that. Make sure that you maintain integrity and keep a level of standards in mind. A comedy should be funny, a horror film should be frightening, a drama should stir emotion, etc. Being honest will garner your review the respect it deserves.

STEP EIGHT

Good luck with your review, stay true to your opinion, and be honest above all else.

32. According to the information provided in STEP THREE, what is the purpose of a good lead?

   (A) to confuse the reader
   (B) to allow the reader freedom to finish reading the review or not
   (C) to force the reader to take notes
   (D) to grab the reader's attention

33. How is the information organized throughout the article?

   (A) Writing a review from initial background information through the inclusion of specific details and opinions.
   (B) Writing a review from the beginning of a film to the end.
   (C) Writing a review from the film credits to the way it is set up by the producers.
   (D) Writing a review by imitating the professional on television.

34. The author of the article uses a series of steps to organize the information to—

   (A) introduce the reader to film editing.
   (B) introduce the reader to background information about a film.
   (C) guide the reader in an organized and step-by-step manner through writing a film review.
   (D) guide the readers to watching more movies in their spare time.

35. The structure of the document is important because—

   (A) it allows the reader to skim the material easily.
   (B) it allows the reader to organize the information needed to write a review in a logical manner.
   (C) it confuses the reader and causes him/her to become discouraged.
   (D) it focuses the reader on the specific needs of writing a documentary film.

36. Which of the following statements BEST summarizes the information presented in the article?

   (A) The important steps needed to write a novel that will be adapted for a film.
   (B) The steps to take before filming a documentary.
   (C) The step-by-step approach to writing an honest and engaging film review.
   (D) The most important information to know about watching a film.

Read the following passage and answer questions 37 through 40.

What to Do with an Old Athletic Shoe

Depending on the condition of your old athletic shoes, many of us either give them away or throw them away. However, for those of you attempting to embrace green living and being good to the environment, you might want to consider a few of the following ways to reuse old athletic shoes.

SUGGESTION # 1

Green up your room or apartment! Athletic shoes, especially hightops—the ones that come up around the ankle—actually make excellent flowerpots. Take an old shoe, fill it up with soil, and plant some flowers in it.

SUGGESTION #2

Entertain your dog! Why buy expensive dog toys when you have a perfectly suited item for the job? Using your old shoes as dog toys will not only entertain your dog, but it will prevent the shoes from adding to the already limited space of a landfill. Remove all the laces and metal parts from the shoes that may cause your dog to choke, and then just give them a toss. Your best pet friend is bound to have fun.

SUGGESTION # 3

Become a sculptor or artist! Found art is the new art (well not so new; artists have been using found items for years and years). Try making a collage or sculpture from used objects like old shoes.

SUGGESTION # 4

Recycle your athletic shoes. Really! Nike, the shoe corporation, has a Reuse-a-Shoe program. By sending your old shoes to this program, the shoes will be reused as padding under a basketball court, an athletic track, or a playground surface.

SUGGESTION # 5

Change the job of your old athletic shoes—use them for something else! There are times when you need an old pair of shoes to get you through a dirty job: gardening and painting are good ways to use old shoes. By cutting off the back part of the shoe, you can use them for slip-ons when you go out to get the newspaper or mail.

SUGGESTION #6

Try giving them to those who are in need of any kind of shoe! The Salvation Army and Goodwill are two great places to donate your old shoes that still have a bit more life in them. Other places include homeless shelters and charities that cater to people who are victims of natural disasters.

37. Based on the information in the document, which of the following statements is accurate?

(A) There are many ways to reuse old athletic shoes.
(B) Athletic shoes should be thrown away at all times.
(C) Athletic shoes can be turned into a special meal for elephants.
(D) There are new careers available for athletic shoes that are homeless.

38. This document provides the MOST information about—

(A) the history of Goodwill and the Salvation Army.
(B) the many uses for shoelaces.
(C) the number of shoes that can fit into a Volkswagon Beetle.
(D) the many ways to reuse old athletic shoes.

39. What statement below supports the idea that recycling old athletic shoes helps save the environment?

(A) Recycling old shoes makes everyone happy.
(B) Recycling and reusing old athletic shoes helps prevent the spread of communicable diseases.
(C) Recycling old athletic shoes takes pressure off garbage persons.
(D) Recycling and reusing old athletic shoes decreases the amount of space taken up in landfills.

40. Which of the following suggestions for using old athletic shoes is NOT found in this article on recycling?

(A) Shoes can be used as flowerpots.
(B) Shoes can be used as dog toys.
(C) Shoes can be used as shelving.
(D) Shoes can be used as padding under an athletic track, playground, or basketball court.

Read the following play and answer questions 41 through 45.

The following one-act play is reprinted from *The Atlantic Book of Modern Plays*. Ed. Sterling Andrus Leonard. Boston: Atlantic Monthly Press, 1921.

The Beggar and the King

a play in one-act

by Winthrop Parkhurst

Characters: King
           Servant
           Beggar

[A chamber in the palace overlooks a courtyard. The season is midsummer. The windows of the palace are open, and from a distance there comes the sound of a man's voice crying for bread.]

[The King sits in a golden chair. A golden crown is on his head, and he holds in his hand a sceptre, which is also of gold. A Servant stands by his side, fanning him with an enormous fan of peacock feathers.]

The Beggar: *(outside)* Bread. Bread. Bread. Give me some bread.

The King: *(languidly)* Who is that crying in the street for bread?

The Servant: *(fanning)* O king, it is a beggar.

The King: Why does he cry for bread?

The Servant: O king, he cries for bread in order that he may fill his belly.

The King: I do not like the sound of his voice. It annoys me very much. Send him away.

The Servant: *(bowing)* O king, he *has* been sent away.

The King: If that is so, then why do I hear his voice?

The Servant: O king, he has been sent away many times, yet each time that he is sent away he returns again, crying louder than he did before.

The King: He is very unwise to annoy me on such a warm day. He must be punished for his impudence. Use the lash on him.

The Servant: O king, it has been done.

The King: Then bring out the spears.

The Servant: O king, the guards have already bloodied their swords many times driving him away from the palace gates. But it is of no avail.

The King: Then bind him and gag him if necessary. If need be cut out his tongue. I do not like the sound of the fellow's voice. It annoys me very much.

The Servant: O king, thy orders were obeyed even yesterday.

The King: *(frowning)* No. That cannot be. A beggar cannot cry for bread who has no tongue.

The Servant: Behold he can—if he has grown another.

The King: What! Why, men are not given more than one tongue in a lifetime. To have more than one tongue is treason.

The Servant: If it is treason to have more than one tongue, O king, then is this beggar surely guilty of treason.

The King: *(pompously)* The punishment for treason is death. See to it that the fellow is slain. And do not fan me so languidly. I am very warm.

The Servant: *(fanning more rapidly)* Behold, O great and illustrious king, all thy commands were obeyed even yesterday.

The King: How! Do not jest with thy king.

The Servant: If I jest, then there is truth in a jest. Even yesterday, O king, as I have told thee, the beggar which thou now hearest crying aloud in the street was slain by thy soldiers with a sword.

The King: Do ghosts eat bread? Forsooth, men who have been slain with a sword do not go about in the streets crying for a piece of bread.

The Servant: Forsooth, they do if they are fashioned as this beggar.

The King: Why, he is but a man. Surely he cannot have more than one life in a lifetime.

The Servant: Listen to a tale, O king, which happened yesterday.

The King: I am listening.

The Servant: Thy soldiers smote this beggar for crying aloud in the streets for bread, but his wounds are already healed. They cut out his tongue, but he immediately grew another. They slew him, yet he is now alive.

The King: Ah! That is a tale which I cannot understand at all.

The Servant: O king, it may be well.

The King: I cannot understand what thou sayest, either.

The Servant: O king, that may be well also.

The King: Thou art speaking now in riddles. I do not like riddles. They confuse my brain.

The Servant: Behold, O king, if I speak in riddles it is because a riddle has come to pass.

[The Beggar's voice suddenly cries out loudly.]

The Beggar: *(outside)* Bread. Bread. Give me some bread.

The King: Ah! He is crying out again. His voice seems to me louder than it was before.

The Servant: Hunger is as food to the lungs, O king.

The King: His lungs I will wager are well fed. Ha, ha!

The Servant: But alas! his stomach is quite empty.

The King: That is not my business.

The Servant: Should I not perhaps fling him a crust from the window?

The King: No! To feed a beggar is always foolish. Every crumb that is given to a beggar is an evil seed from which springs another fellow like him.

The Beggar: *(outside)* Bread. Bread. Give me some bread.

The Servant: He seems very hungry, O king.

The King: Yes. So I should judge.

The Servant: If thou wilt not let me fling him a piece of bread, thine ears must pay the debts of thy hand.

The King: A king can have no debts.

The Servant: That is true, O king. Even so, the noise of this fellow's begging must annoy thee greatly.

The King: It does.

The Servant: Doubtless he craves only a small crust from thy table and he would be content.

The King: Yea, doubtless he craves only to be a king and he would be very happy indeed.

The Servant: Do not be hard, O king. Thou art ever wise and just. This fellow is exceedingly hungry. Dost thou not command me to fling him just one small crust from the window?

The King: My commands I have already given thee. See that the beggar is driven away.

The Servant: But alas! O king, if he is driven away he will return again even as he did before.

The King: Then see to it that he is slain. I cannot be annoyed with the sound of his voice.

The Servant: But alas! O great and illustrious king, if he is slain he will come to life again even as he did before.

The King: Ah! that is true. But his voice troubles me. I do not like to hear it.

The Servant: His lungs are fattened with hunger. Of a truth they are quite strong.

The King: Well, propose a remedy to weaken them.

The Servant: A remedy, O king?

[He stops fanning.]

The King: That is what I said. A remedy—and do not stop fanning me. I am exceedingly warm.

The Servant: *(fanning vigorously)* A crust of bread, O king, dropped from yonder window—forsooth that might prove a remedy.

The King: *(angrily)* I have said I will not give him a crust of bread. If I gave him a crust to-day he would be just as hungry again to-morrow, and my troubles would be as great as before.

The Servant: That is true, O king. Thy mind is surely filled with great learning.

The King: Therefore, some other remedy must be found.

The Servant: O king, the words of thy illustrious mouth are as very meat-balls of wisdom.

The King: *(musing)* Now let me consider. Thou sayest he does not suffer pain—

The Servant: Therefore he cannot be tortured.

The King: And he will not die—

The Servant: Therefore it is useless to kill him.

The King: Now let me consider. I must think of some other way.

The Servant: Perhaps a small crust of bread, O king—

The King: Ha! I have it. I have it. I myself will order him to stop.

The Servant: *(horrified)* O king!

The King: Send the beggar here.

The Servant: O king!

The King: Ha! I rather fancy the fellow will stop his noise when the king commands him to. Ha, ha, ha!

The Servant: O king, thou wilt not have a beggar brought into thy royal chamber!

The King: *(pleased with his idea)* Yea. Go outside and tell this fellow that the king desires his presence.

The Servant: O great and illustrious king, thou wilt surely not do this thing. Thou wilt surely not soil thy royal eyes by looking on such a filthy creature. Thou wilt surely not contaminate thy lips by speaking to a common beggar who cries aloud in the streets for bread.

The King: My ears have been soiled too much already. Therefore go now and do as I have commanded thee.

The Servant: O great and illustrious king, thou wilt surely not—

The King: *(roaring at him)* I said, Go! *(the Servant, abashed, goes out.)* Forsooth, I fancy the fellow will stop his bawling when I order him to. Forsooth, I fancy he will be pretty well frightened when he hears that the king desires his presence. Ha, ha, ha, ha!

The Servant: (returning) O king, here is the beggar.

[A shambling creature hung in filthy rags follows the servant slowly into the royal chamber.]

The King: Ha! A magnificent sight, to be sure. Art thou the beggar who has been crying aloud in the streets for bread?

The Beggar: *(in a faint voice, after a slight pause)* Art thou the king?

The King: I am the king.

The Servant: *(aside to the Beggar)* It is not proper for a beggar to ask a question of a king. Speak only as thou art spoken to.

The King: *(to the Servant)* Do thou likewise. *(to the Beggar)* I have ordered thee here to speak to thee concerning a very grave matter. Thou art the beggar, I understand, who often cries aloud in the streets for bread. Now, the complaint of thy voice annoys me greatly. Therefore, do not beg any more.

The Beggar: *(faintly)* I—I do not understand.

The King: I said, do not beg any more.

The Beggar: I—I do not understand.

The Servant: *(aside to the Beggar)* The king has commanded thee not to beg for bread any more. The noise of thy voice is as garbage in his ears.

The King: *(to the Servant)* Ha! An excellent flower of speech. Pin it in thy button-hole. *(to the Beggar)* Thine ears, I see, are in need of a bath even more than thy body. I said, *Do not beg any more.*

The Beggar: I—I do not understand.

The King: *(making a trumpet of his hands and shouting).* DO NOT BEG ANY MORE.

The Beggar: I—I do not understand.

The King: Heavens! He is deafer than a stone wall.

The Servant: O king, he cannot be deaf, for he understood me quite easily when I spoke to him in the street.

The King: *(to the Beggar)* Art thou deaf? Canst thou hear what I am saying to thee now?

The Beggar: Alas! I can hear every word perfectly.

The King: Fft! The impudence. Thy tongue shall be cut out for this.

The Servant: O king, to cut out his tongue is useless, for he will grow another.

The King: No matter. It shall be cut out anyway. *(to the Beggar)* I have ordered thee not to beg any more in the streets. What meanest thou by saying thou dost not understand?

The Beggar: The words of thy mouth I can hear perfectly. But their noise is only a foolish tinkling in my ears.

The King: Fft! Only a—! A lash will tinkle thy hide for thee if thou dost not cure thy tongue of impudence. I, thy king, have ordered thee not to beg any more in the streets for bread. Signify, therefore, that thou wilt obey the orders of thy king by quickly touching thy forehead thrice to the floor.

The Beggar: That is impossible.

The Servant: *(aside to the Beggar)* Come. It is not safe to tempt the patience of the king too long. His patience is truly great, but he loses it most wondrous quickly.

The King: Come, now: I have ordered thee to touch thy forehead to the floor.

The Servant: *(nudging him)* And quickly.

The Beggar: Wherefore should I touch my forehead to the floor?

The King: In order to seal thy promise to thy king.

The Beggar: But I have made no promise. Neither have I any king.

The King: Ho! He has made no promise. Neither has he any king. Ha, ha, ha. I have commanded thee not to beg any more, for the sound of thy voice is grievous unto my ears. Touch thy forehead now to the floor, as I have commanded thee, and thou shall go from this palace a free man. Refuse, and thou wilt be sorry before an hour that thy father ever came within twenty paces of thy mother.

The Beggar: I have ever lamented that he did. For to be born into this world a beggar is a more unhappy thing than any that I know—unless it is to be born a king.

The King: Fft! Thy tongue of a truth is too lively for thy health. Come, now, touch thy forehead thrice to the floor and promise solemnly that thou wilt never beg in the streets again. And hurry!

The Servant: *(aside)* It is wise to do as thy king commands thee. His patience is near an end.

The King: Do not be afraid to soil the floor with thy forehead. I will graciously forgive thee for that.

[The Beggar stands motionless.]

The Servant: I said, it is not wise to keep the king waiting.

[The Beggar does not move.]

The King: Well? *(A pause.)* Well? *(In a rage)* WELL?

The Beggar: O king, thou hast commanded me not to beg in the streets for bread, for the noise of my voice offends thee. Now therefore do I likewise command thee to remove thy crown from thy forehead and throw it from yonder window into the street. For when thou hast thrown thy crown into the street, then will I no longer be obliged to beg.

The King: Fft! *Thou* commandest *me! Thou,* a beggar from the streets, commandest *me,* a king, to remove my crown from my forehead and throw it from yonder window into the street!

The Beggar: That is what I said.

The King: Why, dost thou not know I can have thee slain for such words?

The Beggar: No. Thou canst not have me slain. The spears of thy soldiers are as straws against my body.

The King: Ha! We shall see if they are. We shall see!

The Servant: O king, it is indeed true. It is even as he has told thee.

The Beggar: I have required thee to remove thy crown from thy forehead. If so be thou wilt throw it from yonder window into the street, my voice will cease to annoy thee any more. But if thou refuse, then thou wilt wish thou hadst never had any crown at all. For thy days will be filled with a terrible boding and thy nights will be full of horrors, even as a ship is full of rats.

The King: Why, this is insolence. This is treason!

The Beggar: Wilt thou throw thy crown from yonder window?

The King: Why, this is high treason!

The Beggar: I ask thee, wilt thou throw thy crown from yonder window?

The Servant: *(aside to the King)* Perhaps it were wise to humor him, O king. After thou hast thrown thy crown away I can go outside and bring it to thee again.

The Beggar: Well? Well? *(He points to the window.)* Well?

The King: No! I will not throw my crown from that window—no, nor from any other window. What! Shall I obey the orders of a beggar? Never!

The Beggar: *(preparing to leave)* Truly, that is spoken like a king. Thou art a king, so thou wouldst prefer to lose thy head than that silly circle of gold that so foolishly sits upon it. But it is well. Thou art a king. Thou couldst not prefer otherwise.

[He walks calmly toward the door.]

The King: *(to the Servant)* Stop him! Seize him! Does he think to get off so easily with his impudence!

The Beggar: *(coolly)* One of thy servants cannot stop me. Neither can ten thousand of them do me any harm. I am stronger than a mountain. I am stronger than the sea!

The King: Ha! We will see about that, we will see about that. *(To the Servant)* Hold him, I say. Call the guards. He shall be put in chains.

The Beggar: My strength is greater than a mountain and my words are more fearful than a hurricane. This servant of thine cannot even touch me. With one breath of my mouth I can blow over this whole palace.

The King: Dost thou hear the impudence he is offering me? Why dost thou not seize him? What is the matter with thee? Why dost thou not call the guards?

The Beggar: I will not harm thee now. I will only cry aloud in the streets for bread wherewith to fill my belly. But one day I will not be so kind to thee. On that day my mouth will be filled with a rushing wind and my arms will become as strong as steel rods, and I will blow over this palace, and all the bones in thy foolish body I will snap between my fingers. I will beat upon a large drum and thy head will be my drumstick. I will not do these things now. But one day I will do them. Therefore, when my voice sounds again in thine ears, begging for bread, remember what I have told thee. Remember, O king, and be afraid!

[He walks out. The Servant, struck dumb, stares after him. The King sits in his chair, dazed.]

The King: *(suddenly collecting his wits)* After him! After him! He must not be allowed to escape! After him!

The Servant: *(faltering)* O king—I cannot seem to move.

The King: Quick, then. Call the guards. He must be caught and put in chains. Quick, I say. Call the guards!

The Servant: O king—I cannot seem to call them.

The King: How! Art thou dumb? Ah!

[The Beggar's voice is heard outside.]

The Beggar: Bread. Bread. Give me some bread.

The King: Ah. *[He turns toward the window, half-frightened, and then, almost instinctively, raises his hands toward his crown, and seems on the point of tossing it out the window. But with an oath he replaces it and presses it firmly on his head.]* How! Am I afraid of a beggar!

The Beggar: *(continuing outside)* Bread. Bread. Give me some bread.

The King: *(with terrible anger)* Close that window!

[The Servant stands stupidly, and the voice of the Beggar grows louder as the curtain falls.]

CURTAIN

41. Read this line from the play.

For thy days will be filled with a terrible boding and thy nights will be full of horrors; even as a ship is full of rats.

What is the meaning of the word *boding* as it is used in this line?

   (A) pretentious
   (B) omens
   (C) impudence
   (D) resentment

42. How does the reader know that this piece of literature is a short play?

   (A) The story is told through character dialogue and uses stage directions.
   (B) The sentence structure.
   (C) The play has characters.
   (D) There is a narrator.

43. This type of story would be considered a—

   (A) tragedy.
   (B) comedy.
   (C) dramatic monologue.
   (D) drama.

44. How does the beggar react to the king's demands that he quit begging?

   (A) He apologizes to the king.
   (B) He tells the servant to stand still.
   (C) He asks the king to throw his crown out the window.
   (D) He promises the king that he will stop begging.

45. Which statement BEST describes the king's reaction to the beggar's request?

   (A) The king refused and demanded the servant to close the window.
   (B) The king agreed and did what the beggar asked.
   (C) The king told the servant to kill the beggar's wife.
   (D) The king gave the beggar some food.

WRITING

The following passage is a rough draft of an essay. It contains a variety of errors that may include grammar, punctuation, sentence structure, or organization. Read the passage and answer questions 46 through 49.

ROUGH DRAFT

Mono Lake

(1) Mono Lake is an unusual lake that is located in the central part of California. (2) It is an alkaline and hyper-saline lake that is a critical nesting habitat for several bird species and is an unusually productive ecosystem as well. (3) It is believed to have formed approximately 760,000 years ago and that Mono Lake is what is left of a much larger lake that covered part of Nevada and Utah at one time. (4) This make Mono Lake one of the oldest lake in North America.

(5) Because the lake contains about 280 tons of dissolved salts, fish cannot survive in the lake. (6) However, Mono Lake is famous for its Mono Lake brine shrimp. (7) This particular species of brine shrimp is about as large as a thumbnail, but more importantly, the only place on earth where they are found is in Mono Lake. (8) During the warmer summer months there is an estimated 4-6 trillion brine shrimp in the lake which feel off of microscopic algae that grows there. (9) There is no nutritional value in brine shrimp for humans, but the shrimp are a staple to birds that are native to the region.

(10) By 1982 the lake lost 31 percent of is 1941 surface area. (11) Negit Island which sits in the middle of the lake became bridge by land and this in turn exposed the nests of gulls to predators and this once vital breeding colony was forced to abandon the site. (12) There has been ongoing controversy that surrounds the lake. (13) Much of water that feeds into the lake by the Owens River was diverted in 1941 to help provide water for the Los Angeles area. (14) Because so much water was diverted, evaporation began to exceed the inflow and the surface level of Mono Lake fell rapidly. (15) This drop exposed the alkaline sands and tufa towers that had at one time been submerged.

46. Which of the following sentences would BEST begin the story?

    (A) Mono Lake is very strange and salty.
    (B) With a critical nesting habitat, Mono Lake is in the center of California.
    (C) One of the oldest lakes in North America, Mono Lake, is a critical nesting habitat and has a flourishing ecosystem.
    (D) Mono Lake used to be quite large, but now it is just old.

47. What is the BEST way to combine the sentences numbered 5 and 6?

    (A) Containing a lot of salt, fish can't live in the lake but brine shrimp can.
    (B) Because the lake contains about 280 tons of dissolved salts, fish cannot survive, but Mono Lake brine shrimp are famous.
    (C) Mono Lake has brine shrimp that can live in salty water, but any fish will die.
    (D) Fish die in the lake because of the salt, but brine shrimp can live and they are famous in Mono Lake.

48. Which of the following BEST describes what is wrong with paragraph three?

    (A) The information is scattered and unorganized.
    (B) The information is dishonest.
    (C) There are too many sentences.
    (D) The sentences are incomplete and fragmented.

49. Which of the following would be the BEST way to repair sentence 4, which has an error in subject/verb agreement?

    (A) This will make Mono Lake one of the oldest lake in North America.
    (B) This will be making Mono Lake one of the oldest lake in North America.
    (C) This make Mono Lake one of the oldest lakes in North America.
    (D) This makes Mono Lake one of the oldest lakes in North America.

The following passage is a rough draft of an essay. It contains a variety of errors that may include grammar, punctuation, sentence structure, or organization. Read the passage and answer questions 50 through 53.

ROUGH DRAFT

The Olympic Games

(1) The Olympic Games are an international multi-sport competition that is divided into winter and summer sporting events. (2) The <u>seasonal games is held</u> every four years and until 1992, they were held in the same year, but since that time, the winter and summer games are separated by two years.

(3) The history of the Olympic Games begins in Greece where the earliest known games were held in 776 BC. (4) The Olympic Games were held until AD 393. (5) The revival of the games was spurred by a Greek poet/newspaper editor in <u>1833 and in 1859 the first modern</u> international Olympic Games were held. (6) A man named Evangelos Zappas sponsored the games and paid for refurbishing the stadium in Athens, Greece where they were held in 1870 and 1875.

(7) By 1894 the IOC (International Olympic Committee) was founded. (8) In the summer of 1896, the first IOC's Olympic Games were held in Athens. (9) Today, participation in the Olympic Games has expanded to include athletes from nearly every nation in the world. (10) Improved <u>satellite communications and global telecasts have help to increase</u> the popularity and support of the games.

(11) History is made almost every year that the games are held. (12) Records are broken and athletic events are added. (13) In addition to the sports and the athletes making history, the locations of the events also make history. (14) In 2008 the Summer Olympic Games will be held in Beijing, China with 302 different events in 28 different sports. (15) That is the first time ever that they have been held there and the world will be watching.

50. Which of the following is the BEST way to correct the underlined portion of sentence 2?

    (A) seasonal game wasn't held
    (B) seasonal game will be held
    (C) seasonal games are held
    (D) seasonal games isn't held

51. Which of the following is supported by details and evidence in the essay?

    (A) The Olympic Games are fun and exciting.
    (B) The Olympic Games date back to Ancient Greece.
    (C) The Olympic Games are dangerous and unhealthy.
    (D) The Olympic Games are always held in Greece.

52. The error in the underlined portion of sentence 5 is—

    (A) with spelling.
    (B) with punctuation.
    (C) unidentifiable.
    (D) grammatical.

53. Which of the following sentences improves the underlined part of sentence 10?

    (A) satellite communications and global telecasts help increase
    (B) satellite communications and global telecasts have helped increase
    (C) satellite communications and global telecasts has helps increase
    (D) satellite communications and global telecasts have help increase

The following passage is a rough draft of an essay. It contains a variety of errors that may include grammar, punctuation, sentence structure, or organization. Read the passage and answer questions 54 through 57.

ROUGH DRAFT

The Pacific Ocean

(1) The Pacific Ocean is the largest ocean on Earth. (2) It was named by the Portuguese explorer Ferdinand Magellan from a Latin word "Mare Pacificum" which means "peaceful sea." (3) Although it is shrinking in size from plate tectonic movement and the Atlantic Ocean is increasing in size for the same reason, the enormity of this body of water is almost incomprehensible.

(4) Extending 9600 miles (15,500 kilometers) from the Arctic in the north and the Antarctica in the south, the Pacific Ocean is bordered on the west by Asia and Australia and by the Americas on the east and measures 12,300 miles (19,800 kilometers) at its widest point. (5) In square miles, the Pacific Ocean <u>boasts</u> a whopping 65.3 million square miles (169.2 million square kilometers). (6) It covers roughly 46% of the Earth's water surface. (7) However, this immense body of water covers 32% of the Earth's total surface area. (8) In other words, the Pacific Ocean is larger than all of the Earth's landmasses put together and there is room for another continent the size of Africa.

(9) The deepest point of the Pacific was in the western part of the North Pacific. (10) The Mariana Trench is 35,798 feet deep (10,911 meters) and the lowest point on Earth. (11) The average depth of the ocean however, is 14,000 feet (4,280 meters). (12) There are about 25,000 islands found in the Pacific Ocean. (13) Most of these islands are located below the equator, <u>which divides the ocean into the North Pacific and the South Pacific.</u> (14) Because the ocean straddles the 180° Meridian (the international dateline, part of the Pacific is in the Earth's Eastern Hemisphere and part is in the Western Hemisphere.

(15) The Pacific Ocean is the granddaddy of all oceans. (16) Its breadth and depth are difficult to understand when you look at a map. (17) However, when the actual numbers are laid out, this ocean's size comes into proper perspective. (18) The word "enormous" doesn't do justice to its size.

54. Which of the following BEST defines the meaning of the underlined word *boasts* in sentence 5?

    (A) a large boat
    (B) take charge of
    (C) brag about
    (D) ignore

55. If a student wanted to learn more about the Pacific Ocean and did not have access to the Internet, what would be the BEST source to find information?

    (A) radio
    (B) television
    (C) encyclopedia
    (D) thesaurus

56. What is the most effective substitution for the underlined part of sentence 13?

    (A) dividing the ocean into the North and South Pacific.
    (B) which cuts the ocean into two parts, the North and the South.
    (C) which separates the ocean in half.
    (D) making a north and a south ocean of the Pacific Ocean.

57. Which revision of sentence 9 uses active voice only?

    (A) The deepest point of the Pacific could have been found in the western part of the North Pacific.
    (B) The deepest point of the Pacific is in the western part of the North Pacific.
    (C) The deepest point of the Pacific was found in the western part of the North Pacific.
    (D) The deepest point of the Pacific had been found in the western part of the North Pacific.

For questions 58 to 64 choose the word or phrase that best completes the sentence.

58. Which of these three swimmers has the _____ qualifying time?

    (A) more fast
    (B) most fastest
    (C) more faster
    (D) fastest

59. _____ is one of the best Olympic athletes that I have ever seen.

    (A) Him
    (B) Her
    (C) I
    (D) She

60. When he _____ the flowers, he tripped on the sidewalk and fell.

    (A) delivered
    (B) delivers
    (C) was delivers
    (D) had delivered

61. What we didn't expect is that _____ would be chosen for the television commercial.

    (A) she and I
    (B) she and me
    (C) her and me
    (D) her and I

62. Cory left the decision up to _____.

    (A) us
    (B) they
    (C) she
    (D) we

63. Many athletic events _____ stamina and agility.

    (A) requires
    (B) require
    (C) does required
    (D) is requiring

64. The _____ dogs bark almost all day long.

    (A) too
    (B) to
    (C) two
    (D) tow

For questions 65 to 72 choose the word or phrase that best completes the sentence.

65. Chihuahua is the _____ state in Mexico.

    (A) larger
    (B) previously larger
    (C) largest
    (D) more larger

66. Horseradish _____ for its pungent fleshy root, which is useful in seasoning.

    (A) has cultivated
    (B) is cultivated
    (C) cultivating
    (D) is cultivating

67. Machu Picchu _____ the best preserved Incan settlement today.

    (A) is
    (B) are
    (C) was
    (D) wasn't

68. _____ be going to Boston College next fall.

    (A) She was
    (B) She'll
    (C) She wasn't
    (D) She's

69. The new Prius has _____ room in the trunk, but gets better gas mileage than the previous model.

    (A) lesser
    (B) least
    (C) smaller
    (D) less

70. Dylan _____ wild lifestyle led to his early death.

    (A) Thomas
    (B) Thomas'es
    (C) Thomas'
    (D) Thomases'

71. John Coltrane, a jazz saxophonist, _____ attention when he played with the Miles Davis quintet.

    (A) attracts
    (B) attracted
    (C) attracting
    (D) can attract

72. _____ going to take a trip to South Africa next winter.

   (A) There
   (B) Their
   (C) They
   (D) They're

DIAGNOSTIC EXAM SECTION 1 WRITING TASK

- Read the instructions for the writing task carefully. You may need to read it several times.
- Brainstorm and organize your thoughts on paper.
- Aim for at least four paragraphs; five is better.
- Be certain that you have a well-developed introduction, body paragraphs, and conclusion.
- Support your thesis by using specific details and examples.
- Use effective word choice.
- Be aware of sentence beginnings; avoid repeating them.
- Vary sentence length to make your writing more interesting.
- Reread your essay to catch errors in grammar, spelling, punctuation, and sentence formation.

Writing Task:

Consider the cliché: Is the glass half empty or half full? Think about it for awhile, brainstorm, and then write a persuasive essay in which you take a stand on the topic. Try to convince someone who believes the opposite that you are correct. Support your essay with examples.

- Write your essay on the answer sheet in the appendix of this book.
- Adding a title is not mandatory.
- Either printing or cursive writing is acceptable.
- Write clearly and neatly—make the reader's job easier.
- Using a dictionary or thesaurus is not permitted.
- GOOD LUCK!

NOTE: There are scored writing samples for this writing task at the end of this test. After you have written your response, compare your writing to those already scored to see how your writing compares. Pay particular attention to the essays with the highest scores. You will need a 3 or a 4 to pass this task.

Diagnostic Exam: Section 1

Question #	Answer	Strand	Standard	
1.	D	Word Analysis	1.0	1.2
2.	A	Word Analysis	1.0	1.1
3.	A	Literary Response and Analysis	1.0	3.4
4.	B	Literary Response and Analysis	1.0	3.11
5.	C	Literary Response and Analysis	1.0	3.9
6.	B	Literary Response and Analysis	1.0	3.7(8)
7.	D	Literary Response and Analysis	1.0	3.12
8.	A	Literary Response and Analysis	1.0	3.11
9.	D	Word Analysis	1.0	1.1
10.	B	Literary Response and Analysis	1.0	3.3
11.	C	Literary Response and Analysis	1.0	3.4
12.	A	Literary Response and Analysis	1.0	3.4
13.	B	Literary Response and Analysis	1.0	3.6
14.	D	Literary Response and Analysis	1.0	3.8
15.	A	Literary Response and Analysis	1.0	3.1
16.	C	Literary Response and Analysis	1.0	3.3
17.	A	Literary Response and Analysis	1.0	3.6
18.	C	Literary Response and Analysis	1.0	3.7
19.	B	Word Analysis	1.0	1.2
20.	C	Literary Response and Analysis	1.0	3.7
21.	A	Word Analysis	1.0	1.1
22.	C	Reading Comprehension	1.0	2.4
23.	C	Reading Comprehension	1.0	2.5
24.	D	Reading Comprehension	1.0	2.7
25.	B	Reading Comprehension	1.0	2.8
26.	D	Reading Comprehension	1.0	2.8
27.	A	Word Analysis	1.0	1.1
28.	C	Reading Comprehension	1.0	2.4
29.	D	Reading Comprehension	1.0	2.5
30.	A	Reading Comprehension	1.0	2.7
31.	B	Reading Comprehension	1.0	2.8
32.	D	Reading Comprehension	1.0	2.8
33.	A	Reading Comprehension	1.0	2.1
34.	C	Reading Comprehension	1.0	2.1 (8)
35.	B	Reading Comprehension	1.0	2.1
36.	C	Reading Comprehension	1.0	2.4

Diagnostic Exam

Question #	Answer	Strand	Standard	
37.	A	Reading Comprehension	1.0	2.5
38.	D	Reading Comprehension	1.0	2.7
39.	D	Reading Comprehension	1.0	2.8
40.	C	Reading Comprehension	1.0	2.8
41.	B	Word Analysis	1.0	1.1
42.	A	Literary Response and Analysis	1.0	3.1
43.	D	Literary Response and Analysis	1.0	3.1
44.	C	Literary Response and Analysis	1.0	3.3
45.	A	Literary Response and Analysis	1.0	3.5
46.	C	Writing Strategies	1.0	1.9
47.	B	Writing Strategies	1.0	1.9
48.	A	Writing Strategies	1.0	1.4
49.	D	Writing Strategies	1.0	1.2
50.	C	Word Analysis	1.0	1.1
51.	B	Writing Strategies	1.0	1.4
52.	B	Writing Strategies	1.0	1.9
53.	A	Literary Response and Analysis	1.0	3.7 (8)
54.	C	Word Analysis	1.0	1.2
55.	C	Writing Strategies	1.0	1.9
56.	A	Writing Strategies	1.0	1.5
57.	B	Word Analysis	1.0	1.1
58.	D	Grammar and Mechanics of Writing	1.0	1.3
59.	D	Grammar and Mechanics of Writing	1.0	1.3
60.	A	Grammar and Mechanics of Writing	1.0	1.3
61.	A	Grammar and Mechanics of Writing	1.0	1.3
62.	A	Grammar and Mechanics of Writing	1.0	1.2
63.	B	Grammar and Mechanics of Writing	1.0	1.2
64.	C	Grammar and Mechanics of Writing	1.0	1.2
65.	C	Grammar and Mechanics of Writing	1.0	1.1
66.	B	Grammar and Mechanics of Writing	1.0	1.1
67.	A	Grammar and Mechanics of Writing	1.0	1.1
68.	B	Grammar and Mechanics of Writing	1.0	1.1
69.	D	Grammar and Mechanics of Writing	1.0	1.1
70.	C	Grammar and Mechanics of Writing	1.0	1.2
71.	B	Grammar and Mechanics of Writing	1.0	1.2
72.	D	Grammar and Mechanics of Writing	1.0	1.3

DIAGNOSTIC EXAM
WRITING TASK SCORED EXAMPLES

Writing Task:

Consider the cliché: Is the glass half empty or half full? Think about it for awhile, brainstorm, and then write a persuasive essay in which you take a stand on the topic. Try to convince someone who believes the opposite that you are correct. Support your essay with examples.

4

SCORE POINT 4
STUDENT RESPONSE

Without question, the glass is always half full! To understand the underlying meaning to this cliché, think of the positive and negative sides to life, situations, experiences and just about every person on the planet. Adopting a positive attitude as a mantra is the only way to face life. A negative attitude is that half-empty glass, and the half-empty glass will always leave you wanting or wishing for more, frustrated and depressed. Seeing the positive side to life is fulfilling, motivating, and rewarding.

Let's say that your friend George left his house to go to school. He jumped into his car, put the key in the ignition and there was no response. The battery was dead. Generally, this guy has a quick temper, but today for some reason he just handled it without going crazy or losing his temper. Calling a friend, who was just leaving for school as well, the problem was solved. Getting into his friend's car, there was a group of elementary school kids. Amazed at the young faces crowded in the back seat, George asked what was going on. His friend Smitty explained that he takes these kids to school for his mom. To cover her carpool duty and after school he tutors them back at his house. George had no idea that his friend did this, and offered to help out. So, taking what could have been a very negative morning with the dead car, George discovers something that he never would have discovered had his car started that morning. George begins helping a group of kids that need help, and while his assistance is much appreciated, he too is fulfilled with having the opportunity to give back. That's the glass being half full!

One day your sister Mary is getting ready for a big debate. She is nervous and maybe nervous isn't quite as strong a word for the way she is feeling. You approach Mary and ask if there is anything you can do to help her out. Mary suddenly begins to cry. She is so worried about forgetting everything the debate team had studied for the past six months; she just lets her guard down. But you, seeing this as an opportunity to help, give her a hug and tell her things are going to be fine. You follow that with a few kind words and maybe something funny. And then, you pull her into the kitchen, make her a sandwich and within minutes, her smile returns and she is back to her old self. That's taking a half-full glass and filling it up. Being kind is motivating—motivating because this once sad situation has been turned into something completely opposite.

How many times have you heard your friends complain about having to do chores around the house or doing things that they have to do, and would rather not. But these negative complaints can be turned into rewards. Take the positive approach. Look at the task at hand and tackle it. The sooner it gets done, the sooner the rest of your life can continue. There really is no sense in whining or complaining—just do it. Be positive, put a smile on your face and go for it.

Approaching everything in life with a positive attitude is the only way to approach life. Seeing the negative in everything brings you down, down down. Who needs down? No one! Life, as they say, is too short for taking the low road. Take the high road and come out on the other side a much better person. We all know people who complain incessantly and say negative things about everything and everyone. They are not particularly fun to be around—but taking the half-full philosophy even about these people, the good thing that they do for you is remind you about how good it is to be positive and to feel good about life. Definitely, the glass is half-full.

3

SCORE POINT 3
STUDENT RESPONSE

Is the glass half-empty or is it half-full? It should be half-full. A half-filled glass is better than its opposite, half-empty. Having a positive attitude is what it takes to keep it half-filled or fill it up. Your choice. Seeing the good things in potentially negative situations is the way to keep positive. It is like learning a positive lesson from everything that you believe is negative. Stay positive and keep that glass half-full is the way to be.

Missing the bus, not making the team, losing your wallet, tripping in front of two million people—who wants to endure such things? I would guess no one. But, situations like these enter your life, everyone's life at some time. It's the way that you handle them that matters. Missing the bus for instance—you miss one, you get on another. You might be a bit late for an appointment, but you sit down next to someone who becomes one of the most motivating people you have ever met and a good friend for a long long time. That's looking at things in a positive manner—yes, you missed the bus, but you also never would have met this new friend if you hadn't.

You've been working out really hard, putting in a lot of time and really improving your game. Weeks and weeks of early morning work outs and afternoon scrimmages have occupied your time. You truly want to make the team, but the day comes when the roster is posted, and you name isn't on it. Do you turn around with a bad attitude, complain, scream and yell? No. What's the point in that? Think about it. Look at the names on the roster. Congratulate them, be happy for them and get on with your life. It just wasn't your time. And, as it ends up, something better comes along—you get that new guitar you've been wanting or the neighborhood YMCA offers you a job coaching basketball. Life is good and there are always positive things that come from negative ones.

Approaching life by looking at things in a positive way, is far more productive. Negativity breeds negativity. If you think negative, negative seems to find you. The opposite is true with the half-full glass. Positive attitude equals positive results regardless of the situation. Look at all things from the perspective that you will always take something away that is helpful or instructive.

2

SCORE POINT 2
STUDENT RESPONSE

The glass should be half-full. And, what that means is to have a good attitude about things that you deal with in life. Whether you are dealing with your parents, or your friends, be positive. Don't say negative things. That doesn't help any situation. Look at things in the bright side.

If you look at things in a bad way, the sky will fall all over your head. And where does that get you. Don't go into work or school with a grumpy attitude, because everyone around you will think you are a jerk. Be positive. And sometimes that is not always easy, but if you give it a try, you will feel better inside and out.

Make your life feel like your glass is always half-full. Don't have a bad attitude. Don't talk back to your parents, don't dis your friends. Good attitude is where it is. Keep on the sunny side.

1

SCORE POINT 1
STUDENT RESPONSE

When someone asks you if the glass is half-empty, tell them no. Its not half-empty. It is almost full. That means you have a good attitude. Good attitude is good. Walking around acting like you have a grump on, is not good. No one will like you—-they'll walk by and say—hey look at that guy, he sure is a punk with his bad ol attitude.

Thing good things. do good things. Don't be sad, be happy as that old song goes.

Word Analysis, Fluency, and Systematic Vocabulary Development—Part I

The California High School Exit Exam is directly tied to the California Content Standards. The content standards are basically (and very simply defined) the specific skills that you are learning in the classroom every year according to the state's education department. At the top of the list—rated number one in importance is READING. Reading is a lot more than just reading! Understanding the *words* that you are reading and making sense of them is vital to improving your overall skills as a reader. In this chapter, we will be looking at **words** and how they are used in sentences. On the exam, there are times when you need to be able to choose an actual or **literal** definition. There will be other times when you will need to select the **figurative**, **denotative**, or **connotative** meaning of the word or to know what an **idiom** is. You're asking yourself, "and just what does all that mean?" Read on.

> **TIP**
>
> Study and focus on the chapters in your areas of weakness *first*.

CHAPTER FOCUS

- Literal—meanings of words
- Figurative—meanings of words
- Denotative—meanings of words
- Connotative—meanings of words
- Idioms—common sayings that mean something different than what is actually said

---

LITERAL MEANINGS

Choosing the literal meaning of a word from a list of answers is a frequent occurrence on the CAHSEE. The test makers don't come right out and say "choose the literal meaning of this word" in their questions, but when they want to know if you can choose the correct definition, that is *really* what they mean. The literal meaning of a word is simply the *actual* or *exact* definition of the word as it is used in the sentence. That's it—nothing more! No need to add or infer meanings that aren't there. A car is a car (something that carries people and moves on four wheels), a fish is a fish (something that swims and breathes in water), and a dog is a dog (a four-legged animal that barks). Not a black Mercedes with leather interior, or a fabulous Ford, or a tiny Toyota. Not a rainbow trout, Atlantic salmon, or mahi mahi. Not a poodle, Labrador retriever, or dachshund. Just a car, a fish, and a dog!

Test Samples

On the exam, you will be asked to read a short essay or story followed by questions asking for the meaning of the word(s) used in the essay. Although the word **literal** will not be used specifically in the question, you will know by the phrasing of the question itself. Look at the two samples below. Both are asking for literal meanings.

EXAMPLE

1. What does the word *inquisitive* mean in the sentence below taken from the essay?

    Experimenting with household objects can often get young people in trouble, but for one intelligent, inquisitive boy, it created the foundation of his future.

    (A) one who doesn't understand
    (B) one who gets confused
    (C) one who knows a lot of information
    (D) one who asks many questions

Your Answer:

ANALYSIS

Looking carefully at the answer choices, you will see that there are two that can be eliminated almost immediately as the weakest links! We are looking for an answer that tells us that what this young man experimented with "created the foundation of his future." Answers **A** and **B** refer to someone who is perhaps not particularly bright. Answer **C** is closer, but it refers to actual intelligence. Therefore, **D is the correct answer.** An *inquisitive* person is someone who asks way too many questions—but in a good way. That's the literal meaning of the word.

EXAMPLE

2. What do the words *remain stationary* mean in the sentence below from the essay?

    This marvelous engine was used for sawing wood and other tasks that required it to remain stationary, but it was mounted on wheels to propel itself from one location to another.

    (A) move from one place to another
    (B) stays in one place and does not move
    (C) move in two directions
    (D) stay in more than one place

Your Answer:

ANALYSIS

If you are not certain what the word *stationary* means, look at the word that is italicized just before it. *Remain*—stays in one place. The two italicized words mean almost the same thing. Now look at the answers. Answers **A** and **C** move around, but **B** and **D** both have the word "stay." Look again at **D**: "Stay in more than one place?"–that's a little weird. Therefore, logically we must conclude that Answer **B** is used correctly.

FIGURATIVE MEANINGS

If someone were to make the comment to you that "two heads are better than one," you might think about this statement in two ways. One, the literal meaning would have you thinking "Wow, there are times when I really could use another head on my shoulders, especially on nights when I have a lot of homework—one could do math and the other English." The second way to consider the comment is figuratively. Thinking of this figuratively, the meaning of the statement changes completely. "Two heads are better than one" means that two people, each with one head (meaning brain), thinking together or brainstorming about something is better than just one person with one head. Why? Because. With two heads, you can bounce ideas off each other and come up with twice the number of solutions. So, two heads **are** better than one—figuratively speaking.

In other words, figurative meanings go beyond literal meanings. Writers use this device to make their word images stronger and more colorful—their writing becomes less boring. Poets are especially fond of using figurative language in their poems. **Simile, metaphor,** and **personification** are examples of figurative language—let's take a closer look at them.

Similes (Pronounced sim-i-lees)

Similes are everywhere and they are easy to spot. When a writer compares two different things using the words *as* or *like*, you will know that it is a simile or a **figure of speech**—hence, **figurative** language.

> Love is *like* a rose.
> I feel *like* a sitting duck out of water.
> His temper is *as* explosive *as* a volcano.
> Clouds are *as* white *as* puffy marshmallows.
> His brain is *like* a sponge.

Metaphors

These are used to compare two different things, but without using *as* or *like* in the comparison. With metaphors, the thing actually becomes what it is being compared to. In fact, the word *is* (or other form of *is* such as *are* for plural or *am* for first person singular) is often found in metaphors!

> Love *is* a rose.
> His brain *is* a sponge.
> I *am* a rock.
> Clouds *are* white puffy marshmallows.

Notice the difference between **similes** and **metaphors?** Similes are *like* something else and metaphors *are* or *become* something else. In other words, metaphors make bold, strong, dynamic (*am* or *is*) comparisons, while similes make less bold and rather soft or gentle (*like* or *as*) comparisons.

Personification

This describes something (an *inanimate* object, to be precise) that is not really a person, such as an animal, an idea, or an object, that is given traits of a human to make it appear as if it were almost human. Sometimes, these objects will hear, talk, feel, or do other things that seem rather strange, but at the same time it seems rather poetic. Writers use personification to make their work come alive!

> The moon is content as he glides across the midnight sky.
> The trees bend with stiff backs as the wind blows through their branches.
> The cheerful flowers shout their joy to the glorious sun.
> The acrobatic surf rolls and tumbles onto the shore.

To test your knowledge of figurative language/meanings, the test makers will ask you to read a poem or a short, very colorful passage of prose (paragraph writing). The questions will follow. Let's see how well you understand figurative language. Read the following poem and then answer the questions. This will test your understanding of **similes, metaphors,** and **personification.**

EXAMPLE

3. Which line in this stanza does NOT have a simile?

From *The Night before Christmas* by Clement C. Moore

His eyes how they twinkled! His dimples how merry!   (1)
His cheeks were like roses, his nose like a cherry!   (2)
His droll little mouth was drawn up like a bow,   (3)
And the beard on his chin was as white as the snow;   (4)

(A) lines 4 and 3
(B) line 2
(C) line 1
(D) lines 1 and 2

NOTE

First of all, read the question very carefully and closely. Sometimes the questions are worded almost the opposite of what you're used to reading.

Your Answer: Ⓓ

ANALYSIS

The question is asking for the line that does *not* have a simile. The key words to look for in finding a simile are *as* and *like*. In this example, there is only one line that does not have *like* or *as*, and that line is 1. Therefore, **C** is the correct answer!

EXAMPLE

4. The metaphor in this poem by Emily Dickinson is stated in which line?

Hope is the thing with feathers	(1)
That perches in the soul,	(2)
And sings the tune without the words,	(3)
And never stops at all,	(4)
And sweetest in the gale is heard,	(5)
And sore must be the storm	(6)
That could abash that little bird	(7)
That kept so many warm.	(8)
I've heard it in the chillest land,	(9)
And on the strangest sea;	(10)
Yet, never, in extremity,	(11)
It asked a crumb of me.	(12)

(A) line 12
(B) line 2
(C) line 7
(D) line 1

Your Answer:

ANALYSIS

A **metaphor** is a comparison of two unlike things. Frequently, you will see the word *is* or *am* included, but not all the time, so beware! In this poem, we see the metaphor in the very first line! *Hope is the thing with feathers*—the poet is comparing **hope** to a **bird** that sings and *never stops at all!* The correct answer is **D.**

EXAMPLE

5. There are two things being personified in this poem by Carl Sandburg. Name them.

"Summer Grass" by Carl Sandburg

Summer grass aches and whispers.	(1)
It wants something; it calls and sings; it pours	(2)
out wishes to the overhead stars.	(3)
The rain hears; the rain answers; the rain is slow	(4)
coming; the rain wets the face of the grass.	(5)

(A) grass and rain
(B) grass and stars
(C) stars and rain
(D) whispers and wishes

Your Answer:

ANALYSIS

Carefully look at the poem. Remember, **personification** transforms or *morphs* inanimate objects by adding human characteristics or traits. Immediately, we see that the grass *aches* and *whispers* and *calls* and *sings* and *pours* out wishes (lines 1–3). That's personification. But, check out line 4! The rain *hears* and *answers*! **A** is the correct answer. It is the only one that mentions grass and rain together.

Idioms

These are common, everyday expressions that really don't mean what they say literally. They reflect the way people talk in normal conversations—and people use them all the time! The basic idea of **idioms** fits nicely in this area of review. They are actually entertaining to look at both literally and figuratively. There are hundreds of idioms, but here are a few examples to play around with. The figurative meanings are given. On a separate sheet of paper, <u>draw a picture of the **literal** meaning of the idiom</u>; it will help you to remember them. P.S. Idioms are very strange to people who are learning English for the first time; after looking at them, you will see why! Read through the following lists of idioms and their explanations. There are far too many idioms to include here, but once you become familiar with them, they will be easy to recognize.

BREAK THE ICE

to say or do something that will reduce the social awkwardness or coldness at a meeting or social event (a party).

ONCE IN A BLUE MOON

something that happens very seldom or rarely.

SECONDHAND

information from somewhere other than the original source.

PICK SOMEONE'S BRAIN

to get information from someone who is more knowledgeable than you are about something.

FOLLOW YOUR NOSE

Instead of following guidelines or rules, to follow your instincts or intuition.

CATCH SOMEONE'S EYE

to attract someone's attention, such as a waiter or waitress, or someone cute at a party.

I'LL EAT MY HAT

expression to emphasize that the probability of something actually happening is not likely.

PUT A SOCK IN IT

to keep quiet or stop talking!

THE LION'S SHARE

the best or largest part of something.

BIRDS OF A FEATHER FLOCK TOGETHER

people with the same or similar interests or traits seem to stick together.

IDIOMS AND THEIR MEANINGS

- **Achilles' heel:** a weak spot in someone who is usually quite strong
- **all thumbs:** clumsy
- **apple of one's eye:** someone special who is adored and well-protected by another
- **at the end of your rope:** to be in a situation that is frustrating and you are almost at the point where you can't deal with it anymore

EXAMPLE

Complete the following sentence with an idiom that best suits the situation.

Some clowns and comedians pretend to be _____ by tripping and falling throughout their routines to make their audiences laugh.

(A) at the end of their rope
(B) all thumbs
(C) an Achilles' heel
(D) an apple of one's eye

Your Answer:

ANALYSIS

Although idioms are used primarily in everyday speech and not in formal writing, they are very much alive in the English language. In looking at the sentence above, you will need to think about what it is that clowns and comedians do. They make you laugh, right? Some clowns and comedians are famous for tripping and falling or otherwise appearing clumsy. To be all thumbs means to be clumsy, therefore the correct answer is **B.** Answers **A** and **C** could be possibilities, but they are not as likely as **B.** The answer **D** makes no sense at all and can be eliminated immediately.

- **bark is worse than the bite:** not as angry or bad-tempered as it appears
- **beat around the bush:** to explain something in a roundabout way, not to the point
- **bend over backwards:** to try very hard
- **bite the bullet:** to have to deal with a difficult situation
- **bite the dust:** to die or to lose a battle
- **black sheep of the family:** a family member who is different/odd or estranged from the family
- **blue moon:** once in a "blue moon" is a rare occurrence
- **break the ice:** to resolve the social awkwardness of a situation
- **bring home the bacon:** to earn enough to support one's family
- **bury the hatchet:** to make peace with someone

TIP

Read the **questions** carefully—note any **boldface** or underlined or *italicized* words—make sure you understand the question before you answer.

EXAMPLE

To *bend over backwards* means to _____.

(A) become friends again
(B) tell a lie
(C) try very hard at something
(D) tell a long story instead of a short one

Your Answer:

ANALYSIS

Knowing the figurative meanings behind idioms is extremely helpful in this case, otherwise using the process of elimination and trying to make an educated guess would be the next best thing. The answer is **C.** To *bend over backwards* is to try your best or to try your hardest at something. To eliminate answers, think of the literal meaning—why would you be leaning over backward? To become friends again, to tell a lie, or to tell a long story instead of a short one? Probably not.

- **cat got your tongue:** unable to speak
- **chip off the old block:** a child who is like his/her mother or father in character and appearance
- **cloud nine:** to be on "cloud nine" is to be extremely happy
- **cold feet:** to have "cold feet" is to be frightened or afraid to do something
- **cold shoulder:** to ignore, to be unfriendly, or to be rude to someone
- **cross your fingers:** to hope/wish for good luck or a happy outcome
- **cry crocodile tears:** crying that is insincere or feigned
- **dark horse:** someone whose abilities are unknown or not proven
- **devil to pay:** means that if you do something questionable, the consequences would be adverse—much like having to pay the devil (bad guy) because of your actions
- **dress to kill:** to wear your finest clothes
- **drive someone up a wall:** to annoy or bother someone tremendously

---

EXAMPLE

Maria went to a party last night and felt as though everyone was giving her the cold shoulder. In this sentence, what is the figurative meaning of cold shoulder*?*

(A) to be extremely happy
(B) to wear your finest clothes
(C) in need of a sweater because of the weather
(D) to be ignored or treated in an unfriendly manner

Your Answer: Ⓓ

ANALYSIS

The key to knowing how to answer this question is knowing what the meaning of *figurative* is. If you didn't know the meaning, you might guess **C,** which would be the literal meaning. The correct answer is **D.** The first two answers make no sense at all and could be eliminated right away.

- **early bird catches the worm:** an early arrival has its advantages
- **ears are burning:** a feeling as though someone is talking about you
- **egg on your face:** looking foolish for making the wrong decision or choice
- **eyes are bigger than one's stomach:** taking more food than one can eat
- **face the music:** to accept the consequences of a decision
- **feather in one's cap:** getting credit for one's work or achievement
- **flash in the pan:** a brilliant idea that amounts to nothing
- **foot in one's mouth:** to make a mistake or say something that could be offensive or hurtful
- **get in someone's hair:** to bother or annoy someone
- **get the ball rolling:** to initiate action or get something under way
- **go fly a kite:** to tell someone to go away

EXAMPLE

Identify the figurative meaning of *flash in the pan*.

(A) a brilliant idea that amounts to nothing
(B) to accept the consequences
(C) to tell someone to go away
(D) to initiate action

Your Answer: (A) (B) (C) (D)

ANALYSIS

Again, the need to know the meaning of *figurative* is imperative. If you weren't sure what the question was asking, think about the saying literally. Draw a picture of it in you mind: *a flash in the pan*—something bright or shiny that doesn't last long. Now, look at the answers. Which one might translate to mean something similar. Right away, the first answer **A** jumps out, and it is the correct answer. But because you need to read the remaining answers, **B** and **C** could be eliminated right away, leaving **D**. The answer **D** might be close, meaning something that is just getting started, but not as close as answer **A**.

- **hatchet job:** to discredit a prominent person
- **hit the ceiling:** to become very angry
- **hit the hay:** to go to bed
- **hold down the fort:** to take care of things as a substitute
- **hook, line, and sinker:** the entire thing
- **if the shoe fits, wear it:** to admit the truth
- **in stitches:** laughing hysterically

- **in the hole:** to owe money or to be in debt
- **jump down someone's throat:** to become extremely angry at someone
- **jump the gun:** to rush or be too hasty
- **keep it under your hat:** to keep something a secret or to yourself
- **kick the bucket:** to die
- **kick up your heels:** to have a lot of fun, celebrate
- **knock one's socks off:** to impress, excite, or get someone enthused over something

EXAMPLE

I don't remember ever having such a good time; we were in stitches *almost the entire evening.* The saying *in stitches* is considered _____.

(A) a myth
(B) personification
(C) a simile
(D) an idiom

Your Answer: Ⓓ

ANALYSIS

The key to answering this question is in knowing literary terms. If you were unsure, eliminate answers one by one according to your knowledge. The correct answer is **D.** A myth would be out of the question. A simile uses either *as* or *like*. Personification could be a stretch, but it definitely is an idiom.

- **let sleeping dogs lie:** don't bother something/someone who could cause trouble
- **let the cat out of the bag:** to tell something beforehand
- **lose your shirt:** to lose a great deal of money
- **make ends meet:** to be able to pay one's debts and live within one's means
- **mind your Ps and Qs:** watch what you say in speech and how you behave
- **money talks:** having money can be influential
- **nip it in the bud:** to take care of a situation in the early stages before it gets out of control
- **on ice:** set aside for later use
- **on last legs:** to be sick and not doing well
- **out of the woods:** out of trouble or danger
- **out on a limb:** in a risky situation
- **paint the town red:** to have a good time; excessive partying
- **pay through the nose:** pay too much for something

- **people who live in glass houses shouldn't throw stones:** those who are equally at fault, should not criticize
- **play it by ear:** to improvise as you go along or take it as it comes
- **pull someone's leg:** to kid around or tease someone
- **pull strings:** to exert influence over a situation

EXAMPLE

When Benny comes to town we are really going to go out and *paint the town red.* When one *paints the town red,* one parties excessively, which is the _____ meaning of the saying.

(A) literal
(B) figurative
(C) denotative
(D) caustic

Your Answer:

ANALYSIS

Again, knowing literary terms is key to answering this question. In looking through the answers though, answer **D** can be eliminated. Answers **A** and **C** are similar in meaning, but *painting the town red* is not something that is literal—to *paint the town red* literally, would be taking a can of red paint and a paint brush and *painting the town red.* The correct answer is **B**.

- **raining cats and dogs:** to rain heavily
- **raise a stink:** to complain or protest strongly
- **read someone the riot act:** to discourage ill behavior by lecturing about the consequences of the behavior
- **rule of thumb:** a guess or estimate
- **scratch someone's back:** to return a favor
- **shake a leg:** to hurry
- **shoot the breeze:** to chat
- **snow job:** to be dishonest or speak insincerely
- **spill the beans:** to reveal a secret
- **take the bull by the horns:** to deal with a difficult situation by facing it head-on
- **throw in the towel:** to give up
- **tongue-in-cheek:** not serious, kidding
- **turn over a new leaf:** to begin again, to renew

- **up your sleeve:** hidden or concealed
- **wet blanket:** dull or boring person who spoils things for others
- **white elephant:** an unwanted or odd object
- **wolf in sheep's clothing:** what appears harmless on the outside, may not be so underneath

---

EXAMPLE

Which of the following is the figurative meaning of the idiom *throw in the towel*?

(A) an unwanted object
(B) to begin anew
(C) to give up
(D) dull or boring

Your Answer: Ⓓ

ANALYSIS

To key into finding this answer, look at the idiom itself. To *throw in the towel* means what? What do you do when you throw in the towel? Look at all of the answers. Answers **B** and **D** could be eliminated right away leaving answers **A** and **C**. It could be answer **A**, but that is closer to a literal meaning. The correct answer is **C**, because idioms are not literal, they are figurative expressions.

Denotative—or Denotations

Denotative word meanings are just like literal meanings.

Denotative (or denotation) is another word for the exact meaning or definition of a word. The denotation of the word *cake* for instance is simply that it is a baked mixture of flour, eggs, and sugar. The denotation is usually serious and straightforward. However, writers often use denotation hand-in-hand with:

Connotative—or Connotations

The **connotative** meanings bring word definitions to a more emotional level. They are meanings that go beyond the literal or denotative meanings. Connotative meanings are the meanings that the reader attaches or associates with the word. As in the example above, *cake* may mean a baked mixture of flour, sugar, and eggs denotatively, but **connotatively** you might think of a beautifully decorated birthday cake, a wedding cake, or any other holiday cake. Connotations usually cause us to react emotionally to a word. Take a look at the lists of words that follow. One list demonstrates the denotative meaning and the other the connotative meaning. Think about what comes to your mind when you review both lists.

Denotation	Connotation
skinny	slender
statesman	politician
parch	dry, arid
beggar	degenerate
filth	contamination
shout	announce
dog	cur
goofy	insane
cook	chef
long	extensive
fastidious	fussy
cocky	arrogant
small	cramped

Directions: After reading the next list of words, write your immediate connotative reaction to them in the column on the right. Your reaction may be positive or negative.

Word	Your Connotative Reaction
antique	_____
old	_____
odor	_____
aroma	_____
bland	_____
mild	_____
ornate	_____
gaudy	_____
snake	_____
dentist	_____
demanded	_____
requested	_____
stingy	_____
thrifty	_____

As you can see, connotative meanings and denotative meanings are different and alike in a way. Denotative meanings are just as they are—simple definitions—while connotative meanings touch something in your brain, your heart, or your soul—and that is what writers do intentionally. The words may in fact be synonyms, but the emotional response to the word is what separates the two dramatically.

Now let's move on to the review on the next few pages. Don't be afraid to look back at the chapter before you attempt the quizzes.

Chapter Review

Now, let's review what you have learned so far—from the beginning. These quizzes are not simulations of the actual test. They are intended for review only. The actual test will be in a multiple-choice format like the tests at the end of the book. The answers will be found in the appendix in the back of the book.

DEFINITION REVIEW QUIZ

Directions: In the following sentences, use one of the words from the word bank below to complete the definition.

Word Bank: literal, denotative, connotative, idiom, figurative, simile, metaphor, personification.
NOTE: Some words might be used more than once.

1. The _____ meanings of words come straight from the dictionary without adding any other meaning to it.

2. *To kill two birds with one stone* is called an _____.

3. _____ meanings of words tend to make you think or feel something specific about the word itself. In other words, you add your own definition or response to it.

4. *Taking the bull by the horns* is also an _____.

5. *School is like a dream* is an example of a _____, which is a part of _____ language.

6. _____ meanings go beyond literal meanings; they add color and personality to writing.

7. *Clouds tiptoe across the sky* is an example of _____. Poets use this device a lot!

8. _____ and _____ meanings are very similar.

9. *I am a rock!* is a _____.

10. *His droll little mouth was drawn up like a bow* is an example of a _____.

FIGURATIVE LANGUAGE REVIEW

Directions: Identify each of the following examples of figurative language by writing simile, metaphor, or personification on the line before the example.

1. _____ as big as an elephant

2. _____ the dancing trees swayed gently in the breeze

3. _____ strength is her mantra

4. _____ the coatrack stood sentinel in the entryway

5. _____ love is a fragile blossom

6. _____ blind as a bat

7. _____ the chattering printer gossiped forever

8. _____ bald like an eagle

9. _____ the moon dances its way across the sky

10. _____ school is a gateway to life

11. _____ cars skate across the icy path

12. _____ the cheery sunflowers tell us to smile

13. _____ cool as a cucumber

14. _____ he is the light of my life

15. _____ snow is like feathers from heaven

16. _____ the clever bell shouted each hour of the day

17. _____ crazy like a loon

18. _____ gentle spring bounces in after the harsh, mean winter

19. _____ the silent books suddenly shout "Read me!"

20. _____ bright as the sun

IDIOMS REVIEW

Directions: Match the idiom with its definition. Write the letter of the correct definition on the blank line before the word it defines.

1. _____ bite the dust
2. _____ the Achilles' heel
3. _____ go fly a kite
4. _____ hook, line, and sinker
5. _____ break the ice
6. _____ on its last legs
7. _____ raise a stink
8. _____ bury the hatchet
9. _____ out on a limb
10. _____ in the hole
11. _____ hit the hay
12. _____ spill the beans
13. _____ white elephant
14. _____ rule of thumb
15. _____ face the music
16. _____ pull strings
17. _____ hold down the fort
18. _____ bite the bullet
19. _____ jump the gun
20. _____ up your sleeve

a. to exert influence in a situation
b. to take care of things as a substitute
c. to die or lose a battle
d. to make peace with someone
e. to owe money or to be in debt
f. to accept the consequences of a decision
g. a vulnerable or weak spot
h. go away
i. to deal with a difficult situation
j. to go to bed
k. a guess or estimate
l. an unwanted or odd object
m. to be too hasty or rushed
n. the entire thing
o. to complain or protest strongly
p. a sick or ailing person or something old or breaking
q. something hidden or concealed
r. to resolve the social awkwardness
s. to reveal a secret
t. in a risky situation

Word Analysis, Fluency, and Systematic Vocabulary Development—Part II

In this chapter, we will focus on words from the root up because the basis of word development through history is truly from the ground up—it's called **etymology**. Many words begin with or contain a part of a word that is the same as another word and that is called a **root word**. With the knowledge of root words, understanding the basic background and meaning of many other words is made much easier. For instance, take the root word "sol," which means the sun. If you add endings (called suffixes) to the root word "sol," you'll get these words that all have to do with the sun—*solar*, *solstice*, and *solarium*. In keeping with learning vocabulary from the ground up, many of our words arrived via Greek, Roman, and Norse mythology (such as *echo* and *narcissistic*). The stories behind the words are interesting and will help you to better understand the words.

> **TIP**
>
> Get help—if you don't understand something ask someone—a teacher, a friend, a tutor, a parent—anyone who has the knowledge and is willing to help.

CHAPTER FOCUS

- Root words
- Words from Mythology
- Chapter Review and Quizzes

ROOT WORDS: LEARNING VOCABULARY FROM THE GROUND UP

Learning **root words** will allow you to understand the meanings of words with similar roots without using the dictionary. Again, *your* learning style is unique to you. How you learn them is always the challenge. Some people learn better by hearing, others by seeing, and still others by doing both. Read them aloud. Write them on cards. Do what you have to do to remember them. They are important! NOTE: The **root** is in **bold** type and its meaning is in parentheses ( ).

- **a (without)** agnostic, amoral, atrophy, atypical
- **ab/abs (off, away from, apart, down)** abnormal, abduct, abhor, abstract

- **ac/acr (sharp/bitter)** acerbate, acidity, acute, acrid, exacerbate
- **act/ag (to do, to drive, to force, to lead)** act, agent, agile
- **ad/al (to, toward, near)** adapt, addict, advice, allure, alloy
- **al/ali/alter (other, another)** alias, alibi, alien, alienation, altruist, allegory
- **am (love)** amateur, amorous, enamored, amity, paramour, amiable, amicable
- **amb (to go, to walk)** ambitious, amble, preamble, ambulance
- **amb/amph (around)** amphitheater, ambience
- **amb/amph (both, more than one)** ambiguous amphibian, ambivalent
- **anim (life, mind, soul, spirit)** animosity, unanimous, equanimity
- **ante (before)** ante, anterior, antecedent, antedate, antebellum
- **anthro/andr (man, human)** anthropology, android, misanthrope, philanthropy, anthropomorphic
- **annu/enni (year)** annual, anniversary, biannual, biennial, centennial
- **anti (against)** antidote, antiseptic, antipathy
- **apo (away)** apology, apostle, apocalypse
- **apt/ept (skill, fitness, ability)** adapt, aptitude, apt, inept, adept
- **arch/archi (chief, principal)** architect, archetype, archipelago
- **archy (ruler)** anarchy, hierarchy, monarchy, matriarchy, patriarchy
- **art (skill, craft)** artisan, artifact, artful, artless, artifice, art, artificial
- **auc/aug/aux (to increase)** augment, auction, auxiliary
- **auto (self)** automobile, automatic, autopsy, autocrat, autonomy

EXAMPLE

In the following sentence, what does the word *monarchy* mean?

The British *monarchy* is under attack by the foreign press for blatant misconduct.

(A) a colorful butterfly
(B) any monetary unit
(C) a form of government ruled by a king or queen
(D) a country in Europe

Your Answer: Ⓐ Ⓑ Ⓒ Ⓓ

ANALYSIS

Don't get confused. Read the sentence carefully. **The correct answer is C.** However, if you were in a hurry and didn't read carefully, answer **A** might have caught your eye because, after all, there *is* a monarch butterfly. But, the sentence mentioned that the monarchy was under attack by the foreign press; what are the chances that a monarch butterfly would behave poorly, which "misconduct" means? Fat chance! Answers **B** and **D** are there to throw you off, especially if you are not paying attention.

- **be (to be, to have a certain quality)** beguile, bequeath, belittle, bemoan, befriend, bewilder
- **bel/bell (war)** belligerent, antebellum, rebel
- **ben/bon (good)** benefit, benefactor, benign, bonus, bona fide
- **bi (twice, doubly)** biplane, biannual, binoculars, bilingual
- **bio (life)** biology, biotic, biosphere, biopsy
- **bri/brev (brief, short)** brevity, brief, abbreviate, abridge

EXAMPLE

What does *antebellum* mean in the following sentence? NOTE: This word is made up of two roots: *ante* and *bel*.

The *antebellum* South was a land of aristocratic landowners and their indentured servants.

(A) after the war
(B) the area just above the South
(C) before the war
(D) during the Civil War

Your Answer: Ⓓ

ANALYSIS

Two roots, two roots, two roots in one! From the last section we have the root **ante,** which means **before.** Add to that, **bell**um. **Bell** means **war.** Put them together and you have **before the war. The correct answer is C.** The other answers are confusing if you are unfamiliar with what went on in the United States before, during, and after the Civil War. It pays to know your roots!

- **cad/cid (to fall, to happen by chance)** cascade, coincidence, cadence, recidivism, decadent
- **cand (to burn)** candle, incandescent
- **cant/cent/chant (to sing)** chant, enchant, accent, recant
- **cap/cip/cept (to take, to get)** capture, recipient, emancipate, anticipate
- **cap/capit/cipit (head, headlong)** captain, principal, capitulate, caption
- **card/cord/cour (heart)** cardiac, cordial, accord, encourage
- **carn (flesh)** carnivorous, carnal, carnage, reincarnation
- **cast/chast (cut)** caste, castigate, chastise, chaste
- **caust (to burn)** caustic, holocaust
- **ced/ceed/cess (to go, to yield, to stop)** cessation, incessant, abscess, recede, antecedent, access, concede, recess, exceed, precede
- **centr (center)** central, concentrate, eccentric, egocentric

- **cern/cert/cret/crim/crit (to separate, to judge, to distinguish, to decide)** discern, criterion, discrete, secret, concern
- **chron (time)** chronicle, chronology, chronic, synchronize
- **circu (around, on all sides)** circumscribe, circumvent, circuit, circumference
- **cis (to cut)** incision, concise, scissors, precise, excise
- **cit (to set in motion)** incite, solicit, excite
- **cla/clo/clu (shut, close)** seclude, cloister, foreclose, recluse, enclose, closet
- **claim/clam (to shout, to cry out)** reclaim, clamor, acclaim, exclaim
- **cli (to lean toward)** recline, decline, climax
- **co/col/com/con (with, together)** conjugal, coalesce, coalition, connect, confide, cohesive, commiserate
- **crat/cracy (to govern)** democracy, aristocracy, bureaucracy, autocracy
- **cre/cresc/cret (to grow)** crescendo, increment, accrue, creation, increase
- **cred (to believe, to trust)** credible, credo, credence, incredulous, incredible, credentials
- **cryp (hidden)** cryptic, crypt, cryptography
- **cub/cumb (to lie down)** succumb, incumbent, recumbent, cubicle
- **culp (blame)** culpable, exculpate, inculpate, mea culpa, culprit
- **cour/cur (running, a course)** courier, occur, recur, current, incur

---

EXAMPLE

What does *secluded* mean in the following sentence?

The pioneers built their cabins in the *secluded* wilderness, but they were often close to a river.

(A) screened or sheltered from view
(B) in the city
(C) above the forest
(D) clearly in view

Your Answer: Ⓒ

ANALYSIS

Thinking back to the roots, what comes to mind? **cla/clo/clu** means **to be shut off from** or **closed in**. Looking at the answers there is only one that clearly is correct. **A is the correct answer.**

- **de (away, off, down, completely, reversal)** descend, defame, delineate, defile, deface, decipher
- **dem (people)** demographics, democracy, epidemic
- **di/dia (apart, through)** dialectic, diagnose, dialogue
- **dic/dict/dit (to say, to tell, to use words)** dictate, dictionary, predict, verdict, indicted, diction
- **dign (worth)** dignitary, dignify, indignant, dignity
- **dis/dif (away from, apart, reversal, not)** diffuse, dissipate, disperse, disseminate, dissuade
- **dac/doc (to teach)** doctrine, didactic, doctor
- **dog/dox (opinion)** dogma, dogmatic, paradox, orthodox
- **dol (suffer, pain)** doldrums, doleful, dolorous
- **don/dot/dow (to give)** dowry, donate, donor, pardon, antidote
- **dub (doubt)** dubious, indubitable
- **duc/duct (to lead)** duct, conduct, abduct, conducive, seduce, induct
- **dur (hard)** durable, endure, duress
- **dys (faulty)** dyslexia, dysfunctional, dystrophy

EXAMPLE

In the following sentence, what does the word *doctrine* mean?

All religions have a unique set of *doctrines* that are followed by their members.

- (A) a set of tablets
- (B) a healing person
- (C) principles and beliefs
- (D) a briefcase full of documents

Your Answer:

ANALYSIS

Doc means **to teach.** So, looking at the answers logically, there could be some confusion with these answers. A healing person is a doctor, but that is not the correct **doc** word; therefore **B** is **not correct.** The other two answers refer to writings, but are still not the correct answers. There is one answer left—**C,** "principles and beliefs" **is the correct answer.** *Doctrines* is a word that is often connected with religious groups.

- **epi (upon)** epitaph, epidermis, epidemic, epilogue
- **equ (equal, even)** equitable, equivocal, equilibrium, equation
- **err (to wander)** error, aberrant, errant, erroneous
- **esce (becoming)** incandescent, effervescent, adolescent, convalesce
- **eu (good, well)** euphoria, euthanasia, euphemism, eulogy
- **e/ef/ex (out, out of, from, former, completely)** exalt, expire, extricate, exonerate, exclude, evade, exult, effervesce
- **extra (outside of, beyond)** extraneous, extrasensory, extraordinary

---

EXAMPLE

In the following sentence, what does the word *extricate* mean?

The determined animal managed to *extricate* himself from the hunter's trap.

(A) a newspaper
(B) unusual circumstances
(C) to add meaning to
(D) to release or disentangle from

Your Answer: Ⓓ

ANALYSIS

ex means **out of.** Reading the sentence carefully, key words such as **determined** and **trap** help key you into the answer. **A** is one of those nonsense answers. **B** could be confusing if the sentence was read too quickly because it sounds like this is an unusual circumstance, and **C** really doesn't make sense; therefore **D is the correct answer.**

- **fab (to speak)** fabulous, fable, affable
- **fac (to do, to make)** facsimile, benefactor, factory
- **fer (to bring, to carry, to bear)** offer, transfer, proliferate
- **ferv (to boil, to bubble, to burn)** fervor, fervid
- **fid (faith, trust)** confident, fidelity, perfidy, infidel, bona fide
- **fin (end)** final, finale, definitive
- **flam (to burn)** flame, flamboyant, inflammatory
- **flect/flex (to bend)** flexible, genuflect
- **flict (to strike)** conflict, inflict, afflict
- **fore (before)** foreshadow, forgo, forebear
- **frac (break)** fraction, fracture, infraction
- **fund/found (bottom)** foundation, fundamental, founder
- **fus (pour)** transfusion, profuse, infusion

EXAMPLE

In the following sentence, what does the word *transfusion* mean?

During life-threatening surgery, a blood *transfusion* is often necessary.

(A) injection of blood into a person or animal
(B) to send out of the country
(C) a simple diagram
(D) taken away

Your Answer:

ANALYSIS

Fus means **to pour.** Immediately, Answer **C** can be eliminated. **B** and **D** might be food for thought because the word *transfer* might come to mind. But, we are talking about a transfusion—a pouring of blood into a person or animal—and therefore **A is the only logical answer.**

- **gen (birth, creation, kind, race)** generate, genetics, homogeneous, genealogy, gender, genre, congenital
- **grand (big)** grandiose, grandeur
- **grat (pleasing)** grateful, gratuity, gratuitous
- **grad/gress (to step)** graduate, progress, gradual, digress

EXAMPLE

In the following sentence, what does the word *congenital* mean?

Because of recent scientific discoveries in the field of genetics, *congenital* birth defects are declining.

(A) a gathering of people
(B) rejection of faith
(C) existing at birth
(D) happiness

Your Answer:

ANALYSIS

Gen means **birth, creation, race, kind.** Answers **D** and **B** are the two obvious wrong answers. Answer **A** might possibly cause confusion because congregation and congenital begin with the same prefix. But, **C is the correct answer.** A congenital defect exists at birth.

- **her/hes (to stick)** coherent, adherent, cohesive, adhesive
- **hetero (different)** heterosexual, heterogenous
- **hom (same)** homogenous, homonym, homosexual
- **hyper (over, excessive)** hyperactive, hyperbole
- **id (one's own)** idiot, idiom, idiosyncrasy
- **inter (between, among)** interstate, interim, intermittent
- **intra (within)** intramural, intrastate, intravenous
- **ject (to throw, to throw down)** eject, inject, dejected
- **join/junct (to meet, to join)** joint, junction,
- **jur (to swear)** perjury, jury

EXAMPLE

In the following sentence, what does the word *junction* mean?

There was an accident at the *junction* of the 405 and the 110 freeways and traffic was delayed.

(A) a junkyard
(B) a place where two things join or cross
(C) a grammatical error
(D) a syncopated rhythm in a song

Your Answer:

ANALYSIS

junct/join means **to meet or to join.** Answers **C** and **D** really make no sense at all. Answer **A** might possibly be confusing because of its similar sounding beginning. However, **B** is the obvious answer knowing that the root means **to meet or join.**

- **lect (to choose)** elect, select, collect
- **lev (life, rise)** levitate, elevator, alleviate
- **loc/log/loqu (word, speech)** soliloquy, colloquial, dialogue, prologue, epilogue
- **luc/lum/lus (light)** lucid, luminous, illustrate
- **mag/maj/max (big)** magnify, major, majestic, maximum
- **mal/male (bad, ill, evil, wrong)** malodorous, malicious, malaise, malevolent
- **man (hand)** manual, manufacture
- **mater/matr (woman, mother)** maternal, maternity, matriarch
- **min (small)** minutiae, miniature, diminish
- **mis/mit (to send)** remit, remission, transmit, emissary
- **mon/monit (to warn)** summons, admonish, monitor, monument

- **morph (shape)** anthropomorphic, metamorphosis
- **mort (death)** immortal, morgue, morbid
- **mut (change)** mutation, mutant, commute

EXAMPLE

In the following sentence, what does the word *metamorphosis* mean?

The *metamorphosis* of the butterfly from its original state as a caterpillar is remarkable to witness.

(A) a mechanical being
(B) a change of shape or form
(C) figurative language
(D) a numbering system from ancient civilizations

Your Answer:

ANALYSIS

Answers **A, C,** and **D** make the least sense when you look carefully at the sentence. **B is the correct answer.** Knowing now that *morph* means **shape,** the answer is easier to detect.

- **nom (rule, order)** astronomy, economy, gastronomy, taxonomy
- **nat (to be born)** natural, native, cognate
- **nox (harm, death)** noxious, obnoxious
- **nom/nym (name)** synonym, anonymous, nominate, acronym, homonym, nom de plume
- **nov/neo/nou (new)** novice, novelty, renovate, neophyte, nouveau riche
- **omni (all)** omnipresent, omniscient, omnipotent
- **pac/peac (peace)** peace, pacify, appease
- **pan (all, everywhere)** panorama, pandemic, panacea, pantheon
- **par (equal)** par, parity, disparity, apartheid
- **para (next to, beside)** parallel, paraphrase, paradox, parable, paralegal
- **path (feeling, suffering, disease)** apathy, sympathy, empathy, pathology, psychopath, sociopath
- **pater/part (father, support)** paternal, patriarch, patron, patronize
- **ped (child, education)** encyclopedia, pedagogue, pediatrician
- **ped/pod (foot)** pedal, pedestal, podiatrist, podium
- **pen/pun (to pay, to compensate)** penalty, punitive, repent

- **pend/pens (to hang, to weigh, to pay)** depend, expend, stipend, spend, expenditure, compensate, pendulum
- **peri (around)** perimeter, periscope, peripheral
- **phone (sound)** symphony, telephone, megaphone, cacophony
- **plac (to please)** placid, placebo, placate
- **port (to carry)** import, portable, deport, export
- **post (after)** posterior, posterity, posthumous
- **pre (before)** prelude, premonition, presume, preempt, premeditate
- **pro (much, for, a lot)** profuse, prodigal, proliferate, prodigy, prolific
- **prob (to test, to prove)** probe, reprobate
- **pug (to fight)** pugnacious, impugn, repugnant

EXAMPLE

In the following sentence, what does the word *noxious* mean?

The fumes emitting from the factory pipes were *noxious* and the neighboring houses were evacuated.

(A) pleasing to the senses
(B) a nonspecific virus
(C) nothing to worry about
(D) unpleasant and harmful

Your Answer:

ANALYSIS

Read the sentence carefully and think about what it is stating. Fumes that were bad enough to force a neighborhood to be evacuated would certainly be unpleasant and harmful. Therefore, **D is the correct answer.**

- **que/quis (to seek)** acquire, acquisition, request, inquisitive, query
- **qui (quiet)** quiet, tranquil, disquiet
- **sacr/sanct/secr (sacred)** sacred, sanctuary, sanctify, sacrament, sacrilege
- **sci (to know)** conscious, science, omniscient
- **scribe/scrip (to write)** scrip, scribble, inscribe, scripture, transcript
- **se (apart)** seclude, secede, sequester, segregate
- **sec/sequ (to follow)** sequel, sequence, consequence, second
- **sens/sent (to feel, to be aware)** sensory, sense, resent, consent, dissent
- **sol (sun)** solar, solstice, solarium

- **sol (to loosen, to free)** absolve, dissolve, soluble, resolve, solvent
- **spec (to look, to see)** spectator, perspective, aspect, spectacles, circumspect, retrospective
- **sta/sti (to stand, to be in place)** stationary, obstinate, obstacle, stagnant
- **sub/sup (below)** subordinate, sublime, subversive, suppress, subsidiary
- **super/sur (above)** superlative, surmount, surveillance, surpass

---

EXAMPLE

In the following sentence, what does the word *sequestered* mean?

The jury was *sequestered* by the judge because he did not want them to hear the publicity given to the case by the news media.

(A) secretive
(B) an adventure
(C) punitive measures
(D) kept apart from, secluded

Your Answer: Ⓓ

ANALYSIS

After reading the sentence carefully, **B** is an obvious wrong answer because why would a judge send a jury out on an adventure? **C** is incorrect for the same reason— why would a judge punish the jury? **A** might be troublesome if you did not know the root to the word *sequestered*. **The correct answer is D.** A jury is kept away from the news media in particularly sensitive cases that receive a lot of attention from the press.

- **tain (to hold)** contain, detain, pertain, sustain
- **theo (god)** theology, theocracy
- **tract (to drag, pull, draw)** attract, contract, detract, tractor
- **trans (across)** transport, transfer, transaction, transition
- **ven/vent (to come, move, toward)** convene, adventure, event, avenue, circumvent
- **ver (truth)** verify, verdict
- **vers/vert (to turn)** aversion, controversy, divert, cover, avert, revert
- **vi (life)** viable, vivacity, vivid
- **vid/vis (to see)** evident, television, vision, provident, vista
- **voc/vok (to call)** advocate, convoke, equivocate, vocal, vocabulary
- **vol (to wish)** benevolent, malevolent, voluntary

EXAMPLE

In the following sentence, what does the word *convene* mean?

The meeting of the Snowboarding Club will *convene* at the normal time on Wednesday.

(A) to come together
(B) a conversation
(C) enter a contest
(D) inner portion of a circle

Your Answer: Ⓐ Ⓑ Ⓒ Ⓓ

ANALYSIS

After reading the sentence carefully and then looking at all of the answers available, there is one that stands out knowing the root of the word *convene*. **The correct answer is A.** Answers **B** and **C** both have **con** words in them, which could confuse some people, but of course are incorrect. Answer **D** makes no sense at all considering the sentence.

WORDS FROM MYTHOLOGY

Occasionally in your readings, you will encounter a word that originated from mythology. Writers often refer to or name certain gods, goddesses, or other mythological beings in poetry, drama (especially Shakespeare and other classically trained writers), novels, and occasionally in the newspaper (certain politicians are compared to a wide variety of mythological beings—and not always complementary!). Below is a list of some of the more common words that are derived from mythology. In *Webster's International Dictionary* alone, of the 166,724 words, 41,214 are Greek in origin, many mythologically derived. Become familiar with them.

> **REMINDER**
>
> It is difficult to predict which of these words will surface on the exam but it will pay off to have them logged into your mind and ready to be called upon when needed.

- **Achates (faithful)** A companion and friend through thick and thin. This man fled the burning city of Troy with Aeneas.
- **Achilles' heel (a vulnerable spot)** His mother dipped him in the river Styx in an effort to make him immortal, but she held onto one of his heels. Later, in a battle, he was struck by a poisoned arrow in the heel and died.
- **Adonis (handsome man)** A youth who was so handsome that he managed to capture the heart of the goddess of love herself, Aphrodite.
- **Aeolian/aeolistic (giving a moaning or sighing sound, like the wind)** Created by Zeus, Aeolus, the god of the winds, was to keep the winds from sweeping away the sea and the earth. This association with the wind was so strong that two adjectives were created from it: *Aeolian* the windlike sound or anything carried or produced by the wind, and *aeolistic,* meaning a long-winded speech.
- **amazon (a large, strong, masculine woman)** One of group of fierce, female warriors who lived in Scythia, in Asia Minor.

- **Antaean/antaean (having superhuman strength)** The word is from Antaeus who was a Greek giant, the son of Poseidon (Sea) and Gaia (Earth). He was invincible as long as he remained in contact with his mother the Earth, who continually renewed his strength.

- **Apollonian (harmonious, balanced, ordered)** The Greek god Apollo is the god of hunting and healing. He personified order and rationality, which was considered the bright side of the universe and of man.

- **arachnid (spiders, scorpions, mites, and ticks)** Named after Arachne, a Greek maiden who challenged the goddess Athena to a weaving contest.

- **Argonaut (an adventurer engaged in a quest)** The crew of the ship *Argo* that the goddess Athena helped the Greeks to build from Zeus's sacred talking oak. The crew was called the Argonauts and they were bold and brave adventurers.

- **Argus-eyed (dedicatedly observant)** Argus had one hundred eyes. He was asked by Hera, Zeus's wife, to guard the maiden Io so that Zeus would not resume his affair with her.

- **atlas (one who carries a heavy burden; a bound book of maps)** Atlas, a Greek Titan who was condemned to carry the weight of the world on his shoulders after helping Cronus fight against the Olympians. Although most of the Titans were banished, Atlas received the worst punishment: He was to bear the weight of the heavens on his shoulders forever.

- **aurora (dawn; a beginning; an early period)** Dawn was personified by the Greeks as the goddess Eos, but the Romans named her Aurora. She would ride across the sky with her brother, the Sun, in his chariot, spreading light from east to west. The dew that covers the earth in the mornings is said to be the tears of Aurora, crying over the death of her son Memnon who was killed by Achilles during the Trojan War.

EXAMPLE

In the following sentence, what does the word *arachnophobia* mean?

The world is filled with people who have *arachnophobia* and shout out the minute they see one.

(A) breathing
(B) two arms and two legs
(C) fear of spiders
(D) reach for the stars

Your Answer: Ⓒ

ANALYSIS

Reading the sentence carefully, there is one answer that appears to be correct right away especially if you know the mythological word **arachnid.** Arachnid has to do with spiders. The suffix *phobia* is added, which means fear. **C is the correct answer.** Arachnophobia means fear of spiders.

- **bacchanal (a wild party; an orgy)** Bacchus was another name for Dionysus, the Greek god of vegetation, fertility, and of course, wine. Those who were devoted to Bacchus believed they were closer to God after drinking wine. Naturally, things got a little out of hand with these groups of devotees over the years and they were finally outlawed by the Roman Senate in 186 B.C.

- **berserk (irrational; reckless; frenzied)** Berserkers were warriors who wore bearskin coats, according to Norse myths. They were so brave and confident that no one could hurt them; they refused to wear the traditional coat and went to battle wearing only the fur.

- **caduceus (symbol of the medical profession, a winged staff with serpents entwined around it)** In Greek mythology, the god Hermes was selected to be Zeus's messenger. Hermes was given a special cap, a pair of winged sandals, and a wooden kerykeion (a staff) from which white ribbons fluttered. How the ribbons became serpents is the real story behind the symbol.

- **cereal (commonly a breakfast food, a grain product)** Named after the Roman goddess of grain and agriculture, Ceres. Ceres assured fertile crops and a good harvest.

- **chaos (disorder and confusion)** The creation of earth is from Chaos who then bore the sky, Uranus. According to ancient Greeks, the god of all things rose from Chaos and separated earth from the heavens.

- **chimera (an illusion or fabrication of the mind)** In Greek mythology, the chimera was a fire-breathing she-monster. She had the body of a goat and the tail of a serpent. Today we call the products of an overactive imagination *chimeras.*

- **circean (dangerously bewitching)** An enchantress, Circe lured Odysseus' crew into a castle. The men were fed a magic potion and then turned into pigs. Circe is the personification of evil pretending to be the delight of all earth. Odysseus, by the way, came to their rescue and forced Circe to turn them back into humans.

- **cornucopia (horn of plenty—symbolic of abundance, a bountiful harvest)** We think of Pilgrims when we see this horn-shaped basket, but the word really originated in Greek mythology. Zeus was nursed as an infant by a goat belonging to the nymph Amalthea. To show his appreciation, he broke off one of the goat's horns and gave it to his nanny. From that time on, it was constantly full of whatever food or drink was wished for.

- **cosmos (harmony and order; the orderly universe)** Because the Greeks believed that the original state of the world was Chaos, order was imposed gradually when the sky and earth were formed and then the sun, moon, plants, animals, and man.

- **Cupid's arrow (lovestruck)** The Roman goddess Venus had a son named Cupid. For entertainment, he would fly around shooting arrows into the hearts of gods and men. Cupid was often portrayed as blind, which demonstrated the unpredictable nature of love. You've heard the term "love is blind"; now you know from whence it came.

- **cyclopean (huge, massive)** A giant with one circular eye who was extremely powerful. The three Cyclops (Brontes, Steropes, and Arges) were offspring of Uranus (Sky) and Gaea (Earth).

- **Daedalian (ingenious, intricate)** A master ironsmith, who is given credit for inventing the ax, the awl, the level, and the labyrinth. But Daedalus had no sense of right or wrong and managed to get into some tight fixes because of it.

- **demon (an evil spirit; a person with great drive)** Demon comes from the Greek word Daimon, which was a generalized term for a supernatural being, such as the spirits of the dead and the spirit that Zeus assigned to each human being at his birth. Not all demons, however, were considered evil.

- **Dionysian (opposite of Apollonian [above], unrestrained, disorderly)** Knowing that Dionysus is the Greek god of wine gives away the meaning of this word. He was also worshipped as the god of fertility, vegetation, woodlands, and wilderness. Think of it this way: Dionysian = wild and crazy; Apollonian = order and rational thinking.

- **dwarf (a small person or smaller-than-normal variety of plant or animal)** From Norse mythology, dwarfs arrived from the lowly maggot, if you can believe that. Evidently, Eddas (Norse myths) state that the world was made out of the slain giant Ymir who was being eaten by the maggots. He condemned them to eternal darkness and to their own underground realm.

EXAMPLE

What does the word *bacchanal* mean in the following sentence?

It seems as though the Greeks had one *bacchanal* party after another.

(A) bachelor
(B) meeting of intellectuals
(C) gardening
(D) a wild party or orgy

Your Answer: (A) (B) (C) (D)

ANALYSIS

Right away, not knowing the word *bacchanal*, you might be thrown off by the first answer, **A**. Bacchanal/bachelor are pretty close; therefore, reading the rest of the answers carefully and rereading the sentence might help. Answer **B, meeting of intellectuals,** could also throw you off if you confuse it with baccalaureate, which is a ceremony for graduates. **C** is an unlikely answer. Answer **D** makes the most sense. *Bacchanal* means a wild party or orgy; therefore, **answer D is correct.**

- **echo (repetition of a sound)** As a punishment by Hera to the mountain nymph Echo for her incessant chattering, Hera took away her power to begin a conversation; all she could do is repeat what others said. She unfortunately fell in love with Narcissus, but her love was unrequited. She hid in the mountains, caves, and forest and refused to eat or sleep. All that remains of her is the endlessly repeating words of those who venture into her lonely haunts.

- **Electra complex (excessive attachment of a girl to her father with hostility toward her mother)** Clytemnestra murdered her husband Agamemnon on the day he returned from the Trojan War. Electra, their daughter, believed the killing to be unjust and hated her mother for it. Electra wanted nothing more than to avenge her father's death. Years later she encouraged her brother Orestes to kill the mother, which he did; he was then punished by the Furies (winds) for it until the gods absolved him of his crime.

- **elf (a diminutive person; a small, lively creature)** From Norse mythology, there were two kinds of elves: dark elves and bright elves. The dark elves lived underground and the bright elves lived in a kingdom between heaven and earth. Most of us think of the bright elves—the ones who help Santa every year.

- **Elysian Fields (paradise, a place of peace and bliss)** Sounds great, doesn't it? The words come from early Greek mythology. Elysian Fields were located on earth and it is the place at the world's end where those who are favored by the gods are sent when they die.

- **erotic (having to do with physical love, arousing desire)** The word arrives via Eros, the son of Aphrodite, the Greek version of the Roman Venus and Cupid. Same story, but this word developed a connotation that is far more passionate and sensual.

- **a face that could launch a thousand ships (a great beauty)** This statement refers to Helen of Troy who, according to the Greeks, was the most beautiful woman in the world. She was kidnapped from her husband Menelaus. Because of an oath to defend his honor, the Greek princes rallied behind Menelaus and "launched a thousand ships" to help find her.

- **fury (usually depicted as a woman—an angry, violent person)** In Greek mythology, the Furies existed to avenge violations of the natural order such as murder and other crimes. They were called the Erinyes and it is said that there were three of them. They were depicted as hideous old women with bat wings and snake hair, and had eyes that dripped blood. The Furies barked like dogs, carried whips, and pursued their victims to their death.

- **giant (larger than normal being, larger than life)** Gaia and Uranus had several sets of beings before humans arrived. The Giants were the fourth set of beings. The Giants (24 of them) rose up against Zeus because he had banished their brothers the Titans to Tartarus. It is said that they were huge, hairy monsters with serpent tails for feet and would hurl huge boulders at the Olympians. This rebellion was known as the Gigantomachy.

- **golden age (a period of great prosperity)** During Cronus's reign, mortal people who lived on earth lived very much like the gods. They never grew old, they knew no sorrow, hard work, or pain, and when death did come, they had no fear; they simply went to sleep. It is a time when people look back with nostalgia and longing.

- **beware of Greeks bearing gifts (watch out for people with hidden motives)**
  This term relates to the Trojans who were tricked by the Greeks with a large
  wooden horse left at their gates. Laocoon, a priest, forewarned his fellow
  Trojans that "I fear the Greeks even when they bear gifts," but his warnings
  were not heeded.

EXAMPLE

In the following sentence, what does the term *Elysian Fields* mean?

We all dream of some day finding our own *Elysian Fields*, where we can live happily
ever after, but that time has yet to come.

(A) strawberry patches
(B) a baseball park
(C) paradise, a peaceful place
(D) a shopping mall in the suburbs

Your Answer:

ANALYSIS

This sentence has a major clue that gives evidence to its meaning. Look at the "live
happily ever after" part. If you have no idea what *Elysian Fields* means, reading that
clue and comparing it to the answers, you could easily guess that **C is the correct
answer.**

- **hot as Hades (sweltering hot)** Unlike us, the Greeks and the Norse believed
  that Hades was a cold, dark place never penetrated by the sun. It was referred
  to as the Underworld. But, the change in temperature occurred in the Bible
  where the Hebrew words referred to the afterworld in which sinners would die
  in the flames of Hell.

- **halcyon days (days of perfect peace to be recalled with nostalgia)** Alcyone
  was the daughter of Aeolus, the keeper of the winds. Her husband Ceyx
  wanted to take a sea voyage to consult an oracle, but Alcyone begged him not
  to because she knew the winds were capable of great damage and destruction.
  He went anyway and was drowned the first day of the voyage. Alcyone waited
  patiently for him to return but she had a dream that he was dead and would
  never return. She rushed down to the water's edge and saw her husband's body
  just off shore. As she tried to reach him, the gods felt sorry for her and turned
  both of them into birds (kingfishers). Each winter for seven days before and
  after the winter solstice, the birds build their nests and raise their young on top
  of the waves. At this time of the year, there is no rain and there are no clouds
  covering the sky so that Alcyone and Ceyx can raise their young in peace and
  tranquility.

- **harpy (a shrewish or grasping person, especially a woman)** To call someone
  a harpy is quite insulting. In Greek mythology, Harpies were creatures with the
  head of a woman and the body of birds of prey and an incredible stench about
  them.

- **hector (bully; boastful person)** *Hector* is believed to come from the Trojan prince who walked around as though he were a god's and not a man's son. However, he was one of the bravest and noblest heroes who fought for Troy.

- **Herculean/herculean (extraordinary strength, or requiring such strength)** Heracles (Greek) Hercules (Roman), probably the best-known character of the Greek heroes, had enormous strength and was larger than most men; in fact, he was almost a giant. He was Zeus's illegitimate son (his mother slept with Zeus, believing him to be her husband Amphitryon), which explains his size and strength.

- **hermaphrodite (one with the characteristics of both sexes)** Hermaphroditus, the son of Hermes (associated with virility) and Aphrodite (the goddess of love) inherited his father's virility and his mother's beauty. The nymph Salmacis fell in love with him, but he rejected her advances. Pleading to the gods for help, she prayed to be united with him and her prayers were answered literally. Their bodies grew together and formed the first hermaphrodite.

- **hero (a person of great courage who performs noble deeds)** Our word *hero* comes from the Greek *heros*. Heroes from the myths were extremely strong and brave and were favored by the gods. Many were part god and part man, or demigods.

- **hydra-headed (hard to eliminate)** The term comes from Hydra, a creature who had the body of a dog and nine heads. When one of its heads was cut off, it grew two more in its place. Hydra's blood was poison, as was its breath. It was a challenge to destroy, but Heracles finally did.

- **hyperborean (very far north; frigid)** Boreas was the Greek god of the north wind. His icy breath was believed to bring the freezing cold weather to the northern countries.

- **Icarian (foolishly daring)** The son of Daedalus, Icarus and his father needed to escape from a small island and using a ship was not an option. Daedalus constructed two sets of wings held together with wax. They took off flying and Daedalus warned his son not to fly too close to the sun, but giddy with excitement, Icarus flew higher and higher. His father lost track of him and the next thing he knew, he looked down to see the feathers floating on the water.

EXAMPLE

In the following sentence, what does the word *Herculean* mean?

In times of crises, humans achieve sudden and unexpected *Herculean* strength that serves to aid victims in a variety of circumstances.

(A) a type of linoleum
(B) a weakling
(C) a wrestler's uniform
(D) extremely strong

Your Answer:

ANALYSIS

Because of its familiarity, this would be one of those questions on a test that most people would love to see. Answers **A** and **C** are wrong. Answer **B** is the exact opposite, an antonym. The only answer that makes sense is **D.**

- **jovial (merry, jolly)** The word *jovial* relates in a roundabout way to Jupiter. Jupiter or Jove was the supreme god of Rome. Although he was thought to be a stern fellow, his name in Latin (*Jovialis*) relates to the planet. Jupiter the planet was thought to be a good planet to be born under as it was thought that those born under the planet were happy and cheerful people.

- **labyrinth (a maze, a complicated arrangement)** A twisted, turning, confusing maze that was originally constructed by Daedalus to contain the monster Minotauar that was half man and half bull.

- **laurels, *covered with* (to receive honors or recognition)** Military heroes and the winners of competitions were given wreaths for their heads made of laurel leaves.

- **lethargy (state of being lazy, sluggish)** The word *lethargy* evolved from Greek mythology's Underworld. There were five rivers that one had to cross, called Lethe. To cross the river causes one to forget all past life experiences.

- **lunatic (deranged person)** In both Greek and Roman mythology, the moon was personified as a goddess. She was believed to have been able to induce spells of madness in those who irritated her. *Lunaticus* was a person who was under her spell.

- **martial (having to do with war or fighting)** Related to the Roman god Mars, who was viewed as the protector of Rome.

- **mentor (a teacher or counselor)** In Homer's *Odyssey,* Mentor was a wise old friend who stayed behind in Ithaca. Odysseus left the entire household and the upbringing of his son Telemachus to Mentor.

- **mercurial (swift, changeable)** This word evolved from the Roman god who was the messenger of the gods. He was walking, talking, running, and flying the day after he was born. Mercury was fast and quick and spent most of his time flying through the heavens carrying messages.

- **Midas touch (able to be successful at anything)** Midas was the King of Phrygia. He was granted a wish by the god Dionysus for being kind to one of his followers. Being the selfish and greedy person that he was, he wished that everything he touched would turn to gold. The wish, backfired, however, because everything he touched literally turned to gold, including the food he ate. Eventually, he was cured and managed to gain a bit of wisdom from the experience.

- **muse (an inspiration)** Originally three in number (later nine) the Muses are said to be the daughters of Zeus and Mnemosyne (Memory). Each one is responsible for the inspiration of a specific area of the arts such as art, history, poetry, tragedy, dance, comedy, music, and astronomy.

EXAMPLE

In the following sentence, what does the word *mercurial* mean?

Spiderman, Batman, Superwoman, and Superman all appear to have *mercurial* flying speed.

(A) slow, sluggish
(B) fast, quick
(C) humorous, funny
(D) masterful

Your Answer: Ⓓ

ANALYSIS

If you are aware of pop culture, the answer to this question is obvious. It is **B.** Relating a word to something that is familiar is always a good way to remember it. This question may not appear on the exam, but you will most likely remember the word *mercurial*.

- **narcissistic (conceited, self-absorbed)** A very handsome young man whose mother was told by a seer or prophet that the boy would live to a great old age if he never got to know himself. He was so handsome that many young men and women attempted to make advances for him, but he rejected them all. When the nymph Echo was rejected by him she asked for help, and Narcissus was cursed to love someone unattainable, himself. This happened when he saw his reflection in a pool of water. Obviously incapable of reaching the reflection, he lay down and died. His body vanished and a flower stood in its place.

- **nectar/ambrosia (something extremely delicious)** From Greek mythology, *nectar* and *ambrosia* are something so delicious that they are considered the drink and food of the gods.

- **nemesis (an unconquerable enemy or stumbling block)** The Greeks believed that the goddess Nemesis was sent to punish others. It was she who punished Agamemnon for the pride in his victory and caused Narcissus to fall in love with himself. Today, a nemesis is someone or something that gets in the way of accomplishing what we set out to accomplish.

- **nepenthe (anything that produces euphoria)** Helen of Troy (the face that launched a thousand ships) overheard the sorrowful stories of the men who had fought in the Trojan War and was so moved that she slipped a drug that would lift their spirits and take away the pain, anger, and grief. Literally, the word means *ne* (not) *penthos* (sorrow).

- **nestor (a wise old man)** Nestor was the oldest, wisest, and most respected member of the Greek forces. He survived the Trojan War and is said to have lived to be three hundred years old.

- **dressed to the nines (dressed in one's finest clothes)** The nine Muses of Greek mythology were elegant and beautiful. They appeared to be perfect and that is what is meant when we hear the saying, "dressed to the nines,"— someone who is attempting to strive for the best.

- **nymph (a beautiful young woman)** Any female spirit who lived on earth according to the Greeks were called *Nymphs*. There were different types of nymphs, the forest variety, as well as the fountain, mountain, and river variety of nymph. Each had a unique personality—some were a little questionable.

- **ocean (body of salt water that covers two-thirds of the earth; an immense expanse or large quantity)** Oceanus was the realm of the Greek Titan named Oceanus. He was the son of Uranus (Sky) and Gaea (Earth). The difference between Oceanus and his brothers and sisters was that he did not side against Zeus and was not exiled to Tartarus. Instead, he continued to rule over his great river.

- **odyssey (a long journey)** The word evolves from the long journey taken by Odysseus, the mythical king of Ithaca. The first part of his nearly twenty-year journey was spent fighting the Trojans. The second half was spent trying to get home.

- **Oedipus complex (a male's excessive attachment to his mother/hostility to his father)** To make a long story short, this term comes from Greek mythology. A prophecy came true that Oedipus would kill his father and marry his mother. A shepherd adopted Oedipus and as an adult he killed a stranger in an argument (not knowing it was his real father). After arriving in the city of Thebes, he was given the widow of King Laius, whom he married. She was his mother. She bore him four children before they realized that their relationship was incestuous.

- **Olympian (godlike, majestic)** This word evolved from the Greeks. Both Mt. Olympus and the Olympians who lived there were obviously larger than life; hence the word *Olympian*.

- **oracle (a person who speaks with authority and wisdom)** The Greeks and Romans believed that the gods spoke to mortals through oracles, giving them advice and predicting the future.

- **orphean (charming; enchanting)** Orpheus was the son of one of the nine Muses, Calliope, and his father was the king of Thrace whose subjects were the most musical of the ancient Greeks. Some say that he was the son of Apollo from whom he inherited his lyre and his musical talent. Orpheus was able to stop arguments as well as entertain with his music. He moved Hades to tears and managed to get his wife Eurydice released from his grasp, but he was asked to not turn back and look at her until they reached the upper world. Orpheus could not resist the temptation and lost his wife forever.

EXAMPLE
In the following sentence, what does the word *nemesis* mean?
Watching television and playing video games seem to be his *nemesis* and his grades are suffering because of it.
(A) an obstacle
(B) name calling
(C) a hobby
(D) an encouragement

Your Answer:

ANALYSIS

Read the sentence carefully. What is preventing this person from improving his grades? Television and video games! Now, look at the answers. Which of the four fit into the meaning of the word? **D** is an antonym; **C** is way out there; and **B?** The only thing that might cause some concern is that they both begin with the same letter, but "name calling" doesn't make sense otherwise. **A is the correct answer.**

- **panacea (cure-all)** Panacea was the daughter of the Greek god of medicine. Her father was struck down by Zeus, but she was believed to be able to heal all mankind's illness and injuries. Today the term *panacea* is used as the answer to all our problems.

- **pander (cater to low tastes)** Named for the son of Lycaon, Pandarus fought on the side of Troy. Athena tricked him into shooting Menelaus, which broke the truce between the Trojans and the Greeks.

- **Pandora's box (a source of all sorts of trouble)** A beautiful woman created by Zeus to take revenge on men. She was given irresistible traits by the Olympians and delivered to Epimetheus (Prometheus' brother) who immediately fell in love with and married her. She brought with her a dowry that contained all the evils unknown to man. The only positive thing in the jar was Hope. Pandora was instructed to never touch the jar, but giving in to temptation, she opened the lid and all the ills that have since plagued mankind escaped—Old Age, Insanity, Jealousy, Sickness, Vice, etc. Even though it was originally a jar, it was translated to mean box in later years.

- **panic (feel sudden, irrational fear)** The sudden fear of the ancient Greeks when hearing the nocturnal revelry of **Pan** (the half man with horns and half goat) and his followers.

- **climb Parnassus (to begin a career in the arts)** The mount on which Apollo is said to have lived on earth. The god of poetry, music, and dance played on his lyre there and enchanted all who heard its strains.

- **patience of Penelope (endless patience)** Penelope was the wife of Odysseus. She was left behind when he went to fight in the Trojan War that lasted ten years. It took Odysseus ten more years to get back to Ithaca. When he returned, Penelope was still faithfully waiting.

- **mount Pegasus (to soar to heights, do inspired or creative work)** winged horse named Pegasus sprang forth from the body of the Gorgon Medusa when Perseus cut her head off. It is said that Pegasus became the pet of the Muses who are the goddesses of the arts.

- **phaeton (a light, horse-drawn carriage)** A young man who rode to his death in a carriage, Phaëthon, although not immortal, begged his father the sun god Helios to allow him to guide the chariot of the sun across the sky. Helios watched as Phaëthon rose into the sky. Without the weight of the master, the horses of the sun went wild, crashing into stars. Phaëthon dropped the reins and the chariot plunged to earth, setting the world on fire. Zeus knocked the chariot and its driver into the river below putting out the flame. Of course, Phaëthon did not survive.

- **rise from the ashes like a phoenix (to make an unexpected comeback)** A bird that, according to Herodotus, was the size and shape of an eagle with red and gold plumage. It would sit on a nest of fragrant spices awaiting its death (some say the bird lived for 1,461 years). The sun ignited the nest and flames consumed the aged bird. A short time later a worm appeared in its ashes and the worm became the new Phoenix, who then made the trip to Heliopolis carrying its parent's ashes as an offering to the sun god.

- **Promethean (creative or daringly original)** Named for the Greek Titan who at first fought on the side of Zeus, but changed sides once man was created. Zeus tried to punish Prometheus by chaining him to a rock and setting a vulture on him. The vulture ate his liver out each day and at night the liver grew back. Prometheus is credited with having taught mankind to cultivate land, tame horses, navigate by the stars, and to forge metal into tools and weapons.

- **protean (versatile, always changing)** Proteus, a Greek sea god, who was able to change shape at will and could turn himself into any creature or object in order to slip away from his questioners.

- **psyche (the human soul, the self)** Odysseus meets his mother in the Underworld and she explains to him that when we die our life force leaves our body and our soul (psyche) slips away and flutters in the air.

- **pygmy (a dwarf plant, animal; small human)** The word comes from the Greek word for fist. It originally stood for a unit of measurement that was equal to the distance from a man's knuckles to his elbow, which is about thirteen inches. But, the word *pygmy* represented the mythical dwarfs or very small humans who lived on the shores of the river Oceanus.

- **Rx (symbol for prescriptions or treatment)** An ancient sign used by apothecaries in Rome, where it meant *recipere* (take this).

> ### EXAMPLE
>
> In the following sentence, what does the term *patience of Penelope* mean?
>
> Raising eight children alone must take the *patience of* three *Penelopes*.
>
> (A) prescription
> (B) impatient
> (C) endless patience
> (D) chattering

Your Answer: Ⓐ Ⓑ Ⓒ Ⓓ

ANALYSIS

Understanding words in context is not as difficult as it sounds. To know that raising eight children would be difficult, one would need a lot of patience and understanding. **The only logical answer of the four is C.**

- **saturnalia (period of unrestrained partying)** A kind of Mardi Gras atmosphere celebrated at the end of December marking the winter sowing season. Saturn was the Roman god of sowing and the harvest. The planet Saturn and Saturday are named after him.

- **satyr (a lecherous man)** Mythological forest deities, these were the followers of the god Pan who was half man and half goat. They were known for their devotion to the god of wine, had a reputation for unrestrained lust, and no woman was safe from their advances. The medical terms *satyromaniac* and *nymphomaniac* refer to the male and female conditions of insatiable sexual appetite.

- **between Scylla and Charybdis (having to choose between two undesirable choices)** In Greek mythology, this saying means to be between the two monsters that were actual navigational hazards. On one side, a large rock posed a threat to all ships that tried to pass through the narrow channel. To avoid it, the ship had to sail closer to the coast, which was in the range of a dangerous whirlpool. We continue to use expressions like "between a rock and a hard place," and "between the devil and the deep blue sea," to convey images of a difficult situation, no matter what choice is made.

- **sibylline (prophetic; mysterious)** An ancient woman who goes into a trance and utters predictions.

- **siren (a temptress, a device that gives off a shrieking sound)** From Greek mythology, the Sirens were three water nymphs whose singing, while not unpleasant, was a dangerous thing to hear. Sailors hearing their alluring song would run their ships aground and never sail again.

- **Sisyphean labor (a never-ending task)** After angering the gods more than was acceptable, Sisyphus was given an extremely frustrating punishment. He was to roll a huge block of stone up a hill, only to have it topple back to the ground just before reaching the top.

- **sphinx (a mysterious, inscrutable person)** The Sphinx originated in Greek mythology. She was a bloodthirsty monster, said to have the face and breasts of a woman, the body of a lion, the wings of an eagle, and a serpent's tail. She was sent to Thebes by Hera to punish its people. She asked a riddle to those walking by: "What creature walks on four legs in the morning, two in the afternoon, and three in the evening?" When they couldn't answer, she strangled them and then ate them on the spot. When Oedipus answered the question, she leapt to her death.

- **stentorian (loud; booming)** Stentor's voice was thought to be as loud and booming as that of fifty men together as it echoed through the Greek camp during the Trojan War.

- **stygian (dark, gloomy)** The river Styx in the Underworld had to be crossed in order to get to the area of Hades that was the departed souls' destiny. Greek myths depict the area as dreary, and cheerless, a place where the sun never warms the air or lifts the shadows. The word **stygian** is used figuratively to describe an atmosphere of gloom and depression.

- **syrinx (a musical instrument/panpipe)** Pan was a lecherous satyr who attempted to rape a virtuous nymph named Syrinx. She called out to the gods for help and was turned into a bunch of reeds. Pan made the reeds into a mouth pipe and became renowned for the beautiful sounds he produced from it.

EXAMPLE

In the following sentence, what does the word *sibylline* mean?

We read a mystery in class last year whose protagonist seemed *sibylline*; she was very old and could see into the future.

(A) simple
(B) protean
(C) homeless
(D) prophetic

Your Answer: (A) (B) (C) (D)

ANALYSIS

This sentence is not completely unusual. Often, when we look at words in context, the answer is right in front of us. The difficult part is in knowing the proper terms or synonyms that match the word in the answer. In this case, *sibylline* means an ancient woman who could tell the future. Someone who can predict the future is prophetic. The **correct answer is D. A** and **C** are completely wrong and **B** might only pose a problem because it is a mythological word, and because it begins with the same letter as "prophetic." This might cause you to stop and ponder, but thinking logically, there is only one answer.

- **tantalize (to tease, to invite but remain unattainable)** After having offended the gods, Tantalus was sent to Tartarus (the section of the Underworld where sinners are punished). He was sentenced to eternal frustration after having attempted to serve his son as dinner to the gods. Zeus restored the life of Tantalus' son, but forced Tantalus to stand in a pool of water up to his chin. When he leaned over to drink, the water would suddenly retreat, leaving mud. When Tantalus stood up again, the water flooded back. The cycle repeated.

- **thersitical (loudmouth, scurrilous)** The ugliest of all Greeks who had come to Troy, Thersites liked to fling vulgar insults at royal masters and was hated for it. Finally, Odysseus had enough and hit him with his staff. After mocking Achilles for being in love, Achilles hit Thersites so hard that his soul was sent to Tartarus.

- **thunder (sound associated with electrical storms; loud booming noise)** The Norse god of the sky was named Thor. He rode across the heavens in his chariot, hurling his magic hammer. The hammer was his lightning bolt and the chariot's rumbling was thunder.

- **titan (leader in one's field; someone of great ability or power)** Larger than life, the first Titans were the first and largest beings in the universe. There were twelve Titans who were the children of Gaea and Uranus (Earth and Sky). They lost the war with the Olympians and were banished to the Underworld.

- **Triton among minnows (one who stands out; a superior individual)** The Tritons were the demigods of the deep. Their job was to attend the supreme god of the sea Poseidon, their father.

- **Trojan (someone with great perseverance and stamina)** The Trojans fought the Greeks for nearly ten years. They lost only when they were tricked by the wiliness of Odysseus and his Trojan horse (see below).

- **Trojan horse (someone or something that subverts from within; a deceptive scheme)** A very large wooden horse constructed with a trap door through which Odysseus and his men climbed. The horse was left outside the Gates of Troy and when the Trojans saw that the Greeks were gone, they rolled the horse inside and began to celebrate the end of the war—they thought. When the Trojans went to sleep, the Greeks crawled out and signaled for reinforcements. Then they began to sack the city of Troy, killing all the men and enslaving the women.

- **troll (an ugly person)** From Norse mythology, the troll is an ugly, weird-acting, malicious creature. Most of you will remember the troll under the bridge in the story "The Three Billy Goats Gruff."

- **typhoon (a violent cyclonic storm; a hurricane)** Named for Typhon, the mythical Greek monster who was the son of Earth and Tartarus. He was the largest of all monsters born with coiled snakes for legs and a serpent's head instead of hands. He terrorized the gods and wounded Zeus who eventually killed him by hurling a thunderbolt at him.

EXAMPLE

In the following sentence, what does the word *titans* mean?

Devoted scientists often appear to be *titans* in their respective fields.

(A) losers
(B) leaders in their fields
(C) insensitive to the needs of others
(D) tight

Your Answer: Ⓒ

ANALYSIS

D, A, and **C** are wrong. Although **D** could possibly throw you if you were attempting alliteration, **B is the correct answer.**

- **unicorn (a mythical, one-horned beast that often symbolizes virility and supreme power)** Although the one-horned creature is seen in the myths of many different countries, Greek and Roman writers told outrageous tales of the beast, which tell of magical powers of the horn and for centuries were thought to have medicinal value. Finally, the Apothecaries' Society of London removed the unicorn horn from its list of effective medications. What the citizenry believed to be unicorn powder was identified as being made from narwhal tusks.

- **Valhalla (a special place for persons worthy of honor)** From Norse mythology, Valhalla was a place reserved in the afterworld for those who died in battle. The Norsemen placed a high value on military might and fierce fighting so they were taken to "the hall of the slain" after dying in battle.

- **Venus (a beautiful woman)** The Roman goddess of love, she was identified with the Greek goddess Aphrodite who was believed to inspire love and lust in all living things. *Venereal, venom, venerate,* and *venerable* are words that evolved from *Venus.*

- **volcano (a vent in the earth's crust through which steam and molten rock issue)** Named after the god of fire Vulcanus, which is identified with Hephaestus the son of Zeus and Hera. He was a master in metalworking and it is said that he created Zeus's thunderbolt and Achilles' armor. The fire god's forges are the holes in the earth where the fire appeared.

- **werewolf (a man who occasionally turns into a wolf)** This word arrives via Greek and Scandinavian myths. Our word is from the Anglo-Saxon *were* (man) and *wulf* (wolf). However, *lycanthrope,* the original Greek word, means *lykos* (wolf) and *anthropos* (man). Lycacon was a king of Arcadia. It is said that he served Zeus a meal of human flesh, which Zeus detected and this made Zeus unhappy. Zeus then killed Lycacon's son with a thunderbolt and turned Lycacon into a wolf.

- **wheel of fortune (symbol of luck or chance)** Named for the Roman goddess Fortuna who, it is said, could grant a mortal all his wishes or take everything away when she spun her wheel of fortune.
- **zephyr (gentle breeze)** The god of the west wind in ancient Greece was called Zephyrus. The west wind is the early sign of spring, replacing the cold north winds indicative of winter.
- ♀ **Greek symbol for female (the sign of Aphrodite, goddess of love)** The circle with the cross beneath it is thought to represent her hand mirror or looking glass.
- ♂ **Greek symbol for male (represents Ares, the god of war)** The circle and arrow stand for either the helmet and plume or the shield and spear worn by Greek warriors as they charged into battle.

EXAMPLE

In the following sentence, what does the word *zephyr* mean?

The slow start of the annual sailing regatta was due to the faint *zephyrs* blowing this morning.

(A) gentle breezes
(B) hurricanes
(C) snowstorm
(D) tsunami

Your Answer: Ⓐ Ⓑ Ⓒ Ⓓ

ANALYSIS

If you absolutely did not know what the word *zephyrs* meant, the answers could be weeded out easily once the sentence was read again. The first clue is "slow start," the second clue is "faint." Both indicate something amiss and it is not a hurricane, snowstorm, or a tsunami (fifty-foot waves). The logical answer and **the correct answer is A.** Zephyrs are gentle breezes.

Chapter Review and Quick Quizzes

ROOT WORDS

In order to check your understanding and to review the roots presented in the first part of this chapter, take the following quick quizzes. You will find the answers in the appendix at the end of the book.

Directions: Match the root with its meaning. Write the letter of the correct answer in the space to the left of the word.

SECTION I

ANSWER	ROOT WORD	MEANING
_____	1. a	a. away
_____	2. ab/abs	b. to go, to walk
_____	3. ac/acr	c. to do, to drive, to force, to lead
_____	4. act/ag	d. skill, craft
_____	5. ad/al	e. against
_____	6. al/ali/alter	f. year
_____	7. am	g. man, human
_____	8. amb	h. to increase
_____	9. amb/amph	i. sharp/bitter
_____	10. amb/amph	j. around
_____	11. anim	k. both, more than one
_____	12. ante	l. self
_____	13. anthro/andr	m. off, away from, apart, down
_____	14. annu/enni	n. to, toward, near
_____	15. anti	o. before
_____	16. apo	p. life, mind, soul, spirit
_____	17. atp/ept	q. other, another
_____	18. arch/archi	r. ruler
_____	19. archy	s. chief, principal
_____	20. art	t. skill, fitness, ability
_____	21. auc/aug/aux	u. without
_____	22. auto	v. love

SECTION II

ANSWER	ROOT WORD		MEANING
_____	1. be	a.	life
_____	2. bel/bell	b.	war
_____	3. ben/bon	c.	to be, to have a certain quality
_____	4. bi	d.	brief, short
_____	5. bio	e.	twice, doubly
_____	6. bri/brev	f.	good

SECTION III

ANSWER	ROOT WORD		MEANING
_____	1. cad/cid	a.	head, headlong
_____	2. cand	b.	time
_____	3. cant/cent/chant	c.	to fall, to happen by chance
_____	4. cap/cip/cept	d.	hidden
_____	5. cap/capit/cipit	e.	to separate, judge, distinguish, decide
_____	6. card/cord/cour	f.	flesh
_____	7. carn	g.	running a course
_____	8. cast/chast	h.	to lean toward
_____	9. caust	i.	shut, close
_____	10. ced/ceed/cess	j.	to burn
_____	11. centr	k.	to go, to yield, to stop
_____	12. cern/cert/cret/crim/crit	l.	to believe, to trust
_____	13. chron	m.	center
_____	14. circu	n.	blame
_____	15. cis	o.	around, on all sides
_____	16. cit	p.	heart
_____	17. cla/clo/clu	q.	with, together
_____	18. claim/clam	r.	cut
_____	19. cli	s.	to grow
_____	20. co/col/com/con	t.	to cut
_____	21. crat/cracy	u.	to burn
_____	22. cre/crese/cret	v.	to set in motion

_____	23. cred	**w.**	to govern
_____	24. cryp	**x.**	to lie down
_____	25. cub/cumb	**y.**	to sing
_____	26. culp	**z.**	to take, to get
_____	27. cour/cur	**aa.**	to shout, to cry out

SECTION IV

ANSWER	ROOT WORD		MEANING
_____	1. de	**a.**	to give
_____	2. dem	**b.**	worth
_____	3. di/dia	**c.**	hard
_____	4. dic/dict/dit	**d.**	away from, apart, reversal, not
_____	5. dign	**e.**	suffer, pain
_____	6. dis/dif	**f.**	to say, to tell, to use words
_____	7. dac/doc	**g.**	faulty
_____	8. dog/dox	**h.**	apart, through
_____	9. dol	**i.**	opinion
_____	10. don/dot/dow	**j.**	doubt
_____	11. dub	**k.**	people
_____	12. duc	**l.**	to teach
_____	13. dur	**m.**	away, off, down, completely, reversal
_____	14. dys	**n.**	to lead

SECTION V

ANSWER	ROOT WORD		MEANING
_____	1. epi	**a.**	good, well
_____	2. equ	**b.**	upon
_____	3. err	**c.**	outside of, beyond
_____	4. esce	**d.**	equal, even
_____	5. eu	**e.**	becoming
_____	6. e/ef/ex	**f.**	out, out of, from, former, completely
_____	7. extra	**g.**	to wander

SECTION VI

ANSWER	ROOT WORD		MEANING
_____	1. fab	a.	before
_____	2. fac	b.	to burn
_____	3. fer	c.	to bring, to carry, to bear
_____	4. ferv	d.	pour
_____	5. fid	e.	to speak
_____	6. fin	f.	end
_____	7. flam	g.	break
_____	8. flect/flex	h.	to bend
_____	9. flict	i.	to boil, to bubble, to burn
_____	10. fore	j.	to do, to make
_____	11. frac	k.	bottom
_____	12. fund	l.	to strike
_____	13. fus	m.	faith, trust

Directions: Write the root of the <u>underlined</u> word on the line at the beginning of the sentence.

SECTION VII

> ***Root Bank:*** gen, grand, grat, grad, her, hetero, hom, hyper, id, inter, intra, ject, junct, jur

_____ 1. The <u>junction</u> between the two railway tracks was washed out by the typhoon.

_____ 2. Japan has a primarily <u>homogenous</u> society; most of its people are Japanese.

_____ 3. The corporate offices hope that its employees will <u>generate</u> business.

_____ 4. To <u>graduate</u> from high school in California, you have to pass the exam.

_____ 5. In wrapping gifts, most people use <u>adhesive</u> tape.

_____ 6. An <u>idiom</u> is a phrase that can be interpreted both figuratively and literally.

_____ 7. An <u>interstate</u> highway is built to connect more than one state.

_____ 8. Before giving an <u>intravenous</u> injection, a nurse needs to have thorough training.

_____ 9. The passenger was <u>ejected</u> from the car during the accident because he was not wearing a seat belt.

_____ 10. The Rose Parade floats are displayed in all their <u>grandeur</u>.

_____ 11. When you are happy with the service in a restaurant, you usually leave a <u>gratuity</u>.

_____ 12. When a witness lies under oath, he or she has committed <u>perjury</u>.

_____ 13. The United States has a <u>heterogeneous</u> society. It is made up of many different nationalities.

_____ 14. Many people believe that when children consume sugar, they become <u>hyperactive</u>.

SECTION VIII

> ***Root Bank:*** lect, lev, log, lus, mag, mal, man, mater, min, mit, monit, morph, mort, mut

_____ 1. The police department was <u>monitoring</u> the situation in hopes that tempers would settle down.

_____ 2. The <u>manufacture</u> of prescription medicines is controlled by the FDA.

_____ 3. The students <u>elected</u> to have a longer lunch instead of having a break after second period.

_____ 4. Environmental pollution is said to be causing the <u>mutation</u> of a certain species of frog.

_____ 5. A woman often has uncanny <u>maternal</u> instincts when caring for her newborn.

_____ 6. Magicians claim to be able to <u>levitate</u> their volunteers five inches from the surface of the table.

_____ 7. There was an unusual <u>metamorphosis</u> of the character in Franz Kafka's novel; he believes that he becomes a dung beetle.

_____ 8. As space becomes less abundant, <u>miniature</u> versions of animals and plants become more and more popular.

_____ 9. To be <u>immortal</u> means to be able to live forever.

_____ 10. Her intentions were <u>malicious</u>, not thoughtful and kind.

_____ 11. The <u>dialogue</u> between the two characters in the play was hilarious.

_____ 12. In <u>illustrating</u> her point, the student displayed a graph of the statistics.

_____ 13. The news of the disaster was <u>transmitted</u> over the airwaves.

_____ 14. Using a <u>magnifying</u> glass to look at the details of a leaf was necessary.

SECTION IX

> **Root Bank:** nom, nat, nox, nym, nov, omni, pac, pan, par, para, path, pater, ped, pod, pen, pend, peri, phone, plac, port, post, pre, pro, prob, pug

_____ 1. An <u>omniscient</u> narrator of a novel is all-knowing, which means he knows everything that is going on with each character.

_____ 2. The widows were offered much <u>sympathy</u> and condolences upon losing their husbands in the mining disaster.

_____ 3. The candidates were <u>nominated</u> in early November.

_____ 4. The <u>telephone</u> is my sister's best friend.

_____ 5. A <u>novice</u> is under much pressure to adhere to the demands of the program.

_____ 6. Not all Californians are <u>natives</u> of the state. Many people have moved here from other places.

_____ 7. His reaction to the news was very <u>placid</u>.

_____ 8. My <u>paternal</u> grandfather was an important part of my life.

_____ 9. Busy harbors deal with the <u>import</u> and <u>export</u> of manufactured goods.

_____ 10. To <u>pacify</u> the baby, the mother changed his diapers and gave him a bottle.

_____ 11. The <u>noxious</u> fumes were dangerous and the employees of the factory were evacuated.

_____ 12. Our fund-raising efforts were on <u>par</u> with those of the previous year.

_____ 13. The <u>podiatrist</u> was able to cure the old woman's foot problems.

_____ 14. She was awarded the Pulitzer Prize <u>posthumously</u>.

_____ 15. A <u>pediatrician</u> specializes in caring for children.

_____ 16. Charles Dickens was one of the most <u>prolific</u> writers of his time.

_____ 17. The jury decided unanimously that the murder was <u>premeditated</u>.

_____ 18. With the <u>panoramic</u> photograph, we were able to see the entire valley.

_____ 19. Some rock stars appear to be rather <u>pugnacious</u> and their names are often in the news.

_____ 20. The team was given a <u>penalty</u> for unsportsmanlike conduct.

_____ 21. An <u>acronym</u> is a group of letters that abbreviate a long name; for instance, FBI is an acronym for the Federal Bureau of Investigation.

_____ 22. The <u>probe</u> included tests of many organs to rule out disease.

_____ 23. The students were <u>compensated</u> for their hard work by earning good grades and getting into good colleges.

_____ 24. The frontage road was <u>parallel</u> to the highway and it was less congested and more relaxing to drive.

_____ 25. As a punishment, our P.E. class had to run the <u>perimeter</u> of the field ten times.

Directions: Match the *root* with its meaning. Write the letter of the correct answer in the space to the left of the word.

SECTION X

ANSWER	ROOT		MEANING
_____	1. que/quis	a.	sacred
_____	2. qui	b.	to look, to see
_____	3. sacr/sanct/secr	c.	to stand, to be in place
_____	4. sci	d.	to know
_____	5. scribe/scrip	e.	above
_____	6. se	f.	apart
_____	7. sec/sequ	g.	below
_____	8. sens/sent	h.	to seek
_____	9. sol	i.	to follow
_____	10. spec	j.	to feel, to be aware
_____	11. sta/sti	k.	to write
_____	12. sub/sup	l.	sun
_____	13. super/sur	m.	quiet

SECTION XI

ANSWER	ROOT		MEANING
_____	1. tain	a.	to come together, move, toward
_____	2. theo	b.	god
_____	3. tract	c.	truth
_____	4. trans	d.	to call
_____	5. ven/vent	e.	to hold
_____	6. ver	f.	to see
_____	7. vers/vert	g.	across
_____	8. vi	h.	to wish
_____	9. vid/vis	i.	life
_____	10. voc/vok	j.	to drag, pull, draw
_____	11. vol	k.	to turn

WORDS FROM MYTHOLOGY

Take these review quizzes to insure that you have initiated the learning process for the exam. You will revisit many of these names and words stemming from mythology in your readings for the rest of your life.

> **Directions:** Match the name or word with its meaning. Write the letter of the correct definition in the space on the left.

SECTION XII

ANSWER	NAME OR WORD		MEANING
_____	1. Achates	a.	harmonious, balanced, ordered
_____	2. Achilles' heel	b.	handsome man
_____	3. Adonis	c.	dedicatedly observant
_____	4. Aeolian/aeolistic	d.	giving a moaning or sighing sound, like the wind
_____	5. amazon	e.	referring to spiders, scorpions, mites, and ticks

_____	**6.** Antaean/antaean	**f.**	one who carries a heavy burden; a bound book of maps
_____	**7.** Apollonian	**g.**	a vulnerable spot
_____	**8.** arachnid	**h.**	dawn; a beginning; an early period
_____	**9.** Argonaut	**i.**	a large, strong, masculine woman
_____	**10.** Argus-eyed	**j.**	an adventurer engaged in a quest
_____	**11.** atlas	**k.**	faithful
_____	**12.** aurora	**l.**	having superhuman strength

SECTION XIII

ANSWER	NAME OR WORD	MEANING
_____	**1.** bacchanal	**a.** dangerously bewitching
_____	**2.** berserk	**b.** lovestruck
_____	**3.** caduceus	**c.** symbol of the medical profession, a winged staff with serpents entwined around it
_____	**4.** cereal	**d.** an illusion or fabrication of the mind
_____	**5.** chaos	**e.** harmony and order; the orderly universe
_____	**6.** chimera	**f.** a small person or smaller-than-normal variety of plant or animal
_____	**7.** circean	**g.** a wild party; an orgy
_____	**8.** cornucopia	**h.** opposite of Apollonian, unrestrained, disorderly
_____	**9.** cosmos	**i.** commonly a breakfast food or grain product
_____	**10.** Cupid's arrow	**j.** an evil spirit; a person with great drive
_____	**11.** cyclopean	**k.** irrational; reckless
_____	**12.** Daedalian	**l.** horn of plenty; symbolic of abundance; a bountiful harvest
_____	**13.** demon	**m.** ingenious, intricate
_____	**14.** Dionysian	**n.** disorder and confusion
_____	**15.** dwarf	**o.** huge, massive

SECTION XIV

ANSWER	NAME, WORD, OR PHRASE	MEANING
_____	**1.** echo	**a.** paradise, a place of peace and bliss
_____	**2.** Electra complex	**b.** a diminutive person, a small, lively creature
_____	**3.** elf	**c.** a great beauty
_____	**4.** Elysian Fields	**d.** larger than normal being, larger than life
_____	**5.** erotic	**e.** usually depicted as a woman, an angry violent person
_____	**6.** a face that could launch a thousand ships	**f.** excessive attachment of a girl to her father with hostility toward her mother
_____	**7.** fury	**g.** repetition of a sound
_____	**8.** giant	**h.** a period of great prosperity
_____	**9.** golden age	**i.** watch out for people with hidden motives
_____	**10.** beware of Greeks bearing gifts	**j.** having to do with physical love, arousing desire

SECTION XV

ANSWER	NAME, WORD, OR PHRASE	MEANING
_____	**1.** hot as Hades	**a.** a bully, a boastful person
_____	**2.** halcyon days	**b.** a person of great courage who performs noble deeds
_____	**3.** harpy	**c.** a shrewish or grasping person, especially a woman
_____	**4.** hector	**d.** hard to eliminate
_____	**5.** Herculean/herculean	**e.** foolishly daring
_____	**6.** hermaphrodite	**f.** sweltering heat
_____	**7.** hero	**g.** very far north, frigid
_____	**8.** hydra-headed	**h.** extraordinary strength
_____	**9.** hyperborean	**i.** days of perfect peace to be recalled with nostalgia
_____	**10.** Icarian	**j.** one with the characteristics of both sexes

Directions: Select the correct answer from the three choices. Write the letter of the correct answer in the space at the left.

SECTION XVI

ANSWER	WORD(S)	MEANING

_____ 1. jovial
    a. disheartened
    b. sad
    c. merry, jolly

_____ 2. labyrinth
    a. a complicated maze
    b. a clear path
    c. a triangle

_____ 3. cover with laurels
    a. losers of major sporting events
    b. to receive honors or recognition
    c. what occurs after falling into shrubbery

_____ 4. lethargy
    a. state of being lazy
    b. ambitious
    c. studious

_____ 5. lunatic
    a. the moon
    b. an intelligent and stable person
    c. a deranged person

_____ 6. martial
    a. marriage
    b. having to do with war or fighting
    c. having to do with shopping

_____ 7. mentor
    a. a teacher or counselor
    b. a deranged person
    c. a confidant

_____ 8. mercurial
    a. easygoing
    b. swift, changeable
    c. stable

_____ 9. Midas touch
    a. to fail at everything
    b. having to do with war or fighting
    c. able to be successful at anything

_____ 10. muse
    a. lazy
    b. an inspiration
    c. funny

SECTION XVII

ANSWER	WORD(S)	MEANING

1. narcissistic
   a. an orange and yellow flower
   b. a kind and generous person
   c. conceited, self-absorbed

2. nectar
   a. a fruit
   b. a body part
   c. something extremely delicious

3. nemesis
   a. an unconquerable enemy or stumbling block
   b. to regurgitate
   c. a friend and co-worker

4. nepenthe
   a. anything that produces euphoria
   b. a snake
   c. a medicine used for infections

5. nestor
   a. where birds live
   b. a wise old man
   c. a pregnant woman

6. dressed to the nines
   a. dressed in one's finest clothes
   b. dressed in work clothes
   c. dressed in gym clothes

7. nymph
   a. a beautiful young woman
   b. an ugly old hag
   c. a sea creature

8. ocean
   a. body of salt water that covers two-thirds of the earth; an immense expanse or quantity
   b. a small body of water
   c. a flying bird

9. odyssey
   a. an automobile with large wheels
   b. a long journey
   c. rest and relaxation

10. Oedipus complex
    a. a male's excessive attachment to his mother and hostility to his father
    b. a Greek city
    c. a shopping mall

11. Olympian
    a. godlike, majestic
    b. fearful and wimpy
    c. a city in Greenland

_____ 12. oracle
    a. a prisoner
    b. a person who speaks with authority and wisdom
    c. a powerful officer in the army

_____ 13. orphean
    a. charming and enchanting
    b. ugly and morose
    c. an orphan

SECTION XVIII

ANSWER	WORD(S)	MEANING

_____ 1. panacea
    a. illness
    b. cure-all
    c. pastry

_____ 2. Pandora's box
    a. a source for all sorts of trouble
    b. a wooden box for storing pandas
    c. a special hat

_____ 3. panic
    a. sudden irrational fear
    b. safe and cozy
    c. a filthy pan

_____ 4. climb Parnassus
    a. a mountain in the French Alps
    b. a hill in Lucerne
    c. to begin a career in the arts

_____ 5. patience of Penelope
    a. quick to anger
    b. endless patience
    c. anxious and out of sorts

_____ 6. mount Pegasus
    a. to sit on a fence
    b. to climb to the top of a mountain
    c. to soar to heights; to do inspired or creative work

_____ 7. phaeton
    a. a light at the end of the tunnel
    b. a dangerous emission from petroleum
    c. a light, horse-drawn carriage

_____ 8. rise from the ashes like a phoenix
    a. to make an unexpected comeback
    b. to smoke out dangerous criminals
    c. to fly easily in a windstorm

_____ 9. Promethean
    a. creative or daringly original
    b. unusually dull
    c. sleepy and unmotivated

_____ **10.** protean a. the life of the party
  b. versatile, always changing
  c. boring

_____ **11.** psyche a. birth
  b. death
  c. the human soul, the self

_____ **12.** pygmy a. a giant of all beings
  b. a dwarf plant, animal; a small human
  c. normal and average

_____ **13.** *Rx* a. a subscription to a magazine
  b. a sign of peace
  c. a symbol for prescriptions or treatment

SECTION XIX

ANSWER	WORD(S)	MEANING

_____ **1.** saturnalia a. a period of unrestrained partying
  b. a time of peace and solitude
  c. a planet

_____ **2.** satyr a. a lecherous man
  b. a kind and generous man
  c. an automobile with a long trunk

_____ **3.** between Scylla and Charybdis a. easily decided
  b. plants of South America
  c. having to choose between two undesirable choices

_____ **4.** sibylline a. a schizophrenic person
  b. prophetic; mysterious
  c. an aged and kindly woman

_____ **5.** siren a. a polite form of forgiveness
  b. silence
  c. a temptress; a device that gives off a shrieking sound

_____ **6.** Sisyphean labor a. a never-ending task
  b. easily accomplished
  c. before five o'clock

_____ **7.** sphinx a. a king
  b. a friendly gentleman
  c. a mysterious, inscrutable person

_____ **8.** stentorian a. loud; booming
  b. soft spoken politician
  c. a type of western cowboy hat

	9. stygian	a. happy and faithful
		b. dark and gloomy
		c. confusing
	10. syrinx	a. a stereo component
		b. a device used to give medicine
		c. a musical instrument/panpipe

SECTION XX

ANSWER	WORD(S)	MEANING
	1. tantalize	a. to give in to completely
		b. tasteful
		c. to tease; to invite but remain unattainable
	2. thersitical	a. soft spoken, gentle
		b. having to do with the theater
		c. loudmouth, scurrilous
	3. thunder	a. a soft featherlike touch
		b. a loud booming noise, sound associated with electrical storms
		c. to walk gently
	4. titan	a. a leader in one's field, of great ability or power
		b. a small dwarflike person
		c. one who accomplishes nothing
	5. Triton among minnows	a. a weak person
		b. a large fish
		c. one who stands out, a superior individual
	6. Trojan	a. a weakling
		b. someone with great perseverance and stamina
		c. a loud and narcissistic person
	7. Trojan horse	a. someone or something that subverts from within; a deceptive scheme
		b. an honorable idea
		c. a colorful wood carving from Spain
	8. troll	a. a handsome prince
		b. a fresh loaf of bread
		c. an ugly person
	9. typhoon	a. a gentle wind
		b. a powerful businessman
		c. a violent cyclonic storm

SECTION XXI

ANSWER		WORD(S)		MEANING

_____ 1. unicorn
- a. a mythical one-horned beast that often symbolizes virility and supreme power
- b. a one-eyed monster that is kind and gentle
- c. a small elflike beast of the woods

_____ 2. Valhalla
- a. where onions are grown in California
- b. a city in Hawaii
- c. a special place for persons worthy of honor

_____ 3. Venus
- a. a star that twinkles in the northern sky
- b. a beautiful woman
- c. a French dessert made of chocolate

_____ 4. volcano
- a. a vent in the earth's crust through which steam and molten rock issue forth
- b. a science experiment using clay
- c. a tide pool in the Galapagos

_____ 5. werewolf
- a. a lost wolf in the forest
- b. a wolf wearing sheep's clothing
- c. a man who occasionally turns into a wolf

_____ 6. wheel of fortune
- a. a game symbolizing loss of equity
- b. a symbol of luck or chance
- c. a large-spoked wheel on a wagon

_____ 7. zephyr
- a. a gentle breeze
- b. a tornado
- c. an instrument that angels play

CHAPTER 4

Word Analysis, Fluency, and Systematic Vocabulary Development—Part III

TIP

Begin preparing for the CAHSEE early—as in months before the exam—not the night before.

Additional and important aspects of vocabulary development that will be covered in this chapter are the understanding of **synonyms** and **antonyms**. Most words have synonyms—words that mean the same or almost the same, and likewise antonyms, or words that mean the opposite. In your readings, you will come across words that you don't understand, but if you look at the definition in a dictionary, thesaurus, or synonym finder, chances are you will understand at least one of the words listed. Being able to understand at least one of the terms will in turn help you to understand the reading. Synonyms are extremely helpful in understanding and learning new vocabulary. Antonyms are additional help in clarifying meaning.

Homonyms are words that sound the same or are similar sounding, but have different meanings. These words are easily confused. The only way to clarify this confusion is to learn them and to be able to use them in the proper context. For instance, take the word **fly.** A fly is a pesky, annoying insect with wings (a noun). But, **fly** is also a verb, as in what airplanes or birds do: Let's fly to France. Fly/fly— same word, different meanings. Understanding words as they are used in the sentence is important; this is often referred to as understanding **words in context.**

CHAPTER FOCUS

- Synonyms
- Antonyms
- Homonyms: Words with Multiple Meanings
- Chapter Review and Quizzes

WORDS AND THEIR SYNONYMS

Read through the following list of words and their synonyms. The synonyms will help with a more in-depth understanding of word meanings.

NOTE

Often you may find a synonym in the definition of a word.

WORD	SYNONYMS
abandon	leave, desert
abbreviate	shorten, reduce, condense
abreast	beside, alongside, next to
absurd	ridiculous, foolish, silly
baffle	mystify, confuse, puzzle
barbarian	savage, brute
benevolent	humane, good, kind
calamity	bad luck, misfortune
charitable	kind, generous, considerate
chic	stylish, up-to-date, fashionable
defile	corrupt, debase, pollute
dispute	argue, debate, quarrel
dutiful	faithful, obedient
ebullient	buoyant, exuberant, high-spirited
elaborate	ornate, decorative
elevate	raise, lift

ANTONYMS

Words that have the opposite meaning are called **antonyms.** *White* is the opposite of *black. Up* is the opposite of *down.* Let's review the list of words that we used for synonyms, but this time we will add words that mean the opposite, the **antonyms.** A combination of synonyms and antonyms add even more clarity to words than dictionary definitions, which can be confusing at times.

WORD	SYNONYMS	ANTONYMS
abandon	leave, desert	join, unite
abbreviate	shorten, reduce, condense	lengthen, extend
abreast	beside, alongside, next to	single file, far away
absurd	ridiculous, foolish, silly	sensible, reasonable
baffle	mystify, confuse, puzzle	inform, clarify, enlighten
barbarian	savage, brute	cultivated, civilized
benevolent	humane, good, kind	mean, cruel, evil
calamity	bad luck, misfortune	blessing, boon, good luck
charitable	kind, generous, considerate	selfish, stingy
chic	stylish, up-to-date, fashionable	out-dated, old-fashioned
defile	corrupt, debase, pollute	purify, cleanse
dispute	argue, debate, quarrel	agree, concur
dutiful	faithful, obedient	willful, disobedient, unruly
ebullient	buoyant, exuberant, high-spirited	gloomy, depressed
elaborate	ornate, decorative	simple, unadorned
elevate	raise, lift	lower, drop

SYNONYMS: WORDS WITH ALMOST THE SAME MEANING

When learning new words, it is helpful to find synonyms for the words that are unfamiliar to you. Synonyms are words that can be used as substitutions and still mean the same thing or nearly the same thing.

Choose the word(s) that is a synonym for the word listed below.

1. COAX

   (A) ignore
   (B) persuade
   (C) hold together
   (D) inhabit

   Your Answer: Ⓐ Ⓑ Ⓒ Ⓓ

Choose the word(s) that is a synonym for the word listed below.

2. BOND

   (A) brute
   (B) convince
   (C) hold together
   (D) letter

   Your Answer: Ⓐ Ⓑ Ⓒ Ⓓ

Choose the word that is NOT a synonym for the word listed below.

3. POPULATE

   (A) inhabit
   (B) live
   (C) dwell
   (D) find

   Your Answer: Ⓐ Ⓑ Ⓒ Ⓓ

Choose the word that is a synonym for the word listed below.

4. MONITOR

   (A) watch
   (B) polluted
   (C) exhaust
   (D) manipulate

   Your Answer: Ⓐ Ⓑ Ⓒ Ⓓ

Check Your Answers

For number **1** the word **COAX** means to persuade, **B.** The answer to number **2** is **C;** to **BOND** means to **hold together.** Question **3** is tricky. Test makers like to throw in questions like this to see if you are awake. It asks for the word that is **NOT** a synonym for the listed word. The answer is **D; inhabit, live, and dwell** are all synonyms. **Find** is not. Question **4** is **A.** Nurses *monitor* their patients and probably their patience all the time. They *watch* them.

HOMONYMS: WORDS WITH MULTIPLE MEANINGS

It's happened to all of us. We are reading along very comfortably, when suddenly we approach a word that seems odd in that it is used in a way that we haven't seen it used before. Chances are it is a word that, although it is spelled the same and sounds the same, it has a different meaning. These words are called **homonyms.** There are hundreds of them. Some are easy to understand and some are very obscure. But, in both reading and *your* writing, the need to understand the way in which they are used is vital to clarifying meaning. In this section, you will find lists of homonyms. Interspersed between lists will be testlike questions that will give you practice for the exam. For those homonyms that you do not understand and that are not used in practice questions (and there are many—a book could be written on them), it is suggested that you write the definition and then use the word correctly in a sentence to help you understand them (see sample).

1. **ad:** an advertisement *In order sell my truck, I placed an ad in the newspaper.*

2. **add:** to join one thing to another as an increase *The doctor will add another medication to help cure the patient's illness.*

1) ad	add		29) cereal	serial	
2) aid	aide		30) choral	coral	corral
3) air	err	heir	31) chute	shoot	
4) aisle	I'll	isle	32) cite	sight	site
5) all	awl		33) clause	claws	
6) away	aweigh		34) coarse	course	
7) bail	bale		35) colonel	kernel	
8) ball	bawl		36) corps	core	
9) band	banned		37) creak	creek	
10) bare	bear		38) dew	do	due
11) base	bass		39) doe	dough	
12) beach	beech		40) earn	urn	
13) beau	bow		41) ewe	yew	you
14) been	bin		42) fair	fare	
15) berth	birth		43) faze	phase	
16) bloc	block		44) feat	feet	
17) board	bored		45) fir	fur	
18) bough	bow		46) flair	flare	
19) brake	break		47) flea	flee	
20) bread	bred		48) flew	flu	flue
21) bridal	bridle		49) flour	flower	
22) broach	brooch		50) foreword	forward	
23) cache	cash		51) foul	fowl	
24) capital	capitol		52) gait	gate	
25) carat	carrot		53) gene	jean	
26) cast	caste		54) gored	gourd	
27) cede	seed		55) grate	great	
28) cent	scent	sent	56) grisly	grizzly	

57) groan	grown	
58) hair	hare	
59) hall	haul	
60) halve	have	
61) heal	heel	
62) heard	herd	
63) idle	idol	
64) it's	its	
65) knight	night	
66) knot	not	
67) lead	led	
68) leak	leek	
69) liar	lyre	
70) links	lynx	
71) loan	lone	
72) locks	lox	
73) main	mane	
74) medal	meddle	
75) mince	mints	
76) moor	more	
77) moose	mousse	
78) morning	mourning	
79) naval	navel	
80) oar	or	ore
81) pair	pare	pear
82) palate	palette	
83) patience	patients	
84) peace	piece	
85) peak	peek	pique
86) pi	pie	
87) pistil	pistol	
88) pleas	please	
89) plum	plumb	
90) pole	poll	
91) poor	pore	pour
92) presence	presents	
93) principal	principle	
94) profit	prophet	
95) rack	wrack	
96) raise	rays	raze
97) rap	wrap	
98) rapt	wrapped	
99) read	reed	
100) read	red	
101) reek	wreak	

102) rest	wrest	
103) retch	wretch	
104) right	write	rite
105) rye	wry	
106) sail	sale	
107) seam	seem	
108) seas	seize	sees
109) sew	so	sow
110) shear	sheer	
111) sighed	side	
112) sighs	size	
113) slay	sleigh	
114) soar	sore	
115) soared	sword	
116) stair	stare	
117) stake	steak	
118) stationary	stationery	
119) suite	sweet	
120) taught	taut	
121) tear	tier	
122) tense	tents	
123) tern	turn	
124) their	they're	there
125) threw	through	
126) throne	thrown	
127) thyme	time	
128) tide	tied	
129) to	too	two
130) toe	tow	
131) toad	towed	
132) vale	veil	
133) vain	vane	
134) vial	vile	
135) wail	whale	
136) waist	waste	
137) wait	weight	
138) way	weigh	
139) we	wee	
140) week	weak	
141) weed	we'd	
142) whine	wine	
143) wood	would	
144) yoke	yolk	
145) yore	your	

1. Select the sentence with the correct usage of the word *bough*.

   (A) The *bough* of the ship is damaged.
   (B) The *bough* on the shirt is polka dotted.
   (C) The *bough* of the tree broke last night during the storm.
   (D) The *bough* of the sail fit the sloop.

   Your Answer: Ⓐ Ⓑ Ⓒ Ⓓ

2. Select the sentence with the correct usage of the word *heir*.

   (A) His *heir* was black with some gray.
   (B) His *heir* will inherit a fortune in stocks and bonds.
   (C) The *heir* became nervous at the sounds.
   (D) The barber became tired of cutting *heir* all day.

   Your Answer: Ⓐ Ⓑ Ⓒ Ⓓ

3. Select the sentence with the correct usage of the word *coral*.

   (A) The *coral* group left after their performance.
   (B) The horses are in their *coral*.
   (C) When you *coral* the animals, they will not escape.
   (D) *Coral* reefs off the coast of Australia are dangerous for ships.

   Your Answer: Ⓐ Ⓑ Ⓒ Ⓓ

4. Select the sentence that does NOT use the word *fare* correctly.

   (A) The county *fare* is always interesting to visit in the fall.
   (B) The bus *fare* to Huntington Park is inexpensive.
   (C) From home to the market, the taxi *fare* is reasonable.
   (D) Airline *fares* are inexpensive these days.

   Your Answer: Ⓐ Ⓑ Ⓒ Ⓓ

5. Select the sentence that uses the word *genes* correctly.

   (A) Scientists are discovering more and more about *genes*.
   (B) Wear your *genes* to the game tonight.
   (C) In China, *genes* are hard to find.
   (D) Oh *Genes*! Don't you have anything better to do than fish?

   Your Answer: Ⓐ Ⓑ Ⓒ Ⓓ

6. Select the sentence that does NOT use the word *mane* correctly.

   (A) The lion's *mane* is coarse and brown.
   (B) The *mane* idea is not clear.
   (C) She braided the horse's *mane*.
   (D) Most animals do not have *manes*.

   Your Answer: Ⓐ Ⓑ Ⓒ Ⓓ

7. Select the sentence that uses the word *palette* correctly.

   (A) My *palette* was burned from eating pizza last night.
   (B) Pilgrims slept on *palettes* of straw.
   (C) The *palette* held a ton of bricks.
   (D) An important artist's tool is the *palette*.

   Your Answer: Ⓐ Ⓑ Ⓒ Ⓓ

8. Select the sentence that does NOT use the word *presence* correctly.

   (A) Your *presence* will be missed if you quit the team.
   (B) It's your brithday! Open your *presence*.
   (C) Her *presence* on the board of directors made a difference.
   (D) His *presence* was disruptive.

   Your Answer: Ⓐ Ⓑ Ⓒ Ⓓ

9. Select the sentence that uses the word *wretch* correctly.

   (A) Ebenezer Scrooge is a miserable *wretch*.
   (B) When you *wretch* out don't fall.
   (C) The *wretching* has to stop now!
   (D) When will you *wretch* Los Angeles?

   Your Answer: Ⓐ Ⓑ Ⓒ Ⓓ

10. Select the sentence that uses the word *thyme* correctly.

    (A) Don't waste *thyme*!
    (B) She will dry the *thyme* that she grew for cooking.
    (C) What *thyme* do you have to go to the doctor?
    (D) When you go to Disneyland you can expect to have a good *thyme*.

    Your Answer: Ⓐ Ⓑ Ⓒ Ⓓ

11. Select the sentence that does NOT use the word *vile* correctly.

    (A) The *vile* weather ruined our plans for the weekend.
    (B) The smell in the auditorium was *vile*.
    (C) The biology students use *viles* at least once a week.
    (D) Do you have to be so *vile* when you speak of your enemy?

    Your Answer: Ⓐ Ⓑ Ⓒ Ⓓ

Check Your Answers

1. C	**5.** A	**9.** A
2. B	**6.** B*	**10.** B
3. D	**7.** D	**11.** C
4. A*	**8.** B*	

NOTE

The answers marked with an asterisk (*) are questions that had a distinct change in direction. All three asked that you select the sentence that was NOT used correctly. Reading directions is important. Hope you weren't caught sleeping!

Chapter Review and Quick Quizzes

In the first part of this chapter, we learned about **synonyms** and **antonyms.** Basically, when a question on the exam asks for a word that means the same or almost the same, if you are unfamiliar with the word, you will need to use the process of elimination. Of the four answers offered, chances are you will be familiar with one or more of the words. Eliminate those that you can, and make an educated guess as to the correct answer. If you positively eliminate all but two answers, that gives you a fifty-fifty chance of getting it right. Being in possession of an extensive vocabulary is vital to success on this and other exams that you will encounter in the near future. Continually build upon your vocabulary—there are always new words to learn—words that can make a difference in your life.

The second part of the chapter focused on **homonyms**—words with multiple meanings. You were given an extensive list of homonyms. Some are easier than others, and some are more confusing and easily misused. For review purposes, take the following quizzes. You will find the answers in the appendix at the end of the book.

Directions: Using the word bank, fill in the blank with the word that is used correctly in the sentence.

Word Bank: bawled, ad, bear, aisle, banned, awl, bale, aide, heir, aweigh

1. A large corporation will place an expensive _____ in the newspaper on Sunday.

2. The _____ managed to secure his boss's seat on the flight.

3. She was _____ to the estate of a famous and very successful industrialist.

4. When you walk down the _____ of a grocery store, making decisions can be difficult.

5. He used an _____ to make holes in the leather belt he was working on.

6. A sailor shouted "Anchors _____" and the ship left for the distant island on the other side of the Pacific Ocean.

7. Farmers spend many hours in the sun when they _____ hay.

8. The child _____ for his mother who had left him behind.

9. The young troublemakers were _____ from the theater.

10. I cannot _____ to watch the film because it has too much violence.

Directions: Using the word bank, fill in the blank with the word that is used correctly in the sentence.

Word Bank: bored, berth, beech, block, bin, bow, bass, bred, brake, bow

11. The _____ drum was pounding loudly throughout the song.

12. The leaves of the _____ tree were falling.

13. She tied the _____ onto the package that she was wrapping.

14. The _____ was filled with grain.

15. The cruise ship was anchored at a _____ in Long Beach.

16. The store is located on the next _____ just past the corner.

17. He was _____, so he went outside to play basketball.

18. The _____ of the ship was damaged by the undetected iceberg.

19. The left _____ on my bicycle needs to be adjusted.

20. The two dogs were _____ so that their unusual traits would continue.

Word Bank: brooch, bridle, carat, capital, serial, ceded, caste, coral, scent, cache

21. The horse's _____ was tangled in knots.

22. The elderly woman's golden _____ had many diamonds on it.

23. There was a _____ of weapons found hidden in the forests of Colombia.

24. You must use _____ letters for proper nouns and proper adjectives.

25. The diamond ring that she is wearing must be at least a ten-_____-size jewel.

26. India has a _____ system in place within their society.

27. The politician, realizing that he was losing, _____ the race for governor.

28. The _____ of her perfume permeated the room and caused many to sneeze.

29. The _____ number on an appliance is important to take note of in case of a manufacturer recall.

30. The surfer risked his life to ride a twenty-foot wave over a _____ reef.

Directions: Using the word bank, fill in the blank with the word that is used correctly in the sentence.

Word Bank: course, urn, chute, due, pare, cite, claws, dough, squeak, kernel

31. The laundry _____ was clogged and caused a backup in the laundry room of the hospital.

32. All officers are asked to _____ anyone who does not obey the laws.

33. Cats use their _____ for protection and for climbing.

34. The Tour de France bicycle _____ is rugged and requires great endurance.

35. The farmer planted the odd-looking corn _____ in hopes that it would grow.

36. Please _____ the apples before you bake them.

37. The floors of the ancient palace _____ as a warning of someone approaching. These floors are called "nightingale floors."

38. Your library books are _____ next week.

39. The _____ was too sticky to knead so we added more flour.

40. The flowers were placed in a large copper _____ to be displayed prominently in the entryway.

Word Bank: yew, flue, forward, flee, feat, phase, flour, fare, fur, flare

41. The _____ tree is an evergreen tree with red berries.

42. The subway _____ is minimal compared to the cost of owning and maintaining a car.

43. Don't worry about your two-year-old; it is just a _____ he is going through.

44. Climbing Mt. Everest is an amazing _____ for anyone to accomplish.

45. Animal Rights activists are disturbed by those who wear _____ coats.

46. The _____ burning in the street indicated that there was danger ahead.

47. The forest fire caused many residents to _____ from their homes.

48. The chimney _____ was closed, causing all of the smoke to remain in the room.

49. We added more _____ to the cookie dough.

50. If you move _____, the line will continue smoothly.

Directions: Using the word bank, fill in the blank with the word that is used correctly in the sentence.

Word Bank: foul, hare, haul, grisly, gait, jeans, halve, groan, grate, gourd

51. The batter hit two _____ balls before hitting a homerun to win the game.

52. His _____ was so unusual that you could recognize him without seeing his face.

53. Her _____ had holes in the knees and were faded to light blue, but she continued to wear them.

54. The African native will use a dried _____ as an instrument.

55. The _____ covering the drainage ditch was broken and dangerous.

56. The scene after the accident was _____.

57. I heard the injured man _____ from his hospital bed.

58. The _____ hopped and ran from the wolf that was chasing him.

59. The sanitation engineers _____ trash and other castoffs daily on the job.

60. We will _____ the profits and give them to our two favorite charities.

Word Bank: idol, lead, heel, knight, herd, lyre, its, knot, leek, lynx

61. Achilles' _____ was his one vulnerable spot and eventually caused his death.

62. The _____ of elephants stormed through the jungle in search of water.

63. That rock star became the teenager's _____ .

64. Do you know what caused _____ decline?

65. She was expecting a handsome, brave _____ to ride up on his stallion and save her, but that didn't happen.

66. The sailor uses a different _____ for each task.

67. Old painted surfaces are known to contain _____, which is poisonous.

68. The French chef used a fresh _____ in cooking his delicious dish.

69. A _____ is a stringed instrument that is shaped like a "U."

70. The _____ is a member of the cat family. It has spotted fur and keen eyesight.

Directions: Using the word bank, fill in the blank with the word that is used correctly in the sentence.

Word Bank: meddle, loan, ore, naval, minced, mousse, moor, lox, mane, mourning

71. Real estate agents suggest that you obtain a _____ before looking for a new home.

72. A type of smoked salmon is called _____ .

73. The horse's _____ was brushed and then braided with multi-colored ribbons.

74. Don't _____ in my business!

75. The clams were _____ and then added to the tomato sauce.

76. The _____ on the coast of England is at times eerie and mysterious.

77. She used a can of _____ on her hair to keep it straight.

78. There is a _____ dove who sadly cries outside my window.

79. The abandoned _____ station was to be used for an international airport.

80. Mining iron _____ is a dangerous profession.

Word Bank: poll, pistil, pare, piece, pie, patience, palette, piqued, pleas, plumb

81. If you will _____ the apples, we can make a pie.

82. The artist used a colorful _____ for his paintings.

83. Many people say that "_____ is a virtue."

84. Adding one individual _____ to another, the quilter constructs a quilt for the guild.

85. The sound of the singer's voice _____ my interest and I wandered over to the stage where he was singing.

86. Pumpkin _____ is my favorite part of the meal at Thanksgiving.

87. The _____ is the seed-producing part of the flower.

88. After hearing many _____ and much begging, the kindly aunt took her nieces to Disneyland.

89. Without a _____, a carpenter's job would be difficult and his work uneven.

90. After taking an informal _____, the students decided to take a field trip to the museum after all.

Directions: Using the word bank, fill in the blank with the word that is used correctly in the sentence.

Word Bank: principal, profit, pore, wrap, read, rapt, presence, wracked, razed, reed

91. A clogged _____ can cause skin problems.

92. The _____ of the National Guard was appreciated by all.

93. In a few years, our school's _____ will retire.

94. Because _____ margins are down, the company's stock prices went down as well.

95. He _____ his brain trying to remember where he left his glasses.

96. The old dilapidated building was _____ and replaced by a modern structure.

97. Make certain that you _____ yourself up well before going out into the freezing cold weather.

98. To see the children so _____ in attention while listening to the story was heartwarming.

99. The _____ to my clarinet needs to be replaced.

100. She _____ the book last week and thought it was one of the best.

Word Bank: wretched, sow, wreak, sheared, wrest, seam, rite, sale, seize, wry

101. They didn't realize that the storm would _____ such havoc on the community.

102. The sword fighter managed to _____ away his opponent's weapon.

103. The witches in the play *Macbeth* are _____.

104. Growing up is considered a _____ of passage.

105. His _____ smile was noticed by the entire audience.

106. The store will have a major _____ over the holiday weekend.

107. The _____ to your pants is torn.

108. "Carpe Diem" means to _____ the day!

109. The farmers will _____ seed in the spring.

110. The sheep need to be _____ after the winter cold has gone.

Directions: Using the word bank, fill in the blank with the word that is used correctly in the sentence.

> **Word Bank:** staring, sighed, slaying, sword, soar, taut, sigh, suite, stake, stationery

111. The runners _____ with relief after reaching the finish line.

112. When the politician made an error in judgment during his speech, the disapproving campaign manager displayed an unhappy _____.

113. It is said that the _____ of dragons was the job of the brave and fearless knights.

114. If we all had wings we could _____ like birds.

115. The knight's _____ was double-edged and very sharp.

116. Will you stop _____ at me?

117. Fasten that corner of your tent down with a _____ so that the wind will not blow it away.

118. We went to the _____ store to order the invitations to the wedding.

119. The accounting firm is located in a _____ of offices on the 27th floor.

120. The _____ wire strung across the stage enabled the circus performer to walk across it.

> **Word Bank:** they're, tern, tide, tents, tear, towed, too, threw, throne, thyme

121. There was a _____ of joy streaming down her face.

122. The red-striped circus _____ are immense in size.

123. The _____ is a seabird with long pointed wings and forked tail.

124. They are running to catch the train because _____ late.

125. The pitcher _____ the ball over ninety miles an hour.

126. The prince will ascend the _____ when his father dies.

127. An herb used in cooking is called _____.

128. The rising and lowering of the _____ is caused by the attraction of the moon and the sun.

129. My sister wants to go _____.

130. The tugboats _____ the ship into port.

Directions: Using the word bank, fill in the blank with the word that is used correctly in the sentence.

Word Bank: toad, weak, waste, veil, weight, yore, vial, wee, vane, wail, weighed, we'd, yolk, would, whine

131. The sound that a _____ makes is "ribbit, ribbit."

132. We will escape under a _____ of darkness.

133. The weather _____ shows which way the wind is blowing.

134. The _____ of blood was confused with something else and had to be redrawn.

135. The _____ of the sirens is painful to my ears.

136. We must take more care to not _____ natural resources.

137. The _____ of the world seems to be bearing down on our shoulders.

138. Trucks have to stop to be _____ on the freeways to make certain that they do not carry too much and cause damage to the road.

139. The _____ children were having a great time singing at the party.

140. I am _____ from being sick for so long.

141. If we want to complete the job before dark, _____ better hurry.

142. If only she would not _____, life would be more pleasant.

143. Your uncle _____ like you to go to the zoo with him today.

144. The egg _____ is the unhealthy part of the egg, according to health experts.

145. In days of _____, life seemed much simpler.

Word Analysis, Fluency, and Systematic Vocabulary Development—Part IV

Don't be afraid to underline, write notes in the margins of the test booklet—that is not a crime and can be extremely helpful.

Before true understanding can take place, you must be able to identify the meanings of the words that you are reading. Without understanding, the words run together and don't make sense *at all*. Before looking at example test questions for literal meanings, we will look at some of the words used in the short readings of the exam. Review these words and their definitions. The words chosen for this chapter are taken from the CAHSEE, and they are representative of the level of vocabulary needed to pass it. If you are unfamiliar with them, become familiar! To learn new words, some people prefer to make note cards, others read the words over and over (at least three to five times), and others complete vocabulary foursquares (see the example on page 129 and the page that can be copied at the end of the book), which is a very visual way of learning words. This will help you lock the definition information into your brain where it will be ready to use when you need it. The definitions provided, by the way, are the literal or actual definitions of the words as they are used in the sentences of the short readings. At the end of the chapter, there will be short quizzes to test your understanding of the vocabulary words that are used on the exit exam.

CHAPTER FOCUS

- Vocabulary development—literal meanings
- Vocabulary foursquares—instruction

CAHSEE VOCABULARY

Reading Vocabulary Review I

Word	Definition
foundation _____	a basis upon which something is built
stationary _____	fixed, unchanging, immobile
propel _____	to drive forward or onward
experimenting _____	trying a new procedure, idea, or activity
required _____	demanded as necessary
inquisitive _____	inclined to ask questions, curious
mounted _____	attached to a support
intelligent _____	having a high degree of mental capacity
curious _____	marked by a desire to investigate and learn
curiosity _____	desire to know
tinker _____	to fool around with, to putter with
darning _____	mending or repairing with a needle
intended _____	planned or designed for a specific use
immigrant _____	a person who comes to a country to live permanently
mechanical _____	relating to machinery or tools
journey _____	an act of traveling from one place to another
variety _____	having different forms or types
carriage _____	a wheeled vehicle, especially horse-drawn, used to carry people or things
protest _____	to object or to disapprove
impressed _____	deeply influenced
incentive _____	something that promotes determination or action
encouraged _____	spurred on, inspired to continue
operable _____	to be able to use
commonplace _____	ordinary, commonly found
genius _____	extraordinary intellectual power or aptitude
dramatic _____	striking in appearance or effect

VOCABULARY FOURSQUARE

Complete one for each word you need to learn!

Write the word here	Draw a picture of the word
Write the definition here	Write synonyms here / Write antonyms here

Synonyms—words that have the *same* or *similar* meanings.

Antonyms—words that mean the *opposite* of the defined word.

Example:

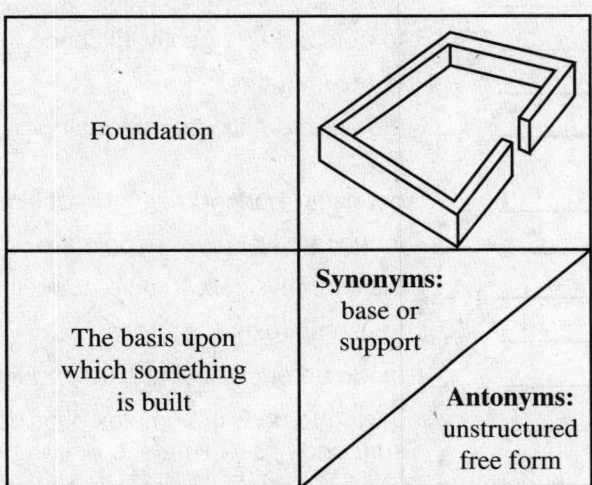

Foundation	
The basis upon which something is built	**Synonyms:** base or support / **Antonyms:** unstructured free form

Reading Vocabulary Review II

Study the list of the following testing words. Become familiar with those you are unfamiliar with through the methods mentioned in the vocabulary review section of Chapter 2.

Word	Definition
falconry _____	the art of training hawks to hunt
ancient _____	having had an existence for many years, or relating to a remote period in time
medieval _____	relating to or characteristic of the Middle Ages
royalty _____	privileged class, of royal status or power
jousting _____	fighting on horseback as knights used to do
enthusiast _____	a person who is extremely excited or interested in something, (enthusiastic)
predatory _____	inclined to injure or exploit others for personal gain
establish _____	to bring into existence
coax _____	to persuade, or gently influence
bond _____	to hold together
horizon _____	the apparent junction or joining of the earth and sky
patience _____	not hasty, bearing pain or problems calmly
populated _____	inhabited, wherever people are
polluted _____	making physically impure or unclean
deplete _____	to use up, exhaust a resource
cumulative _____	made up of additional parts, adding up to
environmental _____	having to do with complex physical surroundings—climate, soil, living things
counter _____	having the opposite effect
impose _____	to bring about by force
exhaust _____	to use up, deplete
regulate _____	to govern according to rule
monitor _____	to watch
generate _____	to bring into existence, to cause
efficient _____	producing desired effects easily
conversely _____	reversing the order of
aerodynamic _____	moving easily without wind resistance
drag _____	something that slows motion
maintenance _____	the upkeep of property or equipment
rebate _____	to return money to consumer for reward
preserve _____	to keep safe from injury or harm

Reading Vocabulary Review III

More words to study! Some of them may be familiar; others not so familiar. Remember to learn the words that you don't know. These are words that are found in the readings on the exam. Study on!

Word	Definition
frost _____	frozen covering of tiny ice crystals
liberty_____	the state of being free
hubbub _____	noise, excitement, an increase in activity
dismantled _____	taken apart
eager _____	excited, anxious
deliberately_____	intentionally, on purpose
slink_____	to slither away quietly without being noticed
dense_____	thick, difficult to see through
thicket _____	a dense growth of shrubbery or bushes
intermittently _____	off and on, not constant
aroused _____	awakened from sleep, or stimulated
tremble_____	to shake nervously
impulse _____	a sudden spontaneous inclination to do something without thinking
undertaking_____	setting about to do something
perturbed_____	annoyed
lurking_____	lying in wait or hiding in the shadows for evil purposes
ominous_____	feeling that something bad will happen
perilous _____	dangerous
shrill _____	high piercing noise, sharp
gruff _____	rough, surly
inedible _____	cannot be eaten
bondage _____	state of being tied to something forcefully
idle_____	without activity
impending_____	something about to happen, hovering threateningly
colossal _____	giant, extremely large
whimper _____	a quiet cry or whine
suppressed _____	held in, not let it out
seized_____	taken possession of

Reading Vocabulary Review IV

Yet another set of words for you to review. Take your time with them. Be aware that any of these words could possibly appear on your CAHSEE. So, study!!!

Word	Definition
majestic	stately, grand
pastoral	pleasingly peaceful, innocent
diverse	differing from one another, unlike
intensifies	strengthens, increases in density
enlivens	gives life or action to
intercultural	between cultures
eccentricities	odd or whimsical mannerisms
hordes	a large crowd or swarm
oblivious	lacking conscious knowledge or memory
stamina	strength, endurance
precipice	a hazardous place
mimicked	imitated
propelled	driven as the force or speed of a jet or airplane
contaminate	to soil, stain, or corrupt
graciously	with kindness and courtesy
promptly	quickly, right away
ensure	to make sure or certain, to guarantee
drape	to hang something (usually cloth) over
foyer	an entry into a building, a lobby
applicant	someone who applies for a position
distress	a situation causing danger, worry, or suffering
prominently	standing out above/beyond, noticeable
perimeter	the outer limits of a designated area
aggressive	driving forceful energy
dominate	to rule over others with commanding preeminence
receptionist	a person hired to greet customers, patients, telephone callers, etc.
pronounce	to declare authoritatively or as an opinion
protruding	jutting out, causing to project
iridescent	a lustrous or attractive quality, rainbowlike (soap bubbles, oil on water)

Reading Vocabulary Review V

Study the list of testing words below. Become familiar with those you are unfamiliar with through the methods mentioned in the vocabulary review section of Chapter 2.

Word	Definition
seine _____	a large fishing net made to hang vertically in the water
minnows _____	any large group of very small freshwater fish used as live bait
plunge _____	to cast, throw, or jump forcefully into something
silt_____	a sedimentary material made of very fine particles between the size of sand and clay
resume_____	to begin or take up again after an interruption
startle_____	to cause to make a quick involuntary movement; to alarm
algae _____	chiefly aquatic organisms that range in size from single cell to giant kelp
tertiary _____	third in formation, place, order, or rank
alteration _____	condition resulting from a change or modification
habitats _____	an area or environment where an organism or ecological community normally lives
polls _____	a place where votes are cast and registered
suffrage _____	the right or privilege of voting
canals _____	a waterway used for travel, shipping, irrigation

Reading Vocabulary Review VI

Study the list of testing words below. Become familiar with those you are unfamiliar with through the methods mentioned in the vocabulary review section of Chapter 2.

Word	Definition
engage _____	to attract or hold the attention of
emerge _____	to come forth from
tow-headed_____	a head of white-blond hair resembling tow (flax to be spun into thread)
coveralls _____	long denim jeans with attached bib
listlessly _____	lacking energy or not inclined to exert effort
nickelodeon _____	an early movie theater charging five cents admission; a player piano or a jukebox
regal_____	magnificent or splendid, befitting a monarch
lured_____	tempted or attracted with the promise of reward or pleasure
precursor_____	one that precedes another, a forerunner, a predecessor
retreat_____	a place affording peace, quiet
sultry _____	very humid and hot, torrid
soar _____	to rise suddenly above normal

Chapter Review and Quick Quizzes

READING VOCABULARY REVIEW QUIZZES

Directions: Write the letter of the matching definition in the box to the left of the number.

VOCABULARY REVIEW I-A

ANSWER	WORD	DEFINITION
_____	1. dramatic	a. basis upon which something is built
_____	2. foundation	b. ordinary, commonly found
_____	3. genius	c. to be able to use
_____	4. propel	d. to spur on, to inspire to continue

_____	5. commonplace	e.	striking in appearance or effect
_____	6. experimenting	f.	to attach to a support
_____	7. operable	g.	extraordinary intellectual power
_____	8. stationary	h.	fixed, unchanging, immobile
_____	9. encourage	i.	to drive forward or onward
_____	10. mounted	j.	trying a new procedure, idea, or activity

Directions: Fill in the blanks with the word that best completes the sentence.

Word Bank: curious, curiosity, tinker, darn, intended, immigrants, mechanical, journey, variety, carriage, protest, impressed, incentive

VOCABULARY REVIEW I-B

1. Henry Ford was a very _____ person. He asked a lot of questions.

2. Getting an allowance is an _____ for me to do my chores.

3. My grandfather liked to _____ around in the garage with all of his tools.

4. Sometimes they say that "_____ killed the cat."

5. The teacher was _____ with the results on the test. Everyone earned an A.

6. Not many people these days take the time to _____ their socks. They just buy new ones.

7. The students held a very loud and boisterous _____ against wearing school uniforms.

8. The new uniform policy was _____ to discourage certain behavior, but no one thought it would work.

9. Before the car was invented, people moved around with horse-drawn _____.

10. America attracts many _____. It is a land of opportunity.

11. The ice cream store had a large _____ of ice cream available.

12. The dog, tired of being ordered around, took a _____ far away from his master.

13. Soda Pop, the character in *The Outsiders* was a very _____ person. He loved to work on cars.

Directions: Write the letter of the matching definition in the space to the left of the number.

VOCABULARY REVIEW II-A

ANSWER	WORD		DEFINITION
_____	1. patience	a.	to hold together
_____	2. falconry	b.	to persuade or gently influence
_____	3. horizon	c.	having had an existence for many years
_____	4. ancient	d.	not hasty, bearing pain or problems calmly
_____	5. bond	e.	relating to or characteristic of the Middle Ages
_____	6. coax	f.	privileged class, of royal status or power
_____	7. royalty	g.	the apparent junction or joining of the earth and sky
_____	8. predatory	h.	to fight on horseback with long poles
_____	9. establish	i.	a person extremely excited or interested in something
_____	10. jousting	j.	inclined to injure or exploit others for personal gain
_____	11. enthusiast	k.	the art of training hawks to hunt
_____	12. medieval	l.	to bring into existence

Directions: Choose the correct definition for the listed word and write the letter in the space on the left.

VOCABULARY REVIEW II-B

ANSWER	WORD	DEFINITION

_____ 1. preserve
  a. to slow motion
  b. to upkeep property or equipment
  c. to return money to consumer for reward
  d. to keep safe from injury or harm

_____ 2. rebate
  a. to move easily without wind resistance
  b. to return money to consumer for reward
  c. to watch
  d. to keep safe from injury or harm

_____ 3. maintenance
  a. the upkeep of property or equipment
  b. to soil, to make impure
  c. having the opposite effect
  d. to bring about by force

_____ 4. drag
  a. to keep safe from injury
  b. to use up, deplete
  c. to slow motion
  d. to enter from the side

_____ 5. aerodynamic
  a. something that slows motion
  b. describing upkeep on property or equipment
  c. institution of new policies
  d. the ability to move easily without wind resistance

_____ 6. conversely
  a. holding together
  b. the reverse order of
  c. efficient
  d. thick growth of shrubbery

_____ 7. efficient
  a. producing the desired effects easily
  b. desperate to live
  c. submerged
  d. professionalism in the workplace

_____ 8. generate
  a. to persuade
  b. a very thickset person
  c. to bring into existence, to cause
  d. very angry, tempestuous

_____ 9. monitor
- **a.** sharp, cutting edge
- **b.** to watch
- **c.** chest of drawers
- **d.** to reverse the order of

_____ 10. regulate
- **a.** to govern according to rule
- **b.** gleaming with anticipation
- **c.** to tunnel into the earth
- **d.** to break into a home

_____ 11. exhaust
- **a.** secretive, keeping to oneself
- **b.** polite and courteous
- **c.** to contain, reserve
- **d.** to use up, deplete

_____ 12. populate
- **a.** loud, brassy, bold
- **b.** to inhabit, wherever people are
- **c.** an undercover assignment
- **d.** sparse, unpopulated

_____ 13. pollute
- **a.** pure, without disease
- **b.** to fight or brawl
- **c.** to make physically impure or unclean
- **d.** first-class, excellent

_____ 14. deplete
- **a.** to use up to exhaust a resource
- **b.** an article used as a weapon
- **c.** to increase in amount
- **d.** to arrange in a group

_____ 15. cumulative
- **a.** made up of additional parts, adding up to
- **b.** to pounce upon, to jump
- **c.** circumference
- **d.** small amount, ineffective

_____ 16. environmental
- **a.** lenient, not withholding privileges
- **b.** divided into separate areas
- **c.** having to do with physical surroundings
- **d.** perceptive, not needing assistance

_____ 17. counter
- **a.** considerate, polite
- **b.** blind, the inability to see
- **c.** synonymous, one and the same
- **d.** having the opposite effect

_____ 18. impose
- **a.** abandon, ignore
- **b.** to bring about by force
- **c.** a loud, incessant noise
- **d.** to move swiftly

Directions: Fill in the blanks with the word that completes the sentence best.

Word Bank: frost, liberty, hubbub, dismantled, eager, deliberately, slink, dense, thicket, intermittently, aroused, trembled, impulse, undertaking

VOCABULARY REVIEW III-A

1. When the explorer set out upon his journey, it was an _____ no other man had ever attempted.

2. When the _____ arrives in the fall, the harvesters must work fast or lose their crops.

3. The school bell was not functioning properly; it rang _____ on and off all day.

4. Sometimes when she goes shopping she suddenly has an urge to buy something she doesn't need. She is the perfect _____ shopper.

5. The schoolchildren were _____ to leave for summer vacation.

6. The _____ and freedom of the world is at risk during troubled times.

7. During the holidays, the _____, excitement, and activities increase every day.

8. The mechanic _____ the car in order to repair it.

9. On the edge of the forest, there is a dense _____ of brush that is very difficult to get through.

10. When the reindeer landed on the roof, the father was _____ from his sleep.

11. The fog was so _____ it was the cause of a seventy-car pileup on the freeway.

12. The Slitherins in the novel *Harry Potter* seem to _____ like snakes.

13. He _____ ran ahead of us so that he would get the best seat.

14. The students _____ with excitement when the contest winners were announced.

> **Directions:** Write the letter of the correct definition in the space to the left of the word.

VOCABULARY REVIEW III-B

ANSWER	WORD	DEFINITION
_____	1. shrill	a. annoyed
_____	2. perturbed	b. took possession of
_____	3. seized	c. a quiet cry or whine
_____	4. gruff	d. to hold in, not to let it out
_____	5. whimper	e. dangerous
_____	6. inedible	f. lying in wait or hiding in the shadows for evil purposes
_____	7. colossal	g. feeling that something bad will happen
_____	8. lurking	h. without activity
_____	9. perilous	i. high piercing noise, sharp
_____	10. impending	j. rough, surly
_____	11. ominous	k. giant, extremely large
_____	12. idle	l. something about to happen, to hover threateningly
_____	13. suppress	m. cannot be eaten
_____	14. bondage	n. tied to something forcefully

> **Directions:** Choose the correct definition and write the letter in the space on the left.

VOCABULARY REVIEW IV-A

ANSWER	WORD	DEFINITION
_____	1. propelled	a. driven as the force or speed of a jet or airplane
		b. strength or endurance
		c. to simplify, to unburden
		d. to share in expenses

_____   **2.** contaminate

    a. a childlike toy
    b. desperate, in great need or desire
    c. to soil, stain, or corrupt
    d. sarcastic, insulting

_____   **3.** mimic

    a. virtuous and moral
    b. to teach or instruct
    c. in addition to
    d. to imitate

_____   **4.** majestic

    a. nonsensical gibberish
    b. stately, grand
    c. theatrical, always on stage
    d. the wasteland, the moor

_____   **5.** pastoral

    a. pleasingly peaceful, innocent
    b. urban dwellers
    c. the largest portions, giant-sized
    d. to humiliate and insult

_____   **6.** intercultural

    a. laden with guilt
    b. a particle used in the construction of an alloy
    c. between cultures
    d. maternal affection

_____   **7.** enliven

    a. a guaranty or a warranty
    b. somber, sullenness
    c. retarded, imbecile
    d. to give life or action to

_____   **8.** diverse

    a. at daybreak, dawn
    b. a small mouthful, bite
    c. differing from one another
    d. to fail, to bungle up

_____   **9.** eccentricities

    a. odd or whimsical mannerisms
    b. to wrap or envelop
    c. to tinker, or play around with
    d. many-sided, complex

_____   **10.** hordes

    a. to amplify, to make much of
    b. a large crowd or swarm
    c. approximately, nearly
    d. a very minute amount

_____   **11.** oblivious

    a. abundant, plentiful
    b. lacking conscious knowledge or memory
    c. the outer limits or perimeter
    d. multicolored, polychromatic

_____ 12. precipice   **a.** a hazardous place
     b. stubborn, obstinate
     c. caught, without a way out
     d. to confuse or mix up

_____ 13. stamina   **a.** changeable, variable
     b. informal, casual in appearance
     c. strength, endurance
     d. performer, accompanist

_____ 14. intensifies   **a.** to assemble, to gather together
     b. genteel, quiet in demeanor
     c. brawny, very muscular
     d. strengthens, increases in density

Directions: Fill in the blanks with the word that best completes the sentence.

Word Bank: pronounced, protruding, iridescent, receptionist, dominate, aggressive, perimeter, prominently, distress, applicant, foyer, draped, ensure, promptly, graciously

VOCABULARY REVIEW IV-B

1. The _____ glass shimmered in the bright sunlight and its many colors glistened.

2. The next _____ to arrive for his interview must complete the application form immediately.

3. The man's coat was _____ over his chair and the waiter almost tripped on it.

4. If you study for the exam, you will _____ your success.

5. Do not leave the _____ of the playing field or you will be suspended.

6. The statue stood _____ in the square among all of the fountains.

7. It is always exciting to see which team will _____ over the other in the basketball game.

8. When the storm hit, the small fishing vessel was in much _____, but the captain seemed to handle the waves appropriately.

9. The _____ and main lobby of the new hotel was decorated in a style similar to those in Italy.

10. The doctor's office relies heavily upon the _____ who greets patients, answers the phones, and schedules appointments.

11. With ease, the queen _____ accepted the award for her country.

12. If treated _____, the disease will not spread.

13. Many football players seem to be _____ on the playing field.

14. The jogger didn't see the limb of the tree _____ in the path and tripped on it.

15. The winner of the election was _____ with much enthusiasm.

READING AND VOCABULARY REVIEW

Directions: Match the word and its correct definition. Write the letter of the correct definition in the space to the left of the word. You will find the answers in the appendix in the back of the book.

SECTION V

ANSWER	WORD	DEFINITION
_____	1. seine	a. a sedimentary material made of very fine particles
_____	2. minnows	b. the condition resulting from a change or modification
_____	3. plunge	c. large group of very small freshwater fish
_____	4. silt	d. to cause to make a quick involuntary movement
_____	5. resume	e. a place where votes are cast and registered
_____	6. startle	f. chiefly aquatic organisms that range in size from single cell to giant kelp
_____	7. algae	g. the right or privilege of voting
_____	8. tertiary	h. a large fishing net made to hang vertically in the water
_____	9. alteration	i. an area or environment where an organism or ecological community normally lives

_____ 10. habitats

_____ 11. polls

_____ 12. suffrage

_____ 13. canals

j. a waterway used for travel, shipping, irrigation

k. to cast, throw, or jump forcefully into something

l. third in formation, place, order, or rank

m. to begin or take up again after an interruption

SECTION VI

ANSWER	WORD		DEFINITION
_____	1.	engaging	a. white-blond hair resembling tow (flax to be spun into thread)
_____	2.	emerge	b. lacking energy or not inclined to exert effort
_____	3.	tow-headed	c. magnificent or splendid
_____	4.	coveralls	d. attracting or holding the attention of
_____	5.	listlessly	e. one that precedes another, a forerunner, a predecessor
_____	6.	nickelodeon	f. a place affording peace, quiet
_____	7.	regal	g. very humid and hot, torrid
_____	8.	lured	h. to come forth from
_____	9.	precursor	i. to rise suddenly above normal
_____	10.	retreat	j. long denim jeans with attached bib
_____	11.	sultry	k. an early movie theater charging five cents admission, a player piano, or a jukebox
_____	12.	soar	l. tempted or attracted with the promise of reward or pleasure

Reading Comprehension—Part I

Reading Comprehension! Why all the fuss? You've heard this before, but undoubtedly the most important thing that you learn to do in your lifetime is to **read.** How well you read can dictate the level of success and accomplishments in all areas of your life. READING IS VITAL! READING IS CRITICAL, CRUCIAL, ESSENTIAL, IMPERATIVE, URGENT, COMPULSORY, and the KEY to life! How's that for a string of synonyms? Never underestimate the power of reading. Reading can take you anywhere you want to go literally and figuratively. Read as much as possible and read a wide variety of text—from fiction to nonfiction (including newspapers, magazines, and journals). JUST READ! In this chapter, we will focus on a few tried-and-true techniques to help you understand your reading and then practice three areas of reading comprehension that will definitely be included on the exit exam and any other exam you may take in the next few years: **main idea, details,** and **inference.**

> **TIP**
>
> Review all of the chapters after you feel confident that you have strengthened your weak areas.

CHAPTER FOCUS

- Reading Comprehension Defined
- How to Comprehend
- Main Idea
- Details
- Inference
- Chapter Review and Quick Quizzes

READING COMPREHENSION—DEFINED

The definition of **comprehension** simply stated is to understand; to grasp mentally. **Reading comprehension** is the understanding of the meanings of written or printed words or symbols.

Reading is a tool to help you understand an infinite number of things in life. INFINITE! Comprehending or understanding what you read can help you in driving, setting up a computer, riding a bus, following a road map, taking an exam, and even becoming a better skateboarder. Reading makes life far more interesting. But reading without understanding is not worth the time spent opening a book. Many people have difficulty focusing; they see words on a page and they may read them, but they really don't READ, meaning, they don't understand or comprehend, and it is all just words on the page. Often enough we understand certain types of reading materials, and not others. It takes practice and determination to read things you don't really care to read, but have to read for school, work, or home (warranties, instruction manuals, etc.). But, in the end it is usually worth the effort—like passing the exit exam!

How to Comprehend

Like almost anything in life, you pretty much have to have a plan. For instance, your plan right now is to pass this exam so that you can get on with your life. Comprehending the short readings on the exam is going to help you with that plan. Comprehending the questions being asked is another part of the plan. We've already talked about reading the directions carefully, because the test makers like to make sure that you are awake and not sleeping through the test. Let's concentrate on the plan to understand the readings. Follow these basic steps for comprehension; a thorough explanation will follow.

> **TIP**
>
> Read the passages carefully—you should *feel free to underline* important facts or passages as you read—this helps you to remember and log things in your brain better.

Step 1: Preview the Reading. Look at the title, glance quickly at the reading, and then turn to the question section.

Step 2: Quickly read the questions to see what you need to look for in the reading. The types of questions vary; some require thorough reading, and understanding (inference and main idea), while others do not (details).

Step 3: Read the section with purpose! Knowing the questions ahead of time saves you reading time. You might want to underline sentences as you read to help improve your memory.

Previewing the Reading

By looking at the reading before you delve into it, you will better understand where the writer is taking you. **Previewing** the reading will help you not only on this exam, but in many types of readings that are required of you, especially science, mathematics, foreign languages, and history texts, etc. With the exit exam, you have plenty of time. It doesn't have the time restraints that SATs or other exams have. That's a good thing.

- **Look at the title.** There are many stories and poems that would not make sense if you didn't know the title. Some writers are creative that way. Sylvia Plath's poem "The Mirror" for instance, only mentions the actual subject/topic in the title. Titles are very important to many pieces of literature. Pay close attention to them.

- **Glance at the reading passage.** Scan the reading—check it out—up and down. Note the length and the number of paragraphs. If it is long, log into your thoughts that you'll need more time obviously, but again, that all depends upon the questions asked. **Note:** Normally, you would scan for unfamiliar vocabulary during the previewing, finding words that you are unfamiliar with to look up in the dictionary, but you don't have time on the exit exam, nor will you be allowed to have a dictionary. However, looking for unfamiliar vocabulary is a good thing to do with any reading, especially history, science, and math texts.

Read the Questions

After previewing the title and briefly looking at the passage itself, read the questions!

- **Read the questions first.** By reading the questions first, you will get an idea of what the test makers want you to look for in the reading passage. Don't spend a lot of time on this, but reading the questions definitely allows you to focus on the areas of the passage that are important, at least to passing the exam. The following section of this chapter will discuss in depth the types of questions asked, but if the questions concern specific **details**—asking for dates, measurements, etc.—you can jump right to these facts by **scanning** the reading. If they are asking for the **main idea** or asking that you **infer** something that isn't written, your reading will have to be more thorough. Chances are, you won't get out of a reading passage too easily and a thorough, but fairly quick reading will be necessary.

Purposeful Reading

After reading the questions, look at the task ahead of you as an adventure of sorts, a scavenger hunt. Reading the passage is the most challenging part when you are taking an exam like this. Some passages will be more interesting to you than others, but you need to focus on the intent, which is answering the questions correctly.

- **Scan the reading** to see if the questions are asking for facts only. To scan the reading, take your finger and move it quickly from left to right, looking for the detail that you need—a measurement, a figure of some sort, a date. You should be able to find the paragraph easily. But, don't do this carelessly; a passage with a lot of facts and figures thrown in could confuse you.

- **Focused reading** is needed when the questions are asking "What is the main idea of the passage?" or one of many different inference-type questions such as "What would be a good title for this story?" or "From this story you can conclude that . . ." To focus your reading, you need to visualize the reading sentence by sentence. Do not look at the words individually, but look at them as sections or groupings. Try to draw a picture in your mind of what is being stated. See the example below.

> **NOTE**
>
> To visualize the sentence, draw a picture in your mind.

Charles Lindbergh flew an
airplane by himself across
the Atlantic Ocean in 1927.

- **Underlining important passages.** When you come across information that could possibly be useful for answering the questions, underline it. The information will be easier to find if you need to refer back to it to answer a question.

Step 4: Reread and answer the questions. The questions should be the easy part if you follow these steps.

Reread and Answer the Questions

Once you have followed the steps above—answering the questions should be easier than it would have been if you did not prepare yourself for reading. Reading, just like writing, is a process. Take it step by step. The more you practice, the better you become at it. Let's practice. Follow the steps above and see how it works for you.

Step 1: Preview. Look at the title and passage length.

A One-Woman Campaign

OK—The title—It is about a woman; the passage—is not too long

In the territory of Wyoming on September 6, 1870, for the first time anywhere in the United States, women went to the polls to cast their ballots. By 1870, the women's suffrage movement had battled unsuccessfully for thirty years on the East Coast. The big surprise to everyone was that the first victory for women's right to vote occurred in Wyoming, where there had been no public speeches, rallies, or conventions for the women's suffrage movement. Instead, there had been just one remarkable woman: Esther Morris. Her one-woman campaign is a classic example of effective politics. She managed to persuade both rival candidates in a territorial election to promise that, if elected, they would introduce a bill for women's suffrage. She knew that, as long as the winner kept his word, women's suffrage would score a victory in Wyoming. The winning candidate kept his promise to Esther Morris, which led to this historic Wyoming voting event in 1870.

NOTE

Now, before you begin reading, you know to look for:

1) something surprising;

2) how the one woman succeeded in getting the vote; and

3) you need to pay attention to the time sequence in the passage.

Step 2: Look at the questions relating to the passage.

1. According to the article, why is it surprising that Wyoming was the first territory to allow women to vote?

2. Which sentence from the article explains specifically how Esther Morris succeeded in providing the women of Wyoming with the right to vote?

3. Which statement below BEST illustrates the time sequence of the events in the article?

Step 3: Read the passage with purpose, now that you know what you are looking for and why you are reading it.

Step 4: Answer the questions!

1. According to the article, why is it surprising that Wyoming was the first territory to allow women to vote?

   (A) Few people knew about formal elections.
   (B) There was a small population of women in the territory.
   (C) The community showed no obvious interest in the issue.
   (D) The efforts on the East Coast were moving ahead quickly.

   Your Answer: (A) (B) (C) (D)

> **NOTE**
>
> Underline: When you come upon any key words such as "surprise," underline it!

2. Which sentence from the article explains specifically how Esther Morris succeeded in providing the women of Wyoming with the right to vote?

   (A) "The big surprise to everyone was that the first victory for women's right to vote occurred in Wyoming, where there had been no public speeches, rallies, or conventions for the women's suffrage movement."
   (B) "In the territory of Wyoming in September 6, 1870, for the first time anywhere in the United States, women went to the polls to cast their ballots."
   (C) "She managed to persuade both rival candidates in a territorial election to promise that, if elected, they would introduce a bill for women's suffrage."
   (D) "She knew that, as long as the winner kept his word, women's suffrage would score a victory in Wyoming."

   Your Answer: (A) (B) (C) (D)

3. Which statement below BEST illustrates the time sequence of the events in the article?

   (A) It begins in the present and then goes back in time to explain the preceding events.
   (B) It begins on September 6, 1870 and then goes back in time to explain the preceding events.
   (C) It begins in 1865 and moves to September 6, 1870 and then goes back to 1865.
   (D) It all takes place on the same day—September 6, 1870.

   Your Answer: (A) (B) (C) (D)

ANALYSIS

1. (**C**) The article states that there were "no public speeches, rallies, or conventions for the women's suffrage movement." This is another way to say that the "community showed no obvious interest in the issue." Answer **D** is totally erroneous—the East Coast had been working for thirty years for women's suffrage. Answers **A** and **B** are both faulty—neither fact is mentioned in the article.

2. **(C)** The article states that Mrs. Morris' success was due to "effective politics," which is followed by the statement made in answer **C**. Answers **A** and **B** both state facts, but not how she succeeded. Answer **D** is close, but not the real reason she succeeded.

3. **(B)** Paying attention to the time sequence is a good habit to get into. If you had underlined dates while you were reading, **B** jumps out at you. Answers **A** and **C** are blatantly false. Answer **D** is impossible and way off course.

READING COMPREHENSION: UNDERSTANDING THE MAIN IDEA

The **main idea** is the most important thing a writer wants you to know, the reason that the story or paragraph or article is written. If you add up the details included in the writing, they usually equal the main idea. But beware! Sometimes the main idea arrives right away, bam! in the first sentence of a paragraph, if you're lucky. There are times when the main idea is buried somewhere in the paragraph or writing, usually at the end of the passage. Then again, there are times when it is not actually stated right out in the open and you have to **infer** (imply or assume) the main idea. Read the short passage below. Look for the main idea, of course, but add up the details while you read along as well.

A Chimney Swept

Chimney sweeps, you know, the ones who clean chimneys and wear the same type of outfit that they wore over 100 years ago; the tall black hat and a scarf. In times past, throughout Europe and North America, many people were able to make a living from sweeping chimneys. It is a job that is difficult and not particularly healthy. Although you might think that there are few, if any, chimney sweeps left in the world, you would be mistaken. Because people nowadays are using their fireplaces more, the number of chimney sweeps is growing.

> **Details: Details + Details**
>
> **=**
>
> **Main Idea**

- many people made a living in past as
- wear tall black hats and scarves
- more and more people using chimneys now
- job not good for your health
- the number of chimney sweeps is growing

Main Idea: Choose One from the Following

  A Chimney sweeps continue to work today as in years past.

  B Chimney sweeps wear tall hats and scarves.

  C Chimney sweeps have an unhealthy profession.

ANALYSIS

The answer is A. The other two answers, **B** and **C**, are limited in their scope, too narrow to be the **main idea.** The main idea is that chimney sweeps are still at work.

READING COMPREHENSION—DETAILS

Details are the small parts of the bigger picture. These are the little things that add up to the main idea that we just reviewed. On most examinations, detail questions are probably the easiest to answer. Often the questions focus on where, what (state, size, month, year, color, and so on), when, how many, etc. Following the test-taking process we learned in the previous section, let's try it again, but this time we will focus on looking at and answering detail questions.

Step 1: Preview the title and the passage.

The Macrozamia Tree: The Oldest Living Thing

The Macrozamia trees grow in the mountains of Australia and they have been growing there for more than 10,000 years. The Macrozamia tree resembles a palm tree. Its leaves look like feathers and the trunk is very thick. On the outside of the trunk, a new ring of scales appear each year. These rings are pushed down to the bottom of the trunk as the tree grows. By counting the rings of scales on the trunk, you can usually tell the age of the tree. But, because the trees are so old, some of the rings at the bottom of the trunk have faded and it is difficult to tell the exact age.

The oldest living tree in the United States is in California. It is the redwood tree. Some of these trees are more than 4,000 years old.

The difference between the oldest plants on earth and the oldest animals is quite extensive. The oldest living animals are thought to be the giant turtles on the Galapagos Islands in the Pacific Ocean. These turtles live as long as 200 years.

Step 2: Read/review the questions.

  1. Macrozamia trees grow in _____?

  2. The Macrozamia tree is like a palm tree because _____.

  3. The age of a Macrozamia tree is determined from _____.

  4. In the United States, the oldest living thing is the _____.

  5. The oldest living animals on earth _____.

Step 3: Read the passage—with a purpose. Underline key words as you read.

Step 4: Answer the questions!

1. Macrozamia trees grow _____

   (A) in California.
   (B) on an island in the Pacific.
   (C) in the Australian mountains.
   (D) in the French Alps.

   Your Answer: (A) (B) (C) (D)

2. The Macrozamia tree is like a palm tree because _____

   (A) both have thick trunks.
   (B) both have thin trunks.
   (C) both trees have needles.
   (D) they both have coconuts growing in them.

   Your Answer: (A) (B) (C) (D)

3. The age of a Macrozamia tree is determined from _____

   (A) counting its leaves.
   (B) the length of its trunk.
   (C) the height of its trunk.
   (D) the rings of scales on its trunk.

   Your Answer: (A) (B) (C) (D)

4. In the United States, the oldest living thing is _____

   (A) a redwood tree.
   (B) a Macrozamia tree.
   (C) a turtle.
   (D) the Liberty Bell.

   Your Answer: (A) (B) (C) (D)

5. The oldest living animals on earth _____

   (A) are the sheep in Scotland.
   (B) are the turtles in the Galapagos Islands.
   (C) are the trees in northern California.
   (D) are the whales in Baja California.

   Your Answer: (A) (B) (C) (D)

ANALYSIS

1. **The correct answer is C.** Answer **D** is way off. Answers **A** and **B** are both facts/details from the story, but not the one that is being asked, and this is when reading the questions carefully really matters. Certain details may be logged in your brain from the reading, but when you are answering the questions, be certain to read the question carefully and then read **all** of the answers before choosing the correct one. Don't let familiar facts fool you! Be careful. **2. The correct answer is A. 3. The correct answer is D. 4. The correct answer is A. 5. The correct answer is B.**

Most of the questions on exams that deal with details or facts are fairly straightforward. In answering the questions, it is a matter of accuracy. If you want to make certain that you are correct, always, *always* look back at the reading. It doesn't take that long to check. You want to be accurate and you don't want to make a careless error.

READING COMPREHENSION—INFERENCES

Are you **inferring** that I . . . ? Has anyone ever said that to you? Well, when we talk about inferring, what we mean is that you are taking information in that the writer or speaker wants you to know. You then process it around in your brain and add it to the stuff you already know. Once processed, out comes something that you are assuming to be correct. Inferences are like **deductions, conclusions, suppositions, conjectures, and presumptions** (another string of synonyms!). The tricky thing about inferences on exams is that the information they are asking for is not spelled out in so many words. You have to *infer* it, or draw a conclusion on your own, or make a reasonable guess. Again, you need to add up the details of the passage to come up with the proper inference.

> **Processed Details + Details**
>
> **+**
>
> **Details + Processing**
>
> **=**
>
> **Inference**

Once again we will follow the test-taking process in learning about inference questions. Inference questions require a more thorough reading of the passage because you need to process the information in your brain for awhile. Follow the steps as usual, but you will especially want to use the visualization technique discussed earlier in the chapter to make certain you understand the reading thoroughly. Read the passage carefully.

Step 1: Preview the title and the passage.

Henry Noble: The Grand Imposter

Monsoon rains were pounding the tents and the generators were struggling to maintain power, but the storm mattered little to the members of the medic team. A crew member was in need of an operation. His appendix had burst and it needed to be removed immediately. The doctor quickly and knowledgeably began the operation and forty minutes later, the operation was successfully completed. With antibiotics and rest, the sailor would be fine.

But, there was something seriously wrong. The doctor doing the surgery wasn't really a doctor at all. His name was Henry Noble, a man who spent his life pretending to be something he wasn't. Noble had very little education and wasn't trained for any specific kind of work.

What Noble was particularly good at was pretending. He made up false papers about himself to fool people into hiring him. Noble tried dozens of careers. Among them, he was a professor at several colleges and a guard at a prison in Kansas. Once people discovered his fraud, he would move on to another career.

His most remarkable fraud was working as a doctor. He managed to convince the authorities of his credentials as a physician. But, what is even more remarkable, Noble performed forty-six operations during the Vietnam War, and all of them were successful.

Step 2: Read the questions to help you read with a purpose.

1. Because he _____ Noble was a fraud.

2. As a doctor, his work must have been _____.

3. Noble probably knew something about _____.

4. Catching up with Noble was challenging because _____.

5. This story is primarily about _____.

NOTE

To visualize the sentence, draw a picture in your mind.

Step 3: Read with a purpose; visualize and underline.

Adrift in the middle of a storm,
the ship rolled wildly in the sea,
but the storm mattered little to the medic team . . .

Step 4: Answer the questions!

1. Because he _____ Noble was a fake.

   (A) was uneducated,
   (B) pretended to be trained for his work,
   (C) only looked like a doctor,
   (D) tried many careers,

   Your Answer: Ⓐ Ⓑ Ⓒ Ⓓ

2. As a doctor, his work must have been _____

   (A) lengthy in training for it.
   (B) a career of a lifetime.
   (C) against the law.
   (D) the cause of many deaths.

   Your Answer: Ⓐ Ⓑ Ⓒ Ⓓ

3. Noble was probably knowledgeable about _____

   (A) taking care of sick people.
   (B) the ways of the sea.
   (C) supervising a prison.
   (D) eating on the run.

   Your Answer: Ⓐ Ⓑ Ⓒ Ⓓ

4. Catching up with Noble was challenging because _____

   (A) he wore the best sneakers money could buy.
   (B) he worked at the same job for years.
   (C) he attended different schools.
   (D) he continually changed careers.

   Your Answer: Ⓐ Ⓑ Ⓒ Ⓓ

5. This story is primarily about _____

   (A) a man and his dog.
   (B) a man who was a fraud.
   (C) a sailor on a ship.
   (D) the Canadian navy.

   Your Answer: Ⓐ Ⓑ Ⓒ Ⓓ

ANALYSIS

1. **The correct answer is B.** Remember when making **inferences,** you have to process the information, the **details** that have been given to you. Although two of the answers are correct in that they are facts from the passage, only **B** is correct because it answers the question about Noble being a fraud; he wasn't a fraud because he didn't have an education or that he tried many

careers; he was a fraud because he pretended to be trained for something that he wasn't.

2. **The correct answer is C.** The key words in the question are "must have been." With these words you know that you are going to have to make a decision on your own. The only answer that stands out here as being a reasonable judgment call is **C;** the others are frauds!

3. **The correct answer is A.** Here is another question with a typical inference-type clue word—"probably." It is yet another opportunity to make a decision on your own and, as you can see, if you look at the answers carefully, only one, **A,** appears to have a measure of fulfilling that goal.

4. **The correct answer is D.** The other answers are false.

5. **The correct answer is B.** Both questions 4 and 5 follow a similar sequence. One only needs to consider the details, which add up to the inferences of both questions.

Chapter Review and Quick Quiz

In this chapter, we discovered the importance of comprehension. In reading, as in life, there are going to be things that you will enjoy and things that are not going to be so pleasant. But, because your enjoyment is perhaps less than what you would choose, that in itself doesn't necessarily mean that it is less important. Comprehending what you read is just as important in science, math, and social studies as it is in English, even though I personally prefer the latter. Remember these comprehension techniques and practice them in your day-to-day readings. Visualizing—drawing pictures in your mind or in the margins of the book (if it is your personal copy) is extremely helpful. Underlining important facts—taking notes or outlining—all are valuable in helping you understand what you read. Use what helps you most. The answers are in the appendix.

REMINDERS:
- **Preview the reading.**
  - Look at the title
  - Glance at the reading passage
- **Read the questions first.**
  - Quickly determine what type of questions are given and what specifically you need to look for in the reading.
    - For detail questions, look for dates, numbers, measurements, and other obvious details that are easy to find and make scanning the reading possible
    - For main idea questions, read passage carefully
    - For inference questions, read passage carefully
- **Read with a purpose.**
  - Scan the reading quickly if the questions are asking for details.
  - Use visualization techniques (drawing pictures in your mind) for a focused reading if the questions are main idea or inference.
  - Underline important passages.
- **Reread the questions and then answer them.**

1. The question below is asking for what kind of information?

   The story is mainly about _____?

   (A) details
   (B) main idea
   (C) inference

   Your Answer: Ⓐ Ⓑ Ⓒ

2. The question below asks for what kind of information?

   No airplane had flown over the Atlantic Ocean before _____.

   (A) details
   (B) main idea
   (C) inference

   Your Answer: Ⓐ Ⓑ Ⓒ

3. The question below asks for what type of information?

   Paragraph 4 is mostly about _____.

   (A) details
   (B) main idea
   (C) inference

   Your Answer: Ⓐ Ⓑ Ⓒ

NOTE

Let's make certain that you understand the difference between questions that ask for details, the main idea, and inferential quetions. Take the following quiz. Detailed answers are in the appendix.

4. The question below asks for what kind of information?

    Riders stuck on the Ferris wheel ride must have spent hours _____.

    (A) details
    (B) main idea
    (C) inference

    Your Answer: Ⓐ Ⓑ Ⓒ

5. The question below asks for what kind of information?

    Clarence Smith's idea was _____.

    (A) details
    (B) main idea
    (C) inference

    Your Answer: Ⓐ Ⓑ Ⓒ

Reading Comprehension—Part II

In this chapter, we will look at real-life writings. **Expository** writings are writings that explain something. That's easy to remember mnemonically—**expository = explain.** You will encounter expository writings for the rest of your life. You also need to understand the technical writings that you will encounter when you buy something, when you sign a contract for a loan, or apply for a job. Types of consumer materials are: warranties, contracts, instruction manuals, and applications. Understanding them is important and occasionally, a question about consumer materials appears on the exam, so it is a good idea to become familiar with them. **Primary and secondary sources**—what are those, you ask? A primary source is an original publication written by the original author who originated the idea in the first place, while a secondary source is a publication that is written by another person, but quotes or uses the ideas of the primary source. Does that make sense? If it doesn't now, it will later. We will also look at the way **bibliographies** are set up, and exactly what types of information can be found in a **thesaurus,** the **Reader's Guide,** an **index,** an **atlas,** and of course the **dictionary.** The chances of an encounter with a question about any of the above items are quite high, so it is best to be prepared. We've got a lot of work to do in this chapter!

CHAPTER FOCUS

- Expository Writings
- Consumer Materials—Structure and Function
    - Warranties
    - Manuals
    - Contracts
    - Applications
- Primary and Secondary Sources
- Bibliographic Citations
- Information Sources:
    - Thesaurus
    - Index
    - Dictionary
    - Atlas
    - Reader's Guide
- Chapter Review and Quick Quizzes

UNDERSTANDING EXPOSITORY WRITINGS

Expository writings are everywhere. You will find them in professional journals, editorials in the newspaper, political speeches, and in primary source material. Everywhere! Expository writings present facts, define terms, give opinions, and otherwise give examples to readers that will help them more clearly understand a specific topic. The writer makes a point or presents the **main idea** or a thesis statement and then supports it with facts or **details** in the body of the writing. The details are important in the support of the main idea. Without them, what kind of **exposition** would it be? Let's look at an example of expository writing and afterward we will review its structure and examine just why it is an expository writing.

The Seneca Falls Declaration of Sentiments
Wesleyan Chapel, Seneca Falls, New York, 1848

Drafted by Elizabeth Cady Stanton (patterned after the Declaration of Independence)

When, in the course of human events, it becomes necessary for one portion of the family of man to assume among the people of the earth a position different from that which they have hitherto occupied, but one to which the laws of nature and of nature's God entitle them, a decent respect to the opinions of mankind requires that they should declare the causes that impel them to such a course.

We hold these truths to be self-evident: that all men and women are created equal; that they are endowed by their Creator with certain inalienable rights; that among these are life, liberty, and the pursuit of happiness; that to secure these rights governments are instituted, deriving their just powers from the consent of the governed. Whenever any form of government becomes destructive of these ends, it is the right of those who suffer from it to refuse allegiance to it, and to insist upon the institution of a new government, laying its foundation on such principles, and organizing its powers in such form, as to them shall seem most likely to effect their safety and happiness. Prudence, indeed will dictate that governments long established should not be changed for light and transient causes; and accordingly all experience hath shown that mankind are more disposed to suffer, while evils are sufferable, than to right themselves by abolishing the forms to which they were accustomed. But, when a long train of abuses and usurpations pursuing invariably the same object evinces a design to reduce them under absolute despotism, it is their duty to throw off such governments, and to provide new guards for their future security. Such has been the patient sufferance of the women under this government, and such is now the necessity which constrains them to demand the equal station to which they are entitled.

The history of mankind is a history of oft repeated injuries and usurpations on the part of man toward woman, having in direct object the establishment of an absolute tyranny over her. To prove this, let facts be submitted to a candid world.

He has never permitted her to exercise her inalienable right to the elective franchise.

He has withheld from her rights which are given to the most ignorant and degraded men—both natives and foreigners.

Having deprived her of this first right of a citizen, the elective franchise, thereby leaving her without representation in the halls of legislations, he has oppressed her on all sides.

He has made her, if married, in the eye of the law, civilly dead.

He has taken from her all right in property, even to the wages she earns.

He has made her, morally, an irresponsible being, as she can commit many crimes with impunity, provided they be done in the presence of her husband. In the covenant of marriage, she is compelled to promise obedience to her husband, he becoming, to all intents and purposes, her master—the law giving him power to deprive her of her liberty, and to administer chastisement.

He has so framed the laws of divorce, as to what shall be the proper causes, and in case of separation, to whom the guardianship of the children shall be given, as to be wholly regardless of the happiness of women—the law, in all cases, going upon a false supposition of the supremacy of man, and giving all power into his hands.

After depriving her of all rights as a married woman, if single, and the owner of property, he has taxed her to support a government which recognizes her only when her property can be made profitable to it.

He has monopolized nearly all the profitable employments, and from those she is permitted to follow, she receives but a scanty remuneration. He closes against her all the avenues to wealth and distinction which he considers most honorable to himself. As a teacher of theology, medicine, or law, she is not known.

He has denied her the facilities for obtaining a thorough education, all colleges being closed against her.

He allows her in Church, as well as State, but a subordinate position, claiming Apostolic authority for her exclusion from the ministry, and, with some exceptions, from any public participation in the affairs of the Church.

He has created a false public sentiment by giving to the world a different code of morals for men and women, by which moral delinquencies which exclude women from society, are not only tolerated, but deemed of little account in man.

He has usurped the prerogative of Jehovah himself, claiming it as his right for her a sphere of action, when that belongs to her conscience and to her God.

He has endeavored, in every way that he could, to destroy her confidence in her own powers, to lessen her self-respect, and to make her willing to lead a dependent and abject life.

Now, in view of this entire disfranchisement of one-half the people of this country, their social and religious degradation—in view of the unjust laws above mentioned, and because women do feel themselves aggrieved, oppressed, and fraudulently deprived of their most sacred rights, we insist that they have immediate admission to all the rights and privileges which belong to them as citizens of the United States.

In entering upon the great work before us, we anticipate no small amount of misconception, misrepresentation, and ridicule; but we shall use every instrumentality within our power to effect our object. We shall employ agents, circulate tracts, petition the State and National legislatures, and endeavor to enlist the pulpit and the press in our behalf. We hope this Convention will be followed by a series of Conventions, embracing every part of the Country . . .

EXAMPLE

1. The main idea of this expository document, which was written in 1848, is_____

   (A) to declare that women are happy and content.
   (B) to "declare the causes that impel them" to voice their desire for equal rights.
   (C) to assume that men will always disrespect women.
   (D) to change the history of mankind the world over.

Your Answer:

EXAMPLE

2. Which of the following statements is NOT one of the supportive details that Cady stated in the "Declaration of Sentiments?"

   (A) He has compelled her to submit to laws, in the formation of which she had no voice.
   (B) He has made her, if married, in the eye of the law, civilly dead.
   (C) He has denied her the facilities for obtaining a thorough education, all colleges being closed against her.
   (D) He has made her spend hours in the scorching sun or drenching rain, planting the crops.

Your Answer:

ANALYSIS

The correct answer for Number 1 is B. The answers **A, C,** and **D** are erroneous; **A** and **C** are especially off the wall. **D** might be negotiable had it not mentioned the "world over" because, at this point, the women's suffrage movement was a concern primarily focused in the United States. **The correct answer to Number 2 is D.** Hope you weren't falling asleep here. The question asks for the detail that is **NOT** mentioned in the "Declaration of Sentiments." **D** is the only one in that category.

Structure of Expository Writing

The "Declaration of Sentiments" is a true example of expository writing. It is also an example of a **primary source document,** which we will discuss later. As in most writings, there is an introduction, body, and conclusion. The "Sentiments," drafted for the women's suffrage movement in the mid-1800s introduces the sentiments of women and their mistreatment considering the words of the Declaration of Independence. The introduction is followed by details or facts upon facts that support the thesis. The thesis is the entire first paragraph; the second paragraph includes a hook (makes the reader want to read more), which is also called the motivator and is creative. By imitating the wording of the Declaration of Independence, Cady certainly manages to attract attention to the writing.

To support her introduction, Cady lists the many injustices that need to be addressed. These facts make up the body of her writing. Cady's conclusion, the last two paragraphs, not only summarizes the "Sentiments," but makes a bold statement as well—the clincher! "Now in view of the entire disfranchisement of one-half the people of this country . . ." That's expository writing!

> **Basic Structure of Expository Writings:**
> **Introduction with Thesis/Hook or Motivator**
>   **Supporting Detail**
>   **Supporting Detail**
>   **Supporting Detail**
>   **Conclusion/Clincher**

STRUCTURE AND FUNCTION OF CONSUMER AND WORKPLACE DOCUMENTS

Warranties

These are guarantees that the manufacturer of an item, which has been purchased by a consumer, will promise to repair. Manufacturers will repair or replace specified defects or parts within a specified period of time, usually a year. For instance, a consumer just bought a $500 television set. The manufacturer (RCA, Toshiba, etc.) promises to repair certain things, such as the speakers or wiring, if these are defects and if the television is not accidentally or intentionally broken within a year or two or even five years (depending on the cost and the manufacturer's faith in its product). Most mechanical and electronic items have warranties. The good thing about warranties is that they make you more confident when a defective product needs to be returned. Some major appliance stores offer extended warranties for, of course, expanded prices. Look at the sample of the warranty below. Answer the questions that might appear on the exit exam.

> **Warranty certificates give details of the promise from the manufacturing company.**

CERTIFICATE OF WARRANTY

To protect your purchase from manufacturer defects, ALF Manufacturing Inc. will replace or repair your television set for up to **2 years** from the date of purchase. We guarantee all parts and labor. Remember our motto, "If we can't fix it we'll replace it." We have a national repair network of over 12,000 licensed service professionals.

To speak with our repair and product support network 24 hours a day, please call 800 869-4629 and ask for Customer Service. If you prefer to communicate on-line, please go to our Internet site: www.ALFMANUFINC.org

ALF MANUFACTURING
INC.

EXAMPLE

1. What does ALF offer as a guarantee to their customers?

(A) A 24-hour customer service is available.
(B) If they can't repair it they will replace it.
(C) All parts and labor are guaranteed.
(D) All of the above.

Your Answer: Ⓐ Ⓑ Ⓒ Ⓓ

EXAMPLE

2. The company's motto is _____

(A) Waste not want not.
(B) If we can't fix it, we'll replace it.
(C) Bring your business to us.
(D) We'll replace and repair your television set for up to two years.

Your Answer: Ⓐ Ⓑ Ⓒ Ⓓ

ANALYSIS

The correct answer to Number 1 is D. All of the statements are a part of the company's guarantee to their customers. **The correct answer to Number 2 is B.** Although **D** was mentioned in the warranty, it is not their motto. Answers **A** and **C** are way off and not a part of this company's credo.

Contracts

These are legal documents that you sign, for instance, when you buy something that is very expensive and you are not paying for it with cash, such as a car or a house. Contracts vary in type and legal implications. And all contracts have to be signed, legally. The signature binds you to the formal language of the contract, which can be really confusing at times and that is why they always tell you to "read the **small** print." Typical contracts are: employment contracts, contracts to hire an attorney, contracts to get braces on your teeth, contracts to sign when you hire a plumber or contractor, a marriage contract, contracts to purchase a vehicle, and the list goes on. Below you will find a portion of the service contract for an automobile. Look it over and then answer the questions pertaining to its terms and conditions.

> **A contract is a formal agreement between people, groups, or countries with a binding legal document setting out terms and conditions.**

PROVISIONS OF THIS VEHICLE SERVICE CONTRACT

This CONTRACT is between YOU and US, and is subject to all the Terms and Conditions contained herein.

1. **CONTRACT PERIOD**
    Coverage under this **Contract** begins on the **Contract** Purchase Date and will expire according to the time and/or mileage of the term/miles selected, whichever occurs first, as shown in the **Registration Information.**
    a. New Vehicle Plan expiration is measured in time/mileage from the **Contract** Purchase Date and zero (0) miles.
    b. Used Vehicle Plan requires a mandatory "Waiting Period" before **Coverage** takes effect. The "Waiting Period" = 30 days <u>and</u> 1,000 miles from the **Contract** Purchase Date and Odometer Mileage at **Contract** Purchase Date. 30 days <u>and</u> 1,000 miles will be added to the term of **Your Contract.**

2. **COVERAGE**
    The **Coverage** afforded **You** for **Your Vehicle** is fully described in this **Contract.** Please see section: "Schedule Of Coverages" of this **Contract.**

3. **BREAKDOWN OF COVERED PARTS**

   We will pay or reimburse **You** for reasonable costs to repair or replace any **Breakdown** of a part listed in the **Schedule of Coverages.** <u>REPLACEMENT PARTS MAY BE NEW, REMANUFACTURED, OR REPLACEMENT PARTS OF LIKE KIND AND QUALITY.</u>

4. **DEDUCTIBLE**

   In the event of a **Breakdown** covered by this **Contract, You** may be required to pay a **Deductible.** No **Deductible** payment is required with respect to Towing/Road Service, Rental, Trip Interruption, and Lost Key/Lockout, if they are provided by this **Contract.**

   If **You** have a **Deductible** as shown in the **Registration Information,** the **Deductible** amount will be applied on a repair visit basis. Should a covered **Breakdown** take more than one visit to repair, only one **Deductible** will apply for that **Breakdown.**

5. **TERRITORY**

   This **Contract** applies only to **Breakdowns** that occur and repairs made within the United States of America and Canada.

6. **LIMITS OF LIABILITY**

   a. **Per Repair Visit—Our** liability for any one (1) Repair Visit shall in no event exceed the trade-in value of **Your Vehicle** at the time of said Repair Visit, as listed in the NADA Used Car Guide.

   b. **Aggregate**—The total of all claims and benefits paid or payable while this **Contract** is in force shall not exceed the price **You** paid for **Your Vehicle** (excluding tax, title and license fees).

7. **MAINTENANCE REQUIREMENTS**

   a. **You** must have **Your Vehicle** checked and serviced in accordance with the manufacturer's recommendations, as outlined in the Owner's Manual. **Your** Owner's Manual lists different servicing recommendations based on **Your** individual driving habits and climate conditions. **You** are required to follow the maintenance schedule that applies to **Your** conditions. Failure to follow the manufacturer's recommendations that apply to **Your** specific conditions may result in the denial of **Coverage.** If an Owner's Manual is not provided, **You** can contact the **Administrator** and the servicing recommendations will be provided to **You.**

   b. It is required that verifiable receipts be retained for the service work. Or, if **You** perform **Your** own service, **You** must retain verifiable receipts showing purchases of all required parts and materials necessary to perform the required maintenance showing the date and mileage when the services were performed. Maintenance and/or service work receipts may be requested by the **Administrator.**

8. **TRANSFER OF YOUR VEHICLE SERVICE CONTRACT**

   a. **Your Contract** may be transferable to someone to whom **You** sell or otherwise transfer **Your Vehicle** while this **Contract** is still in force. This **Contract** cannot be transferred if the title transfer of **Your Vehicle** passes through an entity other than the subsequent buyer, or **Your Vehicle** is sold or traded to a dealership, leasing agency or entity/individual in the business of selling vehicles. This **Contract** can only be transferred once and the transfer must be initiated by the original **Contract** Holder.

   b. To transfer, the following must be submitted to the **Administrator** within 30 days of the change of ownership to a subsequent individual purchaser:

      1. A completed transfer form; with
      2. Name and Address of New owner, date of sale to new owner, current mileage; and
      3. $50.00 Transfer Fee made payable to the **Administrator.**

   c. Any remaining manufacturer's warranty must also be transferred at the same time as vehicle ownership transfer. Copies of all maintenance records showing actual oil changes and manufacturers maintenance must be given to the new owner. These maintenance records must be retained along with similar documentation for future maintenance work which the new owner has performed in accordance with the Maintenance Requirements of this **Contract.** If necessary, these documents will be verified by the **Administrator.**

9. OUR RIGHT TO RECOVER PAYMENT

If **You** have a right to recover against another party for anything **We** have paid under this **Contract, Your** rights shall become **Our** rights. **You** shall do whatever is necessary to enable **Us** to enforce these rights. **We** shall recover only the excess after **You** are fully compensated for **Your** loss.

CANCELLATION OF YOUR CONTRACT

   a. **You** may cancel this **Contract** by contacting the **Administrator.** An odometer statement indicating the odometer reading on the date of the request will be required.

   b. **We** may cancel this **Contract** for non-payment of the **Contract** charge, or for misrepresentation in the submission of a claim. **We** <u>may</u> cancel this **Contract** if **Your Vehicle** is found to be modified in a manner not recommended by the manufacturer, or **Your Vehicle** is found to be used as a **Commercial** vehicle and the applicable surcharge has not been marked in the **Registration Information** and payment has not been received for this surcharge.

   c. If this **Contract** is cancelled within the first sixty (60) days and no claims have been filed, **we** will refund the entire **Contract** charge paid. If this **Contract** is cancelled after the first sixty (60) days or a claim has been filed, **We** will refund an amount of the **Contract** charge according to the pro-rata method reflecting the greater of the days in force or the miles driven based on the term/miles selected and the date **Coverage** begins, less a twenty five ($25.00) dollar administrative fee. In the event of cancellation, the lienholder, if any, will be named on a cancellation refund check as their interest may appear.

Your Signature   Date:

_____   _____

EXAMPLE

1. Provision #5 "Territory" refers to _____

    (A) the areas (Canada and the United States) where the contract will cover repairs for breakdowns
    (B) the Oregon Territory explored by Lewis and Clark
    (C) the territory where the car is forbidden to break down
    (D) all of the above

Your Answer:

EXAMPLE

2. Under the "Contract Period," how long does the buyer of a used vehicle have to wait before the coverage takes effect?

    (A) 2 years and 60,000 miles
    (B) 60 days
    (C) 30 days and 1,000 miles
    (D) contract purchase date and 0 miles

Your Answer:

ANALYSIS

Reading the provisions of a vehicle service contract is not particularly exciting reading, but it is important reading. The best advice is to read carefully. Take your time, especially when you are doing this in the real world. But for now, answering a few questions to check understanding is your goal and the goal of the exam makers. The correct answers to the questions are: **1 A** and **2 C.** To find both answers, it takes careful reading to make certain you are not confused by the details.

Manuals

These are offered, for instance, to the consumer or to the employee for many reasons. To the consumer, manuals are used for instructions on how to put something together such as a barbecue grill, a bike, or a computer, to instruct in art, plumbing, or yoga. Employee manuals give specific instructions as to job descriptions. They tell an employee just exactly what he/she is supposed to be doing at their job. Whatever the type of manual, it will be informative and instructional. Some are well written and easy to follow, while others are extremely difficult and full of **jargon,** which is language that is used in one specific field (teacher jargon, doctor jargon, skater jargon, journalist jargon, electrician jargon, and so on) and the people in that field understand it better than people outside the field. Below is a sample of an instruction manual. It is attempting to teach the consumer to throw a Frisbee forehand. Although many manuals have illustrations, this one doesn't. Many instructions are difficult to follow without a visual to help. Read on.

Teaching Beginners How to Throw Forehand

GRIP: Your grip is like this: the middle finger is straight and flat against the inside rim of the disk. The outside rim of the disk makes contact with the web between thumb and index finger. Beginners may need to keep the index and middle fingers separated to gain more control of the disk. The part of the middle finger must still be against the rim of the disk.

STANCE: Assume a stance with the balls of the feet a shoulder width apart. Initially, it appears easier to learn to throw side on and/or with the elbow close to the hip. This may be a crutch later when you have to look upfield and extend around a marker.

The thrower must have the disk cocked, ready to impart spin before throwing. It can either start wound as far back as it can go or wind just before the throw.

SWING: The main trick is to keep the outer tip of the disk down. For the more advanced beginner, the following points may help. The motion of the disk while in the hand should not be so much as an arclike swing, but a whiplash with increasing speed, motion toward the target starts from the shoulder, to the elbow, then wrist, and finally the fingers. Stepping forward and the nonpivot foot may help. The pivot should be on the opposite side as the throwing hand.

RELEASE: Until now, there has been little spin in the disk. The whiplash effect of the swing should culminate in a "snap" imparting maximum spin plane. [i.e, if the spin axis is not perpendicular to the flight plate, the disk launch should lie within this plane]. The time of release is when it all must come together. The last motions imparted to the disk are the ones it takes with it to combat the wind and gravity. Yet, this instant happens so quickly and beginners have so many things to concentrate on that it's hard to tell what went on.

FOLLOW-THROUGH: Any action by the thrower after letting go of the disk cannot influence the flight of the disk. Nevertheless, some specific follow-through tips are suggested in the next section as an aid to correct specific problems in a throw.

EXAMPLE

1. Instruction manuals are provided for instructional use in the _____ and for the _____

   (A) workplace; consumer.
   (B) baby; toddler.
   (C) giant; ant.
   (D) car; passenger.

Your Answer:

EXAMPLE

2. In the instructional manual above, the directions for throwing would be more easily understood if _____

   (A) the instructions were in a foreign language.
   (B) the instructions were double-spaced.
   (C) the instructions were illustrated.
   (D) they were in red ink and not black.

Your Answer:

ANALYSIS

The correct answer to Question 1 is A. The other answers in this set are wrong. The only logical answer is **A. The correct answer to Question 2 is C.** Reading the answer choices carefully is the key. The answer to this question is inferred in the introductory paragraph to the section. However, most of the answers can be eliminated with a thorough and careful reading.

Applications

There is a time in everyone's life that requires the completion of an application. Applications are completed for employment, driver's licenses, renting or leasing apartments, qualifying for auto or home loans, and so on. Below is a typical application for employment. Become familiar with the information that is asked on these forms. Be prepared to answer a few questions regarding this information.

APPLICATION FOR EMPLOYMENT
Print or type all information.

Section 1: Personal

Date of Application: Phone: ( )

Name: Social Security Number:

Address:

Are you over eighteen years of age?   YES   NO

Person to contact in an emergency:

Address: Phone: ( )

Section 2: Availability

Total Hours Available   M   T   W   T   F   S   S

Per Week: Hours Available:

Date Available for Employment:

What transportation will you use to get to work?

Section 3: Education

Circle the highest grade completed   1   5   6   7   8   grade/middle   9   10   11   12   high school   1   2   3   4   college/technical   1   2   3   4   post graduate

If education in progress, give name and address of school:

Section 4: Work Experience (List previous employers, starting with the most recent, whether part or full time)

Employer	Address	From	To	Position	Salary

Are you able to perform all the essential functions of the job for which you are applying with or without accommodations?   (Circle One)   YES   NO

If no, what accommodations will you need?

If hired, do you agree to abide by the safety rules of the company?   (Circle One)   YES   NO

Applicant's Signature: Date:

EXAMPLE

1. What information belongs in Section 2?

   (A) The applicant's name and address.
   (B) The signature of the applicant.
   (C) The hours that the applicant is available to work.
   (D) The emergency information of the applicant.

Your Answer:

EXAMPLE

2. In what section will you circle the highest grade that you completed in school?

   (A) Section 1
   (B) Section 2
   (C) Section 3
   (D) Section 4

Your Answer:

EXAMPLE

3. What is meant by "accommodations" in the last section of the application?

   (A) That you will need to sleep in a hotel room every night.
   (B) The use of a wheelchair, hearing device, or other aid to help in fulfilling job duties.
   (C) That the office be the executive suite on the 37th floor of the building.
   (D) The use of six secretaries.

Your Answer:

ANALYSIS

The answer to Question 1 is C. The layout of the application form makes it easy to find information quickly; that's the good thing about test questions like this. Occasionally though, the test makers may attempt to fool you with the wording of either the questions or the answers. Just read them carefully. **The answer to Question 2 is C.** Again, the information is easy to find with this format. You don't have to plow through a lot of words to get to the information you need. **The answer to Question 3 is B.** According to the federal government, all employers must accommodate those with disabilities providing they are capable of performing the essential functions of the job. This question in the application asks the job applicant whether there is a need for the accommodations (wheelchair, hearing aid, Braille, etc.)

PRIMARY AND SECONDARY SOURCES

Primary sources are exactly that—sources upon which subsequent interpretations or studies are based. Without primary sources, there would be no **secondary sources.** One begets the other. The "Declaration of Sentiments" that was included earlier in the chapter is a sample of a primary source document. The Declaration of Independence is also an example of a primary document. **Secondary sources,** on the other hand, are works that interpret or analyze an historical event or phenomenon. These documents usually contain bibliographies or a works cited page that documents the use of primary sources and other secondary sources.

Primary Source Documents

- diaries
- journals
- speeches
- interviews
- letters, memos
- manuscripts
- memoirs
- autobiographies
- government records
- organization records
- published materials (books, magazine and journal articles, newspaper articles) written at the time of a particular event
- photographs
- audio recordings
- video recordings, films, documentaries
- public opinion polls (taken at time of event)
- research data (anthropological field notes, scientific data, etc.)
- artifacts (physical objects, buildings tools, furniture, clothing, original artworks, etc.)

Secondary Source Documents

- textbooks
- encyclopedias
- biographies
- critiques and reviews of art/literature

> **NOTE**
>
> Primary Source documents enable the researcher to get as close as possible to what actually happened during an historical event or tine period.

- dictionaries
- books and articles that review or interpret research works

EXAMPLE

1. Which of the following is NOT an example of a primary source document?

    (A) memoirs
    (B) autobiographies
    (C) biography
    (D) government documents

Your Answer: Ⓓ

EXAMPLE

2. Which of the following is an example of a secondary source document?

    (A) biographies
    (B) memoirs
    (C) original art
    (D) interviews

Your Answer: Ⓒ Ⓓ

ANALYSIS

The answer to Question 1 is C. Understanding the difference between the two types of sources is the key to knowing the answers to these questions. If you didn't know what types of documents belong to which source, these questions would be difficult. Just remember, that a biography is a **secondary source document** because it is not written by the person it is about; it is written from research and no doubt many **primary source documents.** The **answer to Question 2 is A.**

BIBLIOGRAPHIC OR WORKS CITED CITATIONS

When you write a research paper in one of your classes, chances are that your instructor will ask for a bibliography or a works cited page. This is the page that is needed in order for you to give credit to the sources whose information you borrowed for your paper (which by the way is a secondary-type source). Giving credit to the person whose work you are borrowing is mandatory. Plagiarism is what it is called if you don't, and that's a legal battle that you would want to avoid at all costs. It is much easier to credit your source. An individual **citation** contains only enough information to enable the reader to look up the source if they so desire. There are different ways to document different types of sources (such as periodicals/

magazines, web sites, encyclopedias, etc.), as well as different types of research papers for different classes. Some subjects require that you document according to the rules of the American Psychological Association or APA. But, because this book focuses on English, we will become familiar with the Modern Language Association (MLA) format. What will be asked on the test are specific questions about the setup of a **bibliographic** or **works cited** entry. Look at the following entry carefully. Note the position of each of the components; author, title, city of publication, publisher, and year of publication. Please be aware that punctuation in the entry is extremely important.

> **NOTE**
>
> *Bibliographic Entries*
>
> Author (last name, first name).
> Title of book (underlined). City of Publication: Publisher, Year of publication.

> **NOTE**
>
> The second line of the entry must be indented.

> **Orwell, George. <u>Animal Farm</u>. New York: Harcourt Brace Jovanovich, Inc., 1946.**

EXAMPLE

1. Which of the following bibliographic entries is incorrect?

   (A) Finley, M.I. <u>The World of Odysseus</u>. New York: Penguin Books, 1956.
   (B) Tolkien, J.R.R. <u>The Hobbit</u>. New York: Ballantine Publishing Group, 1937.
   (C) McCourt, Frank. <u>Angela's Ashes: A Memoir.</u> New York: Simon and Schuster, 1996.
   (D) Houston, Jeanne Wakatsuki, and James Houston. <u>Farewell to Manzanar</u>. 1973.

Your Answer:

ANALYSIS

The correct answer to Number 1 is D. The question is asking which entry is **incorrect**. Remember: punctuation is important. Period, colon, and comma placement is the key to answering this question correctly, plus the fact that the incorrect answer left out the city of publication and the publisher. Both should be placed before the date of publication with the proper punctuation.

INFORMATIONAL SOURCES

You can usually count on a test question that asks you what you will find in various informational sources. A thesaurus, *Reader's Guide to Periodical Literature*, an index, an atlas, and the dictionary are the key sources to the questions. Although your school librarian has no doubt explained these to you many times before, it is helpful to review the functions of these informational sources. Study the entries and then answer the preview questions that follow.

Thesaurus

When you know the definition of a word, but you need a word that has the same or similar meaning, you go to a thesaurus or a synonym finder. Thesauruses are set up alphabetically like a dictionary or they are indexed (see sample below). If you have an indexed version, look up the word in the back of the book and then go to the number that it refers to.

Sample of Indexed Thesaurus

Hypochondria 437
sickness 889

437. HYPOCHONDRIA
See also 889. Sickness

1. imagined ill-health, valetudinarianism, anxiety, neurosis, psychoneurosis.
2. depression, melancholy, *Psychiatry.* melancholia, hypochondriasis, despondency, doldrums, dejection, low spirits, megrims, the blues, *Archaic.* hyp.

Dictionary

In addition to helping you define or understand the meaning of a word, a dictionary is also helpful with spelling, syllabication (splitting up the word properly), pronunciation, parts of speech (noun, pronoun, verb, adjective, etc.), etymology (the history of the word and any root or derivatives), as well as capitalization.

Example of a dictionary entry

> **ex•tro•vert** (**ek**-strö-vurt) *n.* a person more interested in the people and things around him than in his own thoughts and feelings, a lively sociable person. **extrovert** *adj.* **extroverted. ex•tro•version** (ek-strö-**vur**-zhŏn) *n.*

- **ex•tro•vert** = syllabication; this separates the word for you in case you ever need to write part of the word on one line and part of the word on another line
- (**ek**-strö-vurt) = pronunciation—phonetically demonstrates how to say the word
- *n.* = part of speech; this word happens to be a noun
- "a person more interested in the people and things around him than in his own thoughts and feelings, a lively sociable person." } — the definition or word meaning
- **extrovert** *adj.* **extroverted.**
  ex•tro•ver•sion (ek-strö-**vur**-zhŏn) *n.* } — additional forms of the word

Readers' Guide to Periodical Literature

The *Readers' Guide to Periodical Literature* is a book found in the library and is one of the most used magazine reference tools used. The *Readers' Guide* is easily identified by its green cover. If you are looking for information on a current topic in a magazine, this is the source to tap. The guide is indexed alphabetically according to subject and author. Before you go to a lot of work in using this guide, make certain your library has the magazines that it refers you to before you search the shelves and waste time. An entry (see below) in this book will provide you with the following information: the topic, page numbers, volume, name of magazine, name of author, subtopic, date, cross-references, title of article, subject entry, and author entry.

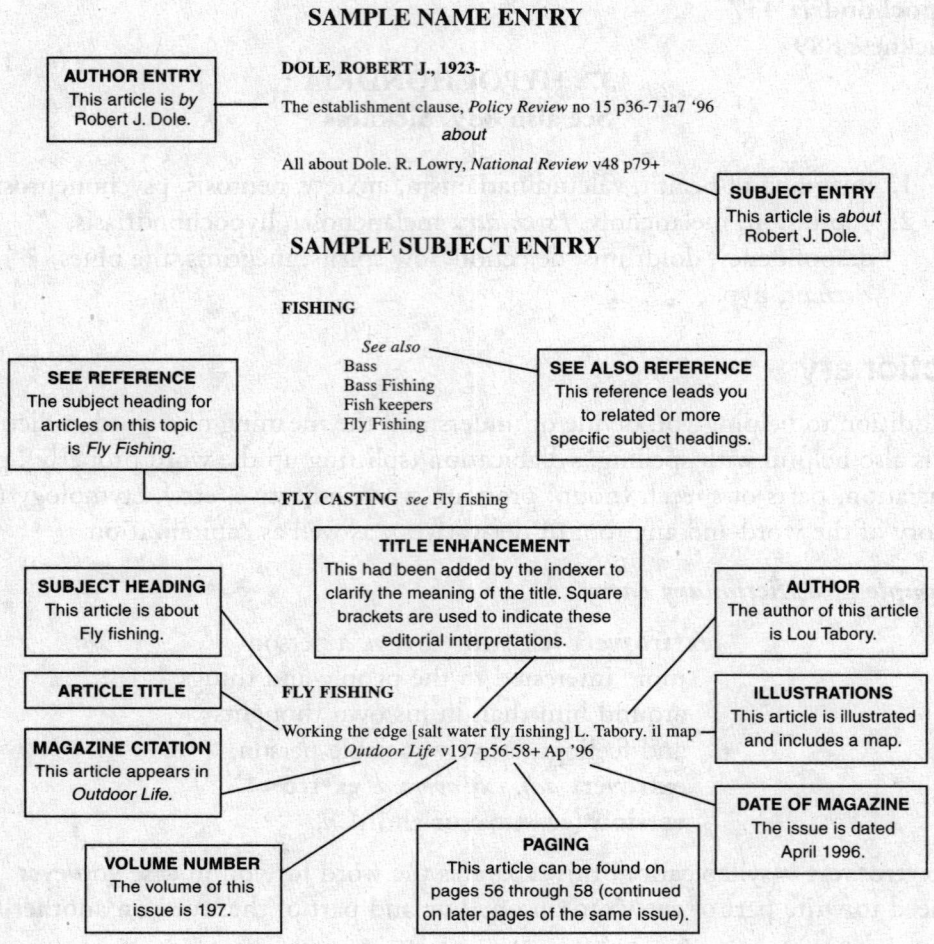

SAMPLE NAME ENTRY

AUTHOR ENTRY
This article is *by* Robert J. Dole.

DOLE, ROBERT J., 1923-
The establishment clause, *Policy Review* no 15 p36-7 Ja7 '96
about
All about Dole. R. Lowry, *National Review* v48 p79+

SUBJECT ENTRY
This article is *about* Robert J. Dole.

SAMPLE SUBJECT ENTRY

FISHING

SEE REFERENCE
The subject heading for articles on this topic is *Fly Fishing*.

See also
Bass
Bass Fishing
Fish keepers
Fly Fishing

SEE ALSO REFERENCE
This reference leads you to related or more specific subject headings.

FLY CASTING *see* Fly fishing

TITLE ENHANCEMENT
This had been added by the indexer to clarify the meaning of the title. Square brackets are used to indicate these editorial interpretations.

SUBJECT HEADING
This article is about Fly fishing.

AUTHOR
The author of this article is Lou Tabory.

ARTICLE TITLE

FLY FISHING
Working the edge [salt water fly fishing] L. Tabory. il map *Outdoor Life* v197 p56-58+ Ap '96

ILLUSTRATIONS
This article is illustrated and includes a map.

MAGAZINE CITATION
This article appears in *Outdoor Life*.

DATE OF MAGAZINE
The issue is dated April 1996.

VOLUME NUMBER
The volume of this issue is 197.

PAGING
This article can be found on pages 56 through 58 (continued on later pages of the same issue).

Index and Other Parts of a Book

- Beginning in the beginning, the **title** page is normally the first page in the book with print on it. The title of the book, the author's name, the publisher's name, and the place of publication are all located on this page.

- The **copyright** page is located usually on the reverse side of the title page. It provides information about the date or dates the book was published. It also has the Library of Congress information (the number that almost all published books are given) or an International Standard Book Number [ISBN], which uniquely identifies the book.

- Often there is a **preface** or a **foreword, introduction,** or an **acknowledgment,** where you will discover some background information to the book, who may have been involved in writing it, and why it was written.

- The **table of contents** lists the divisions of the book into units, chapters, or topics.
- The **body** of the book is the main course—the meat and potatoes.
- An **appendix,** near the end of the book is necessary when additional information is needed to explain something within the book itself. Maps, charts, tables, diagrams, letters, or other documents will be found here.
- A **glossary** provides definitions of words or terms that may be unfamiliar to the reader. It is like a mini-dictionary.
- The **index** is one of the most valuable parts of a book. It is an alphabetical listing of all the important topics included in the book. Although it is a distant cousin to the table of contents, the index is far more detailed, and it tells which page you will find the topic or specific information that you need in the book.
- And, last but not least, a **bibliography**, which we've spoken of earlier in the chapter. The bibliography is where the author credits any primary or secondary sources from which he or she may have borrowed information. It also suggests further readings.

Atlas

An **atlas**—where would we be without one? This is a book of maps. Open an atlas and you will see more than you realize. Cities, states, countries, continents, rivers, mountains, major lakes and bodies of water, deserts, rain forests, and peninsulas appear among the many hundreds of geographical data. Maps contain valuable sources of information. Different types of map offer different types of information:

- **Physical maps** show elevation, natural landscapes (mountains, deserts, etc.), elevations (see example below), mineral resources, vegetation, land use, and ecoregions, among others.

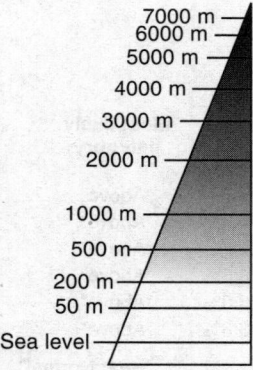

The diagram at left is an approximate key to elevation colors on the relief maps. Dark tones are used for land features (mountains, islands, plains, etc.) and light tones are used for lakes, rivers, oceans, and other water features.

As with the political maps, the relief maps in the World Atlas use the Equidistant Cylindrical projection, which is characterized by severe distortion of area, shape, and distance, particularly near the poles.

- **Political maps** show population density, transportation density, time zones, and of course political information.

Type Styles

ALBANIA	Independent country
ANTARCTICA	Antarctica
GUADELOUPE (FRANCE)	Dependency, overseas territory, etc.
MINNESOTA	Internal division (state, province, etc.)
CHECHNYA	Region with separatist movement(s)
KASHMIR	Disputed territory
Kingston Paris	National capital(s)

Cities

Orlando	Population under 200,000
Zurich	Population 200,000 - 499,999
Lubumbashi	Population 500,000 - 999,000
Jilin	Population 1,000,000 -1,999,999
Melbourne	Population over 2,000,000

Urban areas

■   Population 1,000,000 - 2,999,999

▲   Population 3,000,000 - 4,999,999

●   Population over 5,000,000

Colors

▦   Disputed territory

▨   Antarctic ice shelf

POLITICAL MAPS

Cities with less than 200,000 inhabitants are not shown unless they are either a national capital or the center of a large urban area.

- **Climate and weather maps** show precipitation (rainfall), snow cover, and temperatures.

Precip	Temp	Probability anomaly as shown on map	Probability of occurrence for each class			Most likely category
			A	N	B	
		40%-50%	73.3%-83.3%	23.3%-13.3%	3.3%	"Above"
		30%-40%	63.3%-73.3%	33.3%-23.3%	3.3%	"Above"
		20%-30%	53.3%-63.3%	33.3%	13.3%-3.3%	"Above"
		10%-20%	43.3%-53.3%	33.3%	18.3%-28.3%	"Above"
		5%-10%	38.3%-43.3%	33.3%	28.3%-23.3%	"Above"
		0%-5%	33.3%-38.3%	33.3%	28.3%-33.3%	"Above"
		0%-5%	30.8%-33.3%	33.3%	30.8%-33.3%	"Near Normal"
		5%-10%	28.3%-30.8%	33.3%	28.3%-30.8%	"Near Normal"
		0%-5%	28.3%-33.3%	33.3%	33.3%-38.3%	"Below"
		5%-10%	23.3%-28.3%	33.3%	38.3%-43.3%	"Below"
		10%-20%	28.3%-18.3%	33.3%	43.3%-53.3%	"Below"
		20%-30%	13.3%-3.3%	33.3%	53.3%-63.3%	"Below"
		30%-40%	3.3%	33.3%-23.3%	63.3%-73.3%	"Below"
		40%-50%	3.3%	23.3%-13.3%	73.3%-83.3%	"Below"
		0%	33.3%	33.3%	33.3%	"Climatology"

Also located on most maps are:

- The **compass rose**, which directs you north, south, east, and west on the map. Usually, north is at the top of the map, south at the bottom, east is right, and west is left. The compass rose has been included on maps since the 1300s. It originally was an indicator of the direction of the winds (N, NE, E, SE, S, SW, W, and NW).

- The **legend or key** is in a little box that shows what certain colors or symbols mean. Note the example of the political map legend on the previous page; it illustrates what specific colors and symbols are intended for cities of various sizes.

- The **scale** provides the user with an idea of how large or small an area is. For instance, a one-inch scale could represent 1,000 miles or it could represent 10 miles, depending upon the map. Note the scale on the examples below.

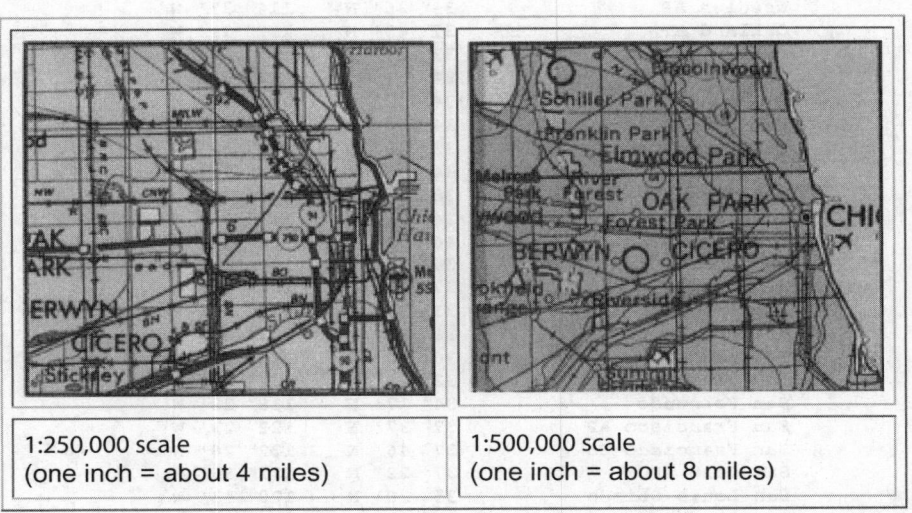

1:250,000 scale
(one inch = about 4 miles)

1:500,000 scale
(one inch = about 8 miles)

- **Longitudinal and latitudinal lines** indicate exactly where in the world the area you are looking for is located. Longitudinal lines are the lines you see running up and down from the North Pole to the South Pole all the way around the globe. Latitudinal lines are the lines that run around the globe and are parallel with the equator. This table gives the latitude and longitude of various major cities in California. The first column gives the latitude in degrees and minutes. The second column gives the longitude in degrees and minutes. The (°) is the symbol for degree, and the (') is a symbol for minute.

CALIFORNIA	Latitude	Longitude
Bakersfield AP	35° 25' N	119° 3' W
Barstow AP	34° 51' N	116° 47' W
Burbank AP	34° 12' N	118° 21' W
Chico	39° 48' N	121° 51' W
Covina	34° 5' N	117° 52' W
Crescent City AP	41° 46' N	124° 12' W
Downey	33° 56' N	118° 8' W
El Cajon	32° 49' N	116° 58' W
El Cerrito AP (S)	32° 49' N	115° 40' W
Escondido	33° 7' N	117° 5' W
Eureka/Arcata AP	40° 59' N	124° 6' W
Fresno AP (S)	36° 46' N	119° 43' W
Laguna Beach	33° 33' N	117° 47' W
Livermore	37° 42' N	121° 57' W
Long Beach AP	33° 49' N	118° 9' W
Los Angeles AP (S)	33° 56' N	118° 24' W
Los Angeles CO (S)	34° 3' N	118° 14' W
Modesto	37° 39' N	121° 0' W
Monterey	36° 36' N	121° 54' W
Napa	38° 13' N	122° 17' W
Needles AP	34° 36' N	114° 37' W
Oakland AP	37° 49' N	122° 19' W
Oceanside	33° 14' N	117° 25' W
Ontario	34° 3' N	117° 36' W
Oxnard	34° 12' N	119° 11' W
Palmdale AP	34° 38' N	118° 6' W
Palm Springs	33° 49' N	116° 32' W
Pasadena	34° 9' N	118° 9' W
Petaluma	38° 14' N	122° 38' W
Pomona Co	34° 3' N	117° 45' W
Redding AP	40° 31' N	122° 18' W
Redlands	34° 3' N	117° 11' W
Richmond	37° 56' N	122° 21' W
Riverside-	33° 54' N	117° 15' W
Sacramento AP	38° 31' N	121° 30' W
Salinas AP	36° 40' N	121° 36' W
San Diego AP	32° 44' N	117° 10' W
San Fernando	34° 17' N	118° 28' W
San Francisco AP	37° 37' N	122° 23' W
San Francisco Co	37° 46' N	122° 26' W
San Jose AP	37° 22' N	121° 56' W
San Louis Obispo	35° 20' N	120° 43' W
Santa Ana AP	33° 45' N	117° 52' W
Santa Barbara MAP	34° 26' N	119° 50' W
Santa Cruz	36° 59' N	122° 1' W
Santa Maria AP (S)	34° 54' N	120° 27' W
Santa Monica CIC	34° 1' N	118° 29' W
Santa Paula	34° 21' N	119° 5' W
Santa Rosa	38° 31' N	122° 49' W
Stockton AP	37° 54' N	121° 15' W
Ukiah	39° 9' N	123° 12' W
Visalia	36° 20' N	119° 18' W
Yreka	41° 43' N	122° 38' W
Yuba City	39° 8' N	121° 36' W

Chapter Review and Quick Quiz

There is a lot going on in this chapter! We reviewed information about **expository** writings, **consumer materials, primary and secondary sources, bibliographic citations,** and **informational sources.** Let's make certain that you understand each of them. Take the following quick quiz for a review. The answers are listed in the appendix at the back of the book.

1. Which of the following is not an example of expository writing?

    (A) newspaper articles
    (B) political speeches
    (C) novels
    (D) editorials

Your Answer: (A) (B) (C) (D)

2. Which of the following is an example of a primary source document?

    (A) a comic book
    (B) the Declaration of Independence
    (C) a novel
    (D) an appliance warranty

Your Answer: (A) (B) (C) (D)

3. Warranty certificates are _____

    (A) not functional.
    (B) used to decorate a product box.
    (C) sold separately at all times.
    (D) guarantees of the manufacturer for an item purchased.

Your Answer: (A) (B) (C) (D)

4. True or False. A contract is a formal agreement between people, groups, or countries with a binding legal document setting out terms and conditions.

    (A) True
    (B) False

Your Answer: (A) (B)

5. Manuals are used for _____

    (A) job descriptions.
    (B) instructions for various appliances.
    (C) care and maintenance of an automobile.
    (D) all of the above.

Your Answer: (A) (B) (C) (D)

6. In general, applications will always ask for _____

   (A) your name, address, and telephone number.
   (B) whether or not you like to wear jeans.
   (C) the color of your hair.
   (D) your shoe size.

Your Answer: Ⓐ Ⓑ Ⓒ Ⓓ

7. Which of the following is NOT an example of a secondary source document?

   (A) textbooks
   (B) encyclopedias
   (C) dictionaries
   (D) poems

Your Answer: Ⓐ Ⓑ Ⓒ Ⓓ

8. A bibliographic citation or works cited citation for a book asks for the
   _____

   (A) author, title, city of publication, publisher, and year of publication.
   (B) author, title, city in which the author resides.
   (C) author, title, publisher and the author's year of birth.
   (D) author, title, city of publication, publisher, and today's date.

Your Answer: Ⓐ Ⓑ Ⓒ Ⓓ

9. A thesaurus is used to locate words that _____

   (A) can be divided into three syllables.
   (B) mean the same or almost the same.
   (C) are biographical.
   (D) have six suffixes.

Your Answer: Ⓐ Ⓑ Ⓒ Ⓓ

10. True or False. A dictionary definition includes syllabication.

    (A) True
    (B) False

Your Answer: Ⓐ Ⓑ

11. The title page is _____ and names the title, author, and publisher.

    (A) at the end of the book
    (B) the first page with printing on it
    (C) used as an index
    (D) the same as a table of contents

Your Answer: Ⓐ Ⓑ Ⓒ Ⓓ

12. True or False. The table of contents lists the divisions of the book into units, chapters, or topics.

    (A) True
    (B) False

Your Answer: Ⓐ Ⓑ

13. The glossary of the book _____

    (A) provides a biography of the author.
    (B) instructs the reader on good reading habits.
    (C) provides a glossy coating to the pages of the book.
    (D) provides definitions of words or terms that may be unfamiliar to the reader.

Your Answer: Ⓐ Ⓑ Ⓒ Ⓓ

14. The index is _____

    (A) in the front of the book and lists the chapters.
    (B) scattered throughout the book to prevent boredom.
    (C) an alphabetical listing of important topics included in the book.
    (D) a random list of names, places, and dates.

Your Answer: Ⓐ Ⓑ Ⓒ Ⓓ

15. The compass rose was originally included on the map to show the direction of _____

    (A) the winds.
    (B) large fish swimming.
    (C) the South Pole.
    (D) the French countryside.

Your Answer: Ⓐ Ⓑ Ⓒ Ⓓ

Literary Response and Analysis—Part I

In this chapter, we will review literary **genres.** Genres are the broad categories under which all literature is typecast or categorized—for instance; fiction, non-fiction, poetry, and drama are all genres of literature. However, within these genres are **subgenres,** which are mini-categories within the large category. Example: within the fiction category its subgenre includes: historical fiction, fantasy, science fiction, mystery, romance, etc. Once we have a clear understanding of genre, we will look at questions on the exam that will ask you to respond to a specific genre.

CHAPTER FOCUS

Understanding Genres

Fiction—The Novel
- Historical Novels
- Science Fiction
- Fantasy Novels
- Mystery or Detective Stories
- Romance Novels

- Bildungsroman
- Picaresque Novels
- Epistolary Novels
- Stream of Consciousness Novels

Nonfiction
- Speeches
- Diaries and Memoirs
- Autobiographies

- Biographies
- Magazine, Newspaper, Journal Articles, and Editorials
- Essays

Poetry
- Ballads
- Blank Verse
- Concrete Poetry
- Didactic Poems
- Dramatic Monologues
- Elegies

- Epic Poems
- Free Verse
- Limericks
- Narrative Poems
- Sonnets

Drama

Chapter Review and Quick Quiz

UNDERSTANDING GENRES

Fiction—The Novel

TIP

If you absolutely do not know the answer, mark the question, leave it and come back to it later.

The first **genre** that we are going to look at is **fiction** (writings that are invented and not true) or more specifically, the **novel.** This genre is by far the most common in all of literature. You probably read several novels each year in your English class. The novel is a long narrative (a writing that tells a story) that deals with characters, settings, and incidents upon which the story is built or developed. The author invents the characters and situations with the intent of entertaining the reader. There are many different types of novels, which are the **subgenres.** Let's take a look at them.

HISTORICAL NOVELS. Usually set in times of great conflict or social change, historical novels attempt to recreate a historically important series of events or depict specific personae, or people vital to that event. Although the foundation of the historical novel is based upon actual events, as are the details of dress, manners, and other aspects of daily life, the author fictionalizes the story in many other ways by adding and subtracting details to move the story along. Examples of historical novels are: Sir Walter Scott's *Rob Roy* and *Ivanhoe*, Victor Hugo's *Les Miserables*, Leo Tolstoy's *War and Peace*, and Margaret Mitchell's *Gone with the Wind.*

EXAMPLE

1. Which of the following novels would be categorized as an example of historical fiction?

   (A) *The Pearl* by John Steinbeck
   (B) *War and Peace* by Leo Tolstoy
   (C) *Fahrenheit 451* by Ray Bradbury
   (D) *The Color Purple* by Alice Walker

Your Answer: Ⓓ

ANALYSIS

The correct answer is B. *War and Peace* by Leo Tolstoy is a historical novel based on the events surrounding the invasion of Russia by Napoleon of France. There are over five hundred characters as well as a variety of themes and action that makes *War and Peace* a monumental work. *The Pearl* and *The Color Purple* are novels that depict characters who deal with major conflict. *Fahrenheit 451* is a science fiction novel written by Ray Bradbury. It is set in the future and deals primarily with censorship and the burning of books.

SCIENCE FICTION. This subgenre is set usually in the future or in an imaginary world. The themes, settings, plots, and characters are based on some scientific or technological speculation or theorization. Jules Verne's *Around the World in Eighty Days* and *20,000 Leagues Under the Sea*, H. G. Wells' *The War of the Worlds* and *The Time Machine*, Ray Bradbury's *Fahrenheit 451* and *The Illustrated Man*, and Arthur C. Clarke's *2001: A Space Odyssey* are examples of the subgenre of science fiction.

EXAMPLE

2. Which of the following novels would be included in the subgenre of science fiction?

    (A) *Romeo and Juliet* by William Shakespeare
    (B) *Wuthering Heights* by Emily Brontë
    (C) *A Farewell to Arms* by Ernest Hemingway
    (D) *The War of the Worlds* by H. G. Wells

Your Answer:

ANALYSIS

Romeo and Juliet is a play about "two star-crossed lovers," which was written by Shakespeare. *Wuthering Heights* is a novel of a family torn apart by the adoption of a homeless waif and the subsequent years of revenge and hate. *A Farewell to Arms* is the love story of a nurse and a wartime ambulance driver. **A, B,** and **C** are incorrect. **The correct answer is D.** *The War of the Worlds* is about an alien invasion. It caused quite a controversy when it was read on the radio; people believed that the invasion was actually happening.

FANTASY NOVELS. These are written for either pure enjoyment or as serious or satirical (writing that blends humor and wit with criticism on human affairs or institutions, most often politics). Fantasy novels are set in an imaginary, unreal, or utopian (an ideal) world and usually involve fantastic or unbelievable characters. Examples of fantasy novels include: *Gulliver's Travels* by Jonathan Swift (a utopian and a political satire), *Alice's Adventures in Wonderland* by Lewis Carroll, J. R. R. Tolkien's *The Lord of the Rings*, and the *Harry Potter* novels by J. K. Rowling.

EXAMPLE

3. Which of the following novels would be considered a part of the subgenre of fantasy?

    (A) *The Lord of the Rings* by J. R. R. Tolkien
    (B) *The Old Gringo* by Carlos Fuentes
    (C) *Don Quixote* by Miguel de Cervantes
    (D) *Moby Dick* by Herman Melville

Your Answer:

ANALYSIS

The correct answer is A. The *Lord of the Rings* is a trilogy of novels set in the world of Middle Earth. J. R. R. Tolkien is widely admired for his fantasies that are based on small people he calls Hobbits. Answers **B, C,** and **D** are novels, but definitely not fantasy, although the whale in *Moby Dick* could possibly be considered fantastic in a sense.

MYSTERY OR DETECTIVE STORIES. This is a subgenre in which a mystery or crime is solved by a detective. The reader is presented with the clues at the same time that the detective uncovers them. Usually, in a detective story, the emphasis is on the plot. However, many authors develop very strong main characters (or protagonists) as well as plot.

EXAMPLE

4. Read the following passage and then select the literary subgenre to which it belongs.

At three o'clock precisely I was at Baker Street, but Holmes had not yet returned. The landlady informed me that he had left the house shortly after eight o'clock in the morning. I sat down beside the fire, however, with the intention of awaiting him, however long he might be. I was already deeply interested in his inquiry, for, though it was surrounded by none of the grim and strange features which were associated with the two crimes which I have already recorded, still, the nature of the case and the exalted station of his client gave it a character of its own. Indeed, apart from the nature of the investigation which my friend had on hand, there was something in his masterly grasp of a situation, and his keen, incisive reasoning, which made it a pleasure for me to study his system of work, and to follow the quick, subtle methods by which he disentangled the most inextricable mysteries. So accustomed was I to his invariable success that the very possibility of his failing had ceased to enter into my head.

(A) Fantasy
(B) Historical fiction
(C) Detective
(D) Picaresque

Your Answer: Ⓐ Ⓑ Ⓒ Ⓓ

ANALYSIS

From reading the passage, the words "crime" and "case" are mentioned and the tone of the writing seems mysterious. Answers **A, B,** and **D** can be ruled out easily by paying close attention to the wording of the passage carefully. **The correct answer is C.**

ROMANCE NOVELS. These depend upon the very fertile imagination of the author rather than on real-life events. The settings, characters, and action are often depicted in a series of episodes that involve adventure in exotic settings, gallant love, heroic deeds, and mysterious events. In the Middle Ages, **chivalric** (the brave knight on the white horse type) **romances** such as *Sir Gawain and the Green Knight* dealt with damsels in distress as well as the knight's many encounters with monsters and giants. Today, we think of the romance novel as the **popular romance** typified by the Harlequin Romances.

EXAMPLE

5. Read the passage below and determine which subgenre of literature it belongs to.

   Mara had never expected to see the man again. She wasn't sure she wanted to see him now.

   But there he stood, dominating the doorway of Books and Such. Mara owned the bookstore just off the picturesque main square in Freeburg, a small, close-knit town in southern Maryland.

   There he stood, Mick Swanson, the man who, a year ago, had pretended to love her and then had broken off their brief but intense relationship as if it meant nothing.

   His neatly trimmed, sandy hair and the tailored overcoat stretching across his broad shoulders gave Mick the air of a man in charge. But there was wariness in those blue eyes that touched Mara more than she wanted to admit.

   (A) Fantasy
   (B) Science Fiction
   (C) Historical
   (D) Romance

Your Answer: Ⓐ Ⓑ Ⓒ Ⓓ

ANALYSIS

The correct answer is D. After reading the passage, one can easily determine the answer with all of the references to "love." The tone of the writing is mushy—gooey, and certainly could not be identified with fantasy, science fiction, or historical fiction. This is definitely a romance novel.

BILDUNGSROMAN. This is a type of novel that follows the development of a character or hero's education or life from youth to experience. The term actually translated from German means "development novel." It was originally coined to describe Wolfgang von Goethe's novel *Wilhelm Meister's Apprenticeship*. Other examples of the bildungsroman are *David Copperfield* by Charles Dickens, Charlotte Brontë's *Jane Eyre*, Hermann Hesse's *Demian*, Saul Bellow's *The Adventures of Augie March*, and Doris Lessing's *Children of Violence*.

EXAMPLE

6. The subgenre of fiction that follows the education of a hero from youth to experience is called _____

   (A) bildungsroman.
   (B) fantasy.
   (C) romance.
   (D) science fiction.

Your Answer: Ⓓ

ANALYSIS

The correct answer is A.

PICARESQUE NOVELS. These are novels whose main character lives by his or her wits and becomes involved in one predicament after another. It usually takes the form of a series of journeys in which the main character's many adventures involve people from all walks of life. The picaresque tales originated in Spain and the most famous of all is the novel by Miguel de Cervantes, *Don Quixote*. Mark Twain's *Huckleberry Finn*, Henry Fielding's *Tom Jones*, and Daniel Defoe's *Moll Flanders* are all examples of the picaresque novel.

EXAMPLE

7. A picaresque novel is one whose main character becomes involved in one predicament after another. Which of the following does NOT represent a picaresque novel?

   (A) *Don Quixote* by Miguel de Cervantes
   (B) *The Grapes of Wrath* by John Steinbeck
   (C) *Moll Flanders* by Daniel Defoe
   (D) *Tom Jones* by Henry Fielding

Your Answer: Ⓓ

ANALYSIS

Make certain you read the questions carefully. This is one of those that could fool you. It asks for the answer that does *not* represent a picaresque novel. **The correct answer is B.** *The Grapes of Wrath* is about a desperate family that moves from Oklahoma to California in search of work during the depression. Choices **A, C,** and **D** are all examples of picaresque novels.

EPISTOLARY NOVELS. These are written through correspondence or letter-writing between characters. It was a form of novel writing that was made popular in the eighteenth century. Examples of the epistolary novel are: Samuel Richardson's *Pamela and Clarissa Harlowe,* but more recently are Alice Walker's *The Color Purple* and John Barth's *Letters.*

EXAMPLE

8. An epistolary novel is one that is written through _____ between one or more characters.

    (A) oral conversations
    (B) written correspondence
    (C) first-person fiction
    (D) third-person fiction

Your Answer:

ANALYSIS

The correct answer is B. The epistolary novel is correspondence between one or more characters. Answers **A, C,** and **D** are wrong. First-person fiction uses "I" as the narration, while third-person fiction uses "he," "she," or "it" in narrating the story.

THE STREAM OF CONSCIOUSNESS NOVEL. This is one that might appear to be a bit unusual at first. It is a type of psychological novel in which the story emerges through the inner workings of one (or more) of the main characters. On the page, the stream of consciousness novel appears to be made of fragmented sentences, unusual capitalization and punctuation and spacing. The author's use of dashes and other typographical oddities are intended to present the character's thoughts as disjointed and illogical, which they usually are. Examples of this type of novel are: James Joyce's *Ulysses,* Virginia Woolf's *Mrs. Dalloway* and *To the Lighthouse,* as well as William Faulkner's *As I Lay Dying.*

EXAMPLE

9. Read the following passage and identify the subgenre to which it belongs.

STATELY, PLUMP BUCK MULLIGAN CAME FROM THE STAIRHEAD, bearing a bowl of lather on which a mirror and a razor lay crossed. A yellow dressing gown, ungirdled, was sustained gently-behind him by the mild morning air. He held the bowl aloft and intoned:

— Introibo ad altare Dei.

Halted, he peered down the dark winding stairs and called up coarsely:

— Come up, Kinch. Come up, you fearful jesuit.

Solemnly he came forward and mounted the round gunrest. He faced about and blessed gravely thrice the tower, the surrounding country and the awaking mountains. Then, catching sight of Stephen Dedalus, he bent towards him and made rapid crosses in the air, gurgling in his throat and shaking his head. Stephen Dedalus, displeased and sleepy, leaned his arms on the top of the staircase and looked coldly at the shaking gurgling face that blessed him, equine in its length, and at the light untonsured hair, grained and hued like pale oak.

Buck Mulligan peeped an instant under the mirror and then covered the bowl smartly.

— Back to barracks, he said sternly.

He added in a preacher's tone:

— For this, O dearly beloved, is the genuine Christine: body and soul and blood and ouns. Slow music, please. Shut your eyes, gents. One moment. A little trouble about those white corpuscles. Silence, all.

(A) Science Fiction
(B) Fantasy
(C) Epistolary
(D) Stream of Consciousness

Your Answer: Ⓓ

ANALYSIS

The correct answer is D. After a brief review of the passage things just don't appear normal do they? Stream of consciousness novels are a bit odd when compared to the "normal" writing of a typical novel. Answers **A** and **B** are obviously incorrect. And, if you didn't know that an epistolary novel was one that is written in the form of letters, you might be confused. But, **D is the correct answer.**

Nonfiction

As you know, nonfiction is a generalized term for writing that is based on truth. The information is real and not imagined like that of novels. Although nonfiction is considered a literary genre, or a main category, it is important to become familiar with the types of nonfiction that are among its many subgenres. Biographies, autobiographies, speeches, diaries, memoirs, essays, editorials, journal articles, and magazine and newspaper articles are all examples of nonfiction.

SPEECHES. These are given by all sorts of people for all sorts of reasons. Most often we listen to speeches being given by a speaker, however, in school, especially in history or English classes; we read and study them to help us understand what exactly was going on during a specific period of time. Most often speeches are given to either inform the listener or to persuade the listener. It would be impossible to go into detail about the number and subjects of speeches given around the world, but the following list of quotes are from speeches that are well known and often referred to not only on examinations, but in daily life as well.

From: Abraham Lincoln's Gettysburg Address given on November 19, 1863: "Four score and seven years ago our fathers brought forth, on this continent, a new nation, conceived in Liberty, and dedicated to the proposition that all men are created equal."

From: Martin Luther King, Jr.'s "I Have a Dream" speech given at the Lincoln Memorial in Washington D.C. in 1963 during the March on Washington: "I have a dream that my four little children will one day live in a nation where they will not be judged by the color of their skin but by the content of their character."

From: President Franklin D. Roosevelt's inaugural address in 1933: "The only thing we have to fear is fear itself."

From: U.S. Supreme Court Justice William O. Douglas's speech on the court: "The court is really the keeper of the conscience, and the conscience is the Constitution."

From: President John F. Kennedy's inaugural address: "Ask not what your country can do for you, ask what you can do for your country."

From: The lunar surface, 240,000 miles from Earth on July 20, 1969, Neil Armstrong said to the world as he took that first historic step: "That's one small step for man, one giant leap for mankind."

EXAMPLE

10. "We have nothing to fear, but fear itself," is a statement made famous by _____, who was speaking at his inauguration in 1933.

    (A) Abraham Lincoln
    (B) Frank Sinatra
    (C) John F. Kennedy
    (D) Franklin D. Roosevelt

Your Answer: Ⓓ

ANALYSIS

The question is very specific in what it is asking, but you need to know a little about American history. First of all, Answer **B** is there and completely wrong because Frank Sinatra was a singer and was never inaugurated as president. Abraham Lincoln and John F. Kennedy (**A** and **C**) were presidents, but their inaugurations are at completely different times than the one stated in the question. So, by process of elimination, **the correct answer is D.**

DIARIES AND MEMOIRS. These are similar in that they are written to remember incidents in our lives; diaries, however, are usually written by people to record events and thoughts on a regular basis. Undoubtedly, one of the most famous of all diaries is *Anne Frank: A Diary of a Young Girl.* Of course, there are hundreds of other notable diaries published; many of them are the writings of politicians and often the writings of well-known authors or poets such as: Jonathan Swift, Ralph Waldo Emerson, Theodore Roosevelt, and Charles Lindbergh. Diaries are often published after the author dies—posthumously. Memoirs, on the other hand, are usually written to record a single period of the author's life that will often coincide with an historical event. Homer Hickam's *Rocket Boys: A Memoir* (a.k.a.: *October Sky*), Ji-li Jiang's *Red Scarf Girl: A Memoir of the Cultural Revolution,* and Frank McCourt's *Angela's Ashes: A Memoir,* are examples of memoirs.

EXAMPLE

11. True or False. Memoirs are usually written to record a specific period of the author's life.

    (A) True
    (B) False

Your Answer:

ANALYSIS

A is the correct answer.

AUTOBIOGRAPHIES. These are written as an account of all or a part of a person's life. In most cases, the writing is in the form of narration or telling the story of important life events, but often, the author manages to weave into the writing introspective thoughts as well as imagination. Autobiographical writings offer glimpses into the author's world through his or her own eyes. We are able to more clearly experience the author's personality, attitudes, and thoughts we probably would not experience otherwise. Examples of autobiographies are: *Up from Slavery* by Booker T. Washington, *Autobiography* by Benjamin Franklin, *The Education of Henry Adams* by, of course, Henry Adams, *I Know Why the Caged Bird Sings* by Maya Angelou, *Confessions* by Jean-Jacques Rousseau, *True Relation* *of My Birth, Breeding and Life* by Margaret Cavendish, and the *Confessions* of St. Augustine.

EXAMPLE

12. True or False. Autobiographies are NOT written by the authors about themselves.

    (A) True
    (B) False

Your Answer:

ANALYSIS

The correct answer is B, False. Autobiographies are written by the authors about themselves.

BIOGRAPHIES. These are written by someone about someone else. As opposed to autobiographies, which are written by someone about themselves. Biographies, usually fact-based writings, <u>ideally</u> (because some of them are unauthorized) are accurate accounts of the person's character, personality, and career. Biographies have been written about people in all walks of life including: artists, actors, inventors, explorers, mathematicians, doctors, businessmen and -women, scientists, anthropologists, saints, composers, musicians, and politicians, to name but a few—and everyone from Archimedes to Max Zorn is included in this large sub-genre of literary works.

EXAMPLE

13. Nonfictional literary works that are written specifically about a real person are called

_____.

    (A) fantasies
    (B) diaries
    (C) biographies
    (D) science fiction

Your Answer: Ⓑ Ⓒ Ⓓ

ANALYSIS

The correct answer is C. Both **A** and **D** are fictional (not real) and diaries (**B**) are writings by people who record their thoughts and impressions of life or events that are happening around them.

Included in this last category of nonfiction are **magazine articles, newspaper articles, journal articles, editorials,** and **essays.**

MAGAZINE ARTICLES. These need little explaining; they are what they are, depending primarily on the type of magazine. There are news magazines, fashion magazines, women's magazines, men's magazines, children's magazines, and motorcycle, sewing, automobile, running, and skiing magazines—magazines for almost all interests and hobbies. The articles are obviously written to help sell the magazine, which means they must be interesting to the reader. The structure of the article again depends upon the magazine type. Most often though, the beginning of the articles usually have a **hook**, as a fisherman would use bait on a hook to attract a fish's attention, or something that will attract the reader's attention and invite or encourage him or her to read further. A hook might be a question or a quote, a strong statement, an interesting fact, or an anecdote (brief story) that catches the reader's attention like this quote:

"I personally believe that each and every one of us was put here for a purpose, and that's to build and not to destroy. And if by chance some day you're not feeling well, you should remember some silly little thing that I've said or done, and it brings back a smile to your face or a chuckle to your heart, then my purpose as the clown has been fulfilled." (Red Skelton)

or this fact:

Sharks are carnivorous. There are over 250 species of the torpedo-shaped fish with strong jaws and bony teeth and at least 10 species are known to attack humans.

These are hooks—something that will interest the reader. The remainder of the article builds upon and around the hook.

EXAMPLE

14. A magazine article often begins with a device that attracts the reader's attention and encourages him or her to read more of the article. This device is called a
_____.

(A) sinker
(B) worm
(C) hook
(D) pole

Your Answer: (A) (B) (C) (D)

ANALYSIS

The correct answer is C. Although the remaining answers are related to the topic of fishing, which is what a hook does—fishes for readers, **A, B,** and **D** are incorrect.

NEWSPAPER ARTICLES. These provide the reader with information that is usually tied to current events or things that are happening at the moment or within a recent period of time. When you read a newspaper article, notice the organization of the article. The manner in which this information is given to the reader is very important. In the newspaper business, they call it the **inverted pyramid**. In the inverted pyramid, you will find the **lead**, which is the really long sentence (or first paragraph) that begins the article and usually includes the "5 Ws and an H" (who, what, where, when, why, and how). The rest of the information that is included is listed according to its importance to the article and that is how the remainder of the pyramid is set up: important information at the top, least important at the bottom. An example of a lead might be:

> "An earthquake measuring 4.3 on the Richter scale, but causing no major damage, was reported by Cal Tech to have been centered in the Big Bear area northeast of Los Angeles and jolted Southern Californian's from their sleep last night at 11:30 P.M. as far away as Oceanside."

Another type of article published in the newspaper is not tied to current events (most of the time), but written for human interest. These articles are called **feature stories** or **features.** Features can be written about any one of a million subjects. Sometimes, they are tied into a current event. For example, if the current event is about the discovery of a new planet or comet, the feature article might be about a powerful telescope or the history of astronomy. Newspaper articles are intended to provide facts about current events or about human interest stories. Whether the article is about international, national, state, or local, political, sports, tragic, or otherwise, the newspaper article keeps the reader informed.

EXAMPLE

15. The first line of a news story is called a _____.
    (A) lead
    (B) editorial
    (C) feature
    (D) tragedy

Your Answer: (A) (B) (C) (D)

ANALYSIS

The correct answer is A. D is easy to eliminate; **B** and **C** are both parts of a newspaper, but **A** is the only one that is a specific part of an article and the obvious correct answer.

EDITORIALS. In keeping with the newspaper/magazine subgenre, editorials are writings that are included in most newspapers and in many magazines. These writings express the opinions of the editors of either the newspaper or the magazine. The editorial may be about an event in the news or an important topic of some sort. For instance, a Supreme Court ruling on censorship of the Internet might prompt an editor to write an opinion piece on the subject. In most cases, these opinions reflect the nature of the paper or magazine: some newspapers are conservative, others are liberal, and yet others take a middle-of-the-road approach, which means they don't take a strong stance either way. In many newspapers, the editorial section (which is usually two pages of writings) includes **letters to the editor** and **op-ed** pieces. Letters to the editor are short writings submitted by readers with varying opinions on a certain topic. Op-ed writings, which are usually on the page opposite the editorials, and usually include opinions that are opposite those of the editor, are intended to provide the reader with a broader view of an issue. A well-informed reader is one who has read or understands both sides of the issue and is capable of making an informed or intelligent judgment on it. Knowing both sides of an issue is extremely important for all citizens.

EXAMPLE

16. Editorials express the opinion of the newspaper or magazine and are written by the _____.

   (A) printer
   (B) staff writer
   (C) editor
   (D) chief executive officer

Your Answer: Ⓐ Ⓑ Ⓒ Ⓓ

ANALYSIS

The correct answer is C. The editorial staff is responsible for writing the editorials of the newspaper. Answers **A, B,** and **D** are all members of the newspaper organization, but none are responsible for the opinion pieces.

JOURNAL ARTICLES. These are articles written by the author for a specific audience, usually a profession or career. For instance, doctors, educators, attorneys, accountants, scientists, and computer engineers who write about their professions, usually submit these writings to a journal that interests people in their field. The articles are used to inform. They are intended to keep people in the profession aware of new methods, techniques, equipment, or studies that could affect what they do professionally on a daily basis. Of course, these articles contain **jargon** that is unique to the profession. For instance, doctors use words that most likely only they would understand. Asking a doctor to read a journal article written for a structural engineer would be as challenging for the doctor as it would be for the structural engineer to understand a medical journal. However, journal articles are vital in keeping members in specific professions informed with the latest research and most current information possible.

EXAMPLE

17. Professional journals are written for a specific audience. The language that is used in the journal is unique to the audience being targeted. This language is called _____.

    (A) slang
    (B) dialect
    (C) academic language
    (D) jargon

Your Answer: (A) (B) (C) (D)

ANALYSIS

The correct answer is D. C might confuse you because most journals use academic language, but not all journals are academic; therefore, **C** is incorrect. Answers **A** and **B** are both wrong because slang is language used informally with friends, and dialects are the words and pronunciations used in a specific area of the country.

ESSAYS. There are many of these around, and they have been around since at least the sixteenth century. Essays are written for many reasons and believe it or not, people who are not in school write essays! Some are published in journals and magazines or in literature anthologies. Here are a few of the essays that you will most likely be asked to write: **expository** (explains something), **narrative** (tells about something), **comparison/contrast** (explains the similarities and differences between two things), **persuasive** (meant to encourage the reader to your opinion), and **autobiographical** (about yourself), among others. The styles in which these essays are written vary as well. Some essays are **formal** and others are **informal**. Formal essays are serious and logically organized, similar to those you write in your English class or your history class. However, informal essays are usually humorous or whimsical and <u>less</u> formal in their structure. Informal essays are intended for entertainment and less conclusive than formal essays. Yes, essays are everywhere. We will discuss essay writing later in the book, because you are going to write one for the exit exam.

EXAMPLE

18. Essays are written in two basic styles: _____ and _____.

   (A) messy and neat
   (B) formal and informal
   (C) confusing and clear
   (D) cohesive and noncohesive

Your Answer: (A) (B) (C) (D)

ANALYSIS

The correct answer is B. Answer **A** is the odd answer out—the one that is most obviously wrong. Answers **C** and **D,** while certainly they could apply to an essay as being either clear or confusing, or structurally cohesive or not, they don't appropriately apply to the manner in which the essay is written in a more authoritarian sense.

Poetry

As the English poet William Wordsworth wrote, poetry is "the spontaneous overflow of powerful feelings . . . recollected in tranquility." Or, as the American poet Marianne Moore states, poetry consists of "imaginary gardens with real toads in them." However you want to describe or define it, poetry is intense, imaginative, and rich in meaning. Written differently on the page than prose (paragraph writing), poets choose their words very carefully. The words are chosen not only for meaning, but for sound and rhythm as well. Poets are able to express meaning through a number of **literary devices;** it has been said that poetry is painting with words. And, if you look closely at poetry, you might find that the poet's use of words is inspiring. We are going to take a look at various types of poems and address the literary devices used in them.

BALLADS. The ballad is a form of narrative poetry (tells a story). It often tells a story of tragedy, for instance, a doomed love affair, family feuds, historical events, battles, shipwrecks, or murders. Ballads also tell the stories of outlaws and rebels like Robin Hood or Jesse James, or admired heroes like John Henry and Casey Jones. Ballads have a distinct rhyme scheme. This is the way the lines are written and which words rhyme at the end. For instance, the ballad rhyme scheme is *abcb*. This means that the first three lines, which are lines *a*, *b*, and *c*, do not rhyme with each other. But, the fourth line rhymes with line *b*, which is the second line. Look at the example of the ballad rhyme scheme that follows:

From: Ballad of Birmingham by Dudley Randall
(On the bombing of a church in Birmingham, Alabama, 1963)

"Mother dear, may I go downtown	(a)
Instead of out to play,	(b)
And march the streets of Birmingham	(c)
In a Freedom March today?"	(b)

Notice how the ending words on lines 1, 2, and 3 do not rhyme? But, notice how the ending words on lines 2 and 4 *do* rhyme—(play rhymes with today). That's the ballad rhyme scheme! Ballads have been written for centuries and are often sung. A slightly more recent example is a song written by Paul Simon in 1966. In this poem, Simon adapts a poem that was written by Edwin Arlington Robinson titled "Richard Cory." Look at the first four lines of the song, which is another example of the ballad rhyme scheme.

They say that Richard Cory owns
One half of this old town,
With elliptical connections
To spread his wealth around.

EXAMPLE

19. A ballad is a narrative poem that is often written about a tragedy, a disaster, a hero, or a rebel. The rhyme scheme of the ballad is _____

   (A) *abab*.
   (B) *abcabc*.
   (C) *abac*.
   (D) *abcb*.

Your Answer: Ⓐ Ⓑ Ⓒ Ⓓ

ANALYSIS

D is the correct answer.

BLANK VERSE. This is unrhymed **iambic pentameter**. And what is iambic pentameter? Well, iambic pentameter is a line of poetry that has words that are unstressed and stressed (or 5 metrical feet). What does that mean? Basically, a line of blank verse has 10 syllables. These 10 syllables are broken up into groups of 2 syllables, which means there are 5 groups and these are called metrical feet. The first syllable of the 10 is unstressed, meaning that it is softer in sound. The second syllable is stressed, which means it sounds louder than the first syllable. Since we are talking about feet, think of it as walking. If you were to walk toe-to-heel, which is opposite of your normal heel-toe walk, putting your toe down first is softer (like walking on tiptoes) than if you did it the other way. Toe-to-heel = unstressed— stressed. In other words, every other syllable in a line of blank verse, which is written in unrhymed iambic pentameter, is either unstressed (soft) or stressed (loud). Look at the example from Christopher Marlowe's play Dr. Faustus:

> Was this the face that launched a thousand ships
> And burned the topless towers of Ilium?

> **Now once again, but this time with *syllabication*:**
> ˘ = unstressed syllable
> ´ = stressed syllable

> Wăs/ thís/ thĕ/ faće/ thăt/ laúnched/ ă/ thóu/ sănd/ shíps
> 1   2   3   4   5   6   7   8   9   10

Blank verse has been used for centuries. William Shakespeare in particular, used blank verse extensively throughout his plays. Below is a sample of blank verse by Robert Frost, an American poet.

> *From* "Mending Wall": By Robert Frost

> Something there is that doesn't love a wall.
> That sends the frozen-ground-swell under it,
> And spills the upper boulders in the sun;
> And makes gaps even two can pass abreast.
> The work of hunters is another thing:
> I have come after them and made repair
> Where they have left not one stone on a stone,
> But they would have the rabbit out of hiding,
> To please the yelping dogs. The gaps I mean,
> No one has seen them made or heard them made,
> But at spring mending-time we find them there.

EXAMPLE

20. True or False. Blank verse is unrhymed iambic pentameter and contains five metrical feet or a total of ten syllables.

   (A) True
   (B) False

Your Answer: Ⓐ Ⓑ

ANALYSIS

The correct answer is A. Blank verse is unrhymed iambic pentameter.

CONCRETE POETRY. It is easier to refer to this type of poem as a shape poem, because the poem is written about and usually in the shape of its subject. For instance, think about a feather; if you were to write a poem about a feather, you would probably mention its airy lightness of being, among other things, and then you would write the poem on the paper, in the actual shape of a feather. See the example below, a poem in the box!

> Have you ever wondered about a box with its lines so simple, so straight and unassuming? Its life is defined by containment—at times cooperative and at others rebellious—screaming at its fullness bursting with discontent. Ah yes, the life of a box, fulfilling, empty, or somewhere in between. Plain brown cardboard, intricately carved wooden teak or mahogany inlaid with mother of pearl or the haughtiness of gold disguising its undemanding ranks. The box, have you ever considered?

EXAMPLE

21. Concrete poetry is a poetry that _____.

   (A) is written in the shape or form of something
   (B) is written with words that are backwards
   (C) is sonnetlike in its structure
   (D) has a rhyme scheme of *abab*

Your Answer: Ⓐ Ⓑ Ⓒ Ⓓ

ANALYSIS

B is a nonsense answer. **C** and **D** have nothing to do with being concrete, or taking a shape that is what concrete poetry does. **The correct answer is A.**

DIDACTIC POEMS. These are poems that teach morals, the good life, or instruct in specific areas of knowledge. This type of poem was favored by the classical Latin poets and eighteenth-century English poets. Below is an example of a didactic poem written by Ovid, a Roman poet who lived from 43 B.C.–17 A.D.

Ovid's

METAMORPHOSES

BOOK XV

Translated by Mr. Dryden, and Others.

The PYTHAGOREAN

PHILOSOPHY.

By Mr. DRYDEN

A king is sought to guide the growing State,
One able to support the Publick Weight,
And fill the Throne where *Romulus* had fate.
Renown, which oft bespeaks the Publick
Voice,

Had recommended *Numa* to their Choice:
A peacefull, pious Prince; who not content
To know the *Sabine* Rites, his Study bent
To cultivate his Mind; to learn the Laws
Of Nature, and explore their hidden Cause.
Urg'd by this Care, his Country he forsook,
And to Crotona thence his Journey took.
Arriv'd, he first enquir'd the Founder's Name
Of this new Colony; and whence he came.
Then thus a Senior of the Place replies,
(Well read, and curious of Antiquities)

EXAMPLE

22. True or False. Didactic poetry is considered instructional or teaching poetry.

   (A) True
   (B) False

Your Answer: (A) (B)

ANALYSIS

The correct answer is A.

DRAMATIC MONOLOGUE. These are poems that allow a single character to speak out about a dramatic situation and the entire episode is overheard by a silent listener. The poet Robert Browning who wrote "My Last Duchess" is famous for his poetry using this technique. The dramatic monologue below was written by Johann Wolfgang Goethe, a German poet, playwright, and novelist.

May Day Celebration (MAILIED)
by Johann Wolfgang von Goethe

Translation by John Sigerson

How grandly nature
Shines upon me!
How glistens the sun!
How laughs the mead!

From countless branches
The blossoms thrust,
A thousand voices
From underbrush,

O maiden, maiden,
How I love thee!
Your eye's a-sparkle—
How you love me!

Just as the lark loves
Singing and sky,
And morning-blooms thrive
On heav'n-mists high—

And joy ecstatic
Fills everyone.
O sun! O earth!
O risk! O fun!

O love, oh, lovely,
So golden fair
Like morning cloudlets
On that hill there!

You prosper grandly
The dew-fresh fields
With breath of flowers;
The whole Earth yields!

So do I love you,
Joy, courage, art
Who give me the youth,
With throbbing heart,

To fashion new songs,
New dances free.
Be ever happy,
As you love me!

EXAMPLE

23. True or False. Poetry that is considered dramatic monologue has more than three speakers or narrators in the poem.

   (A) True
   (B) False

Your Answer:

ANALYSIS

The correct answer is B, false. A monologue is one person speaking. Mono— means one. Dramatic monologue poetry is one-person narration.

ELEGIES. Originally, an elegy in classical times (which refers to ancient Greece), was a poem written in elegiac meter, which is rhyming iambic pentameter, and we all know what that is, right? Well, an elegy is a sad or mournful poem whose mood and tone are both sad and mournful. It is written for someone who has died. The following poem is an example of an elegy.

from Adonais (1821) By Percy Bysshe Shelley

I

I weep for Adonais—he is dead! Oh weep for Adonais! though our tears
Thaw not the frost which binds so dear a head!
And thou, sad Hour, selected from all years
To mourn our loss, rouse thy obscure compeers,
And teach them thine own sorrow, say: "With me
Died Adonais; till the future dares
Forget the past, his fate and fame shall be
An echo and a light unto eternity!"

II

Where wert thou, mighty Mother, when he lay,
When thy Son lay, pierc'd by the shaft which flies
In darkness? where was lorn Urania
When Adonais died? With veiled eyes,
'Mid listening Echoes, in her Paradise
She sate, while one, with soft enamour'd breath,
Rekindled all the fading melodies,
With which, like flowers that mock the corse beneath,
He had adorn'd and hid the coming bulk of Death.

EXAMPLE

24. An elegy is a poem written in a tone that is _____.

   (A) odd and sarcastic
   (B) happy and full of life
   (C) sad and mournful
   (D) friendly and light

Your Answer: (A) (B) (C) (D)

ANALYSIS

The correct answer is C. Answer A is way off, and answers **B** and **D** are total opposites of the true definition of an elegy.

EPIC POEMS. These are very long narrative poems that tell a story of a remote time and place and have characters who are larger than life. The story of the epic poem begins in the middle of the action or, as it is properly referred to, *in media res.* The epic poem uses many literary devices or conventions throughout its length such as catalogs (long lists), formal speeches, and epic similes (longer or extended), among many others. Its style is considered elevated, meaning formal or dignified. There are two types of epics; the folk epic and the literary epic. Folk epics are thought to have been passed along by oral tradition (or told aloud like storytelling), and their original authors are uncertain or unknown. The *Iliad*, the *Odyssey, Beowulf, Song of Roland*, the *Poem of Cid*, and *Mahabharata* are considered folk epics and come from various cultures—Greek to East Indian. Literary epics, on the other hand, are poems that are written and meant to be read like John Milton's "*Paradise Lost*" and Dante's "*Divine Comedy.*" Below is a preview of John Milton's *Paradise Lost.*

"Invocation" to Book I of *Paradise Lost*: By John Milton

Of man's first disobedience, and the fruit
Of that forbidden tree whose mortal taste
Brought death into the world, and all our woe,
With loss of Eden, till one greater Man
Restore us and regain the blissful seat,
Sing, Heavenly Muse, that, on the secret top
Of Oreb, or of Sinai, didst inspire
That shepherd who first taught the chosen seed
In the beginning how the Heavens and Earth
Rose out of Chaos: or, if Sion hill
Delight thee more, and Siloa's brook that flowed
Fast by the oracle of God, I thence
Invoke thy aid to my adventurous song,
That with no middle flight intends to soar
Above th' Aonian mount, while it pursues
Things unattempted yet in prose or rhyme

EXAMPLE

25. Epic poems incorporate _____.

   (A) minimal literary conventions
   (B) many literary conventions
   (C) French in at least one part
   (D) short and abrupt conventions

Your Answer: (A) (B) (C) (D)

ANALYSIS

The correct answer is B. Epic poems are known for incorporating many literary conventions. Answer **A** is the opposite and the other two answers make little sense at all.

FREE VERSE. Literally, this is a poem that is free of meter, rhyme, and other formalities of traditional verse. American poet Walt Whitman, French poets Charles Baudelaire and Paul Verlaine, and English poet Gerard Manley Hopkins were the frontrunners of this style of poetry in the nineteenth century. Most twentieth- and twenty-first-century poetry is free verse, although a few poets choose to revisit some of the older forms. Free verse allows the poet more freedom to play with words and sounds without the restrictions of iambic pentameter or rhyme schemes.

Calvary Crossing a Ford by Walt Whitman

A line in long array, where they wind betwixt green islands;
They take a serpentine course—their arms flash in the sun—hark to the
    musical clank;
Behold the silvery river—in it the splashing horses, loitering, stop to drink;
Behold the brown-faced men—each group, each person, a picture—the
    negligent rest on the saddles;
Some emerge on the opposite bank—others are just entering the ford—
    while,
Scarlet, and blue, and snowy white,
The guidon flags flutter gaily in the wind.

EXAMPLE

26. True or False. Free verse poetry is restrictive and follows very precise rhythms and
meter.

    (A) True
    (B) False

Your Answer:

ANALYSIS

The correct answer is B, false. As the name implies, free verse is exactly that. There
are no restrictions to the poems; poets are free to express themselves without following rigid formats of more formal types of poetry.

LIMERICKS. A limerick is a nonsense poem that has a specific pattern. It has five
lines and the rhyme scheme is *aabba*. Lines one, two, and five are longer and
rhyme and lines three and four are shorter and rhyme. These poems were popular
in the nineteenth century. The following example of a limerick is by Edward Lear.

> There was an Old Man with a beard,
> Who said, "It is just as I feared!
> Two Owls and a Hen,
> Four Larks and a Wren,
> Have all built their nests in my beard!"

EXAMPLE

27. A limerick poem is a _____ poem.

   (A) nonsense
   (B) serious
   (C) concrete
   (D) lengthy

Your Answer: (A) (B) (C) (D)

ANALYSIS

The correct answer is A. The limerick is silly and fun and full of nonsense. Answer **B** is the opposite; answers **C** and **D** are completely erroneous.

NARRATIVE POEMS. Narrative poems simply tell a story. If you look at the ballad and the epic poem explanations above, you will see two examples of narrative poems. Narrative poems have a beginning, a middle, and an end. Geoffrey Chaucer's *Canterbury Tales* is another example of a narrative poem. This is a series of tales about a variety of people who make a pilgrimage to a shrine in Canterbury, England. Each has their own tale to tell and all come from a wide spectrum of classes and occupations, which makes for an interesting read.

EXAMPLE

28. True or False. Narrative poems tell a story and have a beginning, middle, and end.

   (A) True
   (B) False

Your Answer: (A) (B)

ANALYSIS

The correct answer is A, true. Narrative poems tell a story and have a beginning, middle, and end.

SONNETS. Sonnets, sonnets—fourteen-lines of iambic pentameter (unstressed, stressed, toe, heel) originating in the thirteenth century by an Italian poet named Petrarch. The form arrived in England via Thomas Wyatt and it was then modified and made famous by William Shakespeare. So, we have the Italian sonnet and the Shakespearean sonnet. In English, the Shakespearean sonnet is easier to construct than the Italian sonnet because we have less rhyming ability in our language than do the Italians. Their rhyme schemes are different. Let's take a look at the rhyme schemes and then look at a sonnet written by Shakespeare.

The Italian or Petrarch sonnet rhyme scheme: **abba, abba, cde, cde**
The Shakespearean sonnet rhyme scheme: **abab, cdcd, efef, gg**

18

Shall I compare thee to a summer's day?
Thou art more lovely and more temperate:
Rough winds do shake the darling buds of May,
And summer's lease hath all too short a date;
Sometime too hot the eye of heaven shines,
And often is his gold complexion dimmed;
And every fair from fair sometime declines,
By chance or nature's changing course untrimmed:
But they eternal summer shall not fade,
Nor lose possession of that fair thou ow'st,
Nor shall death brag thou wand'rest in his shade,
When in eternal lines to time thou grow'st.
So long as men can breathe or eyes can see,
So long live this, and this gives life to thee.

EXAMPLE

29. Sonnets have _____ lines.

(A) twelve
(B) eighteen
(C) six
(D) fourteen

Your Answer: (A) (B) (C) (D)

ANALYSIS

The correct answer is D. The sonnet has fourteen lines—no more, no less.

Drama

This is our final category in the genre section. Dramas have been around for ages. They originated in ancient times with the Greeks who used drama for various religious ceremonies. The evolution of drama continued on into medieval times and the Renaissance, and up to the present. Drama is a literary work that is written using dialogue between characters that was performed on stage in front of an audience. There are all different types of plays: tragedy, comedy, history, farce, absurd, morality, one-act, and on and on. A play is distinct in the way that it is written, as it includes (usually) stage directions, scene settings, and the dramatis personae or characters named for each act. It is not typical reading that you are used to in fiction or nonfiction; it is more interrupted by the details that an author writing a novel would include in a paragraph; instead, a playwright usually adds settings, expressions, and so on as stage directions. There are thousands of playwrights, but the one you will be reminded of over and over again is William Shakespeare. To the English language, he is probably the best known and respected of them all.

EXAMPLE

30. Drama is written with _____.

    (A) spunk
    (B) confusion
    (C) character dialogue
    (D) darkness

Your Answer: (A) (B) (C) (D)

ANALYSIS

The correct answer is C. Answers **A, B,** and **D** are incorrect.

Chapter Review and Quick Quiz

Another chapter with a lot to say! We've covered everything from speeches to drama. Let's see how you remember what you've learned. The answers are in the appendix.

Directions: Match the letter of the correct definition of the literary term, put it in the space to the left.

ANSWER	LITERARY TERM		DEFINITION
_____	1. historical fiction	a.	work that depends on the fertile imagination of the author, romantically farfetched in nature
_____	2. science fiction	b.	narrative poem telling the story of a tragedy
_____	3. fantasy	c.	a broad category in which all literature is placed or typecast
_____	4. mystery	d.	verbalization of specific topic for audience

_____ 5. romance   **e.** work in which a single character speaks out in the poem

_____ 6. bildungsroman   **f.** written records of specific events in one's life

_____ 7. picaresque   **g.** work written by someone about someone else

_____ 8. epistolary   **h.** work that recreates historically important events

_____ 9. stream of consciousness   **i.** two types: formal and informal

_____ 10. speeches   **j.** a story written in dialogue

_____ 11. diaries   **k.** a sad and mournful poem about death

_____ 12. autobiography   **l.** work set in a futuristic or imaginary world

_____ 13. biography   **m.** a 14-line poem, either Italian or Shakespearean

_____ 14. news articles   **n.** writings by people about themselves

_____ 15. editorials   **o.** describing a story written through letter writing

_____ 16. essays   **p.** work in which random thoughts of characters are revealed

_____ 17. ballad   **q.** a mystery or crime solved by a detective

_____ 18. blank verse   **r.** writings that teach morals or about the good life

_____ 19. epic   **s.** a category of writings that are not true

_____ 20. didactic   **t.** a poem that tells a story

_____ 21. dramatic monologue   **u.** work in which the main character becomes involved in one predicament after another

_____ 22. elegy   **v.** long narrative poem with heroes of epic proportions

_____ 23. free verse   **w.** a category of writings that are factual, true

_____ 24. limerick   **x.** written opinions by an editor of a newspaper

_____ 25. narrative   **y.** a five-line nonsense poem

_____ **26.** sonnet

_____ **27.** drama

_____ **28.** fiction

_____ **29.** nonfiction

_____ **30.** genre

z. work set in an imaginary or unreal utopian world

aa. writings that usually contain the 5 Ws and H in the lead

bb. a poem free of rhyme and meter

cc. unrhymed iambic pentameter

dd. work that follows a main character from innocence to experience.

Literary Response and Analysis—Part II

In this chapter, we will be looking at what happens within a **narrative** text. Basically this is anything in the way of writing—short to long—that tells a story. In the last chapter, we looked at a variety of narratives from ballads, histories, epics and biographies, but here we will dig a little deeper and examine what goes on within the text of the narrative.

CHAPTER FOCUS

Understanding Narrative Texts

- Dialogues
- Monologues
- Soliloquies
- Asides
- Character Foils
- Character Traits (Characterization)
- Themes
- Plot and Conflict

- Foreshadowing
- Flashbacks
- Imagery
- Symbols and Symbolism
- Allegories
- Irony
- Narrator/Point of View
- Mood

Chapter Review and Quick Quiz

UNDERSTANDING NARRATIVE TEXTS

Dialogues

A **dialogue** is conversation between two or more people or characters in a narrative text. Dialogue provides clues not only about the characters themselves, but about the plot as well. Reading dialogue is like eavesdropping on someone's conversation, and from the information you receive as a reader in overhearing this conversation, you can either predict what might happen next, or discover what has happened before. Dialogue is written in plays, short stories, scripts, novels, and narrative poems. Dialogues written for scripts are straightforward; they don't bother with a great deal of stage directions for the most part because that's the director's job. On the other hand, scripts for plays are written with fairly specific stage directions because the playwright has something specific in mind when he/she wrote the play.

EXAMPLE

1. Read the two brief dialogues below. Determine which dialogue has been written for a script, and which has been written for a play.

#1 Band Camp California

Fred: Hey Lucy, the reed to my clarinet is broken, do you have a spare?

Lucy: If I had one I wouldn't give it to you.

Fred: Thanks Lucy, it's great to see you again too.

Lucy: Have you totally lost it or have you been playing your clarinet too long?

Fred: Look Lucy, what happened last summer, was last summer. Can we just move on and start over? I admit what we did was a little crazy, but this year is different . . . I've matured you'll see.

#2 The Secret of Life

Characters: Franny, a homemaker
     Lewis, her retired neighbor

Setting: The scene opens in Franny's small, dimly lit and cluttered kitchen. It has one windowed door, which is stage right. There is an old, grungy-looking table covered with a wrinkled plastic tablecloth. There are two chairs at either end of the table and Franny is sitting at one. Wearing an old housecoat with her hair tied in a bandana on her head, Franny seems to be pondering something and stares off across the room when she hears a knock at the door. Seeing that it is her neighbor Lewis, she motions for him to come into the kitchen. Lewis, an elderly man and quite handy to have around is wearing dirty overalls and a stained white T-shirt underneath. He enters the kitchen.

Lewis: *(Loudly, as he is hard of hearing)* Top o' the mornin' to ya' Franny!

Franny: *(Meekly)* Good morning Lew, how are you? Won't you sit and have a cup of coffee with me? *(Franny motions for him to sit as she stands to get the coffee from the stove.)*

Lewis: I'd love to take you up on that. *(Lewis sits down in the chair at the table.)* What you been up to Fran? I know I ain't no psychologist, but I can see somthins' bothrin' ya.' You seem mighty quiet this mornin'.

Franny: Well, Lewis. *(She pauses as she pours the coffee, serves it to him and then sits across the table.)* I don't rightly know how to explain just what I'm feeling, but something's come over me and I think my life has suddenly turned for the . . . well, I'm not real sure.

(A) #1 is written for a play and #2 for a script.
(B) #1 is written for a novel and #2 for a script.
(C) #1 is written for a script and #2 for a poem.
(D) #1 is written for a script and #2 for a play.

Your Answer: Ⓓ

ANALYSIS:

The correct answer is D. The dialogue of #1 was written as a script; note the simplicity and no stage directions, while #2 is specific about characters and stage directions, which is typical for a play. The other answers are either all or partially wrong; two of them, **B and C,** throw in answers that are really off base from the original question.

Monologues

When a character in a play (or in a narrative) is on stage alone, and he or she begins to speak, that is a monologue. It is usually a long speech and it usually reveals something important either about the action or about the thoughts of the character. A monologue is closely related to a **soliloquy,** which you will learn about next. There are two types of monologues. The **interior monologue,** which demonstrates the character's inner thoughts, is similar to **stream of consciousness** that we learned about in the last chapter. The audience or reader can actually hear the character thinking out loud. When a character is overheard speaking to a silent listener, that is known as a **dramatic monologue**. It reveals not only the personality of the speaker, but a dramatic situation as well.

EXAMPLE

2. The monologue is a long speech given by a character who is _____ on stage. It usually reveals something important either about the action or about the thoughts of the character.

   (A) alone
   (B) eating dinner
   (C) crying and sobbing
   (D) dressing

Your Answer: (A) (B) (C) (D)

ANALYSIS

The correct answer is A. A person in the middle of a monologue is alone and speaking on stage. Answers **B** and **C** are rather obscure and answer **D** is just wrong.

Soliloquies

A **soliloquy,** like an interior monologue, occurs when a character in a play is alone on stage and begins to think aloud. It is used to tell the audience what the character is thinking and what his motives or plans are. It is also used to provide information about earlier events that have occurred elsewhere or simply to provide additional background information. On the next page, you will find an example of one of the most famous of all soliloquies. This is Hamlet (à la Shakespeare) thinking aloud.

Act III, Scene 1

Hamlet

To be, or not to be; that is the question;
Whether 'tis noble in the mind to suffer
The slings and arrows of outrageous fortune,
Or to take arms against a sea of troubles,
And, by opposing, end them. To die, to sleep—
No more—and by a sleep to say we end
The heartache and the thousand natural shocks
That flesh is heir to—'tis a consummation
Devoutly to be wished. To die, to sleep.—
To sleep, perchance to dream. Ay, there's the rub,
For in that sleep of death what dreams may come
When we have shuffled off this mortal coil
Must give us pause. There's the respect
That makes calamity of so long life,
For who would bear the whips and scorns of time,
Th' oppressor's wrong, the proud man's contumely,
The pangs of disprized love, the law's delay,
The insolence of office, and the spurns
That patient merit of th' unworthy takes,
When he himself might his quietus make
With bare bodkin? Who would these fardels bear,
To grunt and sweat under a weary life,
But that the dread of something after death,
The undiscovered country from whose bourn
No traveler returns, puzzles, the will,
And makes us rather bear those ills we have
Than fly to others that we know not of?
Thus conscience does make cowards of us all,
And thus the native hue of resolution
Is sicklied o'er with the pale cast of thought,
And enterprises of great pitch and moment
With this regard their currents turn awry,
And lose the name of action.

EXAMPLE

3. A soliloquy is very similar to _____.

   (A) a character in a play
   (B) the climax of a novel
   (C) an interior monologue
   (D) an exterior monologue

Your Answer: Ⓓ

ANALYSIS

The correct answer is C. The soliloquy is very similar to the interior monologue; in fact, they could be considered synonyms. Answers **A** and **B** are nonsense and Answer **D** is there to confuse you—exterior? Interior!

Asides

Interesting name isn't it? But, an **aside** is when an actor on stage turns to the audience or someone standing nearby, and tells it something <u>allegedly</u> without being heard by the other actors. Asides are used for a comic effect or for a melodramatic effect and they reveal (like the monologue and soliloquy) inner thoughts or feelings of the character or a personal evaluation or interpretation of what is going on in the scene at the time.

EXAMPLE

4. True or False. An aside is an actor speaking to a group of actors on stage about an ongoing conflict.

   (A) True
   (B) False

Your Answer:

ANALYSIS

The correct answer is B, false. An aside is when an actor on stage turns to the audience and makes a comment, either comic or dramatic.

Character Foils

This is another interesting name and an interesting concept. **Character foils** are contrast characters or nearly the complete opposites of another character. What comes to mind right away are the Danny DiVito and Arnold Schwarzenegger characters in a film of the recent past (*Twins*). In drama however, the character foil who, for instance, may not be extremely bright, provides the opposite (or foil) for the intelligent or more wise character. The foil's lack of intelligence makes the wise person look even more intelligent.

EXAMPLE

5. The character foil is a near opposite of another character. The foil makes the other character appear _____ in whatever personality trait the character foil is weakest.

   (A) stronger
   (B) weaker
   (C) ill at ease
   (D) wild

Your Answer: (A) (B) (C) (D)

ANALYSIS

The correct answer is A. The character foil, as an opposite, allows the other character to appear stronger in whatever personality strength the character foil is lacking. Answers **B** and **C** could possibly confuse you if you didn't know what a foil was, but answer **D** is the throwaway answer—the first to eliminate.

Character Traits (or Characterization)

Characters come in all shapes, sizes, colors, and types. The technique that an author uses to develop characters is called characterization. A character in any narrative could be a main character (or the **protagonist**), or as a main character he or she/it could be an **antagonist** (someone who works against or who is in opposition of the protagonist). Characters can also be considered **minor characters.** Minor characters add a little bit of flavoring, but they are less important than the main character(s). Before we get into specific traits, you need to know that characters can be **static** or **dynamic:** static characters (remember the root system!) *stay* the same; they hardly change at all. On the other hand, dynamic characters are the opposite of static characters. Dynamic characters *change* from the beginning of the story or narrative, until the end. That's a lot of information in a little bit of time; let's quickly review.

NOTE: Remember the root system—
<u>pro</u> means for or in favor of
<u>ant</u> or <u>anti</u> means against (hence, protagonist and antagonist!)
<u>Sta</u> means stationary or stays the same = static
<u>dyn</u> means energetic or dynamic

- Main character = protagonist = the most important player or character in the story or narrative

- Main character = antagonist = in opposition to the protagonist, the bad guy <u>most</u> of the time

- Minor character = adds flavoring and spice but is less important

- Dynamic character = changes from beginning to end of the story
- Static character = remains the same or the changes are hardly noticeable

Now that *that* is clear, let's continue with the manner in which authors develop their characters (or characterization). Authors provide the reader with a broad spectrum of details about their characters: physical appearance, personality, speech, actions, thoughts and feelings, behavior, and interactions with other characters. Throughout a lifetime of reading, you will meet characters who assume all sorts of traits. Look at the list below (and these are just a few):

OUTGOING	AGGRESSIVE	ANTISOCIAL	CHIVALRIC	ENTHUSIASTIC
FORCEFUL	NEAT	CHARISMATIC	MESSY	APATHETIC
ORGANIZED	SENSITIVE	CHARMING	UNKEMPT	BOHEMIAN
IMPULSIVE	PERSUASIVE	CAREFUL	ATHLETIC	STRONG
HONEST	CONVENTIONAL	CONVINCING	IGNORANT	WEAK
CALM	ALERT	ANNOYING	EVIL	PERSISTANT
QUIET	LETHARGIC	RISK-TAKING	MEAN	PLEASANT
SLY	MANIPULATIVE	GENTLEMANLY	VULGAR	GUARDED
UNDERSTANDING	PERCEPTIVE	LADYLIKE	KIND	COMPETITIVE
DETERMINED	BOLD	SINFUL	CARING	DEXTEROUS
TALKATIVE	INTELLIGENT	IMMORAL	GENEROUS	ENERGETIC
DEMANDING	SOCIABLE	SAINTLY	STERN	

EXAMPLE

6. An antagonist is an important character in a narrative, but this character's role is _____.

   (A) to make the minor characters look bad
   (B) to make the protagonist laugh and sing
   (C) to take the place of the character foil
   (D) to be in opposition of the protagonist

Your Answer: Ⓓ

ANALYSIS

The correct answer is D. The antagonist's job is to be in opposition of the protagonist—almost complete opposites. Answers **A** and **B** are easily eliminated. There is a chance that **C** might confuse you if you were uncertain about the protagonist.

Themes

The author's message or the main idea of a work is the **theme.** Although the theme is not expressed overtly or specifically stated, it is represented through various images, characters, events, or actions. In reading a novel or any other narrative, discovering the theme oftentimes may be more like detective work. At times it is very subtle and difficult to figure out, but at other times it's right there in front of you. Following is a list of themes.

LONELINESS	FAMILY	VIOLENCE
COURAGE	FREEDOM	TRUTH
AMBITION	PATIENCE	REGRET
GREED	LOYALTY	SUCCESS
JEALOUSY	HATE	TRUST
HAPPINESS	HOPE	NATURE
RACISM	INDEPENDENCE	GROWING UP
FRIENDSHIP	LOVE	PEACE
FAITH	JUSTICE	SELF-IMPROVEMENT

EXAMPLE

7. Read the poem below and select the correct theme of the poem.

Those Winter Sundays By Robert Hayden

Sundays too my father got up early
and put his clothes on in the blueblack cold,
then with cracked hands that ached
from labor in the weekday weather made
banked fires blaze. No one ever thanked him.

I'd wake and hear the cold splintering, breaking.
When the rooms were warm, he'd call,
and slowly I would rise and dress,
fearing the chronic angers of that house,

Speaking indifferently to him,
who had driven out the cold
and polished my good shoes as well.
What did I know, what did I know
of love's austere and lonely offices?

(A) regret
(B) peace
(C) war
(D) success

Your Answer: Ⓓ

ANALYSIS

The correct answer is A. Reading the poem carefully, the narrator is remembering his father's simple kindnesses: getting up early on his one day off to make the fire and polishing his son's shoes. The narrator also expresses his regret: in speaking to him indifferently, never thanking him. Regret appears to be the theme of the poem. Answers **B, C,** and **D** don't really fit in.

Plots

These are the actual events or happenings that take place in a narrative. The author chooses the events and arranges them, usually in a time sequence, but occasionally authors toss in a **flashback** (you'll learn about that soon) or they may write using **stream of consciousness**, which causes the plot to become less logically arranged. However, when there is a logical arrangement of the plot, there is a gradual up, reaching the top, and then a gradual decline, or any version close to that (remember—as mentioned earlier, some authors jump into conflict a little earlier than others so the gradual part may not be so gradual).

- **Exposition—or the opening.** This is the beginning of the plot. The author introduces the characters and setting and provides the reader with background information. Sometimes authors take quite awhile to do this (three or four chapters) and you must be patient in reading. Other times they jump right into the action, taking less time with the introductions.
- **Rising action—or complication.** This is where the author begins to describe the conflict or the problem that the characters are about to face. The situation has caused tension to rise at this point of the story.
- **Climax**—the turning point in the story. This is where the problem is at its peak literally, and the characters begin charting their descent and how are they going to solve the problem.
- **Falling Action**—where the author explains how the solution is going to occur.
- **Resolution or Denouement—the ending.** The story is brought to a conclusion here; it may or may not be the way you would like it to be. Endings are a personal thing; others like them happy; others like them tragic or sad.

Now, what you also must understand is that this rise in action is most likely some kind of **conflict.** Conflict also is expressed by the author in many different ways depending on the nature of the narrative. Let's look.

- **External Conflict**
  - Person against nature (storms, beasts, etc.)
  - Person against person (main character against another character)
  - Person against society (character has difficulty with laws, beliefs)
  - Person against fate (a problem out of the character's control)
- **Internal Conflict**
  - Man against himself (making a difficult decision, inner turmoil)

EXAMPLE

8. The denouement of the plot is the same as the _____.

    (A) climax
    (B) rising action
    (C) resolution
    (D) introduction

Your Answer: Ⓐ Ⓑ Ⓒ Ⓓ

ANALYSIS

The correct answer is C. The resolution and the denouement are the same thing. Answer **D** would be easy to eliminate, but **A** and **B** might give you problems if you didn't know exactly what denouement was.

Foreshadowing

This is a technique that authors use to create suspense and to prepare the reader for what is about to happen in their writing. **Foreshadowing** is the hint or clue given earlier in the book that suggests later events without completely giving the plot away. Foreshadowing can be very subtle, meaning there are times in your reading when you might read on and not realize that it was foreshadowing until the event actually happened. S. E. Hinton foreshadows future events through the character Johnny in her book *The Outsiders*. The protagonist, Ponyboy, tells Johnny to be careful with his cigarettes at the abandoned church where they were hiding and later, they find that the church catches on fire. Johnny and Ponyboy rescue several young children, but Johnny is badly injured and burned, and later . . . well, you'll have to read the book to find out what happens. That's foreshadowing.

EXAMPLE

9. Foreshadowing _____.

    (A) is the hints and clues about what might occur later in the book
    (B) is a television show about shadow puppets
    (C) is the introduction of the characters
    (D) is the rising action of the story

Your Answer: Ⓐ Ⓑ Ⓒ Ⓓ

ANALYSIS

The correct answer is A. Foreshadowing is the hints and clues about what might occur later in the book. Answers **C** and **D** are related to the plot, while Answer **B** is one of those throwaway answers.

Flashbacks

These are techniques that allow the author to go back in time through the characters and to present scenes or incidents that happened before the opening of the narrative. Remember when we discussed plots and the rising action and climax and the fact that some authors jump right into the action and then catch the reader up later through flashbacks? Well, now you know. The author may choose to have the reader understand through character dialogue when one character tells another character about the past, or the author may choose to have a character dream about it or simply reflect.

EXAMPLE

10. A flashback is _____.

    (A) telling a story from the end to the beginning
    (B) scenes presented that took place before the action or conflict
    (C) a summer lightning storm
    (D) hinting or previewing what might happen later in the story

Your Answer: Ⓐ Ⓑ Ⓒ Ⓓ

ANALYSIS

The correct answer is B. Flashback tells the readers what happened before all of the action takes place. Answers **A** and **D** might be a little confusing if you are unsure of the answer, but Answer **C** is completely wrong.

Imagery

Imagery is a device used by an author to create an image in the reader's mind. Usually, the words used, appeal to the five senses in some way—visual, auditory (hearing), kinesthetic (touch), olfactory (smell), and taste. In writing, especially fiction and poetry, authors need to get the images across to the reader in order for the reader to visualize what they are attempting to impress upon the reader in their writing. Not having the benefit of a screen that can actually show you the elegant woman's long fur-lined red coat without telling you (like film or television), authors need to be able to get you, the reader, to see that image in your mind. Authors literally paint word pictures in their works. Without imagery, reading fiction and poetry would be far less exciting.

EXAMPLE

11. Read the following two stanzas of a poem and select which of the five senses it most affects.

From; I Wandered Lonely as a Cloud
by William Wordsworth

I wandered lonely as a cloud
That floats on high o'er vales and hills,
When all at once I saw a crowd,
A host, of golden daffodils;
Beside the lake, beneath the trees,
Fluttering and dancing in the breeze.

Continuous as the stars that shine
And twinkle on the milky way,
They stretched in never-ending line
Along the margin of a bay:
Ten thousand saw I at a glance,
Tossing their heads in sprightly dance.

(A) touch
(B) hearing
(C) smelling
(D) vision

Your Answer: Ⓐ Ⓑ Ⓒ Ⓓ

ANALYSIS

The correct answer is D. Wordsworth provides the reader with strong visual imagery in this segment of his poem. "Lonely as a cloud," A host of golden daffodils," "beside the lake," and "beneath the trees" are a few examples of the visual imagery that you could actually paint if you had to.

Symbols and Symbolism

A **symbol** implies a connection between things. A symbol is something that is concrete (something you can touch) that stands for something that is abstract (a feeling, an idea, or an emotion). For instance, a dove implies a connection to peace, a heart is a symbol that implies love, white is a symbol that implies purity or goodness, and the American flag as a symbol implies for Americans freedom and democracy. There are symbols almost everywhere you look. When you read, you will often find symbols that the author has strategically placed to deepen the meaning of the text; this is called **symbolism**. The symbols themselves can be objects and actions, and even the characters themselves become symbols—standing for good or evil, for instance. Regardless of the symbol and whether it is abstract or literal, symbolism adds another dimension to writing.

EXAMPLE

12. True or False. Symbolism is an abstract object that stands for something that is concrete.

    (A) True
    (B) False

Your Answer:

ANALYSIS

The correct answer is B, false. Read the question carefully. The terms abstract and concrete are reversed.

Allegories

Definitely a more challenging concept to understand, an **allegory** is the use of characters, events, or even the settings of a narrative to represent something abstract such as an idea, emotion, or feeling. The reader in this case is treated to a second or underlying meaning in addition to the surface meaning of the narrative. For instance, an underlying meaning might be social, satirical, political, or religious. Many times the author presents the characters as abstractions come to life: a character could represent greed, hope, charity, and envy, for example. George Orwell's novel *Animal Farm* is an allegory. In this book, Orwell uses animals who take over a farm as an allegory that represents communism and its repressive control over the citizens of the former Soviet Union.

EXAMPLE

13. An allegory uses characters, events, or settings to represent something <u>abstract</u>. In this sentence <u>abstract</u> means _____.

    (A) a style of painting
    (B) something bizarre or ludicrous
    (C) a person, place, or thing
    (D) something nonconcrete; an idea, emotion, or feeling

Your Answer: Ⓓ

ANALYSIS

The correct answer is D. An allegory uses characters, events, or setting to represent something that is abstract. Abstract is something you cannot really touch, an idea, an emotion, or a feeling. Answer **B** is way off, Answer **A** is actually true, but not in the sense that it is being used here, and answer **C** lists things that are concrete—things you can actually touch.

Irony

Irony is using a phrase or a word to mean the exact opposite of its normal or the expected meaning. In other words, it is a contrast between what it *really* is and what it *appears* to be. There are three types of irony used in writing:

- **Dramatic irony:** The reader (or audience) sees a character's faults or mistakes; the character himself does not. In Shakespeare's play *Romeo and Juliet*, the dramatic irony occurs when Romeo, believing that Juliet is dead, kills himself; meanwhile, the readers know that she is merely in a drug-induced coma-like state from which she will be awakening soon.

- **Verbal irony:** The author states one thing, but means another, for instance when someone says to you "Thanks a lot," but saying it in a mean or sarcastic way. That person is stating one thing, but meaning another.

- **Irony of situation or situational irony:** A situation that demonstrates a large difference between the reason for a particular action and the result. In Daniel Keyes' short story, "Flowers for Algernon," Charlie Gordon, the main character, who has a very low IQ, hears of an experimental brain operation that will allow him to become intelligent. It has worked for a mouse named Algernon, so he believes that it will work for him as well. Charlie has the surgery and is given a good-luck disk by another character named Gimpy that has "Sta-Brite" (stay bright?) written on it. Sta-Brite is the name of a metal polish. Anyway, the irony of this situation is that Charlie's intelligence does improve, but it subsequently begins to degenerate into a condition far worse than it was originally, so, ironically, Charlie was unable to "Sta-Brite" (stay bright).

EXAMPLE

14. The three types of irony are _____.

    (A) allegory, situational, and abstract
    (B) verbal, dramatic, and irony of situation
    (C) verbal, abstract, and occasional
    (D) irony, allegory, and concrete

Your Answer: Ⓐ Ⓑ Ⓒ Ⓓ

ANALYSIS

The correct answer is B. The three types of irony are verbal, dramatic, and irony of situation. The other three answers include several literary terms that might confuse you if you did not know the background to irony.

Narrator or Point of View

All works of literature must have a narrator, or someone who tells the story. Depending upon which narrator the author uses determines how much information the reader will be given. There are two major points of view: *first-person* and *third-person.* The first-person narrator stands within the story and describes it from an "I" perspective, which means that when you read a story and you see the word "I," you'll know it is a first-person narrator. This narrator reveals only his or her own feelings and thoughts. However the third-person narrator is an outsider looking in and there are three third-person narrator types. The first is third-person *omniscient.* As an outsider, this person knows *everything* about the characters and about what is going on in their minds, emotions, and their actions. This narrator is referred to as *all-knowing.* The second type of third-person narrator is the *third-person limited.* This narrator enters the mind of only one character and presents the details from that person's perspective only. This type of narrator is limited in what can be presented. The final type of third-person is called *third-person objective.* This narrator offers the readers only facts—only the facts. There are no thoughts, feelings, or emotions presented by this narrator. He or she takes an objective point of view. Let's review again.

- **First person:** Using "I" this narrator has a limited perspective in that he or she only sees the situation from his or her perspective. This person sees the story from the inside.

- **Third-person omniscient:** The all-knowing narrator. As an outsider, this person can enter the characters' minds and relate their thoughts, feelings, and actions.

- **Third-person limited:** As a narrator, this person enters the mind of only one character and sees everything from that character's perspective, hence the limited perspective.

- **Third-person objective:** This narrator states only the facts. He or she does not bother with emotions, feelings, or thoughts—just the facts.

EXAMPLE

15. Which of the following narrators is referred to as the "all-knowing" narrator.

    (A) first person
    (B) third-person omniscient
    (C) third-person limited
    (D) third-person objective

Your Answer: Ⓐ Ⓑ Ⓒ Ⓓ

ANALYSIS

The correct answer is B. The all-knowing narrator is the third-person omniscient. Answers **A, C,** and **D** are incorrect.

Mood

You may be familiar with the term "emo." Well, the literary device "mood" is a rather *emotional* concept. Just as doing something or not doing something depends upon the mood you are in at the time, the same is true for the author when he or she is writing the story—*not* his or her mood *personally*, but the mood in the story. When an author chooses the setting, words, details, objects, and images in a piece of literature, he or she is creating a mood for the work. The mood of a literary work may be happy, sad, lonely, dark, somber, jubilant, empty, isolated, etc. The author chooses the appropriate details to match the mood he or she is attempting to portray in the work. The difficult part of mood is weaving it in throughout the characters, and all that goes on in the course of a story or narrative. It is complex.

EXAMPLE

16. The mood in a narrative sets up (a, an) _____ aspect of the story.

    (A) introduction
    (B) psychotic
    (C) emotional
    (D) resolution

Your Answer: Ⓐ Ⓑ Ⓒ Ⓓ

ANALYSIS

The correct answer is C. Answer **B** is exaggerated and answers **A** and **D** deal with plot and are wrong.

Chapter Review and Quick Quiz

If you stop to really think about it, the amount of work and the number of decisions that need to be made regarding characters, plots, mood, theme, and all the other things that go into writing a novel that were discussed in this chapter must certainly leave an author exhausted. But, that's another reason why reading is so much fun—someone else agonized over all the details, and we get to sit back and enjoy their efforts. To check your learning, take this quick quiz. The answers are in the appendix in the back of the book.

Directions: Write the letter of the correct definition in the space to the left of the word it defines.

ANSWER	WORD(S)		DEFINITIONS
_____	1. dialogue	**a.**	speech in which a character alone on stage begins thinking aloud
_____	2. interior monologue	**b.**	most important character in a story

_____ 3. dramatic monologue

_____ 4. soliloquy

_____ 5. asides

_____ 6. character foils

_____ 7. dynamic character

_____ 8. static character

_____ 9. protagonist

_____ 10. antagonist

_____ 11. theme

_____ 12. plot

_____ 13. foreshadowing

_____ 14. flashback

_____ 15. imagery

_____ 16. symbolism

_____ 17. allegory

_____ 18. irony

_____ 19. narrator

_____ 20. mood

c. words that create images that appeal to the five senses

d. a character who does not change during a story

e. something concrete that stands for something abstract

f. speech that reveals characters thoughts

g. the series of actual events in a narrative

h. the use of characters, settings, events to represent something abstract

i. revisiting past events through a character

j. hints or clues given about future events in a story

k. a character in opposition of the protagonist

l. speech in which a character is overheard speaking to a silent listener

m. the emotional aspect of the writing

n. contrasting or near opposites of another character

o. characters that change somehow during the story

p. the voice of the person telling the story

q. conversation between two or more characters

r. remarks by a character to the audience without being heard by other characters

s. a message or main idea of a narrative

t. the use of a word or phrase to mean the exact opposite of what is being said

SECTION II

WRITING

Written and Oral Language Conventions— Part I

That's a fancy title for **grammar.** Grammar is what we are going to be reviewing in this chapter. The English language is filled with rules about everything, but what is confusing is that there is almost always exceptions to the rules, which makes our language challenging in some ways. But, the more you understand about these little things, the better your writing and speaking will become. We will look specifically at clauses, phrases, and punctuation, but wait, there is a method to this madness! By looking at the little things such as phrases and clauses that make up the bigger things called sentences and paragraphs, we are building upon the basics of writing, which is the final step in this review for the exit exam.

CHAPTER FOCUS

Clauses
- Independent or Main
- Subordinate or Dependent (Parts I and II)
- Adjective/Adverbial/Noun Clauses

Phrases
- Prepositional Phrases
  - Adjective
  - Adverb
- Appositives
  - Appositive Review
  - Appositive Phrases

- Verbal Phrases
  - Participial Review
  - Participial Phrases
  - Gerund Review
  - Gerund Phrases
  - Infinitive Review
  - Infinitive Phrases

Punctuation
- End Marks—a brief word
- Apostrophes
- Colons
- Semicolons
- Commas
- Hyphens

Chapter Review and Quick Quizzes

CLAUSES

I wish this was going to be about a bunch of Santas, but sorry it's not. A **clause** is a group of words that has a **subject** and a **predicate** (the verb part) and is used as part of a sentence. All clauses contain a subject and a verb, but not all clauses express complete thoughts. That is why we are going to look at the two kinds of clauses: **independent** (also known as a **main clause,** but we will use the word independent to make it less confusing), and **subordinate clauses** (also called **dependent clauses,** but we will use subordinate clause to be less confusing).

Independent Clause

Think of the word independent; it means not having to depend upon anyone or anything. That's what an independent clause is: a complete thought, and it can stand by itself as a sentence. In other words, it doesn't need any help; it can be a simple sentence. In looking at the samples below, notice that these independent clauses have a subject and a verb and that they express a complete thought. Note: the subject is boxed, and the verb is highlighted in each clause.

- Charles Dickens wrote many books.

- Ben stopped the car.

- The moon is full.

- Meredith ate the apple.

- Dominic sold the painting.

EXAMPLE

1. Select the independent clause from the following list.

   (A) when he drives slowly
   (B) which tell the entire story
   (C) he was a captain
   (D) because I told her

Your Answer: Ⓐ Ⓑ Ⓒ Ⓓ

ANALYSIS

The correct answer is C. The only clause that can stand independently is this one; the others are subordinate clauses and cannot stand alone as a sentence.

Subordinate Clauses—Part I

Subordinate means of lesser importance and perhaps that is a good way to remember the meaning of this clause. Subordinate clauses are underqualified—they do not express a complete thought and cannot stand alone. Although subordinate clauses do have a subject and a verb, they are still dependent upon an independent clause to make them a complete sentence. Review the samples below.

Notice that these clauses begin with words such as: *that, where, which, since,* and *what.* When you see or hear a clause that begins with one of these, you know that it has to have at least one more clause to make it a sentence and one of those clauses must be an independent clause (because the subordinate clause is dependent). The subject of the clause is boxed and the verb is highlighted.

- that I prefer
- where he put the phone
- which she just bought
- since you've been away
- what they saw

EXAMPLE

2. Which of the following clauses is NOT a subordinate clause?

   (A) when the movie is over
   (B) she works in an office
   (C) because I told you
   (D) what a senator does

Your Answer: Ⓐ Ⓑ Ⓒ Ⓓ

ANALYSIS

The correct answer is B. All of the clauses except for **B** are subordinate. They cannot stand alone as a sentence. She works in an office is an independent clause. NOTE: make certain that you read the question correctly. This question used the word <u>NOT</u>.

Subordinate Clauses—Part II

There are three additional (bonus) clauses in the subordinate category. Let's take a look at them. There is an **adjective clause** (modifies or describes a noun or a pronoun), an **adverb clause** (modifies or describes a verb), and a **noun clause** (person, place, or thing). Don't let the actual definitions on the following pages frighten or confuse you; if you keep this organized in your mind, all of this clause talk shouldn't bother you. You know that an **adjective** describes or (the fancy word) "modifies" a *noun* (person, place, or thing) or a *pronoun* (he, she, it, they, we, etc.) right? The red boat sailed on the blue water. Red is an adjective describing/modifying boat and blue is an adjective describing/modifying water. Well, apply this same idea to the adjective clause; it is going to modify a noun (person, place, or thing) or a pronoun (he, she, it, they, we, etc.). When you review these bonus subordinate clauses, just keep your mind organized and connect and apply what you already know about parts of speech (nouns, verbs, pronouns, adjectives, prepositions, and conjunctions) to the clauses and you will be fine.

Adjective Clause

> **NOTE**
>
> The adjective clause "who paints and sculpts very large rotund people," begins with the relative pronoun who and it modifies the noun artist.

An adjective clause is a subordinate clause that modifies a noun or a pronoun, just as a normal adjective (smart, small, blue, or inquisitive) modifies a noun or a pronoun in an everyday sentence. These clauses are usually introduced with a **relative pronoun: that, which, who, whom, whose.** A relative pronoun *relates* the adjective clause to the word it modifies.

Relative Pronouns That Introduce Adjective Clauses:

that, which, who, whom, whose

Example: Botero is the artist *who paints and sculpts very large rotund people.*

Adverb Clause

This is a subordinate clause that modifies a verb, an adjective, or an adverb. Adverb clauses are introduced by a subordinating conjunction, which is a word that connects the adverb clause to the word or words that the clause modifies. The subordinating conjunctions were listed earlier, but review is always good:

Subordinating Conjunctions That Introduce Adverb Clauses:

> **NOTE**
>
> The subordinating conjunction "though" begins the adverb clause "Though the sun refuses to shine" which modifies the verb "plan."

after, although, as, as if, as long as, as soon as, as though, because, before, how, if, in order that, since, so that, than, though, unless, until, when, whenever, where, wherever, whether, while

Example: *Though the sun refuses to shine,* we will continue to plan our trip to the beach.

Noun Clause

A noun clause is a subordinate clause that is used as a noun. It is common for the list of words below to be introduced as a noun clause:

Words That Commonly Introduce Noun Clauses:

> who, whom, what, whoever, whomever,
> whatever, which, whichever, that

NOTE

The noun clause "that Sammy is very angry" is used as the subject in this sentence.

Example: *That Sammy is very angry* is obvious.

EXAMPLE

3. The three types of subordinating clauses are _____,
_____, and _____

(A) adverb, preposition, verb.
(B) adverb, subject, predicate.
(C) noun, adjective, adverb.
(D) noun, adjective, verb.

Your Answer: Ⓐ Ⓑ Ⓒ Ⓓ

ANALYSIS

The correct answer is C. This is one of those questions that could really throw you off if you didn't know exactly what the answer was. The three subordinating clauses are noun, adverb, and adjective. Answer **D** might confuse you if you were wavering back and forth about the answer, but Answers **A** and **B** are more easily eliminated.

PHRASES

A **phrase** is a group of words that are related in some manner, but they do not have a *verb and its subject*. There are several categories of phrases. We will be reviewing the following: **prepositional phrases** with adjective and adverb phrases. **Verbal phrases** with participial, gerund, and infinitive phrases, and finally, **appositive phrases.**

Prepositional Phrases

Before we get into describing what prepositional phrases are, you need to make certain that you remember what a preposition is. A *preposition* is a word that deals with the relationship of a *noun* or a *pronoun* to another word in the sentence. Look below at the list of prepositions. Review them. Study them. Log them into a permanent part of your brain! Knowing these words for what they are will help you in many ways, not just for parts of speech and grammar, but in the writing that we will be working on in a later chapter.

Prepositions—Those with More Than One Word Are Compound Prepositions			
aboard	before	from	out
about	behind	in	over
above	below	in addition to	past
according to	beneath	in front of	since
across	beside	inside	through
after	besides	in spite of	throughout
against	between	instead of	to
along	beyond	into	toward
along with	but (except)	like	under
amid	by	near	underneath
among	concerning	next to	until
around	down	of	up
aside from	during	off	upon
as of	except	on	with
at			within
because of	for	on account of	without

These are prepositions. Now for prepositional phrases. These phrases are easy as long as you know prepositions. A prepositional phrase is a group of words that begins with a *preposition* and ends with a *noun* or a *pronoun*. Review the examples below. The ⬜preposition is boxed⬜ and ▨the noun or pronoun▨ is highlighted.

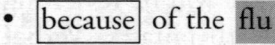

- [because] of the ▨flu▨
- [on] the ▨stove▨
- [through] the ▨window▨
- [out of] the ▨zoo▨
- [within] a ▨month▨

> **REMINDER**
>
> All prepositional phrases begin with a preposition and end with a noun or pronoun.

EXAMPLE

4. Which of the following is NOT a prepositional phrase?

  (A) into the night
  (B) under the clouds
  (C) off the wall
  (D) system is down

Your Answer: Ⓐ Ⓑ Ⓒ Ⓓ

ANALYSIS

The correct answer is D. Just making sure you are paying attention, the question asks which one is *not* the prepositional phrase. The first three phrases all have *prepositions*—into, under, and off. Look at Answer **D.** Down is a preposition right? It's on our list. Well, you need to remember that prepositions are always followed by a *noun* or a *pronoun*. Down is a preposition, but not here. In this question it is used as an adverb.

Adjective Phrases

Simply stated, an adjective phrase is a prepositional phrase used as an *adjective*. Reminder: An adjective is a word that describes or modifies the noun or pronoun and the one-word adjective usually precedes or goes before the noun or pronoun like this: The yellow light means caution. "Yellow" is an *adjective* describing or modifying "light." Similarly, with an adjective phrase the noun precedes the prepositional phrase, making it an adjective phrase. The prepositional phrase hasn't changed; it still has the preposition at the beginning, and the noun or pronoun at the end. Let's take a look at the adjective phrases below; The nouns are boxed and the **adjective phrases** are highlighted.

- The light in the intersection is out of order.
- The package on the shelf is Betsy's.
- Catalina is an island off the coast of California.
- The basket inside the garage is empty.
- The dog with the black spots seems happy.

Adverb Phrases

An adverb phrase, much like an *adverb*, is used to tell *when, where, how, how much,* or *how far*, but in the form of a prepositional phrase. Remember: an *adverb* modifies a *verb*, an a*djective*, or *another adverb*. Let's look at the samples below. The **adverb phrases** are highlighted and the function of the phrase is in parentheses.

- The rain fell over the meadow . (where)

- My friends and I drove throughout the city looking for a CD. (where)

- Peter will finish reading the book by Thursday . (when)

- I will call you early in the morning . (when)

- The clerk answered with a smile . (how)

EXAMPLE

5. Adjective phrases modify _____ or pronouns and adverb phrases modify _____, adjectives, or another adverb.

   (A) verbs, adjectives
   (B) nouns, conjunctions
   (C) nouns, verbs
   (D) interjections and conjunctions

Your Answer: (A) (B) (C) (D)

ANALYSIS

The correct answer is C. Knowing exactly what adverbs and adjectives modify is beneficial for this question. Although Answer **D** can be eliminated quite easily, **A** and **B** might cause a little confusion at first glance.

Verbal Phrases

The **participial**, **gerund**, and **infinitive phrases** are known as verbal phrases. Before delving into their backgrounds, we need to review the definitions of the three verbals standing alone before we get into the phrase part of the review.

PARTICIPLE REVIEW AND PARTICIPIAL PHRASES

- **Participle Review:** a verb that can be used as an adjective
  - **Present** participles end in *-ing*. Example:
    The article was encouraging . Notice that the word encouraging in its true form is a *verb*, but it is used as an *adjective* in this sentence because it describes or modifies the *noun* article.
  - **Past** participles end in *-d* or *-ed*. Example: The student searched the abandoned hall for her backpack. Again, the verb form abandoned is used as an *adjective* in the past tense and modifies the noun hall, making it a past participle.

- Participial phrases: Used as an adjective, the participial phrase is comprised of a participle, its modifiers, and its complements. Review the examples below. The participial phrase is boxed and the noun it modifies is highlighted.

Examples: Flapping its wings , the bird took flight.

Living in California , Eric learned to appreciate the ocean.

Laughing at my joke , Lisa fell from the chair.

EXAMPLE

6. In the following sentence locate the participial phrase: "Destined for fame, my cousin practiced singing every day."

(A) practiced singing every day
(B) my cousin practiced
(C) singing every day
(D) Destined for fame

Your Answer: Ⓐ Ⓑ Ⓒ Ⓓ

ANALYSIS

The correct answer is D. "Destined for fame" is the participial phrase and it modifies the *noun* "cousin." Answers **A, B,** and **C** are incorrect. Taking this a step further, is the word "Destined" past or present participle? (Past) Remember past participles end in *-d* or *-ed,* and present participles end with an *-ing.*

GERUND REVIEW AND GERUND PHRASE

- **Gerund Review:** A form of *verb* that ends in an *-ing* but is used as a *noun. Not* to be confused with the present participle (above), which also ends in an *-ing* but it is used as an *adjective.* That's the major difference. Example: Cooking is an art form for some people. The word cooking —the gerund of this sentence would under normal circumstances be a verb; however, it is used as a *noun.* Gerunds are common but we don't often attach a title to them or think to ourselves "Oh, that's a gerund!" Skating, painting, exercising are commonly used as gerunds.

- **Gerund Phrase:** A gerund phrase includes of course, the gerund and its complement and modifiers. They all act together as a *noun.* Review the following gerund phrases. The gerund phrases are boxed . Remember, gerund phrases act as *nouns,* which mean they might be the *subject* of the sentence, the *direct object,* the *object of the preposition,* etc.

> **TIP**
>
> Usually your first intuition about an answer is correct—so don't change your answers unless you are absolutely certain that you made a selection mistake.

Examples: Approaching the freeway onramp may require caution.

The song spoke of the gentle blossoming of friendship.

By speaking to the audience, the politician was able to relay his message.

EXAMPLE

7. Identify the gerund phrase in the following sentence: "Sweeping the floor was one of his many duties."

 (A) Sweeping the floor
 (B) was one of
 (C) his many duties
 (D) the floor was

Your Answer: (A) (B) (C) (D)

ANALYSIS

The correct answer is A. A gerund phrase contains a gerund, which is a *verb* form that ends in *-ing* and is used as a *noun*. Answers **B, C,** and **D** are incorrect.

INFINITIVE REVIEW AND INFINITIVE PHRASE

- **Infinitive Review:** Another *verb* form that can be used as a *noun*, an *adjective* **or** an *adverb*. This form usually begins with "to." Review the following examples.

  ○ Infinitives as *nouns*: To build the bridge took two years. His ambition is to become a musician. Ann likes to ski but not to skate.

  ○ Infinitives as *adjectives*: The best time to visit California is anytime. If you want information about cameras and photography, that is the magazine to read.

  ○ Infinitives as *adverbs*: The cyclists were eager to ride in the race. The players stopped at halftime to rest.

- **Infinitive Phrases:** An infinitive phrase consists of an infinitive and its modifiers and complements. Again, infinitive phrases can be used as *nouns, adjectives,* and *adverbs*. The infinitive phrases are boxed.

  ○ Infinitive Phrases as *nouns*: To run fast takes a lot of training. To succeed in business takes patience and determination. They wanted to travel around the world beginning in September.

○ Infinitive Phrases as *adjectives*: He is the cyclist to watch in this stage of the Tour de France. He wanted to join the club . They like apples and oranges to eat on the plane .

○ Infinitive Phrases as *adverbs*: The students became quiet to hear the teacher . They are delighted to visit the elderly . The artist was proud to display his sculptures .

EXAMPLE

8. Identify the infinitive phrase in the following sentence: "After surgery, the football player will complete many leg exercises to strengthen his knee."

(A) After surgery
(B) to strengthen his knee
(C) the football player
(D) will complete many leg exercises

Your Answer: Ⓐ Ⓑ Ⓒ Ⓓ

ANALYSIS

The correct answer is B. The infinitive phrase is "to strengthen his knee." It is used as an adverb in the sentence. Answers **A, C,** and **D** are wrong.

Appositives

APPOSITIVE REVIEW AND APPOSITIVE PHRASES

- **Appositives** are *nouns* or *pronouns* that follow another *noun* or pronoun in order to either explain it or to identify it. **Example:** astronaut , John Glenn , was one of America's early space travelers. The word "astronaut" is the appositive and "John Glenn" is the noun(s) that identifies it. **Example:** Lewis and Clark , leaders of an expedition west , are well known in American history. "Lewis and Clark" are the nouns and "leaders of an expedition west" explain.

- **Appositive Phrases** are a phrases made up of an appositive and its modifiers. The appositive is boxed , and the appositive phrase is highlighted .

Examples: The respected and admired French diplomat , Jean Paul Gautier , is visiting Sacramento.

The next train to San Diego , the Coaster , boards in fifteen minutes.

Yo Yo Ma, a well-known and talented cellist, will have a recital next week.

EXAMPLE

9. Identify the appositive in the following sentence: "The writer, Sandra Cisneros, is creative and talented."

   (A) creative and talented
   (B) the writer Sandra Cisneros
   (C) Cisneros is
   (D) writer

Your Answer: (A) (B) (C) (D)

ANALYSIS

The correct answer is B. An appositive is a *noun* or a *pronoun* placed beside another noun or pronoun to identify or explain it. In this case the noun "writer" is placed next to the proper noun "Sandra Cisneros" and is therefore the appositive.

PUNCTUATION

Punctuation is the practice of using marks such as periods, exclamation points, commas, hyphens, and question marks, to separate sentences and to make their meanings clear. Can you imagine if there were no punctuation marks or a sentence without the spaces that separate the words? youwouldntknowwhereathought-beganorendedeverythingwouldblendtogetherandunderstandingwouldbeextremely-challenging. Whether you are writing by hand (as you will be doing on your exam essays) or typing on a computer, punctuation, from a tiny little period to a **C**apital letter, or space between words is mandatory and obviously very necessary.

End Marks—A Brief Word About Them!

Although we all know to use end marks at the ends of our sentences, a few of us forget from time to time. When you get to the writing portion of the CAHSEE, you cannot afford to forget. As a reminder about end marks, please review the following:

- Use a **period** at the end of a statement.

   Example: Autumn is my favorite time of year**.**

- Use a **question mark** at the end of a question.

   Example: How many pencils do you have**?**

- Use an **exclamation point** at the end of an exclamation.

   Example: Look at that view**!**

- Use a **period** or an **exclamation point** at the end of a request or a command.

Example: Please pass the milk**.** (a request)
Give me the milk**!** (a command)

- Use a **period** after most abbreviations.

Example: Mr., Mrs., Ms., Dr., Jr., St., Rd., Blvd., Corp., Inc., A.M., P.M.,
B.C., A.D., B.A., B.S., Ph.D., W.E.B. DuBois,

Example: Government agencies and other widely used abbreviations are written
without periods: FBI, PTA, NAACP, PBS, CNN, VHS, HUD, and
YMCA, etc. Words that are abbreviated (such as television = TV) are
not written with periods.

Apostrophes

These are used for the possessive case of nouns (and some pronouns), to indicate a contraction, and to form some plurals. Let's look at the use of apostrophes in each case.

- **Use of apostrophes in possessive case:**
  - **Possessive case of singular noun** shows ownership or relationship. To form the possessive case of a singular noun, add an apostrophe and then an "s." (singular noun + ' + s = possessive singular noun)
    - the cat's tail
    - Joe's drum set
    - Kyle's guitar
    - one dollar's worth
    - a moment's notice
  - **Possessive case of plural noun ending in "s."** When a plural noun already ends in an "s," add only an apostrophe. This is also true with proper nouns that end with an "s"; add only an apostrophe.
    (plural noun with "s" ending + ' = possessive case of plural noun)
    - the cats' tails
    - Los Angeles' population
    - doctors' opinion
    - ten dollars' worth
    - the students' lockers
  - **Possessive case of plural nouns not ending in "s."** For plural nouns that do not end in "s" add an apostrophe and then an "s."
    (plural noun-no "s" + ' + s = possessive plural noun)
    - men's suits
    - children's toys
    - women's clothing
    - geese's noise
    - mice's tracks
  - **Possessive personal pronouns** do not use an apostrophe with possessive personal pronouns.
    - yours, ours, theirs, hers, its, his, mine

- ◦ **Possessive case of indefinite pronouns.** With some indefinite pronouns, add an apostrophe and an "s" to form the possessive case.
  - Everyone's, everyone's, no one's, somebody's, someone's, anyone's, another's, etc.
- **Use of apostrophes in contractions.** An apostrophe is a shortened form of a word, figure, or a group of words. The apostrophe in the contraction shows where the letter that was left out would be if it were still there. Contractions are short-cuts. Review the following list of contractions. Note that an apostrophe is added where a letter is removed.

Common Contractions	
I am = I'm	2003 = '03
has not = hasn't	let us = let's
she would = she'd	of the clock = o'clock
they had = they'd	where is = where's
cannot = can't	we are = we're
were not = weren't	he is = he's
should not = shouldn't	you will = you'll
there has = there's	is not = isn't
there is = there's	are not = aren't
who is = who's	does not = doesn't
who has = who's	they are = they're
they are = they're	will not = won't

- **Use of apostrophes for plurals.** To form the plurals of letters, numerals, and signs, and for words referred to as words. Review the examples below.
  - ◦ They hope to get all A's and B's on their report cards.
  - ◦ When you write your essay, do not use ampersands (&'s).
  - ◦ You use too many and's in your essay.

EXAMPLE

10. In the following sentence, choose the correct form of the word that is underlined.

"The Senate members approved Senator <u>Kennedys</u> plan for reorganization."

(A) Kennedy's
(B) Kennedys'
(C) Kennedys's
(D) correct as is

Your Answer:

ANALYSIS

The correct answer is A. This form shows ownership; it's Senator Kennedy's plan. Therefore, there is an apostrophe and then an "s." Answer **B** is plural possessive case; Answer **C** is erroneous, as is **D**.

Colons

These are used for the following reasons. Please review them.

- After the salutation of a business letter.
  - ○ Dear Governor Davis:
  - ○ Dear Mayor Hahn:
  - ○ Dear Mr. Miyayami:
- Between the parts of a number indicating time.
  - ○ 9:17
  - ○ 12:30
  - ○ 17:48
- To emphasize a word, phrase, clause, or a sentence that explains or adds impact to the main clause.
  - ○ She has worked here longer than anyone in the district: thirty-two years.
  - ○ There are two things you must remember: drink plenty of water, and get plenty of sleep.
- To introduce a list.
  - ○ We have many things in common: sports, academics, friends, and music.
  - ○ Working for this organization requires: loyalty and long hours.
- To distinguish between a title and a subtitle, volume and page, chapter and verse in literature.
  - ○ *English for Everyone: A Handbook of Grammar, Mechanics, and Usage*
  - ○ *Encyclopedia Britannica* X: 135
  - ○ *Garden of Truth* 23: 1–6
- To formally introduce a sentence, a question, or a quotation.
  - ○ William Shakespeare wrote: "O, it is excellent to have a giant's strength; but it is tyrannous to use it like a giant."

[handwritten margin notes: twenty-one   ninety-nine]

Semicolons

These are related to the colon in a sense; the semicolon is used in a variety of ways. Let's take a look.

- Use to join two or more independent clauses (clauses that could stand alone as a sentence) that are not connected with a coordinating conjunction (and, but, nor, for, or, yet, so).
  - ○ She didn't cause any trouble; she made us laugh and cry at the same time.
  - ○ The dog waited before he pounced; he jumped straight up in the air.
- Use between independent clauses that are joined by a conjunctive adverb (accordingly, besides, consequently, furthermore, however, indeed, instead, meanwhile, moreover, nevertheless, otherwise, therefore) or a transitional

expression (as a result, in addition, for example, in spite of, for instance, that is, in conclusion, in fact).

- ○ Our trip to Japan was all that we expected it to be; nevertheless, it will be an experience we shall never forget.
- ○ The fog continues to block the sun most mornings in June; as a result, the beaches are not too crowded.
- Use to separate independent clauses that are long or contain commas.
  - ○ To the members of the club, meetings and special functions were just a part of the regular routine; but before each and everyone of them, there was always time for socializing.

EXAMPLE

11. In the following sentence, select the word that should be followed by a colon to separate the two clauses:

"The first aid kit contained the following items bandages, antiseptic pads, flares, aspirin, gauze, tweezers, a knife, rain poncho."

(A) kit:
(B) contained:
(C) bandages:
(D) items:

Your Answer:

ANALYSIS

The correct answer is D. Use a colon before a list of items, especially after the expression "the following items." Answers **A, B,** and **C** are definitely wrong.

Commas

These are one of the most used and abused of punctuation marks. As you can see, below is a list of some of the most common usage rules.

- Use between two independent clauses that are joined by *coordinating conjunctions* (but, or, nor, for, yet, and, so).
  - ○ I would like to visit with her, but my life is very hectic right now.
  - ○ Both of the kids went shopping for clothes, so they weren't here when the package arrived.
- Use to separate individual words, phrases, or clauses in a series (a series contains at least three items).
  - ○ At the grocery store I bought eggs, bread, and milk.
  - ○ When I baby-sat last night the children ate dinner, took a bath, and read books.
- Use to separate adjectives that equally modify the same noun.
  - ○ The time passes quickly during the long, hot days of summer.
  - ○ Time passes slowly during the short, cold days of winter.
- To enclose an explanatory word or phrase.

○ Ray Charles, a blind and very talented musician and singer, is touring Europe right now.

○ The two pilots, flying over Fresno, ejected safely and landed in a field.

- Use after *yes, no,* or other mild exclamations such as *well,* or *why* at the beginning of a sentence.

  ○ Yes, I would like to go to the river next weekend.

  ○ Well, I believe there is a better answer to the question.

- Use to set off words used in direct address.

  ○ Dominic, it is your turn to wash the dishes.

  ○ Please, Meredith, call me when you get home.

EXAMPLE

12. In the following sentences, which one is NOT punctuated with commas correctly.

   (A) Please, take me to see your counselor.
   (B) When you go to the store would you pick up some lettuce, tomatoes, and onions?
   (C) Behind the stage door the actors embrace each other in celebration of their opening night.
   (D) Over a period of time, the French have become known for their excellent cooking skills.

Your Answer: Ⓐ Ⓑ Ⓒ Ⓓ

ANALYSIS

The correct answer is C. There should be a comma after *door.* The other sentences are punctuated properly.

Hyphens

These are used to either join two words together or to divide one word into two parts. Let's review the examples below.

- Use a hyphen to divide a word that is too long and won't fit at the end of the line—but remember these rules: divide a word only between syllables (check the dictionary if you are unsure) and do not divide one-syllable words. Also, divide an already hyphenated word at the hyphen and do not separate a word so that one letter remains alone or orphaned.

  ○ Yesterday, there were so many complicated things that had to be completed before our vacation that I was exhausted by bedtime.

  ○ On our way to work today we were stopped in traffic, when my brother-in-law cruised by on his motorcycle.

- Use with compound names, places, and numbers from twenty-one to ninety-nine and for fractions that are used as adjectives.

  ○ Daniel Day-Lewis is a talented dramatic actor.

  ○ Stratford-upon-Avon is the borough where Shakespeare was born.

  ○ There are twenty-three students in my English class.

  ○ I will need one-half cup of milk for the dessert.

- Used to make a compound word.
  - great-great-grandfather
  - brother-in-law
  - sixteen-year-old
- To join a capital letter to a noun or participle.
  - T-shirt
  - U-turn
  - S-shaped
- When two or more words have a common element that is omitted in all but the very last term.
  - There are two-, three-, and four-foot lengths of rope ready to use.
  - The sunglasses were available in blue-, amber-, gray-, and brown-tinted lenses.
- To form new words beginning with the *prefixes self, ex, all, great,* and *half,* and with the *suffix elect,* as well as joining any *prefix* to a *proper noun.*
  - half-eaten
  - half-baked
  - senator-elect
  - post-Depression
  - ex-governor
  - mid-July
- To indicate the life span of a person or the score of a contest or vote.
  - The Dodgers beat the Yankees 6-0.
  - William O. Smithson lived from 1764-1828.

EXAMPLE

13. In the following, which sentence is hyphenated correctly?

   (A) After you turn sixty-five, you will be able to retire from work.
   (B) Can you name the thirty ninth state?
   (C) Kareem Abdul Jabbar is a respected basketball player.
   (D) At the zoo today, we saw many animals and our favorites we-re the giraffes.

Your Answer: Ⓑ Ⓓ

ANALYSIS

The correct answer is A. Numbers between twenty-one and ninety-nine are hyphenated. Answer **B** needs a hyphen between thirty and nine. In Answer **C,** Abdul-Jabbar should be hyphenated, and in Answer **D,** the one-syllable word *were* should not be hyphenated at all.

Chapter Review and Quick Quizzes

After all of this clause, phrase, and punctuation talk, you are probably anxious to test your memory. Let's see what you remember about the chapter. Take the following quizzes and check your answers in the appendix.

Directions: Using the word bank below, complete the sentences by filling in the blanks with the word that best completes the sentence. Some words are used more than once, but they are listed the number of times that they are used in the paragraph.

Word Bank: adjective, adverb, noun, two, subordinate, subordinate, independent, verb, subject, predicate, subject, clause, independent

SECTION I—CLAUSES

A _____ (1) is a group of words that have a _____ (2) and a _____ (3). All clauses contain a _____ (4) and a _____ (5), but not all clauses express a complete thought. There are _____ (6) kinds of clauses: _____ (7) and _____ (8) clauses. _____ (9) clauses express a complete thought, but _____ (10) clauses do not. An _____ (11) clause modifies a noun or a pronoun. An _____ (12) clause modifies a verb, an adjective, or another adverb. A _____ (13) clause is used as a noun.

Directions: Using the word bank below, complete the sentences by filling in the blanks with the word that best completes the sentence. Some words are used more than once, but they are listed the number of times that they are used in the paragraph.

Word Bank: appositive, nouns, -ing, adjective, infinitive, gerunds, phrase, verbal, adverb, phrase, noun, pronoun, adjective, preposition, infinitive, gerund, verbal participial, verb, subject, prepositional

SECTION II—PHRASES

A _____ (1) is a group of words that are related, but they do not have a _____ (2) and a _____ (3). There are _____ (4) phrases, adjective, and adverb phrases. There are _____ (5), _____ (6), _____, (7) and _____ (8) phrases as well as appositive phrases. A _____ (9) phrase begins with a preposition and ends with a _____ (10) or a _____ (11). An _____ (12) phrase is a prepositional _____ (13) used as an _____ (14). An _____ (15) phrase is used to tell when, where, how, how much, or how far. _____ (16) phrases include participial, gerund, and infinitive phrases. Participial phrases are used as an _____ (17). This phrase usually begins with a word that has an _____ (18) ending. Gerund phrases act as _____ (19). Gerunds are verb forms that end in an -ing, but are used as nouns. _____ (20) phrases begin with the word "to" and are used as a noun, adjective, or an adverb. _____ (21) phrases are noun or pronoun phrases that follow another noun or pronoun.

SECTION III—PUNCTUATION

Directions: In the following paragraph there are many punctuation and capitalization errors. Underline the errors and then check the corrected version of the paragraph in the Appendix.

the word machiavellian has become synonymous (a synonym) for political immorality niccolo machiavelli, who lived form 1469–1527 wrote a book titled *the prince* which is remembered for its insistence that while his subjects are bound by conventional or the normal moral obligations, a ruler may use any means necessary to maintain power and it doesn't matter how unscrupulous. therefore machiavellian has come to mean cynical political scheming which is characterized by deceit and bad faith Evidently, niccolo was a thin-lipped man who was very hyperactive and sarcastic isn't it amazing how the memory of one man with theory of political morality can be so appropriate to modern times

Written and Oral Language Conventions—Part II

I t is mind-boggling to think about the amount of work that goes into speaking, reading, and writing English. The rules and their exceptions alone fill books. But, it is all a part of the learning process. This chapter is no different. We have a fair amount to cover in the area of grammar, a continuation of the previous chapter, so we'd better get busy. This is where we are going.

CHAPTER FOCUS

Capitalization

Sentence Construction
- Fragments
- Declarative, Imperative, Exclamatory, Interrogative
- Subject—Simple, Complete, Compound
- Predicate—Simple, Complete, Compound Verbs

Subject/Verb Agreement

Double Negative

Comparison of Modifiers
- Positive Form
- Comparative Form
- Superlative Form

Chapter Review and Quick Quizzes

CAPITALIZATION

The list of capitalization rules is extensive. Much of it comes naturally to you, but reviewing all of the rules is valuable for test taking.

Capitalize . . .

- The first word in every sentence.
  - **M**y shoes need to be repaired.
  - **L**ast night we went to a concert.
- The pronoun I.
- The first word in a full-sentence quotation.
  - Piri Thomas said that, "**E**very child is born a poet and every poet is a child."
- All proper nouns and proper adjectives.
  - **M**rs. **J**ones, **D**octor **S**mith, **L**udwig van **B**eethoven
  - **G**reat **W**all of **C**hina, **S**acramento **K**ings, **C**olorado **R**iver
  - **S**panish dancing, **T**hai food, **J**apanese, **M**orse code
  - **K**orean barbeque, **D**utch chocolate, **N**igerian masks, **V**ictorian dress
- Words that name a particular section of the country; these are proper nouns. But, do not capitalize if the sentence merely indicates direction: Birds fly south in the winter.
  - Many birds spend their winters in the **South.**
  - The **North** was industrialized in the late 1800s.
- Names of planets, stars, and other heavenly bodies.
  - **P**luto, **E**arth, **M**ars, the **M**ilky **W**ay,
- Races, nationalities, languages, and religions.
  - **A**sian, **A**frican-**A**merican, **L**atino, **H**ispanic
  - **F**rench, **S**panish, **J**apanese, **C**anadian, **A**rmenian
  - **G**erman, **D**anish, **E**nglish, **C**hinese, **P**ortuguese
  - **H**indu, **B**uddhism, **C**atholic, **P**rotestant, **M**uslim
- All words in a title except for articles (*a, an, the*), short conjunctions (*and, but, for, nor, or, so, yet*), and short prepositions (*at, for, from, with*).
  - *Romeo and Juliet, Of Mice and Men, To Whom the Bell Tolls*
  - *A Beautiful Mind, Shadowlands,*
  - *Los Angeles Times, Chicago Tribune, Time Magazine*
  - *The Nine Muses: A Mythological Path to Creativity*
  - *"Flying to the Sun: The Story of Icarus"*
- Names of organizations, an association, businesses, government bodies, and a team and its members.
  - **R**eading is **FUN**damental, **D**emocratic **P**arty, **P**alos **V**erdes **P**eninsula **S**nowboarding **C**lub, the **C**ivil **R**ights **M**ovement, the **D**epartment of **H**ealth, **E**ducation, and **W**elfare
- Abbreviation of titles and organizations.
  - **M.D., Ph.D., B.A., FBI, NAACP, B.C., A.D.**
- Brand names of business products.
  - **IBM, H**onda, **D**odge, **H**ewlett-**P**ackard, **S**ony, **F**armer **J**ohn, **W**heaties
- Letters used to indicate a form or shape.
  - **U**-turn, **V**-neck, **S**-shaped
- Mother, father, uncle, and senator when they are being used as part of their title or when they are used in place of proper nouns.

- My **U**ncle **J**eff has a great personality.
- Did you know that **S**enator **B**oxer is from California?
- I told you that **M**om would be upset.

- Nouns or pronouns that refer to a supreme being or deities, holy days, sacred writings, or religious followers.
  - **G**od, **A**llah, the **K**oran, the **T**almud, the **L**ord, **B**ook of **P**salms

- Names of historical events, and periods, special events, and calendar items.
  - The **R**enaissance, the **D**epression, the **M**iddle **A**ges, the **D**ust **B**owl, the **B**attle of **B**unker **H**ill, **S**panish-**A**merican **W**ar, **C**inco de **M**ayo, **V**alentine's **D**ay, the **O**lympic **G**ames, **O**scars

- Names of trains, ships, airplanes, and spacecraft.
  - The *Titanic*, the *Queen Mary, Mayflower*, **A**mtrak, **O**rient **E**xpress, **C**arnival **C**ruises, *Spirit of St. Louis, Apollo 11*

- Names of buildings and other structures.
  - **E**iffel **T**ower, the **E**mpire **S**tate **B**uilding, **T**okyo **T**ower, the **S**ears **B**uilding

- Names of monuments and awards.
  - **W**ashington **M**onument, **L**incoln **M**emorial, **V**ietnam **M**emorial, the **P**ulitzer **P**rize, the **N**obel **P**rize, the **N**ewbury **A**ward

- Cities, towns, and villages.
  - **T**orrance, **L**ong **B**each, **D**el **M**ar, **J**ulian, **P**alm **S**prings, **F**remont

- Streets, roads, highways.
  - **A**rtesia **B**oulevard, the **405** **F**reeway, **I**nterstate **5**, **G**affey **S**treet

- Landforms, continents, bodies of water, public areas.
  - The **C**ascade **M**ountains, **D**eath **V**alley, **S**ahara **D**esert, the **A**lps, **A**sia, **A**frica, **A**ntarctica, **M**t. **E**tna, **G**lacier **N**ational **P**ark, **S**herwood **F**orest

- Titles, the title of a person when it comes before the name, the title used alone or following a person's name only when you want to emphasize the position.
  - The **S**ecretary of **D**efense was speaking at the convention.

- Do **not** capitalize the names of school subjects except languages and course names followed by a number.
  - **E**nglish, **L**atin, **F**rench, **J**apanese, **G**erman, **S**panish, **A**lgebra 101, **B**iology 120

- The words *freshman, sophomore, junior,* and *senior* only when they are part of a title.
  - The **S**enior **B**anquet, **F**rosh-**S**oph. **B**asketball, the **J**unior **P**rom.

- Holidays, months, and days of the week.
  - **T**hanksgiving, **M**emorial **D**ay, **J**une, **J**uly, **A**ugust, **M**onday, **T**uesday

---

EXAMPLE

1. Select the sentence that does NOT have correct capitalization.

   (A) During the long road trip to Tucson, we visited the Grand Canyon.
   (B) The american revolution freed us from england's rule.
   (C) The Declaration of Independence is the heartbeat of our nation.
   (D) Creating the Statue of Liberty must have been an enormous task.

Your Answer:

ANALYSIS

The correct answer is B. American Revolution and England should be capitalized. Answers **A, C,** and **D** are correctly written.

SENTENCE CONSTRUCTION

A sentence is a group of words that expresses a complete thought. It begins with a capital letter, and ends with an end mark of some sort (period, question mark, or exclamation point), depending upon the type of sentence. When you have a group of words that look somewhat like a sentence, but reading it carefully you notice that it really doesn't have a complete thought or, rather, something is missing, it is called a fragment, and these are what you want to avoid in writing sentences. Fragments may have a verb, or subject, or some other important part of the sentence missing to make it that way, and it is our job to make certain we understand the difference. But, before we get into the parts of a sentence and their functions, let's look at the types of sentences there are and how to tell a good sentence from a bad one.

Declarative Sentences

These make a statement. They tell something and are probably the most common type of sentences. They are always ended with a period. Review the following two examples: The first sentence is a normal declarative sentence, the second is a fragment.

- Returning to England next spring will be the highlight of my year. (declarative sentence)

- Returning to England. (fragment—incomplete thought)

Imperative Sentences

These give commands or make requests. In normal circumstances, they are followed by a period, but a very strong command is followed by an exclamation point. Also, note that in commands or requests, the word "you" is understood, meaning you don't have to write it down; people already know you are talking to them. So you don't have to say, "You shut the door." You would say, "Shut the door." Look at the following examples:

- Write your name and address at the top of the card.
- Call the paramedics!

Exclamatory Sentences

These either express strong emotion or feeling or show excitement. These sentences are followed by an exclamation point. Review the samples below:

- Wow, look at that amazing display of awards!
- Watch out!

Interrogative Sentences

These sentences ask questions. They are *always, always* followed by a question mark. Review the examples below.

- What is your favorite movie?
- Where do you think you are going?

EXAMPLE

2. Identify the following type of sentence: "In June, the city of Santa Barbara has a Summer Solstice Celebration."

   (A) exclamatory
   (B) imperative
   (C) interrogative
   (D) declarative

Your Answer: Ⓐ Ⓑ Ⓒ Ⓓ

ANALYSIS

The correct answer is D. This sentence makes a statement and ends with a period. It is definitely a declarative sentence. Exclamatory sentences exclaim something rather dramatically. Interrogative sentences interrogate or ask a question. Imperative sentences are fairly demanding.

The Subject and the Predicate

A sentence is divided into two parts. The subject and the predicate make up the two parts of a sentence. The subject tells whom or what the sentence is about; it includes the *noun.* The predicate, on the other hand, tells something about the subject; it is really the *verb* part or action part of the sentence. Usually, the subject comes before the predicate, but don't be surprised to find the subject somewhere else in the sentence. That's what's so exciting about English; there are always different ways to do things and there are always exceptions to the rules. But, if you will remember that the subject part is the *noun* part, and the predicate part is the *verb* part, this will be a piece of cake. In the examples below, the subjects are in boxes and the predicates are highlighted .

- **Simple Subject.** This is the *main word* in the **complete subject.** See the examples below;

  ○ My foot hurts . ("foot" is the simple subject)

  ○ A two-story building is being built . (building is the simple subject)

- **Complete Subject.** Basically, the complete subject is everything before the verb and includes the simple subject and all the words dealing with it.

  ○ Mota's home run tied the game .

  ○ The giant television screen replayed the run over and over .

- **Compound Subject.** This has two or more connected subjects that have the same verb. Usually, *and* or *or* connect the two subjects.

  ○ Neither snow nor wind will deter our postman from his rounds .

  ○ Vicky, Birgit, Ann, and Juli are the best friends in the world .

- **Simple Predicate.** This is the main word or group of words in the complete predicate, which is the part of the sentence that tells something about the subject.

  ○ My sister paints .

  ○ She is a well-respected artist .

- **Complete Predicate.** This is the group of words that tag along with the simple predicate. Basically, everything from the verb on is the complete predicate.

  ○ John has never played football before today .

  ○ The Peninsula Drama Club will sponsor the Southern Regional Drama Festival .

- **Compound Verbs.** Like the compound subject, the compound verb (notice it is not called "compound predicate") has two or more connected verbs that have the same subject. *And, or,* or *but* usually connect the verbs. See the examples below.

  ○ Alex and his dad leveled and planted a garden plot in the steep slope behind their house .

  ○ While we were home we washed the car, vacuumed the living room, and dusted the furniture .

EXAMPLE

3. Identify the term that best describes the highlighted portion of the sentence. "During this century, guarding and protecting the environment is of the utmost importance ."

   (A) a simple subject
   (B) compound verbs
   (C) compound subjects
   (D) complete predicate

Your Answer: Ⓓ

ANALYSIS

The correct answer is B. This is a tricky question, but it asks you to choose the *best* term that describes the sentence. Although this highlighted part is also a complete predicate, it nevertheless contains two verbs with one subject, thus making it compound verbs, which is the better answer. Answers **A** and **C** are completely wrong.

SUBJECT-VERB AGREEMENT

When you have a *singular* (meaning one) subject, you must have a *singular* verb. When you have a *plural* (meaning more than one) subject, you therefore must use a *plural* verb. It is said that the subject and the verb must agree in number which is another way of saying *singular* subject = *singular* verb, or *plural* subject = *plural* verb. The examples in the table below should help.

Singular Subject	Singular Verb	Example
chair	squeaks	The chair squeaks when you lean back on it.
book	falls	The book falls from the shelf, making a loud noise.
sun	fades	Silently, the sun fades off in the distance.
plant	grows	That large-leafed plant grows well in the shade.
star	shines	The star shines brightly in the desert sky.
vase	shatters	The vase shatters on the floor.
container	sour	A container of milk will sour without refrigeration.
veteran	recover	The injured veteran will recover from his injuries.
student	studies	That student studies in the library every day.
globe	turns	The globe turns hesitantly on its rusted stand.

Plural Subject	Plural Verb	Example
women	challenge	Women of the new millennium challenge men for jobs.
lights	sparkle	Neon lights seem to sparkle more after the rain.
senators	discuss	The senators on the floor discuss the proposed bill.
horses	gallop	The wild horses gallop freely on the island off the coast.
frogs	leap	Newly developed frogs leap uncontrollably at first.
license plates	are	Metal license plates are easily bent on a car's bumper.
neighbors	celebrate	Our neighbors like to celebrate occasions.
runners	struggle	Some marathon runners struggle in the last five miles.
pianists	memorize	Most pianists memorize their recital pieces.
peaches	reach	Peaches reach their peak of sweetness about mid-July.

Now, look what happens if you mix up the agreement of the subjects and verbs. Mixing and matching verbs and subjects from the lists above should allow you to see how funny, as in odd, things sound when the subject and verb don't agree.

- Student celebrate after the exam. (s. subject, pl. verb)
- Students celebrate after the exam. (pl. subject, pl. verb)
- Students celebrates after the exam. (pl. subject, s. verb)

Let's try another one:

- Horse gallop over the plains of Wyoming. (s. subject, pl. verb)
- Horses gallop over the plains of Wyoming. (pl. subject, pl. verb)
- Horses gallops over the plains of Wyoming. (pl. subject, s. verb)

Hopefully, after reading the sentences with the mixed-up agreements you understand the need to make certain that a singular subject has a singular verb; a plural subject has a plural verb. What confuses some people is the fact that we are taught that to make a singular noun plural we add an "s" or "es," but what seems odd is that the *singular verbs* have an "s" or an "es," but the plural verbs don't. How can they agree? Listening or hearing the way they sound together makes all the difference in the world. With all the rules and regulations in the game of English, sometimes all you can do is to listen carefully to the way its sounds, and then make a judgment call.

EXAMPLE

4. Select the sentence below whose subject and verb do NOT agree.

    (A) The baby coughs all night and all day long.
    (B) The highway leading out of town appears to be deteriorating.
    (C) The boys skates down the street.
    (D) The frogs jump into the pond with much excitement.

Your Answer:

ANALYSIS

The correct answer is C. The subject-verb agreement of *boys-skates* is wrong. It should be *boys-skate*. The remaining answers have correct subject and verb agreement.

DOUBLE NEGATIVES

We don't have no milk in the refrigerator. There is barely nothing to eat. There is hardly no soap in the shower. Ouch! Those are double negatives. The use of *two* negative words to express *one* negative idea is a double negative. Avoid them at all costs. Let's see if we can repair the damage we caused in the above sentences.

- We don't have no milk in the refrigerator. ☹
- We don't have any milk in the refrigerator. ☺
- There is barely nothing to eat. ☹
- There is nothing to eat.—or—There is hardly anything to eat. ☺
- There is hardly no soap in the shower. ☹
- There is hardly any soap in the shower. ☺

Review the following words; these are frequently used negative words and they are OK to use; just don't use more than one per sentence.

barely	never	none	nothing
hardly	no	no one	nowhere
neither	nobody	not	scarcely

EXAMPLE

5. Select the sentence from the list below that uses a double negative.

    (A) There never seems to be enough pencils to go around.
    (B) Nobody seemed to notice that I had a bad hair day today.
    (C) Not one of you said "thank you!"
    (D) Hardly none of them liked to swim.

Your Answer:

ANALYSIS

The correct answer is D. The double negatives are "hardly" and "none." They don't belong in the same sentence. The correct way to write this sentence would be, "Hardly any of them like to swim." or "None of them liked to swim." Answers **A**, **B**, and **C** are correct.

COMPARISON OF MODIFIERS

NOTE

Use the comparative form when you are comparing two persons, places, or things.

Use the superlative form to compare three or more persons, places, or things. The chart on this page should clarify this for you.

These are words, phrases, or clauses that describe or place a limit on the meaning of another word. *Adjectives* and *adverbs* are modifiers and they may be used to compare different things. There are three different degrees of modifiers; **positive, comparative,** and **superlative.** How you use them depends upon how many things are being compared and how many syllables the modifier has.

Positive	Comparative	Superlative
bad	worse	worst
weak	weaker	weakest
well	better	best
bad	worse	worst
near	nearer	nearest
fast	faster	fastest
brave	braver	bravest
dry	drier	driest
simple	simpler	simplest
creative	more creative	most creative
happily	more happily	most happily
remorsefully	more remorsefully	most remorsefully
clearly	more clearly	most clearly
important	more important	most important
often	more often	most often
↓ These show decreasing comparison ↓		
safe	less safe	least safe
cautious	less cautious	least cautious
loyal	less loyal	least loyal
cute	less cute	least cute
serious	less serious	least serious

Review the sentences using the following three forms.

- He was **weak** when he first began weight training. (positive)
- He was **weaker** than anyone else in the gym. (comparative)
- He was the **weakest** person in Redondo Beach. (superlative)
- I thought the results of the game were **bad.** (positive)
- I thought the results of the game were **worse** than before. (comparative)
- I thought the results of the game were the **worst** I had ever seen. (superlative)

EXAMPLE

6. In the sentences below, select the one whose modifier is used *incorrectly*.

   (A) Steve believes he is bravest than his brother.
   (B) Steve believes he is braver than his brother.
   (C) Steve believes he is the bravest boy in town.
   (D) Steve believes he is brave.

Your Answer: Ⓓ

ANALYSIS

The correct answer is A. The question asks for the *incorrectly* used modifier. The modifier in this sentence (bravest) is the superlative form, but it is being used with as a comparison. The correct way to write this sentence is the way it is written in Answer **C.**

Chapter Review and Quick Quizzes

Let's see how well you remember what we've reviewed in this chapter. The quizzes that follow should help to spark your memory. The answers are in the appendix in the back of the book.

SECTION I: CAPITALIZATION

Directions: Using the word bank, complete the sentences by filling in the blanks with the word that best completes the sentence. Some words are repeated more than once, but they are listed more than once in the word bank.

Word Bank: organization, capitalize, government bodies, associations, quotations, I, first, proper

Capitalize the _____ (1) word in every sentence, the pronoun _____ (2), the first word in a full-sentence _____, (3) and all _____ (4) nouns and adjectives. You must also _____ (5) words that name a particular section of the country, planets, stars, races, nationalities, language, and religions. _____ (6), _____ (7), and _____ (8) must also be capitalized.

SECTION II: SENTENCES

Directions: Using the word bank, complete the sentences by filling in the blanks with the word that best completes the sentence. Some words are repeated more than once, but they are listed more than once in the word bank.

Word Bank: imperative, declarative, exclamatory, sentence interrogative

A _____ (1) is a group of words that expresses a complete thought. _____ (2) sentences make a statement. An _____ (3) sentence gives a command or makes requests. _____ (4) sentences express strong emotions or feelings. Sentences that ask questions are _____ (5) sentences.

SECTION III: SENTENCE STRUCTURE

Directions: Using the word bank, complete the sentences by filling in the blanks with the word that best completes the sentence. Some words are repeated more than once, but they are listed more than once in the word bank.

Word Bank: negative, verb, plural, subject, verb, superlative, comparative, verb, sentence, agreement, double, predicate

A _____ (1) is divided into two parts. One part, the _____ (2) tells whom or what the sentence is about. The _____ (3) tells something about the subject and contains the _____ (4) part of the sentence. When you have a singular noun you must have a singular_____ (5). When you have a _____ (6) noun, you must have a plural_____ (7). This is called subject-verb _____ (8). _____ (9) negatives happen when there are two _____ (10) words in the same sentence, such as "not" and "no." When you compare two persons, places, or things, you must use the _____ (11) form of the word. When three or more persons are compared you use the _____ (12) form of the word.

Writing Strategies

This is where the fun begins! The CAHSEE initially offered two opportunities to write; one for each session of the test. But the most recent change in the exam eliminated one of the two writings. Lucky you. The writing task will focus on anything from responding to a piece of literature or literary analysis to one of the many different writings that have been covered in the English-Language Arts Content Standards such as: expository, persuasive, biographical, or autobiographical, etc. What we will review in this chapter as well as in Chapter 11 are the skills you need to get through them successfully. Being able to write a well-thought, cohesive essay on the spot is challenging, but if you know specifically what they are looking for, the task seems less demanding. This chapter will get you through some of the nuts and bolts of writing, while Chapter 13 will focus more on the actual writing itself.

CHAPTER FOCUS

Tips for Good Writing
- Sentence Beginnings
- Avoiding Word Repetition
- Word Choice
- Line Length
- Use of Sensory Imagery
- Audience/Tone/Focus

Organization
- The Prompt and How to Deal With It
- Prewriting/Brainstorming
- Rough Outline
- Introduction
- Body Paragraphs
- Conclusion

Chapter Review and Guided Writing

TIPS FOR GOOD WRITING

Sentence Beginnings

When writing a paper of any length, **begin your sentences with different words.** There are a million and one words in the English language, so there is no need to repeat the word you use to begin your sentences. Again, *avoid repeating sentence beginnings.* It is OK to use prepositions (see list below as a reminder) at the beginning of your sentences, but it is frowned upon to use them at the end of your sentence. To avoid boring the reader, begin your sentences with something other than "The" or "I" over and over again. Use a different word to begin each sentence.

Prepositions—Those with More Than One Word Are Compound Prepositions			
aboard	before	from	out
about	behind	in	over
above	below	in addition to	past
according to	beneath	in front of	since
across	beside	inside	through
after	besides	in spite of	throughout
against	between	instead of	to
along	beyond	into	toward
along with	but (except)	like	under
amid	by	near	underneath
among	concerning	next to	until
around	down	of	up
aside from	during	off	upon
as of	except	on	with
at			within
because of	for	on account of	without

Avoiding Word Repetition

Just as you would avoid repeating sentence beginnings over and over, avoid repeating the same words over and over throughout your writing. Some words have to be repeated (*the, a, an*), but most do not. When you write an autobiographical piece, avoid overusing "I"—especially at the beginning of a sentence. Certainly "I" needs to be used in an autobiographical piece, but there are many ways to write a sentence without using "I." Review the samples below.

- I went to the market and to the dry cleaners yesterday afternoon.
- Going to the market and to the dry cleaners were my goals yesterday afternoon.

- I believe that the drought will end long before October.
- From a personal perspective; the drought will end long before October.

Word Choice

Look at the words below and choose the words that sound better when you say them out loud:

drag	haul
rock to sleep	soothe
lucky	fortunate
begin	start
pest	nuisance
pick	select
big	enormous
a lot	numerous, many, infinite

NOTE

If you maintain a rough objective of not repeating the same word more than twice (except in an autobiographical piece) in a paragraph, your writing will be more interesting.

NOTE

"a lot" is *two words*!

- **Words that sound better.** There are words that literally just sound better than others. Be conscious of the words you use. Choosing better-sounding words doesn't mean using *arrogant* or *haughty* words, or words that sound so intellectual or professional that it changes your natural style of writing. But words can make a difference.

- **Avoid colloquial language.** Being aware of your audience (the person reading the paper) is extremely important in writing for an exam. *Do not use colloquial language* or words that you would use with your friends such as *s'up*, or *ain't*, or *dude*. Colloquial language in a formal essay situation like the exit exam is definitely not appropriate.

- **Listen for the tone.** Words can alter the *sound* of your paper; keep that in mind when you write. When you want to sound *bold*, use bold-sounding words: *The time is now! We must be conscious of environmental needs; tomorrow will be too late.* When you want to sound *gentle*, use gentle-sounding words: *If one silently ponders the environmental issues at hand, one might conclude that the need for a more conditioned response to those issues are imminent.* Words make a difference, but choose them wisely.

Line Length

To AVOID boring your reader to tears, try varying the lengths of your sentences; this means varying the number of words in them. For instance, in one paragraph with five sentences, you might have a sentence word count like this: sentence 1 = 8 words, sentence 2 = 5 words, sentence 3 = 12 words, sentence 4 = 7 words, sentence 5 = 10 words. The more you vary the lengths of your sentence, the more interesting your writing becomes to the reader. Even a one-word sentence is effective occasionally. A one-word sentence is bold and can add excitement, but you must be careful to do it at the right time. Imagine an essay or any paper for that matter, written with seven words in every sentence—it would become extremely tedious reading after awhile. Vary the lengths of your sentences!

Use of Sensory Imagery

Another way to put a spark into your writing is to use an occasional descriptive word. An occasional adjective will do wonders for a less exciting line of prose. Again, the key is to not overdo it. Too many adjectives or adverbs will have a negative effect. Look at the samples below to see the change a descriptive word or two can make; notice the difference between underdoing it and overdoing it.

1. Meredith likes ice cream sometimes.
2. Meredith enjoys chocolate ice cream on hot afternoons.
3. Meredith likes nothing more than to while away the hot, summer afternoon sitting in the shade of the weeping willow tree with a bowl of rich dark chocolate ice cream, savoring every morsel of tantalizing flavor.

Let's look closer at the samples. #1 is rather simple and lacks imagination. #2 is much better, and certainly more vivid than #1. Now, look at #3. We've gone from one extreme to another, obviously to make a point, but #3 is definitely overdone and a perfect example of what you *don't* want to do. Something between 1 and 3 is great. Remember to think of the *visualization* trick we learned in the reading comprehension chapter. Drawing a picture of the sentence in your mind might be an effective way to guide you. Remember, you are not writing a novel, just an essay.

Audience/Tone/Focus

We briefly touched upon the importance of audience earlier, but knowing who you are writing for (the audience), is important in that the style of your writing, the tone, and the focus of the paper will all be dependent upon just that. For the exit exam, your audience will be professionally trained readers who are judging the *skill level* of your writing. The importance of these writing tasks for your future is foremost on their mind and should be on yours as well. These essays should be formal in that you are writing for professional people, not your friends or family. That's your audience. Because they are professional doesn't mean that you should lose your natural style of writing or that they won't want to read a humorously written paper, it simply means that you, the writer, need to follow the rules of good writing. The tone of your paper depends on the topic and how it is approached. The tone can be serious, sarcastic, tongue-in-cheek, solemn, objective, enthusiastic, etc. Tone allows for creativity, but again, it all depends on the topic. Focusing on the specific topic or the subject matter gives it emphasis or clarity. Straying from the topic will cause the writing to become disjointed and you will lose the reader, and there in turn goes your score. What's important? Stay focused.

ORGANIZATION

The Prompt and How to Deal with It

TIP

Organize the information you want to write about BEFORE you begin the actual essay.

When you are writing for an examination like the CAHSEE, or any other in-class writing or impromptu essay, it is *vital* to understand the prompt or the topic. What **are** they asking you to write? Don't be surprised if the prompt is on a topic that arrives seemingly out of nowhere—something unusual—chances are good that it might be. If you are lucky, it will be a topic you are comfortable with, but be prepared for some major brainstorming if it isn't. Regardless of what the prompt is, this is what you are going to write about so read it over carefully. Reread it. Underline or jot down notes about the purpose of the essay. Reread it again. Ponder. Think. Reread the prompt. Get your mind *focused* on the task itself. Follow these steps; become very comfortable with the prompt.

- The Prompt: **American society has shifted from eating healthy food straight from the kitchen to prepackaged, ready-to-eat, or fast food from restaurants. Explain the benefits and the drawbacks for this shift in eating habits.**

- Read the prompt very carefully; take your time

- Underline the main ideas and what it is asking. For instance, you might jot down the following and then use them to jumpstart your brainstorm
  - Shift in eating habits
  - Fresh/healthy/from the kitchen
  - To prepackaged/quick/fast food
  - Drawbacks?
  - Benefits?

- Reread the prompt again.

- *Think/Ponder/Deliberate/*Focus.

- Reread yet again.

- Get ready to write.

Completing this little meditative exercise should help you concentrate and really focus on what you are being asked to write. It shouldn't take long—a couple of minutes, maybe five at the most. It is worth the time to get your mind going in the direction it needs to go.

Prewriting/Brainstorming

After reading and thoroughly understanding the prompt, the next step is the prewriting or brainstorming stage. Some people are anxious to jump into the writing and don't feel they need this step in the writing process, but I can guarantee that taking the few minutes that are needed to do this, is well worth the time and the people reading your paper will appreciate it as well. Your paper will be far more *organized* and *logical,* as opposed to just writing what comes to mind and taking a chance that your mind in all its greatness will do the job for you. Take time to brainstorm! There are many ways to brainstorm; use whatever you are comfortable with. Try one of these.

- **Webbing or clustering**
- **Notes or lists**

Most important to know about the brainstorming process is that you should immediately write down whatever comes into your mind about the topic. It doesn't have to be logical at this point, but the more you think and write, the more information you will have to draw from later. You will not use all of the information that accumulates on paper during the prewriting, but it is a great opportunity to get you thinking more concretely about the topic.

> **TIP**
>
> Make certain that you brainstorm or do some prewriting before you write the essays.

NOTE

In the back of your mind, think in threes. Most essays require five paragraphs and you will need three body paragraphs or three main topics to write about.

- For webbing or clustering draw as many lines going in all directions off the main boxes as necessary.

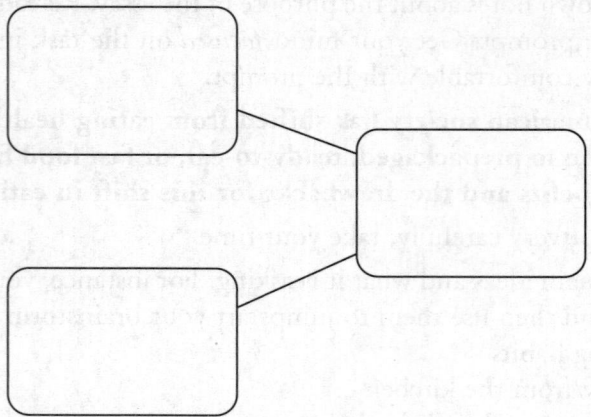

- When using lists, try bulleting (•).
- After you have written all that has surfaced from your mind, look at the information and begin to organize what you have. This is where the next step, outlining, will come in.

Rough Outline

Many people panic when they are asked to outline. Outlining can be a challenging exercise at certain times, but do *not* panic about this outline. Basically, what you really want to accomplish with this outline is to set up your essay in a logical manner, drawing from the information you jotted down while brainstorming. Follow these steps in setting up your outline.

TIP

Remember, you are the only one who is going to see this; it doesn't have to be a work of art, just a functional piece to help you write a good essay.

- INTRODUCTION
- TOPIC PARAGRAPH I
- TOPIC PARAGRAPH II
- TOPIC PARAGRAPH III
- CONCLUSION

✓ Spread these headings out, leaving four or five lines in between to write on, on one side of a piece of scratch paper.

✓ Looking at your brainstorm material, *select the three main topics first.* These should address the prompt directly. Most essays will require five paragraphs, so be sure you choose three strong topics that can be well supported.

✓ Once the main topics are chosen, begin listing or placing supporting evidence under each topic.

✓ For the introduction, you will need to decide on how you are going to hook the reader, either with a strong statement, a question, or a quote, and then introduce your three topics. We will discuss the writing of an introduction below.

✓ For the conclusion, you will need to summarize your writings and then end with a good line of writing. Again, we will discuss the ins and outs of conclusion writing later.

Introduction

The introduction to your essay, or your opening paragraph should do two things; *hook* your reader's attention and *identify the focus* of your writing, which is to explain, persuade, or entertain basically. How you write the introductory paragraph will affect the style, tone, and focus of the entire paper. Your opening paragraph is vital. First of all, you've got to get the reader's attention. There are many ways to do this; choose one that fits your style and go with it.

- Begin with a dramatic or "wow" (eye-opening) statement.
- Open with a funny anecdote or story to set a humorous tone.
- Start with an appropriate quote.
- Ask a thought-provoking question.
- List all of your main points in a straightforward, no-nonsense manner for a serious tone.

Once you have decided how you are going to begin, then begin. The introductory paragraph should include the following:

- The opening line or hook to get the reader's attention.
- A sentence detailing what each of the body paragraphs will be about. Write these details in a logical manner, as the body paragraphs that you write will follow the same order as they are listed in the introduction.
- A focus sentence or thesis statement of what you are going to *prove*. The thesis statement is usually found at the end of the introductory paragraph and is used as a concluding sentence, but it may be used as a boldly written statement right up front as well, serving two purposes: the hook and the thesis statement.

> **Thesis Statement Formula**
>
> =
>
> **A Specific Subject**
>
> +
>
> **A Specific Feature or Feeling**
>
> =
>
> **A Thesis Statement**

Using the thesis statement formula above, let's look at the possibilities for the prompt that was given earlier.

- A Specific Subject = prepackaged, ready-to-eat, fast food
- + Specific Feeling or Feature = unhealthy
- = Thesis Statement = "Prepackaged, ready-to-eat foods, and fast foods so typical in the American diet today are unhealthy."

Body Paragraphs

From your introduction, you have laid out the plan for the body paragraphs. By writing a sentence about each of the body paragraph topics, you have prepared the writer for what's ahead. Each of the paragraphs should continue the tone and focus that you have started in the introduction and each paragraph should have about five sentences. Paragraphs typically are set up like this:

- Topic Sentence (see formula for topic sentence below).

- Supporting details that focus on the topic sentence to help make it clearer, explain, or describe the topic to the reader.

- Concluding or clincher sentence, which is used to summarize or restate the topic.

> **AVOID THESE:**
>
> believe it or not, better late than never, calm before the storm, easier said than done, food for thought, grin and bear it, in the nick of time, last but not least, so far so good, and so on.

> **Topic Sentence Formula**
>
> **=**
>
> **A Limited or Focused Topic**
>
> **+**
>
> **A Specific Impression or Opinion**
>
> **=**
>
> **A Topic Sentence**

Using this formula, let's work on a topic sentence for the prompt we were given earlier:

- Limited Topic = High fat content of convenience foods.

- Specific Impression = Causes obesity, heart disease, high blood pressure.

- = Topic Sentence = Obesity, heart disease, and high blood pressure are just a few of the health problems that plague the American public due to the high fat content of convenience foods.

> **FINAL HINTS FOR CONCLUDING AN ESSAY**
>
> Restate your main idea in a different manner, sum up your ideas and tie loose ends but not in a dull manner, close with a final thought that again allows the reader to take something away from your essay. Let the reader learn something from your efforts.

Conclusion

Concluding paragraphs are intended to stress the important points, speculate the future outcome, suggest a solution, or raise further questions. Frequently, the concluding paragraph summarizes or briefly restates important facts and ties them all together, unifying the essay. It may then end with a thought-provoking statement or detail, giving the reader something to think about long after the reading is completed. Avoid preaching, worn-out endings like morals or clichés. You don't want the reader to be turned off by something trite.

CHAPTER REVIEW AND GUIDED WRITING

To help get you focused for writing, in this chapter we have revised basic ideas and tips that will help you write an essay. We have looked at: avoiding the repetition of sentence beginnings, avoiding word repetition throughout the essay, varying the lengths of your sentences, paying attention to who is reading the essay (the audience), and to the words that you choose. We visited the structure and organization of the essay along with the steps of prewriting, which is brainstorming and outlining. Now, let's practice the prewriting aspect of essay writing; address each of the topics below as if they were going to be your essay topic on the exit exam. Practice these steps with each of them:

- Reading the prompt—over and over.
- Brainstorming—webbing, clustering, listing, etc.
- Outlining—roughly set up your paragraphs as you would if you were going to write the essay

Use a separate piece of paper for each topic. Practice having to think of something different, a topic you may not know much about, but are forced to come up with something to write. Try *all* of the topics, not just those you are comfortable with. In your prewriting, continue brainstorming until you have at least a main topic for three body paragraphs. Think of quotes or strong statements about the topic as you go along.

1. Music has a different meaning for everyone. It is a universal source of healing, comfort, and connection. Explain what music means to you.
2. Respond to the quote by Jacques Barzun: "History's most conspicuous feature is active change."
3. Being a hero or heroine or not being a hero or heroine is all about the difference in doing something or not doing something. Write about heroism.
4. Respond to Eleanor Roosevelt's statement from her speech to the United Nations in 1948 regarding the International Bill of Human Rights: "The unalienable right of all members of the human family is the foundation of freedom, justice, and peace in the world."
5. Physical fitness has been proven to be beneficial in many ways. Prove or disprove this statement.

Writing Applications

As promised, this chapter will walk you through the process of writing an essay for the examination. Following the English-Language Arts Content Standards for ninth and tenth grades, we will focus on the types of writing that could possibly be included on the exam. You will witness the writing process for each of the genres.

CHAPTER FOCUS

Biographical or Autobiographical Narratives

Response to Literature
- Integrating Quotations

Expository Compositions

Persuasive Writing

Business Letters

BIOGRAPHICAL OR AUTOBIOGRAPHICAL NARRATIVES

A narrative is simply telling a story. In an exam situation, you might be asked to relay a personal experience in an autobiographical narrative or about someone else, a biographical narrative. Regardless of the type of paper, the process in getting to the finished product is the same: prewriting with a brainstorm and rough outline and then writing the essay. In a testing environment, chances are that there will be little time for revision, but if you do have time, by all means reread your writing and correct errors neatly. An autobiographical prompt might ask you to respond to one of these:

- an unforgettable or memorable experience
- memories of people
- memories of places
- memories of events
- memories of objects

- memories of family life

A biographical prompt might ask you to respond to:

- someone who has inspired you
- describing an experience through someone else's eyes
- an extraordinary person in your life
- a special person who is
  - helpful/kind
  - talented
  - patriotic
  - weird
  - happy
  - funny

THE PROMPT

In a narrative essay, relate the details of an unforgettable experience in your own life.

Let's take a look at a prompt and begin the writing process.

Prewriting: Brainstorm

walking on the street	listened to speaker
approached by a girl my age	felt uncomfortable
speaking in a familiar language	decided to get out quickly
asked to attend a meeting	invented a sudden and uncontrollable cough
invited to dinner	ran out coughing as fast as I could
there were lots of kids	never looked back

Prewriting: Informal Outline

Introduction: Attention Getting—Hook—Running
Body Par. I: Walking in a new town
Body Par. II: Meeting/Dinner
Body Par. III: Lecture
Conclusion: What you learned

Autobiographical Writing: Unforgettable Experience

Welcome to Your New Home!

My heart was racing, my lungs were aching, my legs exhausted, but there I was in the middle of a strange new town, running as fast as I could to get to my bicycle and then back home. What had just happened to me was an unforgettable incident that took me by complete surprise and when my thoughts return to the incident that occurred so long ago, it forces me to realize the value in trusting one's intuition. When something doesn't seem right, get out, get away as fast as you can, and never look back.

Just having moved to a new town, one that I was exploring by bicycle one sunny Saturday afternoon, I locked my bicycle onto a tree and began exploring on foot, the shops and side streets of my new hometown. The excitement and curiosity of exploring must have been visible on my face, because not three or four blocks from where my bicycle stood, I was approached by a girl who appeared to be my age. She asked if I was new in town and I confirmed her suspicion. Noticing that she had an accent, I asked her where she was from, and she said Germany. We had an immediate connection because I had just returned from spending some time there as an exchange student. During the course of our brief conversation, she asked if I would like to meet some local people, and trusting her I said "Sure."

The young woman gave me the address and directions to a house not far away and said that there would be quite a few people getting together at 3:00 and to come along then. Agreeing, we separated and I continued my exploration. As 3:00 arrived, I found my way to the house. Reaching the door, I heard friendly chatter and was greeted cheerfully and invited to come in. Entering the house, which wasn't a normal house with living room furniture, I saw that it was mostly empty, and that struck me as being rather odd. Hanging on the wall in the empty living room was a large portrait of someone I didn't recognize. I immediately had a very strange feeling. I was escorted into the dining room. There were about twenty young people gathered around a large wooden kitchen table that had plenty of room for everyone. We were offered bowls of chili, cornbread, salad, and milk. I declined the food, stating that I had just eaten, but in reality all sorts of suspicious thoughts were surfacing in my mind: "What if there's poison in the food?"

After everyone had finished eating, we were herded into another room of the house. It was filled with chairs and there was that portrait again. Who is this guy? I wondered, and again my suspicions were being challenged. A young man stood up and began to speak. He began talking about the man in the portrait. The speaker had such incredible charisma when he spoke that it would be mesmerizing, if not for the content of his speech. Listening for about ten minutes, I began to feel extremely uncomfortable. "How do I get out of here," I thought to myself. Not knowing how I arrived at this decision, I suddenly began coughing and choking, I stood up and headed for the door. The speaker questioned where I was going, but I shook my head and continued to cough and ran out of the room. Outside the door, there were two other men who also questioned me, but I continued my acting, motioned to my throat, continued the cough, and ran out the door.

And I ran! Breaking personal speed records, my bicycle was right where I left it. Hopping on, I pedaled as fast as I could. By the time my house was in sight, I was exhausted and out of breath. Sitting down in the comfort of my cozy little home, my thoughts spun around the unexpected incident. I was thankful for the fact that I was able to think quickly enough to get out of an uncomfortable situation, and even more thankful that I was safe at home. Reading the papers years later, I discovered who that man was in the portrait, and knowing what I know now, relying on my intuition was a good thing.

An autobiographical essay obviously will use the pronoun "I" frequently, but this writer manages to use "me" and "I" interchangeably, making the narrative flow easier. As a *hook*, the writer begins in the *middle of the action*. That is a good way to get the story going and the reader into it. Although this story was suspenseful, using this technique with humorous stories is also effective.

GOOD WRITING TIP REMINDERS:
- Vary lengths of sentence.
- Use different sentence beginnings (prepositions, *-ing* words, etc.).
- Watch word choice.

RESPONSE TO LITERATURE

In writing an essay about a piece of literature, on an exam, initially, the most important thing to do is to read the prompt. As instructed in the last chapter, make certain you thoroughly understand and absorb it before you complete the reading. Once you have sorted out what you need to focus on for the writing, the reading will be more focused as well. **Literary analysis** challenges you to present a *thoughtful* interpretation of a literary work. Your well-thought-out interpretation is going to depend upon how well you understand the work and this may take more than one reading. Remember, underline, take notes, do whatever you need to do to understand the reading and then proceed with the writing process. **NOTE:** *The example for this type of essay is going to be the literary analysis prompt that was actually given on the exam the first year.* Again, we will walk through the entire writing process, but know that this is the type of writing that will be expected of you.

The Prompt: In this essay about hummingbirds, the author describes many of the bird's characteristics. In each paragraph, she supports the purpose of her essay. What is the author's purpose for writing this essay about hummingbirds? What details does she give to support her purpose?

Write an essay in which you discuss the author's purpose for writing this essay on hummingbirds. What details and examples does she use to support the purpose of her essay?

Your response will be scored in two ways. One score will be given for how well you understand the selection and for the completeness of your response. A second score will be given for the overall quality of your writing.

Checklist for Your Writing

The following checklist will help you do your best work. Make sure you:

- ☐ Read the selection and the description of the task carefully.
- ☐ Use specific details and examples from the reading selection to demonstrate your understanding of the selections' main ideas and the author's purpose.
- ☐ Organize your writing with a strong introduction, body, and conclusion.
- ☐ Choose specific words that are appropriate for your audience and purpose.
- ☐ Vary your sentences to make your writing interesting to read.
- ☐ Use an appropriate tone and voice.
- ☐ Check for mistakes in grammar, spelling, punctuation, and sentence formation.

The Reading:

Hummingbirds

A flicker of color off to the side catches my eye as I walk along the back fence. It is a warm May morning, and I am outside early to see how the lettuce I've planted is doing. The wire mesh fence that edges my backyard is draped in blue and white morning glories just starting to open in the morning sun. The flicker of color off to my left becomes more pronounced, and I turn, expecting to see a butterfly hovering over the flowers. Instead, a tiny green bird with a red throat is hanging upside down above one of the morning glory blossoms. It is bigger than the butterfly and has a long bill protruding from its tiny head. The bird I have sighted above the morning glories is a male ruby-throated hummingbird, the most common species in the eastern United States.

The hummingbird is found only in the Western Hemisphere and belongs to the *Trochilidae* family, which contains more than 300 species of "hummers," as they are known among enthusiasts. Sporting an emerald green back with gray flanks and an iridescent ruby-red throat, this bird is also called *Joyas Voladoras* or "flying jewels" in Spanish because of its brilliant colors. With an average length of 3.5 inches and weighing only one eighth of an ounce, this hummingbird is incredibly quick, flying at speeds of 30 miles per hour and diving at speeds of up to 65 miles per hour. Hummingbirds' brains make up almost 2.5 percent of their overall weight, making them proportionately, the largest-brained in the bird kingdom, yet the flying muscles comprise some 30 percent of the bird's tiny weight. With these flying muscles, hummingbirds have the fastest wing rate of any bird, which helps them on their migratory paths that can cover up to 2,000 miles between Canada and Panama.

Hummingbirds use their speed to be aggressive feeders and become very territorial. They will fiercely fight one another for sources of food, diving and colliding in midair, and using their bills and claws as weapons. The tremendous speeds at which hummingbirds fly require that they feed constantly. One bird may visit a thousand flowers a day in search of food, munching on gnats, spiders, and sapsuckers, feeding every 10 minutes, and eating almost two thirds of its body weight every day. Like butterflies, they also feed on the pollen and nectar of flowers, sucking out this drink through a long tube-like tongue that absorbs the liquid through capillary action.

The most remarkable aspect of the hummingbirds' wing function is that the wings can rotate fully, making them the only birds that can fly forward, backward, up, down, sideways, or simply hover in space. This ability makes the tiny birds seem like magical creatures. They can hang poised over a blossom, or they can appear to stand still in midair. When hovering in this apparent stationary position, they are actually moving their wings in a figure-eight pattern, and from this position can move in any direction.

On this particular morning, I continue my stroll along the perimeter of the fence. I see two more hummingbirds: one a female that lacks the ruby iridescence at its throat, but that sports a white breast; the other, a male with the ruby gorget. Since it is spring, I wonder if the female is nesting or if her two eggs have hatched. I hope that each season brings more of the tiny, brilliant birds to my backyard, where I can enjoy their aerodynamic antics and their brilliant flashes of color.

Prewriting: Brainstorm

The prompt—what's the author's purpose?

To share her knowledge about the hummingbird

To share her love of the bird

Give details that support her purpose

Each paragraph supports her purpose

1st body paragraph—all about body compositions

       hb found only in W. hemisphere. 300 + species

       Joyas Voladoras or flying jewels in Spanish—brightly colored

       3.5 inches weighs 1/8 of an ounce

       fast—flying speeds 30 mph diving speeds 65 mph

       hb brain 2.5% of body weight—largest-brained in bird kingdom

       flying muscles 30% of body weight

       fastest wing rate of any bird

2nd body paragraph—all about feeding habits

       aggressive feeders—very territorial

       fight for food, diving, colliding use of bills/claws

       tremendous speed = need lots of food

       visit as many as 1,000 flowers/day—every 10 mins

       gnats, spiders, sapsuckers, pollen, nectar of flowers

       long tube-like tongue

3rd body paragraph—all about flying capability

       wing functions—can rotate fully

       only birds that can fly forward, backward, up, down, sideways, hover

       appear to be standing still in midair

       when hovering wings = figure 8 pattern

Prewriting: Informal Outline

Introduction: Hook—Attention Grabber—Did you know that hb
              can fly forward etc.
              Author's purpose is to share knowledge and interest
              Body composition, feeding habits, flying capabilities

Body Paragraph 1: Body composition—brain, weight, length,

Body Paragraph 2: Feeding habits—aggressive, 1,000 flowers, specific
                 foods

Body Paragraph 3: Flying capabilities—all directions, wing functions

Conclusion: Amazing, unique, one-of-a-kind Superbird of the bird
              kingdom

Literary Analysis Essay:

Hummingbirds: The Superbird of the Species

Did you know that hummingbirds can fly forward, backwards, up, down, sideways, or hover in midair? This is one of many fascinating facts shared by the author who appears to be an expert on the subject. The author enthusiastically shares her knowledge of the hummingbird's body composition, its aggressive feeding habits, as well as its unique flying capabilities. From this article, we learn that the hummingbird is truly an amazing creature.

Found only in the Western Hemisphere, the hummingbird is not only one of the tiniest birds in the kingdom, but it is the largest brained and the one of the fastest as well. The hummingbird weighs only one eighth of an ounce and its average length is only 3.5 inches. That's tiny! As the largest-brained bird (proportionately) in the bird kingdom, the hummingbird's brain makes up about 2.5 percent of its body weight. Thirty percent of the hummingbird's body is flying muscles. These muscles allow the bird to have the fastest wing rate and to facilitate their 2,000-mile migration between Canada and Panama.

Considering the hummingbird is so tiny, it is remarkable that they are such aggressive feeders. Because they use up so much energy, they need to feed about every ten minutes and visit about a 1,000 flowers every day. These tiny birds use their bills and claws as weapons to get the food they need. They are extremely territorial. Eating roughly two thirds of its body weight in food every day, the hummingbird enjoys eating gnats, spiders, sapsuckers, pollen, and the nectar of flowers.

The hummingbird has a unique flying capability. It is the only bird that can fly in all directions and hover in midair as well. Its wings rotate fully, which is unusual in and of itself, but when the hummingbird hovers, its wings move in a figure-eight pattern. Flying forwards, backwards, up, down, sideways, and hovering is an incredible aspect of this bird.

After reading this article, it is easy to understand why the author is such a hummingbird enthusiast. This bird sets many records in the bird kingdom. From its speed and unique flying capabilities, to its aggressive and almost constant need to feed, and to its proportionately largest brain, the hummingbird is a fascinating creature. It is truly the Superbird of the bird kingdom.

After first reading the prompt—understanding it thoroughly—and then going on to the reading, it appears to be a fairly straightforward article. The author's tone is one of enthusiasm and therefore, the writer of this essay, carried that tone into her essay. The essayist's introduction *hook* was a question and the subsequent paragraphs supported the request of the *prompt* with *details from the article*. Although this essayist, did not use specific quotes, but reworded everything, she could have inserted an author's quote. Using quotes is a good way to use authentic information to support your writing. See the following to clarify the use of quotes.

- **Integrating quotations.** The use of quotes to support a point in question is valuable. Depending on the type of paper you are writing, the use of quotes will provide official legitimacy to your paper. In nonfiction writing, a quote from an expert in the field can be used to your advantage. In writing about fiction, a dialogue quote from a character that supports the issues you are writing about is advantageous as well. Follow these guidelines when using quotes in your writings:

- Make certain that the capitalization, punctuation, and spelling are the same as that found in the original work.
- Have a short quotation of four lines or fewer, which can be worked into the body of the paragraph that you are working on with quotation marks around it.
- Quotations that are long, five lines or more, should be set off from the rest of the writing. Indent ten spaces and double-space the material. Do not use quotation marks with these longer quotes.
- In using only part of the quote, use an ellipsis (. . .) in place of the words that you are removing from the quote. Use quotation marks as directed above.
- When you add anything to an author's quote use brackets [ ] to show exactly what you have added.

EXPOSITORY COMPOSITIONS

These explain or present information about a specific topic. They may give facts, directions, or explain an idea or define terms. The following are example topics for expository essays. On an exam, one will be chosen for you; it would be a topic broad enough that you should be able to spontaneously gather enough information to write about it.

- **The Causes of:** immigration, good grades, cheating, global warming, litter, water pollution, air pollution, dropouts, corporate greed, etc.
- **The Definition of:** a hero, rap, rock'n'roll, metric system, a conservative, a liberal, soul, the government, a disabled person, generation gap, friendship, loyalty, honesty, a good time, time, patriotism, etc.
- **How to:** operate a video system, grow vegetables, protect the environment, get in shape, impress your teacher, earn extra money, get a job, improve your memory, repair, etc.
- **Kinds of:** friends, dreams, neighbors, clouds, stereos, pain, vacations, heroes, compliments, happiness, censorship, chores, communication, etc.

> **The Prompt:** Define, in a thorough and thoughtful essay, the definition of a school.

Prewriting: The Brainstorm
School is a place to learn
A place to socialize
A place to participate in a club or sport
Study
Experience new things
Make new friends
Teachers, students, lockers, lunch period, classes, gym, sports
Library, offices, principal, counselors, career center
Benches, meeting place, the field
Cafeteria, snack shack, lunch carts—pizza, Chinese, sandwiches,
  Mexican, junk food
Different groups of people
Where you grow and develop physically, emotionally, and
  academically

Prewriting: The Informal Outline
Introduction: The hook, attention grabber—no more pencils, no
  more books
academic /emotional-social/ shaping future in participatory activities
Paragraph 1: academic
Paragraph 2: Character/social development
Paragraph 3: Shaping future
Conclusion: Not just an institution of learning

The Expository Essay:

"No more pencils, no more books, no more teachers' dirty looks." Superficially, when you think of school, something negative seems to surface in your mind. But if you honestly begin to consider school from a more philosophical standpoint, the definition you once had changes dramatically. Learning and academics is the foundation of education, but school not only builds intellect, it builds character and shapes your future as well. School is much more than pencils and books. School is where you begin to become who you are and school guides you to where you want to be.

Of course, you go to school to learn. School is English, science, mathematics, art, physical education, languages, history, social science, journalism, and the list goes on; this is what you "learn" at school. Teachers are there to instruct and to share their expertise. Each grade level builds upon the previous and as you move from one level to the next, your skills become more advanced. What you knew as a freshman seems elementary compared to what you know as a senior. And, that's the nature, the basic premise of school, academic learning.

But, there's more to school than academic learning, much more. School is where you develop as a person, socially and emotionally. Of course, each of us has a friend or group of friends that we socialize with, but socializing isn't all there is to it. When you bond with a few people, they often become confidants, sounding boards, and people to whom you are loyal. These friends help define you as a person. The people that you sit in class with day after day, also become a part of your social development. There are some people you laugh at because they are funny; there are some who are very quiet and seem difficult to get to know; there are others who are loud and boisterous and you only hope they can control themselves so that you won't get held after class. In classes, you meet a variety of people, and you begin to learn about yourself through these observations.

Participating in sports, clubs, and various activities is an indicator of your future as well. Specific interests that are discovered through school-sponsored activities and functions expand upon the depths of your personality. You are developing interests, and broadening your world. An interest in journalism could lead you to a career in that field. An interest in debate or MUN, could spark an interest in politics or diplomacy. The possibilities are almost endless. Participating in school activities really does have the possibility of shaping your future or at least providing guidance.

School is the beginning of your future. If you add together academic learning, social development, and participatory activities, that's the true definition of school. It is not just one-dimensional learning; school is an all-encompassing socially expanding experience that shapes your future, and what you get out of school is dictated by what you put into it. When you hear "No more pencils, no more books," think of all the opportunities to grow and not the one dimension of academics. School is growth.

The expository essay above, takes the three main points that the essayist came upon in his brainstorm and expands upon them. You can clearly see what he is attempting to get across to you, that school is much more than academics. His sentences begin with different words and he manages to develop his paragraphs quite thoroughly.

> **TIP**
>
> Read your writings aloud to catch obvious errors.

PERSUASIVE WRITING

This is one of the most common types of essays assigned, and is one that asks you to convince someone to come over to your side of thinking. In order to do this, you must first form your opinion, and then back it up with facts and details. In general, you must mention the opposing opinion and give details of its weakness without coming right out and saying something degrading or sarcastic. Most important in a persuasive essay is the *need* to be persuasive. Editorials, letters, cartoons, research papers, advertisements, pamphlets, and commercials are examples of persuasive writings.

Common topics for persuasive papers include something that needs improving, something that deserves support, something that everyone should see or do, something that is unfair, etc. Review the writing process and the essay that follows.

The Prompt: Choose a subject that you believe is unfair. In a well-written and well-thought-out essay, persuade the reader to believe as you do regarding the issue.

The Brainstorm: Wearing school uniforms is unfair
Because you lose self-identity
Lack of self-expression
Boring
Ho hummm
Everyone looks the same
Constitutional right

Opposing Argument: less comparison to others—less pressure to be cool
Less to worry about every morning—it is already decided.
Self-expression through shoes and hair

The Informal Outline:

Introduction: Where are the founding fathers when we need them?
Body Paragraph 1: Constitutional right of freedom of expression
Body Paragraph 2: Lack of self-expression
Body Paragraph 3: Opposing—safety issues/less competition, less pressure
Conclusion:

The Persuasive Essay:

Freedoms Lost, Uniforms Gained

Help! Where are our founding fathers when we need them? The recent decree sent forth by the powers that be in our school that *all* students shall wear a white-collared shirt and dark navy pants or skirts should be abolished. Now! The First Amendment speaks of freedom of speech; choosing our own clothes is a freedom tied closely to that amendment and it is being denied us. We have lost our individuality; we have lost our freedom of expression—all in the name of safety. It is unconstitutional and we need to do something about it.

It used to be that getting up in the morning and deciding what to wear was fun. Wearing this with that or that with this, mixing, matching, rolling it up, rolling it down, blue socks, red socks, no socks. It was fun. Now, we get up, go to the closet, and choose a white-collared shirt and navy blue pants, no not the black pants or the jeans, the navy blue ones. Dressing for school has become boring, ho hummmmmmmmmm. Yawn. We no longer are individuals, nor are we independent. All of that is lost, lost to the demands of those who would rather see us all look the same. There goes our individuality.

During lunch, when you look out over the field at everyone dressed in their white and blue, what do you see? A sea of similarity. Bobby looks like Fred, Fred looks like Steve, and Steve looks like Bobby. *Everyone looks the same!* It is as though we are being controlled by an academic big brother. This is much like the government in Ray Bradbury's book *Fahrenheit 451*. They didn't want anyone to think for themselves so they burned all the books so everyone would be on the same level. This is a similar idea; we have no freedom of expression, which is what being a teenager is all about. Freedom of expression is what we long for; conformity is what we live by. But no, oh no, we all look the same and this is not by our choice. We need to do something about it.

The adults who impose this ruling on us unsuspecting students believe that we will all be safe wearing our white and navy, being afraid that someone with an outside group affiliation will disturb the balance of things here at school. They also mistakenly believe that we will be less likely to be judgmental about what someone else is wearing or feel pressured to wear something because it is a fad. That's their argument, their rationale. Group affiliation or association should be under the control of parents and if necessary, the police. And, as far as fads go, that too is a need that teenagers need to fulfill on their own. Teenagers should be able to express themselves and that allows them to grow socially and emotionally. Developing self-expression is what being a teenager is all about.

Yes, without a doubt, our founding fathers would be disappointed in the restrictions and lack of choice that has been imposed upon us. Uniforms are boring. Uniforms deny us our freedom of expression. Uniforms have caused us to lose our identity. We are nothing but white and navy with legs—our minds are dormant—our lives, boring. We want to wear *real* clothes, we want to be normal teenagers, and we want to be free to express ourselves. It's all a part of growing up.

The essayist has a strong opinion, that's for certain. She doesn't like uniforms, but she manages to express herself boldly and not offensively. The topic paragraphs are supported with facts and arguments that are valid to someone her age. The writer also addresses the opposing opinion somewhat harshly, but validates her opposition with facts supporting the social and emotional needs of teenagers. Her conclusion is emotional without being offensive and it leaves the reader knowing her opinion and that was the point.

BUSINESS LETTERS

Business letters are intended to help you get information about something (letters of inquiry), to express an opinion about something (letter to an editor or official), and to order a product or to complain about one (a letter of complaint). Regardless of the type of letter you write, there is a formal format that should be followed. Most letters these days are formatted in a **full-block** style. This means that the left margins are lined up evenly. See the following sample.

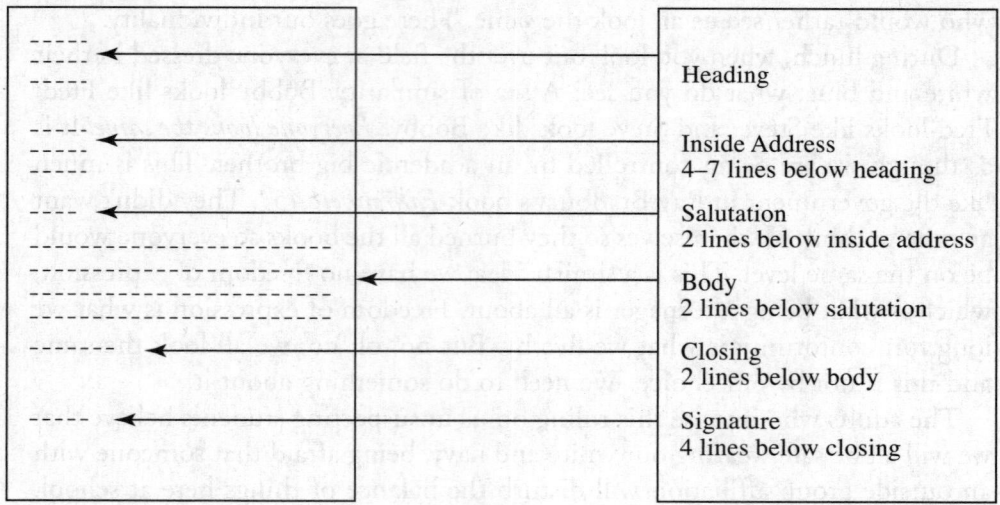

Identification of the parts of a letter:

- **Heading:** Includes the sender's address and the full date. The heading is placed about an inch down from the top of the page.

 2314 Hawthorne Blvd.
 Mayberry, CA 96722
 July 31, 2004

- **Inside Address:** Placed four to seven lines below the heading. It should include the name and complete address of the person/company to whom the letter is being written. If the person has a title, place the title after his or her name.

 Darryl Scoffers, Director
 National Foundation for the Retired
 1413 18th Street SE
 Washington D.C. 20038

- **Salutation:** Placed two lines below the inside address, the salutation is for a specific person or persons. For an individual use: *Dear Mr.* ——, *Dear Ms.* ——, etc. For a company, a group, or an organization, use *Gentlemen, Dear Sirs, Dear Name of Company*, etc. Place a colon (:) at the end of the salutation.

 Dear Mr. Scoffers:

- **Body:** The body of the business letter is placed two lines below the salutation. The information written should be clear and concise, meaning to the point. Businesspeople, like almost everyone else, are busy, and prefer that the direction of the letter is matter of fact and not rambling. Do not indent, and leave a double space between paragraphs.

 It has come to my attention after visiting your establishment last week that your business could benefit from organization. What I observed was a variety of employees not focused on what they were doing and making mistakes because they were continually having to interrupt (or be interrupted) to locate a needed form or supply from a drawer that was being obstructed by something or someone else.

My company, Time Savers, Inc., could be saving you time and money by organizing the way in which your office is set up and operated. Efficiency is our business. Let us help you make it yours. Please call (333) 566-7777 to discuss your options. We have been in business for over twenty years and have hundreds of satisfied customers as references. Let us make a difference in your office.

- **Closing:** Placed two lines below the body and use *Yours truly, Sincerely,* or *Very Truly* for business letters, followed by a comma.

  Sincerely,

- **Signature:** Skip four lines after the closing and then *type* your name. Sign your name between the closing and your typed name.

Thomas Van Horne

Now, put it all together and you have a business letter.

2314 Hawthorne Blvd.
Mayberry, CA 96722
July 31, 2004

Darryl Scoffers, Director
National Foundation for the Retired
1413 18th Street SE
Washington D.C. 20038

Dear Mr. Scoffers:

It has come to my attention after visiting your establishment last week that your business could benefit from organization. What I observed was a variety of employees not focused on what they were doing and making mistakes because they were continually having to interrupt (or be interrupted) to locate a needed form or supply from a drawer that was being obstructed by something or someone else.

My company, Time Savers, Inc. could be saving you time and money by organizing the way in which your office is set up and operated. Efficiency is our business. Let us help you make it yours. Please call (333) 566-7777 to discuss your options. We have been in business for over twenty years and have hundreds of satisfied customers as references. Let us make a difference in your office.

Sincerely,

Thomas Van Horne

Thomas Van Horne

Chapter Review and Guided Writing

As you can see from the last two chapters, there is a lot of thinking organization that goes into writing an essay. From prewriting to the final draft, essay writing takes preparation and thought. You will find that some essays are easier to write than others. But, regardless of whether the topic is easy or challenging, knowing how to set it up and develop your thoughts in an organized manner is the important part. Being able to write a good essay doesn't happen overnight; it is a skill that has to be developed. Following the processes outlined in Chapter 12 and in this chapter will definitely help. But, you've got to continue to practice. Review the prewriting that you completed on the topics from Chapter 12. Using your brainstorms and outlines, begin writing the essays. Follow the suggestions below, which is a walk through the writing process. When you have finished each essay go back over it and look at your sentence beginnings, word choice, sensory imagery (added sparingly), sentence lengths, and structure of each of your paragraphs. Have someone else read them, if possible. Rewrite the essay until you are happy with the end product. You probably won't have time to rewrite the essay on the exit exam, but these essays are to help you achieve a passing score. Practice. Practice.

TIP

Have someone read your writings.

- Read topic thoroughly—over and over until you understand it well.
- Begin brainstorming—webbing, clustering, listing, etc.
- Circle main subtopics that are strong enough to be supported in a paragraph for the body of your essay.
- Make a rough outline of the essay, listing what is going where for each of the paragraphs, including a hook for the introduction.
- Begin writing the essay, being mindful of:
  - Sentence beginnings
  - Word choice
  - Avoiding repetition of words
  - Varying the lengths of your sentences
  - Adding an occasional adjective now and then
  - Staying with the topic in each paragraph
  - Making certain each topic is supported with facts or details and if possible, use a quote (if writing a literary analysis)
- Once the essay is complete with Introduction, Body Paragraphs, and Conclusion, reread it.
- Look at your paper and compare it to the list of things above to be mindful of. Rewrite sentences that repeat words, or change the structure of the sentence if you have been repetitious of sentence beginnings.
- Read the paper *aloud*! You can often catch errors in grammar or punctuation by reading it aloud. How does it sound?
- Repair what needs to be repaired.
- Rewrite the essay and reread; begin the process all over again, if necessary.
- Practice!

Practice Exams

Well, this is it! This is your chance to practice taking the CAHSEE in the comfort of your own room or classroom. Included in this chapter are two full-length CAHSEE practice exams. These exams are primarily made up of actual test questions that are released by the California Department of Education. Additional CAHSEE-like questions are included to balance out the exam and to ensure that it follows the Blueprint (more on that later).

Each exam has 72 multiple-choice questions and a writing task. The CDE includes seven unscored questions in the actual CAHSEE—bringing the total number of questions to 79. These additional questions are experimental in nature and are **NOT** included here. In the making of the tests, the CDE and the makers of the CAHSEE follow what they call a English-Language Arts Blueprint (see below). This Blueprint designates how many questions are included and to which standard they apply. The exams included here follow the Blueprint that was in effect at the time of publication as closely as possible.

Additionally, please note that the CAHSEE only requires ONE writing task. The exams in this book include TWO writing tasks for each test. Writing practice is healthy and beneficial in many ways and all students are encouraged to practice both writing tasks in each exam. Smile!

English-Language Arts Blueprint

Strand	Standards Covered	Number of Multiple-Choice Items	Number of Writing Tasks
Word Analysis	1.1, 1.2	7	-
Reading Comprehension	8.2.1, 2.1, 2.4, 2.5, 2.7, 2.8	18	-
Literary Response and Analysis	3.1, 3.3, 3.4, 3.5, 3.6, 3.7, 3.8, 3.9, 3.10, 8.3.7	20	-
Writing Strategies	1.1, 1.2, 1.4, 1.5, 1.9	12	-
Writing Conventions	1.1, 1.2, 1.3	15	-
Writing Applications	2.1. 2.2, 2.3, 2.4, 2.5	-	1
TOTAL	**72**	**1**	**1**

As for the scoring of the exam, the English-Language Arts section is scored on a scale from 250–450. The multiple-choice scores are totaled and then weighted to account for 80% of the scaled score. The writing task is weighted to account for 20% of the English-Language Arts scaled score.

Answer sheets precede each practice exam—both for the multiple-choice sections and the writing tasks. Good luck with your practice tests. Take a deep breath, focus, and take your time.

Answer Sheet

PRACTICE EXAM 1

1 Ⓐ Ⓑ Ⓒ Ⓓ
2 Ⓐ Ⓑ Ⓒ Ⓓ
3 Ⓐ Ⓑ Ⓒ Ⓓ
4 Ⓐ Ⓑ Ⓒ Ⓓ
5 Ⓐ Ⓑ Ⓒ Ⓓ
6 Ⓐ Ⓑ Ⓒ Ⓓ
7 Ⓐ Ⓑ Ⓒ Ⓓ
8 Ⓐ Ⓑ Ⓒ Ⓓ
9 Ⓐ Ⓑ Ⓒ Ⓓ
10 Ⓐ Ⓑ Ⓒ Ⓓ
11 Ⓐ Ⓑ Ⓒ Ⓓ
12 Ⓐ Ⓑ Ⓒ Ⓓ
13 Ⓐ Ⓑ Ⓒ Ⓓ
14 Ⓐ Ⓑ Ⓒ Ⓓ
15 Ⓐ Ⓑ Ⓒ Ⓓ
16 Ⓐ Ⓑ Ⓒ Ⓓ
17 Ⓐ Ⓑ Ⓒ Ⓓ
18 Ⓐ Ⓑ Ⓒ Ⓓ
19 Ⓐ Ⓑ Ⓒ Ⓓ
20 Ⓐ Ⓑ Ⓒ Ⓓ
21 Ⓐ Ⓑ Ⓒ Ⓓ
22 Ⓐ Ⓑ Ⓒ Ⓓ
23 Ⓐ Ⓑ Ⓒ Ⓓ
24 Ⓐ Ⓑ Ⓒ Ⓓ

25 Ⓐ Ⓑ Ⓒ Ⓓ
26 Ⓐ Ⓑ Ⓒ Ⓓ
27 Ⓐ Ⓑ Ⓒ Ⓓ
28 Ⓐ Ⓑ Ⓒ Ⓓ
29 Ⓐ Ⓑ Ⓒ Ⓓ
30 Ⓐ Ⓑ Ⓒ Ⓓ
31 Ⓐ Ⓑ Ⓒ Ⓓ
32 Ⓐ Ⓑ Ⓒ Ⓓ
33 Ⓐ Ⓑ Ⓒ Ⓓ
34 Ⓐ Ⓑ Ⓒ Ⓓ
35 Ⓐ Ⓑ Ⓒ Ⓓ
36 Ⓐ Ⓑ Ⓒ Ⓓ
37 Ⓐ Ⓑ Ⓒ Ⓓ
38 Ⓐ Ⓑ Ⓒ Ⓓ
39 Ⓐ Ⓑ Ⓒ Ⓓ
40 Ⓐ Ⓑ Ⓒ Ⓓ
41 Ⓐ Ⓑ Ⓒ Ⓓ
42 Ⓐ Ⓑ Ⓒ Ⓓ
43 Ⓐ Ⓑ Ⓒ Ⓓ
44 Ⓐ Ⓑ Ⓒ Ⓓ
45 Ⓐ Ⓑ Ⓒ Ⓓ
46 Ⓐ Ⓑ Ⓒ Ⓓ
47 Ⓐ Ⓑ Ⓒ Ⓓ
48 Ⓐ Ⓑ Ⓒ Ⓓ

49 Ⓐ Ⓑ Ⓒ Ⓓ
50 Ⓐ Ⓑ Ⓒ Ⓓ
51 Ⓐ Ⓑ Ⓒ Ⓓ
52 Ⓐ Ⓑ Ⓒ Ⓓ
53 Ⓐ Ⓑ Ⓒ Ⓓ
54 Ⓐ Ⓑ Ⓒ Ⓓ
55 Ⓐ Ⓑ Ⓒ Ⓓ
56 Ⓐ Ⓑ Ⓒ Ⓓ
57 Ⓐ Ⓑ Ⓒ Ⓓ
58 Ⓐ Ⓑ Ⓒ Ⓓ
59 Ⓐ Ⓑ Ⓒ Ⓓ
60 Ⓐ Ⓑ Ⓒ Ⓓ
61 Ⓐ Ⓑ Ⓒ Ⓓ
62 Ⓐ Ⓑ Ⓒ Ⓓ
63 Ⓐ Ⓑ Ⓒ Ⓓ
64 Ⓐ Ⓑ Ⓒ Ⓓ
65 Ⓐ Ⓑ Ⓒ Ⓓ
66 Ⓐ Ⓑ Ⓒ Ⓓ
67 Ⓐ Ⓑ Ⓒ Ⓓ
68 Ⓐ Ⓑ Ⓒ Ⓓ
69 Ⓐ Ⓑ Ⓒ Ⓓ
70 Ⓐ Ⓑ Ⓒ Ⓓ
71 Ⓐ Ⓑ Ⓒ Ⓓ
72 Ⓐ Ⓑ Ⓒ Ⓓ

Answer Sheet
PRACTICE EXAM 1—WRITING TASK 1

Write your response here:

_____

_____

_____

_____

_____

_____

_____

_____

_____

_____

_____

_____

_____

_____

_____

_____

_____

_____

_____

_____

Answer Sheet

PRACTICE EXAM 1—WRITING TASK 2

Write your response here:

_____

_____

_____

_____

_____

_____

_____

_____

_____

_____

_____

_____

_____

_____

_____

_____

_____

_____

Practice Exam 1 Writing Task 2 Continued:

California High School Exit Exam Practice Test 1

READING

Read the following passage and answer questions 1 through 8.

Beneath the Redwoods

As night began to settle in after a long stormy afternoon, the darkened village of Whistler's Glen, which is nestled among the towering redwood trees in Northern California, slowly began to reappear as cabin lights were lit one by one. Miners who spent long days breathing in the dirt and coal dust of the tunnels they dug far beneath the surface returned to their homes. Many of these men were there temporarily. Most were there to earn a living during this disparaging and devastating economic downturn of the 1930s. But there were two brothers who notably arrived in Whistler's Glen with the idealistic hopes and dreams that would end up inspiring hundreds.

Walter and Harold McLean were born just eighteen months apart. Raised by a stern, firm-handed father and a kindly and quiet-mannered mother, the two boys, although poor and underprivileged in many ways, were prosperous and well off in their outlook and approach to life, and seemingly, since birth. Walter and Harold saw the world in a manner that was admirable considering their unfortunate circumstances—much like the evening lights that lit the tiny village of Whistler's Glen.

When the Great Depression arrived, the McLean family was hit hard. Mr. McLean lost his job, and although Mrs. McLean had cleaned and cooked for a living, times were difficult for everyone, rich and poor alike, and she was laid off as well. Walter and Harold were forced to drop out of school and find work. Having heard about the mines of Whistler's Glen, both boys set out on the rugged journey, hoping of course to find work to help their parents, who were devastated by their present situation. After a journey of several days on foot, they came upon the village that seemed dwarfed by the redwoods that surrounded it. Having no means with which to pay for a room, the boys slept beneath the giant trees which, over the next few months not only sheltered them, but became majestic symbols of strength and undaunted inspiration for Walter and Harold.

After months and months of dirty and hazardous labor in the mines, the boys began to consider life beyond the village. Although they were tied to the area because of their economic hardships, that did not dampen their spirits. Each night after work, Walter and Harold returned to their campsite beneath the redwoods and discussed the future and imagined what it might hold for them. These stories of hope buoyed them through each day.

The months turned to years, and although Walter and Harold had been helping their parents adjust and survive through the worst of the Depression, the two boys managed to save enough money to invest in their futures and to begin to realize the dreams that they had discussed over the years.

Knowing that the United States and much of the world had experienced one of the worst economic periods in history, they wanted to invest in something that could survive, despite the worst of times. They decided to open a small grocery store. Looking at many possible sites and towns near to Whistler's Glen, they knew that they wanted to be close to the trees that had provided them with shelter and inspired their dreams with their elegant yet strong presence.

Over the years, Walter and Harold expanded their enterprise. One store turned into ten and then fifty, and they are scattered all over California. Eventually, the mines of Whistler's Glen were closed and the village deserted. The McLean boys returned to revitalize the area. Their main goal was to preserve its natural beauty and the campsite that they called home for so many years.

Whistler's Glen is now a quaint village with vast parkland that can be enjoyed by all who venture there seeking peace and inspiration from nature.

1. The words *giant* and *majestic* found in paragraph 3 suggest a feeling of—

    (A) poor and weakened.
    (B) small and immature.
    (C) grand and stately.
    (D) large and unimportant.

2. Read this sentence from the story.

"These stories of hope buoyed them through each day."

What does the word *buoyed* mean as it is used in this sentence?

(A) caused them to sink
(B) helped keep their spirits up
(C) made them float
(D) caused confusion

3. How does the challenging situation that Walter and Harold find themselves in seem to make them stronger?

(A) They sleep under the redwood trees because they cannot afford to rent a room.
(B) The Great Depression caused many to lose their jobs.
(C) They continually keep a positive attitude and discuss their hopes and dreams for the future.
(D) Whistler's Glenn is a tiny village that seemed like home to Walter and Harold.

4. In what way does the majestic redwood tree foreshadow a positive end to "Beneath the Redwoods?"

(A) The tree seems to stand tall and proud, and inspired the boys with its enduring nature.
(B) The trees provided shelter for the boys.
(C) The tree stands for strength.
(D) The tree signifies happiness and joy.

5. Which word BEST describes the tone throughout the passage?

(A) ironic
(B) sarcastic
(C) frustrated
(D) hopeful

6. Which of the following BEST represents the intent of the author in writing "Beneath the Redwoods?"

(A) to demonstrate the tragedies of the Great Depression
(B) to prove that optimism in times of distress can bring good rewards
(C) to ensure that the reader understands the meaning of hardships
(D) to prove that the narrator has a positive outlook

7. Which of the following themes of the Great Depression are represented in this story?

   (A) homelessness and frustration
   (B) emotional turmoil and hunger
   (C) unemployment and economic hardships
   (D) travel and sportsmanship

8. Despite the serious calamities that prevailed during the Great Depression, which of the following BEST represents the tone of this story?

   (A) hopelessness
   (B) frustration
   (C) carelessness
   (D) optimism

Read the following passage and answer questions 9 through 15.

Early Summer Mornings

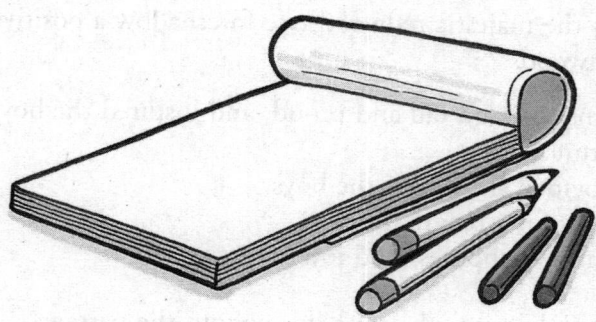

My room faces east. When the sun rises ever so brightly in the morning during the summer, it doesn't care what time I've gone to bed the night before. Most of the time I get up, make breakfast, shower, watch a little TV, or listen to music on my iPod before getting on with the rest of the day. I'm an early riser.

For some reason, this morning I wake up feeling antsy, as though I've had ten cups of coffee. As I pull back the curtains, I notice the sky is dark and gray, and is hiding the sun from its employment.

Going downstairs, the clock in the hall tells me that it is nearly six thirty. I make juice and toast, pour milk on my bowl of cereal, load it onto a tray, and head back up to my room.

Hearing my brother thrashing around in the bathroom getting ready for work, I go downstairs to make his breakfast. Within five minutes, he joins me in the kitchen wearing his work clothes with eyes that appear as though they are taped partially closed. His hair is a bed-headed mess and the imprint of his pillow remains on the right side of his face.

"Good morning," I say.

And he responds with a weak and tired, "Uh huh."

I leave him with his breakfast and morning stupor and return to my room. Some mornings I can get right into the day, but others I like to hover beneath the quilt and think about things.

This morning happens to be one of the latter.

Today is dad's birthday. My mom won't mention it at all, but my brother might, just to cause an argument. I am an artist, and every year on my dad's birthday I draw a picture of him. He looks different every year that I draw his picture. Part of it is because I like to draw using different techniques, but part of it is my imagination and how I think he might look if he were here. Sometimes I think that if he were to return, I would show him these portraits and explain a painting that imitated Monet's style and say, "This is you when I was nine," pointing to a portrait that imitated Picasso's cubism. "This is you when I was fourteen and you'd been gone for five years," pointing to a painting done in dark and serious Rembrant-like tones. He'll look at each painting and know that I love him and will never forgot him.

Right now I am into lines and shapes, like Miro or Klee. Getting out of bed, I gather my pastels, some charcoal, and tape a sheet of heavy art paper to my drawing board.

Saturdays when mom worked, he would take me around town and I would insist on visiting all of the art shops. On my sixth birthday he bought me a box of crayons, the giant box with 99 different colors. On my seventh birthday he bought me oil paints. On my ninth birthday he bought me an easel—not the kind for children, a real one.

"Draw me," he'd ask.

"Dad, I can't."

There were mornings when I would wake up and find a book about DaVinci or Chagall on my pillow.

I should go to school, I'm supposed to be in class learning physics or history or algebra. But I just can't find a good reason to leave this project behind. I will be in trouble tomorrow, but I will deal with that tomorrow. I'll say that it was my dad's birthday and I spent the day with him.

I spend a few minutes thinking about his hair. It is probably a bit more gray than it was last year, and I'll make his hair longer this year. I think I will give him a few extra pounds, too, but I keep his smile fixed in my head.

How am I going to draw his shoulders? I'll put him in a sweater with a dress shirt beneath it. It brings out the color in his eyes and shows how they sparkle.

Sitting there, I think about how much I want to show and how much I want to tell in the painting.

Then I pick up the charcoal and begin to draw. And then I take up the pastels to add color to his eyes, another for his mouth.

Suddenly.

Oh, Dad. There you are.

9. What does the word *employment* mean as it is used in the following sentence?

As I pull back the curtains, I notice the sky is dark and gray and hiding the sun from its employment.

(A) preventing the sun from shining
(B) causing it to rain
(C) making the day gloomy
(D) forcing the sun to shine

10. How does the brother react when he is greeted in the morning by the narrator?

(A) He remains silent.
(B) He has a grumpy and mean reply.
(C) He is cheerful.
(D) He seems to be sleepy and groggy.

11. Why does the main character paint a portrait of his dad every year on the day of his birthday?

(A) Because his father bought him his first big box of crayons.
(B) Although he doesn't see his dad anymore, he has fond memories of him and wants to remember him every year by painting a portrait of what he thinks he might look like now.
(C) He doesn't seem to have anything else to do and he doesn't want to go to school.
(D) The weather is gloomy outside and he would rather just stay in his room and paint than go outside.

12. Which statement best describes the narrator's feelings about his father?

(A) He seems to miss him very much.
(B) He is disappointed in his mother's lack of concern.
(C) Although he cares for his brother, he knows the brother doesn't care about his father.
(D) He is angry that his father isn't there and takes it out on his brother.

13. What does the use of a flashback accomplish in the story "Early Summer Mornings?"

    (A) It allows the narrator to lose track of time.
    (B) It allows the reader to understand the memories of the boy's father—memories that he doesn't want to forget.
    (C) It changes the perspective and the direction of the story.
    (D) It adds color and vividness to the narrative.

14. How is the ending to the story ironic?

    (A) When the narrator has finished the painting of his father, his comment makes it appear as though he really was there, which is wishful thinking and not reality.
    (B) With the narrator's painting completed, his statement represents anger.
    (C) The painting represents the father.
    (D) The narrator has a problem with finishing the painting; he stumbles at the end and doesn't know what else to say.

15. How is the internal dialogue used effectively in the story?

    (A) It represents the narrator's true feelings about his father.
    (B) It demonstrates to the reader the thoughts of the boy's mother.
    (C) It shows how angry he is about his brother's lack of respect.
    (D) It shows the conflict between the narrator and his family.

Read the following poem and answer questions 16 through 20.

The Storm

She seems to reach
For all that is bright and shining.
The cruel storm cloaks this light
With the darkness of immorality,
Coupled with implications of dread and destruction.

Living with the stars overhead and the sea below,
The malicious storm spreads her blustery wings
Throughout the unsuspecting and anxious sky.
She stirs peril into the sea
By bringing waves that forcefully overthrow the meek,
And with the devastating force
Of a witch's cauldron set to boil, boil, boil.

Extending her dominion and supremacy
With widespread arms,
The mountains,
Locked between the restless sea and the troubled sky,
Become the storm's testimony to uncertainty
And her need to impress the earth with dignity and defiance.

The storm triumphs in battle after raging battle.
And with no effort on her part
To sympathize or extend an apology
To all who suffer from her inconsiderate wrath.
And yet the storm, without remorse,
Continues her vicious rites of passage,
Striking all of the unsuspecting
Who might stand in her broad and unwavering path.

16. Read the following two lines from the poem.

    She seems to reach
    For all that is bright and shining.

    How does the imagery of these two lines contradict the rest of the poem?

    (A) There is no contradiction; the lines introduce the bright imagery of the rest of the poem.
    (B) They contradict the rest of the poem by pointing the way toward darkness.
    (C) These lines are the only two lines that have imagery that is positive; the rest of the poem is dark.
    (D) The two lines indicate an impact on the positive before revealing the negative.

17. How does the use of personification affect the tone of the poem?

    (A) It demonstrates the unpredictability of storms.
    (B) It turns nature into an entity.
    (C) It allows the reader to clarify the meaning of a storm.
    (D) It makes the storm seem like a cruel human seeking vengeance.

18. The imagery of the poem is—

    (A) optimistic and positive.
    (B) dark and ominous.
    (C) friendly and persuasive.
    (D) colorful and animated.

19. The words *cruel, darkness,* and *dread* that are found in the first stanza of the poem imply a feeling of—

    (A) fear and evilness.
    (B) cheerfulness and mirth.
    (C) goodness and joy.
    (D) confusion and dismay.

20. Which of the following BEST describes the effect of the tone on the poem itself?

    (A) It colors the poem with cheerfulness.
    (B) It allows the plot to develop.
    (C) It changes the storm into something sinister and unpredictable.
    (D) It allows the author to express frustration with storm damage.

Read the following passage and answer questions 21 through 26.

Continents

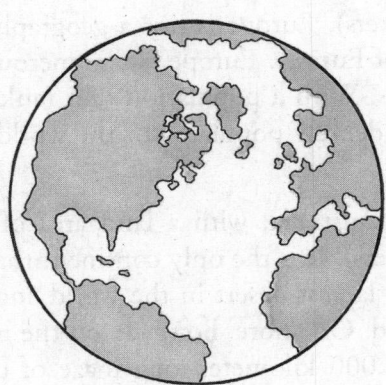

There are seven continents on Earth. From the largest to the smallest, they are: Asia, Africa, North America, South America, Antarctica, Europe, and Australia. Continents cover about 30% of the Earth above the sea, but also extend below sea level and form continental shelves. Although all of the continents are unique in many ways, they all have four things in common. These four common traits are the components that make up the continental crust: shields, stable platforms, sedimentary basins, and folded mountain belts.

Asia is the world's largest continent and has a land mass area of 17, 212,041 square miles (44,579,000 square kilometers). Asia is a part of the Eurasian land mass which it shares with Europe. Because Europe and Asia are not separated by a large body of water, the boundary between the two continents is defined by the Ural Mountains, the Ural River, the Caspian Sea, and the Caucasus Mountains. Asia contains the highest mountain, Mount Everest. It has eighteen of the world's 50 largest rivers and six of the world's largest deserts.

Africa is the second largest continent, with a land area of 11,608,156 square miles (30,065,000 square kilometers). Africa's largest geographical feature is the Sahara Desert. It is the largest desert on Earth. It covers an area of 3.5 million square miles (9,065,000 square kilometers), which is just slightly less than the total area of the United States.

North America is the third largest continent with a land area of 9,365,290 square miles (24,245,000 square kilometers). It stretches from Canada in the north and as far south as the Isthmus of Panama which connects North America to South America.

The fourth largest continent is South America. Its land area covers 6,880,000 square miles (17,819,000 square kilometers). The Andes, a mountain range that stretches nearly the entire length of the continent on its west side, is a prominent physical feature. The Amazon River is the world's largest river by volume and the second largest by length.

Antarctica is the fifth largest continent, with an area of 5,404,000 square miles (14,000,000 square kilometers). The continent is covered by an ice sheet that averages about 2,160 meters thick. Antarctica has no indigenous population. The only humans that live on the continent are at research stations.

The sixth largest continent is Europe. With an area of 3,837,082 square miles (9,938,000 square kilometers), Europe is not a geographically distinct continent. Instead, it is a peninsula of Eurasia. Europe has numerous mountain ranges and a number of navigable rivers. With a population that ranks third among the continents, Europe is the most densely populated of the world's most highly developed areas.

The smallest continent is Australia, with a land area of 2,967,966 square miles (7,687,000 square kilometers). It is the only continent that contains a single country. Australia has the third largest desert in the world and roughly one half of the country or continent is arid. Off shore, however, on the northeast coast, the Great Barrier Reef, which is a 2,000 kilometer-long maze of coral reefs, is the world's largest.

Although the seven continents vary in size and unique geographical features, they each contain common elements that help to define them as continents.

21. What is a synonym for the word *arid* as it is used in the following sentence?

    Australia has the third largest desert in the world and roughly one half of the country or continent is arid.

    (A) dry
    (B) soggy
    (C) damp
    (D) fruitful

22. Which of the following statements BEST summarizes the information presented in the article?

    (A) The seven continents are vast expanses of land and ice.
    (B) The continents are primarily deserts and rivers.
    (C) Despite the differences in size, all seven continents have elements in common.
    (D) All continents contain rock.

23. Based on the information in the article, which statement about continents is accurate?

    (A) Asia is the smallest continent.
    (B) Australia is the largest continent.
    (C) The largest desert on Earth is in Africa.
    (D) Antarctica has the largest population.

24. This article contains the MOST information on—

    (A) the number of rivers found on each continent.
    (B) the number of reefs that each continent contains.
    (C) the number of navigable rivers found on each continent.
    (D) the size and unique geographical features of each continent.

25. What information supports the idea that Europe and Asia could be considered one continent?

    (A) Europe has several navigable rivers.
    (B) Asia has the highest mountain.
    (C) Europe consists of only one nation.
    (D) Europe is not a geographically distinct continent; it is a peninsula of Eurasia.

26. What fact supports the idea that Australia is one of the most arid continents?

    (A) Australia is the smallest continent.
    (B) The Great Barrier Reef is the largest in the world.
    (C) Australia is the only continent with a single country.
    (D) One half of the Australian continent is arid.

Read the following passage and answer questions 27 through 31.

The Hamburger's History

Have you ever wondered how the common, everyday hamburger got its name? Well, the story goes like this—well, at least one of the stories; there are many. During a trip to Asia in the early 1800s, a German merchant couldn't help but notice that the nomadic Tartars (a Turkic-speaking group) softened their beef and venison by storing it under their horse's saddles. Because the motion of the horse pounded the meat into pieces, the Tartars would scrape it together, season it, and then cook it.

The idea of pounded beef found its way back to Europe with the merchant whose hometown was Hamburg. Here, the cooks would broil the meat and began to refer to it as Hamburg meat. From there, German immigrants brought the recipe to the United States and it is believed to have appeared on the menu of Delmonico's Restaurant in New York in 1834, although nothing exists to prove that. The first mention of "Hamburg steak" was made in the *Boston Evening Journal* in 1884. But the hamburger that we all know (without the bun) can be attributed to a man named Charlie Nagree of Seymour, Wisconsin. He introduced the American hamburger at a county fair in Seymour, which is considered the hamburger capital of the world.

The first hamburger to be served on a bun took place in 1904 at the St. Louis World's Fair. This event eventually led an enterprising cook from Wichita, Kansas to seek financial backing, which led to the eventual development of a hamburger restaurant chain called White Castle, which was an instant success. McDonald's, owned by Dick and Mac McDonald in San Bernadino, California began in 1940. They introduced their efficient "Speedee Service System" in 1948, and later sold their franchise to Ray Kroc who expanded the corporation worldwide. The rest is history.

27. What is the definition of the word *nomadic* as it is used in the following sentence.

   During a trip to Asia in the early 1800s, a German merchant couldn't help but notice that the nomadic Tartars (a Turkic-speaking group) softened their beef and venison by storing it under their horse's saddles.

   (A) stable
   (B) patterned
   (C) advance
   (D) roaming

28. Which of the following statements BEST summarizes the information presented in the article?

   (A) The history of the hamburger began in Asia, and as it evolved, the idea traveled to Germany and the United States.
   (B) The hamburger was discovered by the Tartars of Asia.
   (C) The hamburger was not served with a bun, in Germany.
   (D) McDonalds discovered the hamburger in the 1800s.

29. Based on the information in the article, which of the following statements is accurate?

   (A) Hamburgers were invented by White Castle Restaurants.
   (B) McDonald's invented the hamburger in 1940.
   (C) An early form of the hamburger was served in Germany in the 1800s.
   (D) The first hamburger served on a bun was in Asia.

30. This document provides the reader with the LEAST information on—

   (A) the nomadic tribe, the Tartars.
   (B) the history of the hamburger.
   (C) Delmonico's Restaurant in New York City.
   (D) how McDonald's was established.

31. What information supports the notion that the original idea of hamburger meat comes from Asia?

   (A) Ray Kroc bought McDonald's from two brothers in San Bernardino.
   (B) Hamburgers were first served on buns at a World's Fair.
   (C) A German merchant noticed that the Tartars tenderized their beef and venison by storing it under their saddles.
   (D) A merchant brought the idea to Hamburg, Germany.

Read the following passage and answer questions 32 through 40.

How to Choose a Career

Many students have a level of uncertainty regarding the best way to go about deciding a career path that best fits their personal interests, passions, and individual goals. There are several steps to take to make a decision that will affect you for the rest of your life. Take notes, make lists, and jot down ideas as you follow through all of the steps. But most importantly, don't panic. Choosing a career path is important, but you will have time to decide. If you choose to go to college, the first two years of classes allows you time to explore many areas that you may not have considered previously. These classes are a broad spectrum of subjects—from philosophy to literature—and you can look at taking these classes as an additional exploration or opportunity to find the right career path for you. If you choose not to go to college, most jobs require some training, whether it is on-the-job training or at a technical school. Take your time in making the decision, and make sure that you are doing something that means something to you personally.

STEP ONE

To begin to discover what your career interests are, ask yourself the following questions.

- What areas am I interested in?
- What are my strengths?
- What are my best subject areas in school?
- What are my weaknesses?
- What kind of personality do I have?
- What is really important to me?
- What am I passionate about?
- What are my values? (helping society, working alone or with groups, security, status, having a positive impact on others, etc.)

STEP TWO

Take any, or several, career-related interest surveys or tests. There are many that you can take on the Internet or in your college and career center at school. These tests or surveys will show you your areas of interest and possible careers that relate to those areas of interest.

STEP THREE

Draw upon your own life experiences. Think about jobs, classes, volunteer opportunities, and other experiences that you have enjoyed. Use these personal experiences to help you focus on career possibilities.

STEP FOUR

Learn about career options. It is rare that you will have an opportunity to take a class in high school or college that shows you the work place as it actually exists. You will have to take the initiative to discover this on your own. One way is by reading. Most libraries have books that explain all of this. Locate the Bureau of Labor and Statistics publication titled *Occupational Outlook Handbook*. You can read about specific jobs that you are interested in, what specific duties are involved, what qualifications are needed to obtain this type of position, the education or training that is required, as well as the salary ranges.

Another way to experience a prospective job is to find an internship or to work part time in the industry of interest. An internship is an opportunity to experience a job interest firsthand by working with the people who actually work at the job that you are exploring. Many internship opportunities are offered in many different areas of the job market. Actual work opportunities or internships will help you make a more educated decision. You could find that you love the area or that you absolutely dislike it—which is good to know either way. Your school's career center should be able to direct you to these opportunities.

STEP FIVE

After going through the earlier steps, begin to sort out your priorities. You may find that you dislike certain work environments and prefer others, such as offices, hospitals, warehouses, etc. You may find that your interest in a certain area may not sustain a career, so you'll have to eliminate those types of jobs from your list. Regardless of the possibilities that are available—and there are many—you will be learning a great deal about yourself. These discoveries will help you make the right decision when the time comes. But remember, you don't have to live forever with a specific career decision. The job you choose in your twenties may not be the job that you will be working at or interested in when you are in your forties. Many people change careers several times during their lives. That is not to discount those who find their passion and stick with it for the rest of their lives; just know that you can change careers.

STEP SIX

Weigh your options. By now you should have a list of possibilities. Take the time to imagine or visualize working in a certain work environment. Talk to your family and friends who know you well. Listen, but follow your passion—make your own decisions. Evaluate everything possible—training, education, graduate school, job opportunities—are there enough jobs in this area and can I earn enough to survive on? Take your time, be rational, and most importantly, choose the right path for your skills and talents.

32. According to the information provided in Step Three, what is the strategy that would be useful in a search for a career?

   (A) Observe your parents.
   (B) Draw upon your own life experiences.
   (C) Listen to your teachers.
   (D) Don't take a chance at anything.

33. How is the information organized in the article *How to Choose a Career*?

   (A) from taking a survey to asking yourself questions
   (B) from eliminating bad choices to writing notes
   (C) from weighing your options to reading the *Occupational Outlook Handbook*
   (D) from asking yourself questions to weighing your options

34. The author of the article uses a series of _____ to present the information on choosing a career.

   (A) bullets
   (B) steps
   (C) paragraphs
   (D) sentences

35. The structure of the document is important because it allows the reader to develop a personal focus on career choice by providing a progressive series of exercises that—

   (A) confuse the reader.
   (B) simplify the process of choosing a career.
   (C) build upon the previous step, much like laying a foundation.
   (D) complete a series of exercises that are redundant.

36. Which of the following statements BEST summarizes the information presented in the article?

   (A) Choosing a career is extremely easy.
   (B) Take your time when choosing a career.
   (C) There are six progressive steps to take when trying to choose the right career path.
   (D) The best way to choose a career is to read about careers in the library.

37. Based on the information in the document, which of the following statements is accurate?

   (A) Choosing a career is a long and tedious process.
   (B) Choosing a career involves knowing your strengths and weaknesses.
   (C) Going to college is the only way to find a career.
   (D) Spending time on the Internet will help you find the right job.

38. This document provides the LEAST information on—

    (A) various working environments.
    (B) the steps in choosing a career.
    (C) drawing upon life experiences.
    (D) questions to ask yourself.

39. Which statement supports the idea that choosing a career is an important decision?

    (A) It is something that you will be spending a good part of your life doing, and your job should fit your personality.
    (B) Choosing a job depends on your level of education.
    (C) Choosing a job can be rewarding.
    (D) There are many aspects to consider before choosing a job.

40. Which of the following statements supports the idea that working at an internship or a part-time job in an area of interest is helpful in making a career choice?

    (A) A career center should be able to help you find an internship.
    (B) A part-time job is a good way to earn money.
    (C) Internships allow you to actually experience an area of interest firsthand, helping you to make a more educated decision.
    (D) An internship is not a good experience for many students.

Read the following drama and answer questions 41 through 45.

David's Haircut

Characters:
David Moreno—a teenage boy
Jim Moreno—David's father
Sarah Moreno—David's mother
Mr. Gonzalez—the barber

Scene I
(A warm Saturday morning in the Moreno home kitchen.)

Mr. Moreno: Hey David, don't you think it's about time we went to the barber and got that mop of yours cut?

David: Dad, I really wanted to grow my hair out for awhile, can we postpone our little Saturday ritual for a while?

Mr. Moreno: Well, perhaps I should take care of it for you and then we won't have to make the trip down to Mr. Gonzalez's shop. Sarah, where are the shears?

(Laughing, Mr. Moreno chases David around the table pretending to use scissors with his fingers.)

David: Dad, knock it off. PLEASE!!! I'm not a kid anymore.

Mr. Moreno: Who says you're not a kid?

David: I do. After all, I am going to high school next fall and I really think it is time for me to make some of my own decisions. And just because we have gone to Mr. Gonzalez's barbershop together for the past fourteen years, doesn't mean that should always be the way it is.

Mr. Moreno: Well, I'm going to have to think about that.

David: Come on Dad, what's there to think about?

Mr. Moreno: For one, why I should let you grow your hair out?

David: Okay, what can go wrong if I grow my hair out a little bit?

Mr. Moreno: Well, all I know is that if I let you grow your hair out, the next thing you are going to do is dye it purple or orange, or turn it into a Mohawk, or twist it into dreadlocks.

David: Dad, be serious.

Mr. Moreno: I am serious, I'm VERY serious.

David: Why would you think I would do that? Have I ever done anything crazy like that before? Have I given you reason to mistrust me?

(Mr. Moreno pauses for awhile and looks down at the floor as he contemplates what he wants to say to his son.)

Mr. Moreno: No, you haven't given me any reason to mistrust you, David. It's just that I'm . . . well, I'm afraid of losing that little kid that I still see in you . . . holding my hand and walking up the stairs to Mr. Gonzalez's shop . . . the Saturday tradition . . . boys morning out . . . and our special lunch at the diner together.

(David is obviously moved by his father's sentimentality, something that he had never noticed before.)

David: I . . . I . . . I . . . don't know what to say, Dad. And I didn't realize all of that meant so much to you. Wow. But I still feel strongly about making some of my own decisions. And all that I can say is that I will PROMISE that I won't do anything crazy with my hair. . . but even if I did, would you love me less just because I have purple hair, or a tattoo, or a piercing, or something equally artistic?

(He begins to smile as he watches his dad's reaction—which is apparent shock at David's last statement)

I don't think so. Besides Dad, we can still go to lunch—I'd do that every day of the week—that tradition doesn't have to end just because I want to do something different with my hair. In fact, why don't we begin a new tradition? Why don't I start cutting YOUR hair! Mom! Where are the shears?

(Laughing, David begins chasing his dad around the table using his fingers as scissors.)

41. Read this sentence from the drama

    Dad, I really wanted to grow my hair out for awhile, can we postpone our little Saturday ritual for awhile?

    What does the word *postpone* mean as it is used in this sentence?

    (A) accelerate
    (B) hurry
    (C) delay
    (D) frustrate

42. How does the reader know that the story is a short play?

    (A) The story is told through character dialogue and uses a specific format and stage directions.
    (B) The story has characters.
    (C) The story is told through an omniscient narrator.
    (D) The scene descriptions are printed in italics.

43. This story would be considered a—

    (A) tragedy.
    (B) comedy.
    (C) dramatic monologue.
    (D) drama.

44. How does the father react to his son's request to make some of his own decisions?

    (A) He tells his son to go to his room.
    (B) He screams at his son.
    (C) He becomes angry.
    (D) He becomes sentimental.

45. Which statement BEST describes what happens in the story?

    (A) A father and son differ on the meaning of life.
    (B) A father tries to control all aspects of his son's life.
    (C) A son realizes his father's love, and attempts to assure him that he will make good decisions.
    (D) A son tries to run away from home to prove a point to his father.

WRITING

The following passage is a rough draft of an essay. It contains a variety of errors that may include grammar, punctuation, sentence structure, or organization. Read the passage and answer questions 46 through 49.

ROUGH DRAFT

Reality Television

(1) With all of the excitement about reality tv in today's world, many people probably don't know that this form of unscripted television has been around for about 50 years. (2) Early reality shows included various game shows, talent shows and one of the most popular shows called *Candid Camera*. (3) But reality television as we know it today comes in many forms.

(4) The documentary form of reality TV uses various formats. (5) The unique environments of shows like *The Real World;* the homes and lives of various celebrities such as the *Osbournes;* or the videoing of professionals doing their jobs on shows like *Cops*. (6) *American Idol* and *Dancing with the Stars* are examples of reality elimination type shows. (7) *The Weakest Link* and *Who Wants to be a Millionaire* are elimination game shows.

(8) There are reality shows for just about everything imaginable: from dating with *The Bachelor* or *The Bachelorette*; to job search shows like *Project Runway, America's Next Top Model,* or *Hell's Kitchen*. (9) There are reality shows that test athletic and survival skills and a contestants fear level. (10) There are reality shows for personal or family make-overs like *The Biggest Loser* or *Supernanny*. (11) *Extreme Makeover: Home Edition, Divine Design, Designed to Sell* are examples of reality home or room renovation reality television. (12) There are interview reality shows known as trash TV like the Jerry Springer Show or hidden camera type shows such as *Punk'd*.

(13) Reality television is a modern phenomenon. (14) Many people are fascinated by shows that allow the viewer to see another side of life, something different than our own. (15) Some shows are produced with class and sophistication, while others are intended to shock the viewer. (16) Regardless of your personal preference, it seems as though reality TV is here to stay.

46. Which of the following sentences would BEST begin the essay?

   (A) Reality television is a modern-day phenomenon that has captured everyone's attention.
   (B) Reality television is here to stay.
   (C) Reality television is filled with unscripted plots, and the twists and turns of real life.
   (D) Reality television is a confusing and ambiguous genre.

47. The BEST way to combine the sentences numbered 13 and 14 is—

    (A) Reality television is a modern phenomenon that holds the attention of the viewer.
    (B) Reality television takes the viewer to new places.
    (C) Reality television, a modern phenomenon, challenges a viewer's way of thinking.
    (D) Reality television is a modern phenomenon that allows the viewer to see a new and different side of life.

48. Which of the following BEST describes what is <u>wrong</u> with paragraph three, which includes the sentences numbered 8 through 12?

    (A) There is too much information.
    (B) Sentence beginnings are repetitious—all of them begin with "There are."
    (C) It mentions several different types of shows.
    (D) All of the sentences are too short.

49. Which of the following would be the BEST way to repair sentence 5 which is an incomplete sentence?

    (A) Add the words "are interesting" at the end of the sentence.
    (B) Add the words "Among the various formats are" to the beginning of the sentence.
    (C) Add the words "Typical of the varied formats are: the . . ." at the beginning of the sentence.
    (D) Instead of a period, add a colon (:) to sentence 4 and eliminate the capital T on the word "the."

The following passage is a rough draft of an essay. It contains a variety of errors that may include grammar, punctuation, sentence structure, or organization. Read the passage and answer questions 50 through 53.

ROUGH DRAFT

An Unsuspecting Environmentalist

(1) Most people know the name Leonardo DiCaprio. (2) He is a well respected and admired actor who was born in Los Angeles, California in 1974. (3) Over the years DiCaprio has portrayed just about everything imaginable: an aviator, a mentally disabled boy, Shakespeare's Romeo, a poor immigrant who falls in love with a wealthy girl, a check forger and thief, a poet, a heroin addict and an undercover cop and the list goes on and on. (4) But what many people don't realize about Mr. DiCaprio is his dedication to environmental concerns.

(5) Capable of chartering his own flights, Mr. DiCaprio chooses to ride commercial airlines which use less fuel. (6) He drives a hybrid car and uses solar energy in his home. (7) He recently purchased and apartment in a building that is completely

"green." (8) DiCaprio has worked with Al Gore who won the Nobel Prize for his work with the environment by presenting at the American portion of *Live Earth*, a concert that presented over 150 musical groups around the world with the intent of bringing attention to environmental concerns such as global warming.

(9) Despite a face and a reputation that is much easily recognized and admired around the world, Leonardo DiCaprio is a celebrity who gives back to society. (10) He should be applauded for his efforts to bring attention to environmental issues as much as for his work on the silver screen.

50. Which of the following is the BEST way to define the meaning of the word green in sentence 7?

    (A) Everything in the building is colored green.
    (B) The materials used in the construction come from Greenland.
    (C) The use of environmentally friendly and energy-saving materials and products.
    (D) The limited use of fossil fuels were used in the building.

51. Which of the following is supported by details and evidence in the essay?

    (A) that Mr. DiCaprio promotes environmental issues when he is not acting
    (B) that Mr. DiCaprio is young
    (C) that Mr. DiCaprio has been nominated for an Academy Award
    (D) that Mr. DiCaprio flies his own plane

52. The BEST way to write sentence 8 is—

    (A) DiCaprio has worked with Al Gore who won the Nobel Prize for his work with the environment. He presented at the American portion of *Live Earth*. *Live Earth is* a concert that included over 150 musical groups who performed around the world to bring attention to environmental concerns such as global warming.
    (B) DiCaprio has worked with Al Gore who won the Nobel Prize for his work with the environment by presenting at the American portion of *Live Earth*, a concert that gathered over 150 musical groups around the world with the intent of bringing attention to environmental concerns such as global warming.
    (C) DiCaprio has worked with Al Gore who won the Nobel Prize for his work with the environment. He presented the American portion of *Live Earth*, a concert that presented over 150 musical groups around the world with the intent of bringing attention to environmental concerns such as global warming.
    (D) Leave as is.

53. The author of this passage—

   (A) is a lobbyist for "green" industries.
   (B) enjoys seeing films.
   (C) believes that environmental issues should take a backseat to acting.
   (D) admires DiCaprio's dedication to the environment as well as his acting ability.

The following passage is a rough draft of an essay. It contains a variety of errors that may include grammar, punctuation, sentence structure or organization. Read the passage and answer questions 54 through 57.

ROUGH DRAFT

Old School Hip Hop

(1) Hip-hop music has been around for quite awhile. (2) Hip-hop is a genre of music that most often consists of rap or a rhythmic style of speaking that is performed over the sound of beats played on a turntable by a DJ. (3) It began in the early 1970s in New York City. (4) DJs such as Kool DJ Herc and Grandmaster Flash began to extend the percussion breaks in the beat of funk records which is the blending of soul, soul jazz and R & B music. (5) By doing this, they created a sound that was easier to dance to.

(6) Extended percussion breaks were followed by the development of techniques known as mixing and scratching. (7) Scratching was invented by Grandmaster Grand Wizard Theodore in 1977. (8) This led to remixes, which is a new or different version of a song.

(9) As the popularity of hip-hop continued to grow, performers began speaking while the music played. (10) These performers were known as *MCs* or emcees. (11) Hip-hop evolved through the years with MCs adding brief rhymes or rhyming lyrics along with improvisational beats and words. (12) Many of the early raps focused on various aspect of the African American culture. (13) The first hip-hop recordings to be released were by the Fatback Band and The Sugarhill Gang.

(14) While most of old school rap focused on parties and friendships and good time, a song that was written by Melle Mel titled "The Message" started what is called "message rap." (15) In the 80s, hip-hop began to evolve to another level of sophistication and complexity with the addition of multi-layered beats and <u>metaphorical</u> raps. (16)And over the years, the genre has become more and more mainstream and popular with a broad and diverse group of fans.

54. Which revision of sentence 6 uses active voice only?

   (A) The development of mixing and scratching techniques follow the extension of percussion breaks.
   (B) Extended percussion breaks had been followed by the development of techniques known as mixing and scratching.
   (C) Extending the percussion breaks was followed by the development of techniques known as mixing and scratching.
   (D) Mixing and scratching techniques followed the extended percussion breaks.

55. Which sentence would BEST follow sentence 15?

   (A) Hip-hop is a unique form of music.
   (B) The end of hip-hop is forthcoming.
   (C) The evolution of hip-hop music continues.
   (D) Hip-hop is old-fashioned and passé.

56. If a student wanted to learn more about hip-hop, an Internet site would probably be more useful than an encyclopedia because an Internet site would probably—

   (A) provide more up-to-date information on current artists who perform in the genre.
   (B) be able to keep the reader better informed on policies of the genre.
   (C) be able to spell names correctly and quote various performers.
   (D) be able to link the reader to books and radio stations.

57. Which of the following BEST defines the meaning of the underlined word *metaphorical* in sentence 15?

   (A) inquisitive
   (B) statuesque
   (C) symbolic
   (D) intriguing

For questions 58 to 64, choose the word or phrase that best completes the sentence.

58. The black purse has _____ room than the brown one.

   (A) smaller
   (B) less
   (C) least
   (D) smallest

59. The singer managed to sing Jenna's favorite song for her friend and _____.

   (A) his
   (B) she
   (C) her
   (D) I

60. _____ going to be tardy if he doesn't hurry up.

   (A) He's
   (B) He'll
   (C) He
   (D) His

61. When the teacher _____ the award, she was modest and humble.

   (A) expected
   (B) accepted
   (C) excepted
   (D) accepts

62. The frightened surfer knew that he had to paddle as fast as he_____ that his injured friend needed help desperately.

   (A) was able: he knew
   (B) was able but he knew
   (C) was able. He knew
   (D) was able, he knew

63. "We will have to _____ without the secretary," said the frustrated club president.

   (A) precede
   (B) proceed
   (C) preceded
   (D) proceeded

64. The most noted goddess of Roman deities was also the _____ of all.

   (A) most beautiful
   (B) most beautified
   (C) more beautifulest
   (D) beautifulness

For questions 65 to 72, choose the answer that is the most effective substitute for each underlined part of the sentence. If no substitute is necessary, choose "Leave as is."

65. During the commercial <u>break: Betsy made a snack for</u> her mother.

   (A) break. Betsy made a snack for
   (B) break, Betsy made a snack for
   (C) break; Betsy made a snack for
   (D) Leave as is.

66. <u>"Why aren't you going on the field trip?" whined Meagan</u> as she stumbled onto the steps of the bus without her best friend.

   (A) "Why? aren't you going on the field trip" whined Meagan
   (B) "Why aren't you going on the field trip" whined Meagan
   (C) "Why aren't you going on the field trip?" whined Meagan
   (D) Leave as is.

67. The hiking trail to Mt. Olympus is beautiful in the <u>summer but it is unreachable</u> in the winter.

   (A) summer but, it is unreachable
   (B) summer but it is unreachable,
   (C) summer, but it is unreachable
   (D) Leave as is.

68. When Joseph arrived for the meeting <u>this morning he appeared to be frustrated</u>.

   (A) this morning, he appeared to be frustrated.
   (B) this morning he appeared, to be frustrated.
   (C) this morning; he appeared to be frustrated.
   (D) Leave as is.

69. After spending the long holiday at home with his <u>sick brother, Spencer was ready</u> to go back to school.

   (A) sick brother Spencer was ready
   (B) sick brother: Spencer was ready
   (C) sick brother. Spencer was ready
   (D) Leave as is.

70. When Frida turns sixteen next fall, <u>she was able to get her driver's license</u>.

   (A) she had the ability to get her driver's license.
   (B) she was likely to get her driver's license.
   (C) she will be able to get her driver's license.
   (D) Leave as is.

71. <u>Mandi explained her problem at home to us at lunch</u>.

   (A) At lunch, Mandi explained the problem she is having at home to us.
   (B) Mandi explained to us her home problem she is having at lunch.
   (C) Explaining, Mandi her home problem to us at lunch.
   (D) Leave as is.

72. <u>My baby brother sings about the farmer and his animals incessantly.</u>

    (A) My baby brother sings. About the farmer and his animals incessantly.
    (B) My baby brother sings incessantly about the farmer and his animals.
    (C) About the farmer and his animals, my baby brother sings incessantly.
    (D) Leave as is.

TEST 1 WRITING TASK 1

- Read the instructions for the writing task carefully. You may need to read it several times.
- Brainstorm and organize your thoughts on paper.
- Aim for at least four paragraphs; five is better.
- Be certain that you have a well-developed introduction, body paragraphs, and conclusion.
- Support your thesis by using specific details and examples.
- Use effective word choice.
- Be aware of sentence beginning; avoid repeating them.
- Vary sentence length to make your writing more interesting.
- Reread your essay to catch errors in grammar, spelling, punctuation, and sentence formation.

Writing Task:

Throughout your school years you have studied a number of subjects and topics—from English, to mathematics, to history, science, and foreign language. Review these subjects and topics and choose one that interested you more than any other.

Write an essay explaining what exactly it was about this specific subject or topic that you enjoyed. Use specific details and examples to support your decision.

- Write your essay on the answer sheet that precedes this exam.
- Adding a title is not mandatory.
- Either printing or cursive writing is acceptable.
- Write clearly and neatly—make the reader's job easier.
- Using a dictionary or thesaurus is not permitted.
- GOOD LUCK!

NOTE: There are scored writing samples for this writing task after the answer key for this exam. After you have written your response, compare your writing to those already scored to see how your writing compares. Pay particular attention to the essays with the highest scores. You will need a 3 or a 4 to pass this task.

TEST 1 WRITING TASK 2

- Read the instructions for the writing task carefully. You may need to read it several times.
- Brainstorm and organize your thoughts on paper.
- Aim for at least four paragraphs; five is better.
- Be certain that you have a well-developed introduction, body paragraphs, and conclusion.
- Support your thesis by using specific details and examples.
- Use effective word choice.
- Be aware of sentence beginnings; avoid repeating them.
- Vary sentence length to make your writing more interesting.
- Reread your essay to catch errors in grammar, spelling, punctuation, and sentence formation.

Writing Task:

In the story *Early Summer Mornings*, the reader learns of the narrator's personality and emotions through his actions and thoughts that are presented in the story.

Write an essay in which you discuss the unnamed narrator's personal characteristics and how these traits are portrayed throughout the story. How do these characteristics add dimension to the story? Use details and examples to support your ideas.

- Write your essay on the answer sheet that precedes this exam.
- Adding a title is not mandatory.
- Either printing or cursive writing is acceptable.
- Write clearly and neatly—make the reader's job easier.
- Using a dictionary or thesaurus is not permitted.
- GOOD LUCK!

NOTE: There are scored writing samples for this writing task after the answer key for this exam. After you have written your response, compare your writing to those already scored to see how your writing compares. Pay particular attention to the essays with the highest scores. You will need a 3 or a 4 to pass this task.

Practice Test 1

Answer Key

1. **(C)**	16. **(C)**	31. **(C)**	46. **(C)**	61. **(B)**
2. **(B)**	17. **(D)**	32. **(B)**	47. **(D)**	62. **(C)**
3. **(C)**	18. **(B)**	33. **(D)**	48. **(B)**	63. **(B)**
4. **(A)**	19. **(A)**	34. **(B)**	49. **(C)**	64. **(A)**
5. **(D)**	20. **(C)**	35. **(C)**	50. **(C)**	65. **(B)**
6. **(B)**	21. **(A)**	36. **(C)**	51. **(A)**	66. **(D)**
7. **(C)**	22. **(C)**	37. **(B)**	52. **(A)**	67. **(C)**
8. **(D)**	23. **(C)**	38. **(A)**	53. **(D)**	68. **(A)**
9. **(A)**	24. **(D)**	39. **(A)**	54. **(A)**	69. **(D)**
10. **(D)**	25. **(D)**	40. **(C)**	55. **(C)**	70. **(C)**
11. **(B)**	26. **(D)**	41. **(C)**	56. **(A)**	71. **(A)**
12. **(A)**	27. **(D)**	42. **(A)**	57. **(C)**	72. **(B)**
13. **(B)**	28. **(A)**	43. **(D)**	58. **(B)**	
14. **(A)**	29. **(C)**	44. **(D)**	59. **(C)**	
15. **(A)**	30. **(C)**	45. **(C)**	60. **(A)**	

PRACTICE EXAM 1
WRITING TASK 1 SCORED EXAMPLES

> Throughout your school years you have studied a number of subjects and topics—from English, to mathematics, to history, science, and foreign language. Review these subjects and topics and choose one that interested you more than any other.
>
> Write an essay explaining what exactly it was about this specific subject or topic that you enjoyed. Use specific details and examples to support your decision.

4

SCORE POINT 4
STUDENT RESPONSE

Without a doubt the most interesting subject that I have studied throughout my years in school, has to be English. The subject fascinates me because there are so many different components to it. Some, I enjoy more than others. English, as a subject, exposes students to a broad spectrum of literature including: novels (of all kinds), biographies, non-fiction, and poetry. Writing is an important aspect of the subject and last but not the most favorite least is grammar. English is an important and vastly interesting subject that helps in all areas of your life.

Reading novels is one of the most important aspects of English. Every year we are given a list of books to read and study throughout the year and every year the difference in the themes, plots and characters changes and seem to become more fascinating. There are novels about good, bad, evil, crazy and down and out characters. Each novel, poem or other piece of literature that is read for class has, for the most part, a purpose or a message that as a reader can be taken from it. The readings in English class are important to help build skills in creative thinking and simply to advance reading and analytical skill. Just as reading is important, writing likewise fulfills an important niche in our education.

Writing essays or journals or poems in English class helps develop a lifelong skill. Knowing how to organize thoughts and to write clearly is something that everyone should be able to do. Knowing that there are interesting ways to write and knowing how to respond to a variety of topics will aid all students throughout their school years (high school and college) as well as in the real world. I don't know that anyone ever really escapes not having to write something (a letter, a proposal, a note, an email) beyond the school years. Writing in an invaluable skill, but to do it well, understanding basic grammar is essential.

Raise your hand if you enjoy grammar. If that were actually announced in class, there would be one or two students raising their hands. Grammar can be tedious and challenging, but again, like learning to read and write well, it is unavoidable. Some aspects of grammar come easier than others: parts of speech, subject, predicate etc. However there are areas of grammar that are mind-boggling and if they could be avoided, most would choose to do so. Participial and dangling modifiers are two rather confusing culprits. But, overall, grammar has more benefits than drawbacks.

Reading, writing and grammar are the primary focus of an English class. And although these might sound tedious and boring to many students, these topics are foundation builders and lifelong skills needed to survive in the real world. Whether I am reading about Holden Caulfield, writing about The Great Gatsby or working on subject-verb agreement, English is always interesting and always diverse.

3
SCORE POINT 3
STUDENT RESPONSE

There are so many different topic and subjects that are covered in school throughout the years; it is difficult to choose just one. However one of the most interesting for me has to be geography. Geography is amazing. Most people believe that it is nothing more than looking at maps, but it is much more than that. Learning about population, rainfall, continents, rivers, bodies of water, geological formations are just part of the subject. Geography is looking at the world in a new way and in many different ways.

Studying maps is just one aspect of the subject geography. Of course knowing directions, latitudes and longitudes and the names of the continents, the names of the countries and their capitals is important. There is much to learn from studying a map. But there is more to the subject.

The areas of geography that go beyond the obvious are the study of the globe as a whole and continent by continent. Land masses, coral reefs, oceans, seas, lakes, deserts, earthquake faults, islands, peninsulas and climatology are the part of geography that takes a student to a new level of knowledge.

Geography is more than looking at a map and finding a state or a country, it is seeing the world with knowledge that allows you to understand the nature and uniqueness of our planet. Understanding why Africa is the largest continent, yet the poorest or why Australia is the only continent to have a single country. The extent of geography goes beyond any other subject and is far more interesting.

2
SCORE POINT 2
STUDENT RESPONSE

Over my years in school I have learned a lot about a lot of things. But the one I like the most is learning about Benjamin Franklin. Some people think he was a president, but he wasn't. His life was interesting because he did a lot of things in a lot of areas like science, politics and inventions.

Benjamin Franklin lived a long time ago. He had a lot to do with the writing of the Constitution and he was an Ambassador. He also invented things like the lightning rod and bifocal glasses. He also learned about and studied lightning and how it could be turned into electricity.

Franklin seemed to be a very smart man, he also played a lot of instruments and had a family that was interesting too.

Of all of the subjects or topics that I have learned about, Benjamin is the most interesting. He was a busy guy.

1

SCORE POINT 1
STUDENT RESPONSE

The most interesting topic that I have learned about is the beatles. They are a group from the 60s, but there music is the best. I don't know where the world would be without their music. They were pretty good musicians and there singing was ok, but the music they wrote it, is the best ever. They are paul, george, john and ringo. I think I like there sergeant pepper cd the best, there is lots of different songs on that cd.

PRACTICE EXAM 1
WRITING TASK 2 SCORED EXAMPLES

Writing Task:

In the story *Early Summer Mornings,* the reader learns of the narrator's personality and emotions through his actions and thoughts that are presented in the story.

Write an essay in which you discuss the unnamed narrator's personal characteristics and how these traits are portrayed throughout the story. How do these characteristics add dimension to the story? Use details and examples to support your ideas.

4

SCORE POINT 4
STUDENT RESPONSE

In the story "Early Summer Mornings" we read about an unnamed narrator who is young man whose father does not live with the family anymore, although we do not understand why. Throughout the story, the reader discovers a very sensitive person in this young man who seems to be extremely mature, kind and helpful. Most importantly however, the reader learns of the boy's love for his father and the fond memories that he maintains in a ritual that he performs every year on the day of his father's birthday by painting a portrait of his father.

In the beginning of the story, the day begins on an interesting note. The boy feels strange for some reason and at this point the reader doesn't quite understand the reason. However, despite the boy's initial feelings, the reader listens to his thoughts and what we hear indicates a sensitivity and kindness that is admirable. The boy hears his brother in the bathroom getting ready for work and immediately goes downstairs and fixes his breakfast for him. How many brothers do you know that would do that?

Soon after the brother leaves, we hear the narrator speak of his family and acknowledging that today is his dad's birthday. He mentions that his mother wouldn't mention it and that his brother might, but it would only be to cause a disagreement with his mother. It is obvious that the boy had many fond memories of his father and their times together. He loved spending time with him and his father encouraged the young man's interest in art by buying him crayons, pastels and books about different artists. The narrator obviously misses this man very much.

As the narrator obviously tries to hold on to all of his fond memories, he explains his ritual of painting a portrait of his father every year on the day of his birth. He describes the various styles in which he has painted the portraits, and sentimentally describes the years they were completed: "this was done when I was fourteen and you had been gone for five years." The young man's sensitivity to his father and how he imagines he might look right now is evident in the interior dialogue that he shares with the reader.

As the story ends, we follow the boy's thought processes in deciding how to paint his father this year and we intently watch the process and see the end result as the boy puts down his art supplies and comments, "Oh, dad, there you are." "Early Summer Mornings" is a character study of a young man who is mature, sensitive and kind. The reader is cheering this boy on and we want to bring his father back to him. The story is one of optimism and hope, but on an extremely sensitive and caring level.

3

SCORE POINT 3
STUDENT RESPONSE

From the story "Early Summer Mornings" the reader sees first hand what a young boy, the narrator, experiences on his father's birthday. The father no longer lives at home, but the boy continues to keep his memories alive by painting a portrait of his father on his birthday. Throughout the story we observe a nice young man who seems to be caring and devoted to his family, especially his father's memory.

The narrator describes this particularly awkward morning at the beginning of the story and the reader doesn't understand until later why he is feeling this way. In the meantime, we hear his thoughts or interior monologue. He explains that his brother has to go to work and he makes his breakfast for him. Soon the reader learns that today is his father's birthday and he reports that he knows his mother won't say anything about it, but his brother might, just to irritate her. Despite this small taste of negativity in his family members, the young man continues to be kind and thoughtful.

Every year, the reader learns that the boy paints a portrait of his father. It seems as though he has quite a collection of them. We begin to understand that these portraits are his only remaining connection to his father and it is obvious that he cherishes each and every one of them.

As the story concludes, the reader can sympathize with the young man's feelings. This father obviously encouraged him with his art by buying him supplies and books on artists. It is obvious that the young man misses him a great deal. The story is moved along by the author's sensitive detail and as the boy thinks about the painting he is going to complete and until he finishes it and sees his father again, the reader is captured by the emotions of the situation.

2

SCORE POINT 2
STUDENT RESPONSE

The story called "Early Summer Mornings" is sad. I feel bad for the boy who doesn't have a father. But he seems like a good person. He makes his brothers breakfast and paints a picture of his dad. That seems pretty nice.

Sometimes the story talks about the family, his mother and brother. But most of it is about his father. The father bought him some art stuff and other things when he was little.

The boy ends up painting a picture of his dad and tells how he does it different every year. Sometimes he changes his hair or the way he paints. The story is sad because you feel bad for him.

1

SCORE POINT 1
STUDENT RESPONSE

In the story there is a boy who 's father is gone. He want to paint a picture of him, I think, but I don't know why. He is skipping school that day to stay home to do it and he knows he is going to get in trouble for not going to school but he doesn't care. Mostly the boy is sad about his dad and he talks about it and then draws a pitcher.

Answer Sheet

PRACTICE EXAM 2

1 Ⓐ Ⓑ Ⓒ Ⓓ
2 Ⓐ Ⓑ Ⓒ Ⓓ
3 Ⓐ Ⓑ Ⓒ Ⓓ
4 Ⓐ Ⓑ Ⓒ Ⓓ
5 Ⓐ Ⓑ Ⓒ Ⓓ
6 Ⓐ Ⓑ Ⓒ Ⓓ
7 Ⓐ Ⓑ Ⓒ Ⓓ
8 Ⓐ Ⓑ Ⓒ Ⓓ
9 Ⓐ Ⓑ Ⓒ Ⓓ
10 Ⓐ Ⓑ Ⓒ Ⓓ
11 Ⓐ Ⓑ Ⓒ Ⓓ
12 Ⓐ Ⓑ Ⓒ Ⓓ
13 Ⓐ Ⓑ Ⓒ Ⓓ
14 Ⓐ Ⓑ Ⓒ Ⓓ
15 Ⓐ Ⓑ Ⓒ Ⓓ
16 Ⓐ Ⓑ Ⓒ Ⓓ
17 Ⓐ Ⓑ Ⓒ Ⓓ
18 Ⓐ Ⓑ Ⓒ Ⓓ
19 Ⓐ Ⓑ Ⓒ Ⓓ
20 Ⓐ Ⓑ Ⓒ Ⓓ
21 Ⓐ Ⓑ Ⓒ Ⓓ
22 Ⓐ Ⓑ Ⓒ Ⓓ
23 Ⓐ Ⓑ Ⓒ Ⓓ
24 Ⓐ Ⓑ Ⓒ Ⓓ

25 Ⓐ Ⓑ Ⓒ Ⓓ
26 Ⓐ Ⓑ Ⓒ Ⓓ
27 Ⓐ Ⓑ Ⓒ Ⓓ
28 Ⓐ Ⓑ Ⓒ Ⓓ
29 Ⓐ Ⓑ Ⓒ Ⓓ
30 Ⓐ Ⓑ Ⓒ Ⓓ
31 Ⓐ Ⓑ Ⓒ Ⓓ
32 Ⓐ Ⓑ Ⓒ Ⓓ
33 Ⓐ Ⓑ Ⓒ Ⓓ
34 Ⓐ Ⓑ Ⓒ Ⓓ
35 Ⓐ Ⓑ Ⓒ Ⓓ
36 Ⓐ Ⓑ Ⓒ Ⓓ
37 Ⓐ Ⓑ Ⓒ Ⓓ
38 Ⓐ Ⓑ Ⓒ Ⓓ
39 Ⓐ Ⓑ Ⓒ Ⓓ
40 Ⓐ Ⓑ Ⓒ Ⓓ
41 Ⓐ Ⓑ Ⓒ Ⓓ
42 Ⓐ Ⓑ Ⓒ Ⓓ
43 Ⓐ Ⓑ Ⓒ Ⓓ
44 Ⓐ Ⓑ Ⓒ Ⓓ
45 Ⓐ Ⓑ Ⓒ Ⓓ
46 Ⓐ Ⓑ Ⓒ Ⓓ
47 Ⓐ Ⓑ Ⓒ Ⓓ
48 Ⓐ Ⓑ Ⓒ Ⓓ

49 Ⓐ Ⓑ Ⓒ Ⓓ
50 Ⓐ Ⓑ Ⓒ Ⓓ
51 Ⓐ Ⓑ Ⓒ Ⓓ
52 Ⓐ Ⓑ Ⓒ Ⓓ
53 Ⓐ Ⓑ Ⓒ Ⓓ
54 Ⓐ Ⓑ Ⓒ Ⓓ
55 Ⓐ Ⓑ Ⓒ Ⓓ
56 Ⓐ Ⓑ Ⓒ Ⓓ
57 Ⓐ Ⓑ Ⓒ Ⓓ
58 Ⓐ Ⓑ Ⓒ Ⓓ
59 Ⓐ Ⓑ Ⓒ Ⓓ
60 Ⓐ Ⓑ Ⓒ Ⓓ
61 Ⓐ Ⓑ Ⓒ Ⓓ
62 Ⓐ Ⓑ Ⓒ Ⓓ
63 Ⓐ Ⓑ Ⓒ Ⓓ
64 Ⓐ Ⓑ Ⓒ Ⓓ
65 Ⓐ Ⓑ Ⓒ Ⓓ
66 Ⓐ Ⓑ Ⓒ Ⓓ
67 Ⓐ Ⓑ Ⓒ Ⓓ
68 Ⓐ Ⓑ Ⓒ Ⓓ
69 Ⓐ Ⓑ Ⓒ Ⓓ
70 Ⓐ Ⓑ Ⓒ Ⓓ
71 Ⓐ Ⓑ Ⓒ Ⓓ
72 Ⓐ Ⓑ Ⓒ Ⓓ

Write your response here:

_____

_____

_____

_____

_____

_____

_____

_____

_____

_____

_____

_____

_____

_____

_____

_____

_____

_____

_____

Practice Exam 2

Practice Exam 2 Writing Task 1 Continued:

Write your response here:

_____

_____

_____

_____

_____

_____

_____

_____

_____

_____

_____

_____

_____

_____

_____

_____

_____

_____

_____

_____

_____

California High School Exit Exam Practice Test 2

READING

Read the following passage and answer questions 1 through 8.

The Old Metal Teapot

We were on our way home from dropping my brother James off at college, and my dad needed to stretch his legs. He was tired from our long drive back to Hermosa Beach. We were near some strange and minuscule town off Highway 1, somewhere in the middle of the state. Spotting a rustic roadside diner with an antique shop and a two-pump gas station, we pulled over.

The first thing my mom did when she got out of the car was head to the antique shop. Out of curiosity, and with nothing better to do, I joined her. We entered the musty-smelling shop, filled with what looked like a lot of junk to me. An old woman greeted us, speaking with a strange accent that I couldn't identify. She was wearing an odd assortment of clothes, none of which matched—a ragged sweater, a flowery old-fashioned, threadbare dress. But what was strange, even more than her appearance, was her demeanor. It's not that she seemed spooky or crazy; she just seemed, well, mysterious—as though she coveted a dark hidden secret or something.

As we wandered through the cluttered little shop, the old woman limped over to my mom, and handed her a metal teapot. She didn't say anything; she just handed

345

it to her. Mom, not knowing what to say, said thank you and looked curiously at the brass-looking teapot, then at me, raising an inquisitive eyebrow. Obviously, feeling a bit sorry for the old woman, my mom gave her two dollars, and we politely left the peculiar little shop.

Tossing the teapot onto the backseat, we crowded into the diner with my dad for a quick and odd assortment of refreshments. Back at the car, my dad noticed the teapot. "What's that, Carly?" he asked my mom. She explained about the old woman handing it to her and how bad she felt for her that she couldn't just leave without buying something. "Well, that looks like a piece of junk, and we shouldn't really be spending money on hunks of metal like that—not with James and Chelsea in college, and our little Haley sitting in the back seat there, heading off next year." "Oh, Alfonso, it was only two dollars," Mom said.

With five hours to go, I tried to ignore the money argument that ensued. That argument has been on automatic rewind lately, but I do understand. Paying for college is expensive, and they are worried about retirement and my senior year, which is costly too. Not to mention the fact that both of the companies that my parents work for are downsizing and outsourcing, and both of them are worried about losing their jobs. It seems as though everything has hit them all at once.

We eventually arrived home. Emptying the suitcases out of the trunk, suddenly we all heard the sound of something metal clanging, a tinny kind of sound. Looking a bit bewildered, Mom reached into the backseat and grabbed the teapot. Shaking it, she found six quarters. "Wow, it practically paid for itself," she remarked a bit confused.

Mom brought the old kettle inside and put it on the stove, which annoyed my father to death. But three days later, when the electric coffee pot broke, it turned out to be a blessing in disguise, to put it mildly. "What are you doing with that old thing, Carly?" my dad asked. "Making coffee," she said. "The electric pot broke, and I've never done it this way." She poured coffee grounds into the old metal teapot. Dad grabbed a metal spoon and said with authority, "You have to do it like this," dipping the spoon into the dark insides of the teapot. Suddenly, he noticed another coin in the bottom of the kettle. "Carly, did you clean this old thing? There's another quarter," he exclaimed abruptly. "Yes, of course I cleaned it, I don't know where that came from," my mom replied. After emptying the kettle and cleaning it yet again, our day went on as usual, that is, until we all returned home that evening.

After dinner, Mom took the lid off the kettle to boil some water for tea, when suddenly my dad and I heard her scream, "Oh my goodness!" Dad and I rushed back into the kitchen and noticed her holding a handful of cash. "What's going on and where did you get that money?" exclaimed my dad before I could get a word out of my mouth. "I have NO idea where this came from, do you? Are either of you playing a trick on me?" Mom asked. "No, of course not, where would either of us get that kind of money?" responded my father. "This is unbelievable!" my mother continued to chant, with a voice that was obviously shaken.

We helped my mother gather up the bills and sat down to count it. There was more than one thousand dollars. All three of us were speechless and we really didn't know what to do with the money. We were utterly baffled; there is no other word to describe it.

Sitting astonished and dumbfounded around the table, we began to discuss the possibilities—what we could do with it—how it would help pay some of our many debts. We each shared our theories. Dad thought it was a gift from heaven or from a guardian angel, and I of course thought that it had to be from a mystery fairy. But Mom, thinking back on the look in the old woman's eyes when she so determinedly handed her the old metal teapot, knew it was more than a gift. She suddenly hung her head and began to sob with gratitude and disbelief.

Well, the story needs to end, but just so you know, my parents, unsure of what they should do, took the money to the bank and opened an account, saving every dollar that the teapot offered. Eventually, with the help and inexplicable kindness of an old metal teapot, all of our college tuitions were paid off and Mom and Dad didn't have to worry about losing their jobs or retirement. And many other families were helped along the way.

We don't ask how or why it happened anymore, but that kind old woman, who must have known how desperate our lives had become, passed a gift on to us that was and still is unbelievable. If any of us told this story to anyone, they would think we were all crazy.

And, by the way, we did drive back up to that strange little town to talk with the old woman at the antique store, but the store and diner had been leveled and they were building a resort hotel in its place.

1. The words *ragged, old-fashioned,* and *threadbare* found in paragraph 2 invoke a feeling of—

   (A) nostalgia.
   (B) poverty.
   (C) inspiration.
   (D) insipid.

2. Read the following sentence from the story.

   It's not that she seemed spooky or crazy; she just seemed, well, mysterious— as though she coveted a dark hidden secret or something.

   In what way does this foreshadow the events that happen later in the story?

   (A) She really wanted to get rid of another piece of junk from her shop.
   (B) The old woman had a feeling that Carly liked tea and could use a teapot.
   (C) She seemed to know that their coffee pot was going to break soon.
   (D) It is as though the woman knew that the teapot held special powers, and that it would help the family's economic worries.

3. How does the sudden clanging of the coins in the teapot become a turning point for the family?

   (A) The family is able to survive with less worry about jobs and expenses.
   (B) The family regrets bringing the teapot home.
   (C) Their attitudes suddenly change and good things begin to happen to them.
   (D) The family's happiness is in jeopardy because of the teapot's curse.

4. Read the following sentence from the story.

   But what was strange, even more than her appearance, was her demeanor.

   What does the word *demeanor* mean as it is used in this sentence?

   (A) unimportance or irrelevance
   (B) grotesqueness
   (C) character or facial appearance
   (D) meanness and irrationality

5. Despite the cheerful and fortunate ending of the story, which of the following BEST describes the tone of the story?

   (A) confusing
   (B) mysterious
   (C) chaotic
   (D) tragic

6. Which of the following BEST describes the personality of the youngest daughter, Haley?

   (A) calm and understanding
   (B) bitter and sarcastic
   (C) selfish and insecure
   (D) mean and argumentative

7. Which of the following BEST describes the author's intent in choosing this particular family to inherit such good fortune?

   (A) They were selfish and should be punished.
   (B) Their situation was good but not great.
   (C) They were hard working and good people who needed a twist of fate in their favor.
   (D) All of their friends were wealthy.

8. Possible themes of this story are—

   (A) whim and comedy.
   (B) fate and fortune.
   (C) horror and pain.
   (D) love and honor.

Read the following passage and answer questions 9 through 15.

A Hot Game of Scrabble™

It's a really hot day—no, it is scorching. I hate my life. I'm stuck here at home playing Scrabble™ with my stupid cousins who aren't really stupid because they are beating me up in this game. In fact, my cousins are BRAINIACS. But that doesn't lessen the fact that I'm stuck inside on a hot day playing SCRABBLE™! And look at the letters that I've been dealt! An 'S' an 'R,' 'M,''B,' 'P,' and another 'S.' The only vowel I have is a 'U.' Dude, I should be outside doing something with my friends—**S**kateboarding, **R**iding **M**y **B**ike, **P**laying **S**occer or the **U**kulele. Anything but SCRABBLE™!

And it's as though life isn't bad enough. Now don't get me wrong, I really don't hate my life, but this game is beginning to annoy me. Maybe I'm just a bad loser, and add to that my letters DON'T SPELL ANYTHING!

Clack, clack, clack. The sound of these plastic letters is really beginning to annoy me. "Your play," my cousin Thad says, sounding impatient. "Hold on," I reply with a definite sound of 'just give me a minute you jerk' in my voice. So I play the word BURPS and somehow earn twenty-two points—and I follow that grandiose score with an intentionally loud one, just to make the game a little more interesting, and at the same time trying to hold back from laughing myself dizzy.

I look up at my cousins and both Thad and Judd are smirking, rolling their eyes back like they are all that. Of course they could care less about my sophomoric humor. Well, they can smirk all they want, because little do they know that I am NOT enjoying myself ONE BIT and I, too, am smirking under this fake smile on my face. Jeeze. Okay, my next batch of letters. Adding to my leftover 'M' comes 'S,' 'A,' 'T,' 'B,' 'C,' and 'E.' What words can I make out of these? And the only thing I can think of is if I weren't stuck in here on this—did I mention that it is a REALLY hot day—I would be out **S**wimming or **A**t the **B**each, or **C**limbing **M**t. **E**verest, or something equally exciting. NOT PLAYING SCRABBLE™ with my cousins.

Judd rattles his letters—clack, clack, clack—did I mention that the sound is annoying? He plays the word JINXED with a smug look on his face—and with a double letter score for the 'X' he gets thirty more points to add to his already near record-breaking slaughter. Thad is close behind, and as I drift off somewhere else, I visualize these two nerds intentionally grinding my face on the game board and shoving Scrabble™ tiles up my nose and in my ears just to liven up the entertainment. Of course, they wouldn't do such a thing—they are, after all, MY COUSINS—nice boys from Santa Fe Springs.

Thad somehow plays ZOOPHYTE, and he is wallowing in the fact that he just edged past Judd—and I mean right now, this guy wouldn't be able to get his head through the door if he tried, he is feeling that good about himself. Wanting to get back at his brother, Judd impatiently prods me with, "It's your play, Juan, come on!" I remind myself that I just need to chill out—literally—this has to be the hottest day of the year and I'm inside playing SCRABBLE™!!! Great! I spell BAIT on an 'I.'

The room suddenly seems to be getting hotter, and I don't know if it is from all the hot air coming from Thad and Judd, who are gloating at their own skills and inaudibly belittling my ineptness, or the temperature outside has finally reached the boiling point. I'm just about ready to lose my cool; I've just about had it up to here (insert hand gesture up around my neck or above). The thermometer is beginning to break now—especially when the replacement letters arrive after my last brilliant play: OH GREAT! My letters spell 'P,' 'S,' 'W,' 'M,' 'C,' 'E.' How lucky for me, and this is seriously all I have to say: **P**laying **S**crabble **W**ith **M**y **C**ousins **E**rks **M**e!!! Okay already. I know that you don't spell "IRK" with "E"—but that's all I can think of at the moment. Dude, I really have to get out of here.

9. Read the following sentence from the story.

   The room suddenly seems to be getting hotter, and I don't know if it is from all the hot air coming from Thad and Judd, who are gloating at their own skills and inaudibly belittling my ineptness.

   What is the meaning of the word *ineptness* as it is used in the sentence?

   (A) vocal and obnoxious
   (B) quiet and shy
   (C) skillful and viable
   (D) without skill, incompetent

10. The narrator's attitude about playing the game with his cousins is—

    (A) cordial and friendly.
    (B) reserved and timid.
    (C) sarcastic and resentful.
    (D) cheerful and gracious.

11. How is internal dialogue used effectively in the story?

    (A) The narrator's inhibitions are encapsulated.
    (B) The reader is allowed to see the narrator's true personality.
    (C) The cousins don't know what is going on.
    (D) It gives the reader a negative opinion of the narrator.

12. Which statement BEST describes the narrator's feelings about his cousins?

    (A) He thinks that they are smart but sometimes arrogant about their intelligence.
    (B) He thinks that they are dull.
    (C) He thinks that they are ignorant and without purpose in life.
    (D) He thinks that they should go swimming.

13. Why does Juan use the letters of the game to think of things he would rather be doing?

    (A) because he has a good sense of humor
    (B) because his cousins are smarter than he is
    (C) because he is bored and wants to go outside
    (D) because he doesn't know how to play the game

14. Read the following sentence.

I know that you don't spell "IRK" with an "E"—but that's all I can think of at the moment.

What makes this statement ironic?

(A) It shows that the narrator is smarter than he is letting on.
(B) It demonstrates that he doesn't know how to spell.
(C) It shows that he is creative.
(D) It demonstrates that the narrator has better things to do.

15. In what way does the imaginary scuffle in paragraph 5 help the story's plot?

(A) It adds a sense of remorse.
(B) It adds comic relief.
(C) It changes the narrator's demeanor.
(D) It adds sophistication and class.

Read the following poem and answer questions 16 through 20.

The Last Man Standing

Surrounded by worldly shapes
And odd fragments of hope and anticipation
Slowly dissolving into desolation and despair,
The last man standing
Covets immortality.

Crying out to an unknown void,
The last man standing speaks of a vision,
An apparition that challenges his potency
And questions his purpose, his ambition.
Demanding to know why, why, why?
And what and how.

"It tugged at my spirit
And twisted my entrails into knots,"
Muttered the last man standing.
"How am I to answer?" he desperately exclaims.
"There is no one here to help me save
Solitude
And desolation, my only companions."

Silence was the only reply.

The Sun's bony arms were weakened
By the dread and the gloom of the world.
Earth's cities were without sound,
And its seas were vacant and numb to their sickened state.

The last man standing began to reel in disgust and anguish.
He fell to his knees and began to sob.

"Thousands of years of neglect,
Bringing devastating fires and floods, continent-wide famines,
Plagues and diseases unknown to man, hatred and their subsequent wars,
Emaciating hunger, starvation, and death,"
Bellowed the last man standing with fear and trembling.
"All of this suffering has turned my heart to stone, and the sum of these agonies
Rests upon my shoulders alone, and
I CURSE this immortality! I curse this immortality."

16. How does the last line of the poem contradict the last line of the first stanza of the poem?

    (A) At the beginning of the poem, the man longs for immortality; at the end, he changes his mind.

    (B) The man doesn't seem to know what he wants.

    (C) At the beginning of the poem, the man is alone; at the end, he is joined by a group of people.

    (D) The beginning shows desperation and the ending shows fulfillment.

17. Of the following lines from the poem, which is an example of onomatopoeia?

    (A) thousands of years of neglect

    (B) silence was the only reply.

    (C) he fell to his knees and began to sob

    (D) slowly dissolving into desolation and despair

18. Read the following lines from the poem.

Earth's cities were without sound,
And its seas were vacant and numb to their sickened state.

Which of the following BEST describes the emotion of what is going on at this point in the poem?

    (A) joviality and frivolity

    (B) fantasy and horror

    (C) abandonment and hopelessness

    (D) restlessness and curiosity

19. The overall tone of the poem can be described as—

    (A) gloomy and dismal.

    (B) exciting and adventurous.

    (C) precipitous.

    (D) glorified and honorable.

20. Which of the following is echoed in every stanza of the poem?

    (A) I curse this immortality
    (B) He fell to his knees and began to sob
    (C) And desolation, my only companions
    (D) The last man standing

Read the following passage and answer questions 21 through 26.

Butterflies

Have you ever heard of the insect order called Lepidoptera? Lepidoptera is the scientific name for butterfly of which there are more than 15,000 species. We all know what butterflies are, and that they are famous for their unusual life cycle. The life cycle of the butterfly begins with a homely and plodding larval caterpillar stage, and then transforms into the inactive pupa stage, which is similar to dressing like a mummy at Halloween—or at least being snuggled and safe in a protective covering of some sort. The first two stages are not particularly attractive, considering what arrives at the end. But from these two rather unattractive stages comes the grand finale—the Lepidoptera's metamorphosis into a beautiful adult butterfly.

The adult life span of a butterfly may last only a few weeks, depending on the species. Some butterflies are important in the pollination of various crops, and others are destructive to crops; therefore, the reputation of the butterfly is a mixed one. Regardless of their reputation, butterflies have been depicted in art for thousands of years and have become meaningful symbols in various cultures around the world.

Depictions of butterflies have been found as far back as in 3,500-year-old Egyptian hieroglyphics. They continue to be incorporated into art at present, and that tradition will undoubtedly continue. After all, seeing a butterfly in a piece of art is not an uncommon sight. However, the butterfly's role in art and culture extends far beyond its beauty and elegant stature. Symbolically, butterflies have come to mean many things to many different people around the world.

In some cultures the butterfly stands for beauty and metamorphosis, or change for the better. In other cultures the butterfly stands for the fleeting nature of happiness. The early stages and the metamorphosis of the butterfly are also seen metaphorically as the transformations of our own souls. In Japan, a butterfly is considered the personification of a person's soul, but if there are many butterflies seen together, that is viewed as an omen, or sign, of bad luck to come. Similar to the Japanese belief, the Greek word for butterfly is "soul." The Chinese culture views two butterflies flying together as a symbol of love. In Mexico this beautiful insect represents something else entirely different, and is often depicted with the sun, or symbolized as flickering firelight in Aztecan art and history. The Russian word for butterfly is the word for bow tie, which also means grandmother. With an added diminutive (adding a suffix that means "little" such as '-kin' as in munchkin or '-let' as in droplet), the meaning of butterfly becomes "little bowtie," or "little grandmother," or something close to that.

The butterfly, as you can see, is more than just a member of the species Lepidoptera. It is not only a scientific anomaly because of its unique transformation and metamorphosis, but it is also an important cultural symbol and metaphor.

21. What is a synonym for the word *depictions* as it is used in the sentence below?

    Depictions of butterflies have been found as far back as in 3,500-year-old Egyptian hieroglyphics.

    (A) reservations
    (B) dances
    (C) illustrations
    (D) departures

22. Which of the following statements BEST summarizes the general idea of the information presented in the article?

    (A) Butterflies are beautiful.
    (B) Butterflies are symbolic and meaningful in various cultures around the world.
    (C) Butterflies have wings.
    (D) Butterflies are dangerous to some crops and helpful to others.

23. Based on the information in the article, which statement about butterflies is accurate?

    (A) Butterflies are mammals.
    (B) Butterflies are a part of an insect order known as Lepidoptera.
    (C) The Russian word for butterfly is droplet.
    (D) Butterflies originated in Egypt.

24. This article contains the MOST information on—

    (A) the spring mating rituals of butterflies.
    (B) the cultural and symbolic meanings of butterflies.
    (C) the needs of individual butterflies.
    (D) migration patterns of the butterfly.

25. What information supports the idea that the butterfly's metamorphosis is unique?

   (A) Butterflies are noted for their unusual life cycle.
   (B) Butterflies are cultural symbols.
   (C) Butterflies pollinate some crops.
   (D) Butterflies represent renewal.

26. What fact supports the idea that butterflies are a large order of insects?

   (A) Butterflies are a cultural symbol.
   (B) There are over 15,000 species of Lepidoptera.
   (C) Lepidoptera is the scientific name for butterflies.
   (D) Butterflies go through a series of stages before becoming adults.

Read the following passage and answer questions 27 through 31.

The Comic Book

When you think of the word "comic," the first thing that comes to mind is something funny. However, despite its name, the comic book is often not all that humorous. Originally, comic books were a collection of comic strips that were previously printed in newspapers, and most of these comic books actually were funny. The evolution of the comic book developed, however, from these reprinted collections into a unique but varied genre of literature.

In America, the comic book form that we see in bookstores, on magazine shelves at book stands, and in grocery stores, dates back to the early 1930s. The subject matter of a large number of comics in America leans toward the superhero or super-heroine, such as *Superman, Spiderman, Wonder Woman,* and *Spider-Woman.* These are fictional characters that have amazing physical powers and are devoted to saving society from evil. Comic book history in the United States is roughly divided into ages, none of which is agreed upon by comic book scholars. These eras or ages begin with the Platinum Age and move on to the Golden Age, the Silver Age, the Bronze Age, and end with the Modern Age.

The Platinum Age is approximately the early beginnings of the genre. These are the comic books of the early days, the original comic book as mentioned earlier. The early comic books consisted of a collection of newspaper comic strips and any other form of the comic book before the onset of the Golden Age.

Lasting from approximately the late 1930s until the early 1950s, the Golden Age of comics introduced the superhero, specifically *Superman.* He was the first superhero comic book. His stories became so popular during this era that comic books were printed for the first time with new stories, rather than reprinted material from newspapers. Soon, many other superheroes arrived on the comic book scene. *Batman and Robin, Wonder Woman, Captain America, The Green Lantern, Aquaman,* and many others were introduced to the American public. World War II had an impact on comics during the Golden Age. Superheroes were depicted punching out

Adolph Hitler or Japanese soldiers. But superheroes were not the only popular subjects in comics during this time. Walt Disney characters such as *Mickey Mouse* and *Donald Duck* were extremely popular in comic book form. *Tarzan, Roy Ro*gers, various jungle characters, funny animals, romantic, and western-style comic books also sold millions.

From the late 1950s through the early 1970s, the Silver Age of comics witnessed a reinvention of the superhero's personality. A part of this change was a result of a U.S. Senate hearing on juvenile delinquency. Many citizens were blaming the violence and other societal woes that were published in the comic books as a primary cause for troubled young adults. In response to this, comic book publishers developed what they titled a Comics Code, which was intended to police the content of the comics. As a result, the superhero became more troubled and more humanlike. There was an element of science fiction introduced during this era, as well as group heroes such as the *Justice League of America* and *the Fantastic Four*. The end of the Golden Age saw the beginning of a more urban, grittier comic.

The Bronze Age of American comics lasted from the 1970s through the mid-1980s. Although the superhero themes prevailed, the plots became darker and dealt with real-life issues. Drug use was initiated into the genre during this era. Minority issues and social inequities were also addressed, particularly in the *Green Lantern/Green Arrow* comics. Minority superheroes arrived on the scene with mixed reviews. Some believed that minority stereotyping was being perpetuated. The revival of the *X-men* team, however, became a commercial success and historical event of its own. The end of the Bronze Age ushered in the Modern Age, with comics like the *New Universe* and the *X-factor*.

The Modern Age of comics arrived just after the mid-1980s and continues to the present. Characters are even darker than before and have evolved into far more complex characters psychologically. Antiheroes such as *Wolverine, the Punisher,* and *Daredevil* become more of the norm than the good vs. evil superheroes of the past. To counter the restrictions of the Comics Code, the Modern Age witnesses a rise in independent publishers. Fantasy, horror, and suspense comics such as *Conan the Barbarian, The Swamp Thing,* and *The Tomb of Dracula,* are revived. Comic books also evolve into an art form with the publication of books like Art Spiegelman's *Maus.* Today we see the popularity of the graphic novel on the rise, and with it a new generation of comic readers and avid fans of the genre.

Comic books are popular worldwide for a reason. The fast-paced action allows the reader to visualize the plot and to follow a story line that is easier for some readers. There are those who believe that the sophistication of vocabulary and plot found in today's comics and graphic novels are good ways to improve reading skills. The evolution of the comic book has come a long way since the Platinum Age and its publication of previously printed comic strips. It will be interesting to see where it goes from here.

27. What is the definition of the word *delinquency* as it is used in the following sentence?

    A part of this change was a result of a U.S. Senate hearing on juvenile delinquency.

    (A) uprightness
    (B) forthrightness
    (C) misbehavior
    (D) considerate

28. Which of the following statements best summarizes the information presented in the article?

    (A) Comic books are all humorous collections of comic strips.
    (B) Comic books are sold only in comic book stores and they are outlawed in Florida.
    (C) Comic books have gone through a series of evolutions over the past fifty years.
    (D) Comic books depict only superheroes.

29. Based on the information in the article, which of the following statements is accurate?

    (A) The Modern Age of comics began in 1920.
    (B) The X-men series of comics was a complete failure.
    (C) Comic books are the primary cause of juvenile delinquency.
    (D) The Golden Age of comics introduced the comic *Superman.*

30. This article provides the LEAST information on—

    (A) Green Lantern/Green Arrow comics.
    (B) the Golden Age of comics.
    (C) the history of comics.
    (D) the Platinum Age of comics.

31. What information supports the idea that the Bronze Age of comics ushered in the themes and everyday experiences of modern society?

    (A) Superman was introduced to society.
    (B) Drug use, minority issues, and social inequities were introduced.
    (C) Science fiction comics returned.
    (D) Group heroes became famous.

Read the following passage and answer questions 32 through 36.

How to Be a Smart Driver

Learning to drive is a skill that should be taken seriously. It is a privilege that many take for granted. Driving sensibly and defensively is something to strive for at all times. When you get behind the wheel of a car, driving IS your only focus. Friends, cell phones, text messaging, music, eating snacks, or drinking a Monster, as well as other distractions, turn nice people into statistics. These are not the kind of statistics your parents, teachers, and society in general like to read about on the front page of the newspaper. Strive for a perfect driving record—be proud of your ability to focus on the road. Follow these steps to improve your skills as a driver.

STEP 1: Know the rules of the road. Follow the posted speed limits. Stop at ALL stop signs and traffic lights. Be particularly careful in school zones—there are lots of pedestrians and teen drivers who might not be as careful and focused as you—in fact, some of them shouldn't be driving at all. Your driving record will follow you for the rest of your life; protect it and your insurance rates. If you question or are unsure of any rule or regulation—ask. Get help.

STEP 2: Set the rules of conduct in your car. You HAVE to be in charge. Wearing seat belts and limiting distractions should not be an option for you or your passengers.

STEP 3: Avoid emotional upset, better known as ROAD RAGE. Yes, there are far too many incompetent drivers on the road, and the need to be constantly aware of cars on all sides of you, coming and going, comes with the driving territory. Getting angry doesn't help. You need to remain calm and collected because life-changing accidents occur in a matter of seconds. Your ability to avoid or prevent an accident is the result of being calm and focused at all times.

STEP 4: Cell phones should be carried for emergencies ONLY. Driving is not the time to catch up on the latest happening and gossip around school or work. In fact, cell phone distractions have become one of the leading causes of teen auto accidents. Use your cell phone only when stopped—pull off the road if you need to use the phone.

STEP 5: Be prepared. Know who to call if you have car troubles, get into an accident, or lock your keys in the trunk. Make sure you have your driver's license, insurance card, and car registration available. Know where these pieces of information are at all times. Joining the AAA or other automobile service agency is a wise thing to do. Call these agencies and they will get help to you right away—that is why they are in business. Take advantage of their services.

STEP 6: The BIGGEST no-no in the driving world is the use of drugs and alcohol while driving. Getting behind the wheel after you have been involved in either of these activities is a potential death sentence, not to mention it is illegal in all fifty states. Intoxicated drivers kill countless numbers of INNOCENT victims everyday. Don't do it—don't take the risk of dying or of spending many years in jail for killing someone you didn't mean to kill because you were intoxicated. Being a designated driver is one thing—a good thing—but don't take that responsibility lightly. Alcohol and drugs, coupled with a rather large hunk of metal, is a potentially lethal combination.

STEP 7: Peer pressure. Don't cave in. Ensure the trust that your parents have in you by allowing you to drive responsibly. Sometimes friends will try to talk you into doing something that is risky and dangerous, such as driving too fast, showing off, or racing. Be strong. Use YOUR head, and don't cave in to hazardous behavior. How many times have you seen headlines about teen car accidents? All too often a car full of teenagers veers off the road or into the path of an oncoming car. All too often the entire group is killed or sent flying through the window because they were not wearing seat belts. All too often the driver escapes with minor injuries, while the other teens in the car are killed instantly. It is not worth the brief thrill to risk having that on your conscience for the rest of your life.

STEP 8: MOST IMPORTANTLY—THINK—FOCUS—AVOID DISTRACTIONS.

32. According to the information in Step 1, what is the most important information to know about driving?

    (A) Listen for sirens.
    (B) Don't cross the yellow line.
    (C) Know the rules of the road.
    (D) Carry your insurance card.

33. In what format is the information in the article *How to Be a Smart Driver* organized?

    (A) in a series of question and answers
    (B) In a series of rules and regulations
    (C) in a series of lessons
    (D) in a series of steps

34. The author of the article is the most adamantly against—

(A) the use of drugs and alcohol when driving.
(B) carrying your insurance card.
(C) driving on the wrong side of the street.
(D) wearing seat belts.

35. The overall structure is important because it allows the reader to understand what it takes to become a smarter driver. The article is organized—

(A) to confuse the reader about the rules of the road.
(B) to leave the reader thinking about the importance of being responsible behind the wheel in all situations.
(C) to force the reader to admit wrongdoings.
(D) to allow the reader an opportunity to disagree with state driving rules.

36. Which of the following statements BEST summarizes the information presented in the article?

(A) There are several ways to get a driver's license in every state.
(B) Street racing is illegal.
(C) Auto accidents are a major cause of teenage deaths.
(D) Driving is a privilege and huge responsibility that requires focus and sensible thinking.

Read the following passage and answer questions 37 through 40.

How to Stop Procrastinating

To procrastinate means to postpone or delay. Most of us procrastinate at one time or another, and some do this more than others. The following steps should help you in adjusting your level of procrastination.

STEP 1: Explore the reasons behind your procrastination. Is it something you dislike doing? Is it a task that you are afraid of doing poorly or failing? Are you easily distracted? Or, are you a perfectionist who can only begin working when every little detail is in its proper place? There are many reasons for procrastinating, and understanding why it happens is the beginning of the resolution.

STEP 2: Is the task daunting? Overwhelming? Break up a large or difficult project into smaller, more manageable pieces. Make a checklist of tasks or stages that have to be completed. Do one piece at a time and check them off the list. The once-immense task becomes less intimidating. While you are checking them off the list, completion comes closer and closer.

STEP 3: Begin with the easiest portion of a large and complex project, because it is far more motivational. For instance, if you need to write a research paper and are having difficulty with the introduction, move on to the body of the work and go back to the introduction later.

STEP 4: Limit the amount of time that you spend on the project. Work in small blocks of time instead of long and tiring stretches of time. For instance, when studying for an exam, study in one or two hour spans of time with a break in between.

STEP 5: Set completion deadlines. Assign yourself small-scale deadlines. You can even turn it into a game. For example, for a long and tedious reading assignment, commit yourself to reading a certain number of pages in the next hour. Try to stick to this commitment. Reward yourself with a break or snack.

STEP 6: Manage your time. Use a calendar to set up task deadlines, and STICK TO THEM. Know when the project is due and what steps are needed to complete it. Assign yourself tasks that consider the amount of work and the time needed for each task. For instance, editing a project is easier and quicker than completing all of the research. Also, take into consideration the possibility of unexpected events— your computer crashing, running out of ink in your printer, or other technical and personal woes—which is even more reason to adhere to a schedule. Getting behind causes a snowball reaction that turns into an avalanche of unfinished tasks.

STEP 7: Find a place that has limited distractions—quiet, well lit, comfortable. Turn of your television, MP3 player, cell phone, telephone, and anything else that might keep you from accomplishing your goal.

37. Based on the information in the document, which of the following statements is accurate?

    (A) Everyone should procrastinate.
    (B) Procrastination means being reliably on time.
    (C) Breaking down an overwhelming task into smaller tasks is helpful.
    (D) Removing all distractions can be harmful.

38. This document provides the LEAST information on—

    (A) setting deadlines.
    (B) finding a place to work.
    (C) the definition of procrastinate.
    (D) steps to break up a large project.

39. What statement supports the idea that completing the easiest part of the task first is a good idea?

    (A) Completing the difficult tasks first is less discouraging.
    (B) Completing the difficult tasks first is more rewarding.
    (C) Completing the easiest tasks first is more enjoyable.
    (D) Completing the easiest tasks first is encouraging and more motivating.

40. Which of the following statements supports the idea that doing a little bit of the work on a large project is less daunting?

(A) The more work that is done on a project at one time, the better.
(B) Breaking up a large task is less intimidating than tackling the entire project.
(C) Avoiding distractions is of utmost importance.
(D) Procrastinating is normal.

Read the following drama and answer questions 41 through 45.

The High School Bully

Characters:

Vince—orphaned as a child, but now a successful business owner
Mario—an old classmate of Vince's from high school
Catherine—Mario's wife
Waitress in a cafe

Scene I

(For the first time in fifteen years, Vince walks into a cafe in his old hometown where he is visiting the orphanage in which he once lived.)

Waitress: Please sir, have a seat anywhere you'd like.

Vince: Thank you.
(He sits at a table facing the other customers.)

Waitress: Welcome. How are you today? Here is a menu and some water. Is there something that I can get you started with, a beverage or appetizer?

Vince: Thank you. I think I'll have a decaf coffee for now, thanks.

Waitress: That's easy. I'll be right back with that and give you a little more time with the menu.

Vince: Much appreciated.
(As he is reading over the menu, he glances up and sees a couple looking at him and speaking, but he does not recognize either of them and continues to scan the menu.)

Waitress: Here is your decaf, sir. Have you made a decision or do you need a few more minutes?

Vince: I'm ready. I would like the soup and sandwich special. I'll have a turkey sandwich on a wheat roll please, with a bowl of the cream of broccoli soup. Thanks.

Waitress: Great! That'll just be a few minutes.
(As he is waiting for his meal, the couple that was looking at Vince earlier walks over to his table.)

Catherine: Hi, my name is Catherine DiBernardo, are you Vince McGraw?

Vince: Yes, that's me. I'm sorry, have we met?

Catherine: Yes, years ago. We went to St. Peter's High School together. That's my husband, Mario, sitting over there.
(Vince looks up to look at the woman's husband. He waves, but he doesn't remember him.)

Vince: Wow. Gosh. I am embarrassed. I guess my memory just isn't as good as it should be, but I am having difficulty placing both of you. I'm sorry.

Catherine: Oh, please. Don't be embarrassed—it's been such a long time and both Mario and I have changed so much over the years. We really didn't hang out together in high school, so I'm not surprised that you don't remember either one of us. We just wanted to say "hi."

Vince: Thank you for understanding. I've been away so long; this is the first time I've been back in Cloverdale since high school, actually. I'm here to visit with some of the retiring caretakers from the orphanage.

Catherine: Well, it is nice to see you and I hope you have a great visit. Take care and good luck to you.

Vince: Same to you and Mario. Take care.
(Baffled by his loss of memory and not being able to place the couple from his past, the waitress arrives with Vince's meal. He is just about finished, when he hears the crash of dishes hitting the floor and looks up to see Catherine and Mario. They struggle to get Mario into a wheel chair and are apologizing to the waitress who is picking up the broken dishes. Suddenly, the memories all come back to him. Mario was the school bully. Over and over again, this guy shoved Vince into the lockers, made fun of him because he lived at an orphanage, or belittled him because of his big ears and long nose just to make himself look good in front of his friends. This guy made Vince's life miserable, but he didn't recognize him because he is now so thin and old looking. Vince watches the couple leave and notices through the window that they are having trouble getting the ramp down from their van for Mario's wheelchair. He pays his bill and walks outside to help.)

Vince: Do you need some help?

Catherine: Sometimes the ramp mechanism sticks and we can't get it down.

Vince: Here, let me help lift you up into the seat. Put your arms around my neck and hold on.
(He had helped many kids in the orphanage and knew what he was doing.)

Mario: Thank you. You remember now, don't you?

Vince: Yes, I remember.

Mario: Well, I bet you are thinking what goes around comes around, eh?
(He reached over and grabbed both of Vince's hands and gently squeezed them.)

Vince: No, not at all, Mario. I don't think that way. That's not my nature.

Mario: Is the way I feel sitting in this wheelchair the same way that you felt when you lived in the orphanage?

Vince: Close, Mario. But at least you have someone who loves you to push you around in the wheelchair. That's more than I had. You are a lucky man.
(Vince reached into his pocket and gave Mario one of his cards.)

Here, please give me a call sometime and we'll do lunch.

(They both laughed and Vince watched as they drove away.)

41. Read this sentence from the drama.

    I'm here to visit with some of the retiring caretakers from the orphanage.

    What does the word *retiring* mean as it is used in this sentence?

    (A) rewarding
    (B) justified in all actions
    (C) withdraw from service
    (D) aggressive and rebellious

42. How does the reader know that this is a short play?

    (A) The main character is a man.
    (B) The waitress is a minor character.
    (C) The story is told through dialogue and stage directions.
    (D) All of the characters have first names.

43. This story would be considered a—

    (A) comedy.
    (B) tragedy.
    (C) dramatic monologue.
    (D) situational drama.

44. How does Vince react when Mario states—*Well, I bet you are thinking what goes around comes around, eh?*

    (A) Vince feels vindication.
    (B) Vince is kind and polite.
    (C) Vince is angry and resentful.
    (D) Vince is content.

45. Which statement BEST describes what happens in the plot?

    (A) An orphan who was bullied in school runs into the bully fifteen years later who is now confined to a wheelchair.
    (B) A bully is injured and can't move.
    (C) The wife of a bully resents her husband's behavior.
    (D) The waitress brings lunch to the main character.

WRITING

The following passage is a rough draft of an essay. It contains a variety of errors that may include grammar, punctuation, sentence structure, or organization. Read the passage and answer questions 46 through 49.

ROUGH DRAFT

George Bernard Shaw

(1) It would be a safe bet to say that everyone knows who William Shakespeare is. (2) But the bet would be less than safe to wager on who might be the second best English playwright. (3) His name is George Bernard Shaw and although he is Irish and not English, his fame and reputation is second only to that of the great Shakespeare. (4) As a critic, a prolific letter writer, and social reformist, Shaw transformed Victorian theater and did his best to raise his audiences' level of awareness.

(5) Many of Shaw's plays are comedies, but within these comedies are varying degrees of attack on society's troubles as well as expressions of his political and philosophical ideas. (6) The intent of his plays was to shake people up. (7) He strongly believed that if you were not a part of the solution, then certainly you were a part of the problem. (8) In other words if you didn't help solve a problem, then you were probably the one causing it.

(9) Shaw presents varying degrees of harshness and outrage when addresses issues such as class structure, male and female relationships, education, prostitution and slumlords. (10) He was particularly vocal on the subject of prostitution and in the preface to his play *Mrs. Warren's Profession*, he writes: "to draw attention to the truth that prostitution is caused, not by female depravity or male licentiousness, but simply by underpaying, undervaluing, and overworking women so shamefully that the poorest of them are forced to resort to prostitution to keep body and soul together."

(11) *Pygmalion, Major Barbara, Heartbreak House,* and *Saint Joan* to name a few, are plays that go beyond their original intent which is to entertain. (12) Shaw managed to take it to another level completely, to inform and to encourage involvement in solving society's troubled areas.

46. Which of the following sentences would BEST begin the essay?

   (A) George Bernard Shaw is an Irish playwright.
   (B) George Bernard Shaw's reputation for playwriting is second only to William Shakespeare.
   (C) Although Shakespeare is considered the best playwright of all time, George Bernard Shaw is pretty good, too.
   (D) Not a day goes by when the name George Bernard Shaw appears somewhere.

47. The BEST way to combine the sentences numbered 1 and 2 is—

(A) It would be a safe bet to wager on the fact that everyone knows who William Shakespeare is, but a less safe bet to wager on the fact that George Bernard Shaw might be the second best playwright.
(B) William Shakespeare is a safer bet than George Bernard Shaw.
(C) Betting on William Shakespeare being the best playwright would be a safe one, but betting on George Bernard Shaw would put your life in jeopardy.
(D) George Bernard Shaw is a less safe bet than William Shakespeare.

48. Which of the following BEST describes what is <u>wrong</u> with paragraph 4?

(A) It is a conclusion to the essay.
(B) The conclusion is too short.
(C) The conclusion doesn't have punctuation.
(D) The conclusion is humorous.

49. Which of the following would be the BEST way to repair sentence 12?

(A) Shaw managed to take playwriting to another level completely: to . . .
(B) Shaw takes playwriting to different scopes . . .
(C) Shaw leaves the normal world of playwriting behind and takes to another stratosphere . . .
(D) Playwriting for Shaw was like a game to cause anxiety . . .

The following passage is a rough draft of an essay. It contains a variety of errors that may include grammar, punctuation, sentence structure, or organization. Read the passage and answer questions 50 through 53.

ROUGH DRAFT

Yosemite National Park

(1) Yosemite is a national park that is located in Sierra Nevada mountain range located in central California. (2) Although it is named after the river that runs through it, the word 'Yosemite' is an Indian name that means "grizzly bear." (3) A visit to this 1,189 square-mile park might leave you questioning its "grizzly bear" name. (4) Each year 3.5 million people visit this spectacular park to view its towering granite cliffs, waterfalls, streams and Giant Sequoia groves.

(5) Most of the park, in fact 95% of the park is wilderness, but most visitors stay in the Yosemite Valley. (6) Although the valley is only 1% of the park, its rock formations are known around the world. (7) El Capitan, a 3000 foot vertical rock formation is the park's most popular rock climbing feature. (8) It has many climbing routes and it is accessible all year long. (9) Sentinel Rock (3000 feet) and Half Dome (4800 feet) are also spectacular to see. (10) Another popular sight in the valley is Yosemite Falls. (11) At 2,423 feet, it is the highest in North America.

(12) In the higher sections of the park, Tuolumne Meadows, Dana Meadows, Cathedral Range and Kuna Crest are beautiful to explore, especially when the wildflowers are blooming in late spring. (13) The Pacific Crest Trail runs through the park in this area and the highest peak, Mount Lyell is also located here.

(14) Some of the tallest and longest living trees are located in Yosemite. (15) The Giant Sequoia trees are found in three groves within the borders of the park. (16) The Tuolumne Grove has 25 trees, the Merced Grove with 20 trees and the largest grove, the Mariposa, has 200 trees.

(17) Yosemite National Park is an heirloom that should be cherished, nurtured and enjoyed by all. (18) Its beauty, diversity and expanse is a golden spot in the golden state of California.

50. Which of the following is the best way to define the meaning of the word *expanse* as it is used in sentence 18?

   (A) beauty
   (B) miniscule
   (C) vastness
   (D) solidarity

51. Which of the following is supported by details and evidence in the essay?

   (A) Yosemite Falls is the highest in North America.
   (B) Granite is a coarse-grained igneous rock.
   (C) Tuolumne is a French word meaning coarse.
   (D) There are twenty trees in Yosemite National Park.

52. The best way to rewrite sentence 6 is—

   (A) Although the valley is a part of the park, it is famous.
   (B) The valley's rock formations are known just about everywhere.
   (C) The rock formations in the one percent part of the valley are famous.
   (D) The Yosemite Valley is only one percent of the park, but it is known worldwide for its rock formations.

53. The author of this passage—

   (A) likes to climb rock formations everywhere.
   (B) intended to inform the reader about Yosemite National Park.
   (C) believes that there should be national parks in all states.
   (D) has a passion for waterfalls.

The following passage is a rough draft of an essay. It contains a variety of errors that may include grammar, punctuation, sentence structure, or organization. Read the passage and answer questions 54 through 57.

ROUGH DRAFT

The Pacific Ocean

(1) The Pacific Ocean is the largest ocean on Earth. (2) It was named by the Portuguese explorer Ferdinand Magellan from a Latin word "Mare Pacificum" which means "peaceful sea." (3) Although it is shrinking in size from plate tectonic movement and the Atlantic Ocean is increasing in size for the same reason, the enormity of this body of water is almost incomprehensible.

(4) Extending 9600 miles (15,500 kilometers) from the Arctic in the north and the Antarctica in the south, the Pacific Ocean is bordered on the west by Asia and Australia and by the Americas on the east and measures 12,300 miles (19,800 kilometers) at its widest point. (5) In square miles, the Pacific Ocean <u>boasts </u>a whopping 65.3 million square miles (169.2 million square kilometers). (6) It covers roughly 46% of the Earth's water surface. (7) However, this immense body of water covers 32% of the Earth's total surface area. (8) In other words, the Pacific Ocean is larger than all of the Earth's landmasses put together and there is room for another continent the size of Africa.

(9) The deepest point of the Pacific was in the western part of the North Pacific. (10) The Mariana Trench is 35,798 feet deep (10,911 meters) and the lowest point on Earth. (11) The average depth of the ocean however, is 14,000 feet (4,280 meters). (12) There are about 25,000 islands found in the Pacific Ocean. (13) Most of these islands are located below the equator, <u>which divides the ocean into the North Pacific and the South Pacific.</u> (14) Because the ocean straddles the 180° Meridian (the international dateline, part of the Pacific is in the Earth's Eastern Hemisphere and part is in the Western Hemisphere.

(15) The Pacific Ocean is the granddaddy of all oceans. (16) Its breadth and depth are difficult to understand when you look at a map. (17) However, when the actual numbers are laid out, this ocean's size comes into proper perspective. (18) The word "enormous" doesn't do justice to its size.

54. Which of the following BEST defines the meaning of the underlined word *boasts* in sentence 5?

   (A) a large boat
   (B) take charge of
   (C) brag about
   (D) ignore

55. If a student wanted to learn more about the Pacific Ocean and did not have access to the Internet, what would be the BEST source to find information?

    (A) radio
    (B) television
    (C) encyclopedia
    (D) thesaurus

56. What is the most effective substitution for the underlined part of sentence 13?

    (A) dividing the ocean into the North and South Pacific.
    (B) which cuts the ocean into two parts, the North and the South.
    (C) which separates the ocean in half.
    (D) making a north and a south ocean of the Pacific Ocean.

57. Which revision of sentence number 9 uses active voice only?

    (A) The deepest point of the Pacific could have been found in the western part of the North Pacific.
    (B) The deepest point of the Pacific is in the western part of the North Pacific.
    (C) The deepest point of the Pacific was found in the western part of the North Pacific.
    (D) The deepest point of the Pacific had been found in the western part of the North Pacific.

For questions 58 to 64, choose the answer that is the most effective substitute for each underlined part of the sentence. If no substitution is needed, choose "Leave as is."

58. While Meredith visited <u>with Cory: she finished</u> typing her essay.

    (A) with Cory; she finished
    (B) with Cory, she finished
    (C) with Cory. She finished
    (D) Leave as is.

59. When our grandparents leave for South America <u>next month, they will celebrate</u> their 50th anniversary.

    (A) next month they will celebrate
    (B) next month. They will
    (C) next month: they will
    (D) Leave as is.

60. <u>Maria told us about her travels to Honduras last March in class.</u>

    (A) Maria told us in class about her travels to Honduras last March.
    (B) Maria in class told us about her travels last March to Honduras.
    (C) In class, Maria told us about her last March travels to Honduras.
    (D) Leave as is.

61. <u>After, the earthquake, struck</u> San Francisco, the city was devastated and practically demolished.

    (A) After the, earthquake struck
    (B) After the earthquake struck,
    (C) After the earthquake struck
    (D) Leave as is.

62. The French city of Paris is filled with tourists <u>in summer but it is much quieter</u> in winter.

    (A) in summer but, it is much quieter
    (B) in summer, but it is much quieter
    (C) in, summer, but it is much quieter
    (D) Leave as is.

63. <u>"Why do I have to take out the trash?"</u> whined the boy to his mother.

    (A) Why do I have to take out the trash" ?
    (B) Why do I have to take out the trash"
    (C) Why do I have to take out the trash!"?
    (D) Leave as is.

64. <u>A dog bit Adam's leg while riding a bicycle.</u>

    (A) A dog bit Adam's bicycle while he was riding.
    (B) While riding a bicycle, a dog bit Adam's leg.
    (C) While Adam was riding a bicycle, a dog bit his leg.
    (D) Leave as is.

For questions 65 to 72 choose the word or phrase that best completes the sentence.

65. Chihuahua is the _____ state in Mexico.

    (A) larger
    (B) previously larger
    (C) largest
    (D) more larger

66. Horseradish _____ for its pungent fleshy root which is useful in seasoning.

    (A) has cultivated
    (B) is cultivated
    (C) cultivating
    (D) is cultivating

67. Machu Picchu _____ the best preserved Incan settlement today.

    (A) is
    (B) are
    (C) was
    (D) wasn't

68. _____ be going to Boston College next fall.

    (A) She was
    (B) She'll
    (C) She wasn't
    (D) She's

69. The new Prius has _____ room in the trunk, but gets better gas mileage than the previous model.

    (A) lesser
    (B) least
    (C) smaller
    (D) less

70. Dylan _____ wild lifestyle led to his early death.

    (A) Thomas
    (B) Thomas'es
    (C) Thomas'
    (D) Thomases'

71. John Coltrane, a jazz saxophonist, _____ attention when he played with the Miles Davis quintet.

    (A) attracts
    (B) attracted
    (C) attracting
    (D) can attract

72. _____ going to take a trip to South Africa next winter.

    (A) There
    (B) Their
    (C) They
    (D) They're

TEST 2 WRITING TASK 1

- Read the instructions for the writing task carefully. You may need to read it several times.
- Brainstorm and organize your thoughts on paper.
- Aim for at least four paragraphs; five is better.
- Be certain that you have a well-developed introduction, body paragraphs, and conclusion.
- Support your thesis by using specific details and examples.
- Use effective word choice.
- Be aware of sentence beginnings; avoid repeating them.
- Vary sentence length to make your writing more interesting.
- Reread your essay to catch errors in grammar, spelling, punctuation, and sentence formation.

Writing Task:

By the time you enter high school, you have learned about many moments or events in history that have influenced or changed our world in some way. Think about a historical moment or event that you have studied and consider its importance.

Write an essay in which you discuss this event or moment in history. Be certain to explain why it was important, and support the moment or event with details and examples.

- Write your essay on the answer sheet that precedes this exam.
- Adding a title is not mandatory.
- Either printing or cursive writing is acceptable.
- Write clearly and neatly—make the reader's job easier.
- Using a dictionary or thesaurus is not permitted.
- GOOD LUCK!

NOTE: There are scored writing samples for this writing task after the answer key for of this exam. After you have written your response, compare your writing to those already scored to see how your writing compares. Pay particular attention to the essays with the highest scores. You will need a 3 or a 4 to pass this task.

TEST 2 WRITING TASK 2

- Read the instructions for the writing task carefully. You may need to read it several times.
- Brainstorm and organize your thoughts on paper.
- Aim for at least four paragraphs; five is better.
- Be certain that you have a well-developed introduction, body paragraphs, and conclusion.
- Support your thesis by using specific details and examples.
- Use effective word choice.
- Be aware of sentence beginnings; avoid repeating them.
- Vary sentence length to make your writing more interesting.
- Reread your essay to catch errors in grammar, spelling, punctuation, and sentence formation.

Writing Task:

Many students have expressed an interest in starting an environmental project on school grounds by focusing on the removal of trash, recycling cans, bottles, and papers.

Write a persuasive essay that will be printed in your school newspaper that convinces your readers that, by removing the trash and recycling, the students will not only make the school more attractive, but will help the environment as well. Convince your readers by using specific examples and reasons.

- Write your essay on the answer sheet that precedes this exam.
- Adding a title is not mandatory.
- Either printing or cursive writing is acceptable.
- Write clearly and neatly—make the reader's job easier.
- Using a dictionary or thesaurus is not permitted.
- GOOD LUCK!

NOTE: There are scored writing samples for this writing task after the answer key for this exam. After you have written your response, compare your writing to those already scored to see how your writing compares. Pay particular attention to the essays with the highest scores. You will need a 3 or a 4 to pass this task.

Practice Test 2

Answer Key

1. (B)	16. (A)	31. (B)	46. (B)	61. (C)
2. (D)	17. (D)	32. (C)	47. (A)	62. (B)
3. (A)	18. (C)	33. (D)	48. (B)	63. (D)
4. (C)	19. (A)	34. (A)	49. (A)	64. (C)
5. (B)	20. (D)	35. (B)	50. (C)	65. (C)
6. (A)	21. (C)	36. (D)	51. (A)	66. (B)
7. (C)	22. (B)	37. (C)	52. (D)	67. (A)
8. (B)	23. (B)	38. (C)	53. (B)	68. (B)
9. (D)	24. (B)	39. (D)	54. (C)	69. (D)
10. (C)	25. (A)	40. (B)	55. (C)	70. (C)
11. (B)	26. (B)	41. (C)	56. (A)	71. (B)
12. (A)	27. (C)	42. (C)	57. (B)	72. (D)
13. (C)	28. (C)	43. (D)	58. (B)	
14. (A)	29. (D)	44. (B)	59. (D)	
15. (B)	30. (A)	45. (A)	60. (A)	

PRACTICE EXAM 2
WRITING TASK 1 SCORED EXAMPLES

By the time you enter high school, you have learned about many moments or events in history that have influenced or changed our world in some way. Think about a historical moment or event that you have studied and consider its importance.

Write an essay in which you discuss this event or moment in history. Be certain to explain why it was important and support the moment or event with details and examples.

4

SCORE POINT 4
STUDENT RESPONSE

September 11, 2001 is a day that changed the world forever. It was the day that two jet airliners were hijacked by Islamic fundamentalists and flown directly into the Twin Towers in New York City. Thousands were killed and the world continues to mourn them today. The world has not been the same since. The regulations and laws regarding airlines, the establishment of Homeland Security Department, and the initial grounds for the beginning of the war in Iraq are all a result of that one day.

After the attack in New York, all airlines were grounded. But once they were allowed to continue regular schedules, many things had to be changed. These changes included: additional security on the planes themselves, the screening of passengers and added security at airports both inside and out which contributed to much needed safety, but to long lines and weary travelers as well. With the airline industry being regulated, national security had to be revamped.

A new department for Homeland Security was developed. Having been attacked from within our borders by outsiders, new laws and regulations were needed. Much of America had suddenly changed the stagnant complacency in their belief that America was safe and protected. But our government had to drastically change that frame of mind. Homeland Security began guarding and protecting all of our borders. They issued various warnings for cities that could possibly come under attack and industries and businesses that might be targeted. Many changes were made that would never have been consider pre-9-11.

Because of mistrust and the desire to protect our country, President Bush within a short time after 9-11, declared war on Iraq. He believed that they had weapons of mass destruction and were viable enemies because of their previous support of the Islamic fundamentalists. War became inevitable and continues unabated.

September 11, 2001 was a turning point in history for the entire world. It demonstrated our vulnerabilities and complacencies. Although a tragic and horrible nightmare, the lessons that we have learned from this event have been sad and demoralizing. The vast majority of the world would choose to live in peace, but this was a declaration of mistrust, hatred and disgust. No, the world will never be the same again.

Practice Exam 2

3

SCORE POINT 3
STUDENT RESPONSE

Although there are many moments in history that have made great impacts on the world, 9-11 and the attacks on New York City and Washington DC have to stand out. Partially because these attacks are the most recent, but partially because they truly transformed the way the world sees many things. Commercial airline travel and national security are two of the most transformed as a result of the attacks on the World Trade Center and the Pentagon.

Since 9-11, airline travel has changed drastically. What use to be a fairly easy thing to do; has become a project in humility. Travelers now have to be screened, sometimes several times before getting onto a plane. There are new rules for what can be packed and brought on board. Parking, buying tickets and other areas of travel have added security and evaluations because of the attacks. Long lines, taking your shoes, coats and jewelry off at screening points, is now the norm for most travelers.

The United States developed a new department within the government; The Department of Homeland Security. This department is responsible for keeping America safe. They patrol the skies, the airports, the harbors, the borders and waters that surround the US. They keep track of possible attack areas and notify cities and various industries if they feel they should be alerted to possible danger.

The new airline regulations and the new Department of Homeland Security would most like not have occurred if 9-11 had not happened, But because of the tragic and horrifying events that took place that day, life in the US and around the world will never be the same.

2

SCORE POINT 2
STUDENT RESPONSE

America went under attack on September 11, 2001. To me that was the worst event in history and it changed the world. I've learned about many events, but that one stands out.

When the attackers hit the Twin Towers of the World Trade Center in New York, life wouldn't be the same ever again. People cannot fly easily anymore and the way that America is guarded has changed also. It is a sad world now that all those people died and that the men who hijacked the planes were living here in the us and nobody knew what they were up to.

The world has changed since that day. Airports are different and there are long lines and people have to take their shoes off. It is not fun. The attacks on New York changed the world forever. and ever.

1

SCORE POINT 1
STUDENT RESPONSE

I have to say the attacks in new york are the worsts thing in history. because of all the people that died and the buildings wreck. It was not a good thing and it changes the world. now people don't trust a lot of people and plus they are all sad about their families.

Being attacked in new york is the worst the very worst thing ever.

PRACTICE EXAM 2
WRITING TASK 2 SCORED EXAMPLES

Writing Task:

Many students have expressed an interest in starting an environmental project on the school grounds by focusing on the removal of trash and recycling cans, bottles and papers.

Write a persuasive essay that will be printed in your school newspaper that convinces your readers that, by removing the trash and recycling, the students will not only make the school more attractive, but help the environment as well. Convince your readers by using specific examples and reasons.

4

SCORE POINT 4
STUDENT RESPONSE

With all the talk and publicity that our environment is getting these day, don't you think it is about time that we, the students of Marysville HS step up to the planet and do our part to help? Our planet is being abused and misused. We are depleting natural resource so fast that our children and our grandchildren will be lucky to see a tree or any open spaces left. We need to pick up our trash, recycle paper, cans and bottles and reuse as much as possible to SAVE OUR PLANET. Join the Environmental Club and help launch a new recycling and pro-environmental project today!

Have you seen the school grounds after lunch lately? It is a mess. And, as it is right now, the custodians have to pick it all up. They don't have time to separate the trash from the recyclables, so it ALL goes into the trash. That is a tragedy beyond words. We can and HAVE to help out. Everyday at lunch there will be a group of kids monitoring the grounds. We are going to be placing recycling bins everywhere possible. The bins will be labeled: "Cans," "Glass Containers," "Plastic," "Reusable Paper," and "Trash." Please help us out by taking the SHORT time that it takes to separate your trash, because not all of it is trash, it is reusable and will help save the planet.

When you go to the store, choose products in containers that are either recyclable or reusable. Some containers are not recyclable, so avoid those. Another tip, buy a reusable bottle to carry your water in, instead of using so many plastic bottles that get sent to landfills for the most part. Be smart about your product choices. Look at the bottom of the container for the recycling icon—help save the planet.

The Environmental Club really needs your help. Please do your part to help recycle and to make this program a success. Be proud of your school and the planet. We need volunteers to help take the recycling to the large bins that will be taken to the recycling station. Please, please volunteer as much as you can. HELP SAVE THE PLANET!

Recycling, reusing and making a difference on our campus is the right thing to do. You've heard all the arguments, there is nothing more to say. WE NEED YOUR HELP! Take time to recycle your trash while you are on campus and at home, in fact everywhere that you go. Become a world citizen in addition to an American citizen. Help Save the Planet! NOW! PLEASE?

3

SCORE POINT 3
STUDENT RESPONSE

Recycling trash is no longer an option. Recycling trash is now mandatory. The campus is left in such a mess everyday at lunch, the janitors have no time for recycling—they barely have time to pick up after a bunch of kids who should be doing this on their own. We should all be ashamed. Please, help with the new environmental project on campus. Do your part. Use the recycling bins instead of dropping your trash on the ground. The Earth is in danger. We cannot afford to allow reusable containers and other materials to fill massive areas of land where it sits for centuries before it disintegrates. Please recycle.

Recycling is not difficult. There are bins ready to be used for glass, plastic, paper, and cans. USE THEM. We are not going to stand by and allow our school to look like it was hit by a tornado everyday at lunch. Please take the few steps that it takes to separate your trash. It only takes a minute of your time and you will sleep better at night knowing that you did your part for the EARTH.

Please consider joining the environmental project as it begins it's new program this week. We need volunteers everyday to help us in many different ways. This is a plea for your help—we need you—the campus needs you—the Earth needs you. Please help.

Recycling and helping to save our planet is vital to our future. With the depletion of natural resources, global warming, overcrowding and many other desperate issues plaguing the planet, please join in this effort to help save our campus and our world.

2

SCORE POINT 2
STUDENT RESPONSE

Recycling is important and everyone needs to help out. There is a new program to help clean up our campus. Think about joining. It will make our school look better and help the environment too.

The program has beens sitting around everywhere, and you should just not be so lazy and go over to them and drop your cans in one, your glass in another and the plastic stuff in the other one. THer is also one for paper. But don't put your yucky trash in that one, put yucky trash in the trash can.

You really need to help this is a must. Don't waste another minute or waste another piece of good trash. Recycle it.

1

SCORE POINT 1
STUDENT RESPONSE

The environment is in trouble. Our school is a mess at lunchtime and you need to help. everybody needs to help and not just the kids who like to do this stuff.

Put your trash in the right spots. don't waste it on landfills that are too fulled up right now anyway. Put your trash where it belongs and into the right place. recycling is helpful to everybody.

APPENDIX

- Vocabulary Foursquares Page
- Chapter Review Answers
- Scoring Guide—Response to Writing Prompt
- Scoring Guide—Response to Literary/Expository Text

VOCABULARY FOURSQUARES

CHAPTER 1: DIAGNOSTIC EXAM

Multiple-choice questions 1–5 from Chapter 2

1. (C)
2. (B)
3. (A)
4. (D)
5. (D)

Multiple-choice questions 6–10 from Chapter 3

6. (A)
7. (C)
8. (B)
9. (C)
10. (A)

Multiple-choice questions 11–15 from Chapter 4

11. (C)
12. (B)
13. (C)
14. (A)
15. (D)

Multiple-choice questions 16–20 from Chapter 5

16. (D)
17. (A)
18. (C)
19. (B)
20. (C)

Multiple-choice questions 21–25 from Chapter 6

21. (B)
22. (D)
23. (C)
24. (A)
25. (A)

Multiple-choice questions 26–30 from Chapter 7

26. (D)
27. (C)
28. (A)
29. (C)
30. (D)

Multiple-choice questions 31–35 from Chapter 8

31. (C)
32. (A)
33. (C)
34. (B)
35. (D)

Multiple-choice questions 36–40 from Chapter 9

36. (C)
37. (C)
38. (C)
39. (A)
40. (D)

Multiple-choice questions 41–45 from Chapter 10

41. (D)
42. (B)
43. (A)
44. (B)
45. (A)

Multiple-choice questions 46–50 from Chapter 11

46. (C)
47. (D)
48. (A)
49. (A)
50. (B)

Multiple-choice questions 51–55 from Chapter 12

51. (B)
52. (D)
53. (D)
54. (A)
55. (C)

Multiple-choice questions 56–60 from Chapter 13

56. (C)
57. (A)
58. (B)
59. (D)
60. (C)

CHAPTER REVIEW ANSWERS: CHAPTER 2

Definition Review

1. literal
2. idiom
3. connotative
4. idiom
5. simile/figurative
6. figurative
7. personification
8. denotative/connotative (or vice versa)
9. metaphor
10. simile

Figurative Language Review

1. simile
2. personification
3. metaphor
4. personification
5. metaphor
6. simile
7. personification
8. simile
9. personification
10. metaphor
11. personification
12. personification
13. simile
14. metaphor
15. simile
16. personification
17. simile
18. personification
19. personification
20. simile

Idioms Review

1. c
2. g
3. h
4. n
5. r
6. p
7. o
8. d
9. t

10. e
11. j
12. s
13. l
14. k
15. f
16. a
17. b
18. i
19. m
20. q

CHAPTER REVIEW ANSWERS: CHAPTER 3

Section I

1. u
2. m
3. i
4. c
5. n
6. q
7. v
8. b
9. j or k
10. k or j
11. p
12. o
13. g
14. f
15. e
16. a
17. t
18. s
19. r
20. d
21. h
22. l

Section II

1. c
2. b
3. f
4. e
5. a
6. d

Section III

1. c
2. u or j
3. y
4. z
5. a
6. p
7. f
8. r
9. u or j
10. k
11. m
12. e
13. b
14. o
15. r
16. v
17. i
18. aa
19. h
20. q
21. w
22. s
23. l
24. d
25. x
26. n
27. g

Section IV

1. d or m
2. k
3. h
4. f
5. b
6. d or m
7. l
8. i
9. e
10. a
11. j
12. n
13. c
14. g

Section V

1. b
2. d
3. g
4. e
5. a
6. f
7. c

Section VI

1. e
2. j
3. c
4. i
5. m
6. f
7. b
8. h
9. l
10. a
11. g
12. k
13. d

Section VII

1. junc
2. hom
3. gen
4. grad
5. hes
6. id
7. inter
8. intra
9. ject
10. grand
11. grat
12. jur
13. hetero
14. hyper

Section VIII

1. monit
2. man
3. lect
4. mut

5. mater
6. lev
7. morph
8. min
9. mort
10. mal
11. log
12. lus
13. mit
14. mag

Section IX

1. omni
2. path
3. nom
4. phone
5. nov
6. nat
7. plac
8. pater
9. port
10. pac
11. nox
12. par
13. pod
14. post
15. ped
16. pro
17. pre
18. pan
19. pug
20. pen
21. nym
22. pro
23. pen
24. para
25. peri

Section X

1. h
2. m
3. a
4. d
5. k
6. f
7. i

8. j
9. l
10. b
11. c
12. g
13. e

Section XI

1. e
2. b
3. j
4. g
5. a
6. c
7. k
8. i
9. f
10. d
11. h

Section XII

1. k
2. g
3. b
4. d
5. i
6. l
7. a
8. e
9. j
10. c
11. f
12. h

Section XIII

1. g
2. k
3. c
4. i
5. n
6. d
7. a
8. l
9. e
10. b

11. o
12. m
13. j
14. h
15. f

Section XIV

1. g
2. f
3. b
4. a
5. j
6. c
7. e
8. d
9. h
10. i

Section XV

1. f
2. i
3. c
4. a
5. h
6. j
7. b
8. d
9. g
10. e

Section XVI

1. c
2. a
3. b
4. a
5. c
6. b
7. a
8. b
9. c
10. b

Section XVII

1. c
2. c

3. a
4. a
5. b
6. a
7. a
8. a
9. b
10. a
11. a
12. b
13. a

Section XVIII

1. b
2. a
3. a
4. c
5. b
6. c
7. c
8. a
9. a
10. b
11. c
12. a
13. c

Section XIX

1. a
2. a
3. c
4. b
5. c
6. a
7. c
8. a
9. b
10. c

Section XX

1. c
2. c
3. b
4. a
5. c

6. a
7. a
8. c
9. c

Section XXI

1. a
2. c
3. b
4. a
5. c
6. b
7. a

CHAPTER REVIEW ANSWERS: CHAPTER 4

1. ad
2. aide
3. heir
4. aisle
5. awl
6. aweigh
7. bale
8. bawled
9. banned
10. bear
11. bass
12. beech
13. bow
14. bin
15. berth
16. block
17. bored
18. bow
19. brake
20. bred
21. bridle
22. brooch
23. cache
24. capital
25. carat
26. caste
27. ceded
28. scent
29. serial
30. coral
31. chute

32. cite
33. claws
34. course
35. kernel
36. pare
37. squeak
38. due
39. dough
40. urn
41. yew
42. fare
43. phase
44. feat
45. fur
46. flare
47. flee
48. flue
49. flour
50. forward
51. foul
52. gait
53. jeans
54. gourd
55. grate
56. grisly
57. groan
58. hare
59. haul
60. halve
61. heel
62. herd
63. idol
64. its
65. knight
66. knot
67. lead
68. leek
69. lyre
70. lynx
71. loan
72. lox
73. mane
74. meddle
75. minced
76. moor
77. mousse
78. mourning

79. naval
80. ore
81. pare
82. palette
83. patience
84. piece
85. piqued
86. pie
87. pistil
88. pleas
89. plumb
90. poll
91. pore
92. presence
93. principal
94. profit
95. wracked
96. razed
97. wrap
98. rapt
99. reed
100. read
101. wreak
102. wrest
103. wretched
104. rite
105. wry
106. sale
107. seam
108. seize
109. sow
110. sheared
111. sighed
112. sigh
113. slaying
114. soar
115. sword
116. staring
117. stake
118. stationary
119. suite
120. taut
121. tear
122. tents
123. tern
124. they're
125. threw

126. throne
127. thyme
128. tide
129. too
130. tow
131. toad
132. veil
133. vane
134. vial
135. wail
136. waste
137. weight
138. weighed
139. wee
140. weak
141. we'd
142. whine
143. would
144. yolk
145. yore

CHAPTER REVIEW ANSWERS: CHAPTER 5
Vocabulary Review I-A

1. e
2. a
3. g
4. i
5. b
6. j
7. c
8. h
9. d
10. f

Vocabulary Review I-B

1. curious
2. incentive
3. tinker
4. curiosity
5. impressed
6. darn
7. protest
8. intended
9. carriages
10. immigrants
11. variety

12. journey
13. mechanical

Vocabulary Review II-A

1. d
2. k
3. g
4. c
5. a
6. b
7. f
8. j
9. l
10. h
11. i
12. e

Vocabulary Review II-B

1. d
2. b
3. a
4. c
5. d
6. b
7. a
8. c
9. b
10. a
11. d
12. b
13. c
14. a
15. a
16. c
17. d
18. b

Vocabulary Review III-A

1. undertaking
2. frost
3. intermittently
4. impulse
5. eager
6. liberty

7. hubbub
8. dismantled
9. thicket
10. aroused
11. dense
12. slink
13. deliberately
14. trembled

Vocabulary Review III-B

1. i
2. a
3. b
4. j
5. c
6. m
7. k
8. f
9. e
10. l
11. g
12. h
13. d
14. n

Vocabulary Review IV-A

1. a
2. c
3. d
4. b
5. a
6. c
7. d
8. c
9. a
10. b
11. b
12. a
13. c
14. d

Vocabulary Review IV-B

1. iridescent
2. applicant

3. draped
4. ensure
5. perimeter
6. prominently
7. dominate
8. distress
9. foyer
10. receptionist
11. graciously
12. promptly
13. aggressive
14. protruding
15. pronounced

Section V

1. h
2. c
3. k
4. a
5. m
6. d
7. f
8. l
9. b
10. i
11. e
12. g
13. j

Section VI

1. d
2. h
3. a
4. j
5. b
6. k
7. c
8. l
9. e
10. f
11. g
12. i

CHAPTER REVIEW ANSWERS: CHAPTER 6

Answers:

Question 1 asks what the story is "mainly about." You will be looking for an answer that provides the **main idea** of the story. **The correct answer to Question 1 is B—**main idea. This means you must read the passage carefully; visualize and understand thoroughly.

Question 2 is asking for a date of some sort; this is a **detail** that is easily found in the reading—scanning the reading quickly will help you answer this question. **The correct answer to Question 2 is A—**details.

Question 3 asks what a certain paragraph is about. **The correct answer to Question 3 is B—**main idea.

Question 4 asks something that you need to think about or **infer.** You really don't know what was going on inside the mind of the people who were stuck on a Ferris wheel for hours, but you can imagine what was going through their minds. You must therefore infer. **The correct answer to Question 4 is C.**

Question 5 is asking for details of Clarence Smith's idea. Don't let the word "idea" fool you into thinking this is a question about the main idea—it isn't. The question makers simply want to find out what his idea is. **The correct answer to Question 5 is A.**

CHAPTER REVIEW ANSWERS: CHAPTER 7

1. C
2. B
3. D
4. A
5. D
6. A
7. D
8. A
9. B
10. A
11. B
12. A
13. D
14. C
15. A

CHAPTER REVIEW ANSWERS: CHAPTER 8

1. h
2. l
3. z
4. q
5. a
6. dd
7. u
8. o
9. p

10. d
11. f
12. n
13. g
14. aa
15. x
16. i
17. b
18. cc
19. v
20. r
21. e
22. k
23. bb
24. y
25. t
26. m
27. j
28. s
29. w
30. c

CHAPTER REVIEW ANSWERS: CHAPTER 9

1. q
2. f
3. l
4. a
5. r
6. n
7. o
8. d
9. b
10. k
11. s
12. g
13. j
14. i
15. c
16. e
17. h
18. t
19. p
20. m

CHAPTER REVIEW ANSWERS: CHAPTER 10

Section I: Clauses

1. clause
2. subject
3. predicate
4. subject
5. verb
6. two
7. independent
8. subordinate
9. independent
10. subordinate
11. adjective
12. adverb
13. noun

Section II: Phrases

1. phrase
2. subject
3. verb
4. prepositional
5. verbal
6. participial
7. gerund
8. infinitive
9. prepositional
10. noun
11. pronoun
12. adjective
13. phrase
14. adjective
15. adverb
16. Verbal
17. adjective
18. -ing
19. nouns
20. Infinitive
21. Appositive

Section III: Punctuation

The word Machiavellian has become synonymous (a synonym) for political immorality. Niccolo Machiavelli, who lived from 1469–1527, wrote a book titled *The Prince*, which is remembered for its insistence that while his subjects are bound by conventional or the normal moral obligations, a ruler may use any means necessary to maintain power and it doesn't matter how unscrupulous. Therefore,

Machiavellian has come to mean cynical political scheming, which is characterized by deceit and bad faith. Evidently, Niccolo was a thin-lipped man who was very hyperactive and sarcastic. Isn't it amazing how the memory of one man with a theory of political morality can be so appropriate to modern times?

CHAPTER REVIEW ANSWERS: CHAPTER 11

Section I: Capitalization

1. first
2. I
3. quotation
4. proper
5. capitalize
6. Organizations
7. associations
8. government bodies

Section II: Sentences

1. sentence
2. Declarative
3. imperative
4. Exclamatory
5. interrogative

Section III: Sentence Structure

1. sentence
2. subject
3. predicate
4. verb
5. verb
6. plural
7. verb
8. agreement
9. Double
10. negative
11. comparative
12. superlative

Scoring Guide—Response to Writing Prompt

4 The essay—

- provides a *meaningful* thesis that is responsive to the writing task.
- *thoroughly* supports the thesis and main ideas with *specific* details and examples.
- demonstrates a consistent tone and focus, and illustrates a *purposeful* control of organization.
- demonstrates a *clear* sense of audience.
- provides a *variety* of sentence types and uses *precise, descriptive* language.
- contains *few, if any, errors* in the conventions* of the English language. (Errors are generally first-draft in nature.)

3 The essay—

- provides a thesis that is responsive to the writing task.
- supports the thesis and main ideas with details and examples.
- demonstrates a consistent tone and focus, and illustrates a control of organization.
- demonstrates a *general* sense of audience.
- provides a *variety of* sentence types and uses *some descriptive* language.
- may contain *some errors* in the conventions* of the English language. (Errors do **not** interfere with the reader's understanding of the essay.)

2 The essay—

- provides a thesis or main idea that is related to the writing task.
- supports the thesis or main idea(s) with *limited* details and/or examples.
- demonstrates an *inconsistent* tone and focus, and illustrates *little, if any* control of organization.
- demonstrates *little* or **no** sense of audience.
- provides *few, if any,* types of sentence types, and basic, *predictable* language.
- may contain *several errors* in the conventions* of the English language. (Errors **may** interfere with the reader's understanding of the essay.)

Scoring Guide—Response to Writing Prompt (cont.)

1 The essay—

- *may* provide a *weak* thesis or main idea that is related to the writing task.
- *fails* to support the thesis or main ideas with details and/or examples.
- demonstrates a *lack of* tone and focus, and illustrates *no* control of organization.
- may demonstrate *no* sense of audience.
- may provide *no* sentence variety and uses *limited* vocabulary.
- may contain *serious errors* in the conventions* of the English language. (Errors interfere with the reader's understanding of the essay.).

Non-Scorable

The code "NS" will appear on the student answer document for responses that are written in a language other than English, or that are off-topic, illegible, unintelligible, or otherwise non-responsive to the writing task.

*Conventions of the English language refer to grammar, punctuation, spelling, capitalization, and usage.

Scoring Guide–Response to Literary/Expository Text

4 The response—

- demonstrates a *thoughtful,* comprehensive grasp of the text.
- accurately and coherently provides *specific* textual details and examples to support the thesis and main ideas.
- demonstrates a clear understanding of the ambiguities, nuances, and complexities of the text.
- provides a *variety* of sentence types and uses *precise, descriptive* language.
- contains *few, if any, errors* in the conventions* of the English language. (Errors are generally first-draft in nature.)

3 The response—

- demonstrates a comprehensive grasp of the text.
- accurately and coherently provides *general* textual details and examples to support the thesis and main ideas.
- demonstrates a *general* understanding of the ambiguities, nuances, and complexities of the text.
- provides a *variety* of sentence types and uses some *descriptive* language.
- may contain *some errors* in the conventions* of the English language. (Errors do **not** interfere with the reader's understanding of the essay.)

2 The response—

- demonstrates a *limited* grasp of the text.
- provides *few, if any,* textual details and examples to support the thesis and main ideas.
- demonstrates *limited, or no* understanding of the ambiguities, nuances, and complexities of the text.
- provides *few, if any,* types of sentences and uses *basic, predictable* language.
- may contain *several errors* in the conventions* of the English language. (Errors **may** interfere with the reader's understanding of the essay.)

Scoring Guide—Response to Literary/Expository Text (cont.)

1 The response—

- demonstrates *minimal* grasp of the text.
- may provide *no* textual details and examples to support the thesis and main ideas.
- may demonstrate *no* understanding of the ambiguities, nuances, and complexities of the text.
- may provide *no* sentence variety and uses *limited* vocabulary.
- may contain *serious errors* in the conventions* of the English language. (Errors interfere with the reader's understanding of the essay.)

Non-Scorable

The code "NS" will appear on the student answer document for responses that are written in a language other than English, or that are off-topic, illegible, unintelligible, or otherwise non-responsive to the writing task. *Conventions of the English language refer to grammar, punctuation, spelling, capitalization, and usage.

Index